INSIDE THE MAZE

Also by Chris Ryder

The RUC: A Force Under Fire

The Ulster Defence Regiment: An Instrument of Peace?

(with Vincent Kearney)
Drumcree: The Orange Order's Last Stand

INSIDE THE MAZE

The Untold Story of the Northern Ireland Prison Service

Chris Ryder

Methuen

Published by Methuen 2001

10 9 8 7 6 5 4 3 2

This edition published in Great Britain in 2001 by
Methuen Publishing Ltd
215 Vauxhall Bridge Rd, London SW1V 1EJ

Methuen Publishing Limited Reg. No. 3543167

A CIP catalogue record for this book is available from the British
Library

ISBN 0 413 75250 X

Typeset by SX Composing DTP, Rayleigh, Essex
Printed and bound by Cox and Wyman Ltd., Reading, Berkshire

For Genny

Contents

Introduction

Gerry Kelly and David Ervine are figureheads of a new generation of political leaders in long troubled Northern Ireland. Although they come from working class backgrounds in Belfast and are both elected members of the Northern Ireland Assembly, they stand at opposite extremes of the political spectrum. On the face of it, they appear to have little else in common. Kelly is an Irish Republican, utterly committed to removing Northern Ireland from the United Kingdom. Ervine, an Ulster Loyalist, is pledged to defend the Union. But when they debated together in front of some 150 members of the Current Affairs Society at St Patrick's College, Belfast in March 2000, they revealed another commonality: how the time they spent imprisoned for their cause had been a defining influence on their lives.

'I had priorities in jail: one was to escape, the other to get an education,' recalled Kelly.

'I wouldn't be the person I am today had I not gone to jail,' said Ervine.

The jail they are talking about is the Maze prison, a dozen miles west of Belfast, which emerged as one of the most notorious symbols of the conflict in Northern Ireland and ranks in historical terms with Alcatraz, the Tower of London, the Soviet Gulags and the Nazi concentration camps as an extraordinary penal establishment. Its compounds and, later, its infamous H-blocks became one of the most fiercely contested battlegrounds of the conflict. Ten prisoners starved themselves to death, two died trying to escape and several others were murdered within its heavily-guarded walls. Despite its tight security, 38 IRA prisoners staged a mass breakout in 1983, the largest ever escape in British penal history. During the years of violence, 29 prison officers were ruthlessly murdered by terrorists and countless more were attacked, maimed and injured.

Here, for the first time, is the story of the Northern Ireland Prison Service. It explores what happened after the police, army and courts had captured and convicted the terrorists and they were handed over for imprisonment. Even behind bars, however, they refused to give up their fight, going to extreme lengths to ensure they were regarded as political prisoners of war, not 'ordinary decent criminals'. For years the Maze was a university of terrorism. Then, in the 1990s, its inmates played a crucial role in redefining Northern Ireland's political landscape and it became a powerhouse of peace. So this is also an account of how Maze alumni like Kelly and Ervine have played a key role in this process in the Republican and Loyalist heartlands, outside the prisons.

By any normal standards, Gerry Kelly is a ruthless terrorist. Born in 1953 and reared in the Lower Falls and Ballymurphy areas of Belfast, one of a family of eleven, he became an active member of the outlawed Irish Republican Army when the violent troubles in Northern Ireland erupted at the beginning of the 1970s. It was outrage at the events of Bloody Sunday, in January 1972, when British soldiers shot dead thirteen unarmed civil rights marchers, that caused him to enlist. Later the same year he escaped from Mountjoy Prison in Dublin where he had been sent after being caught with weapons near the Irish border. The following year he was arrested at Heathrow airport, London, trying to flee back to Ireland after playing a key role in causing a series of car bomb attacks at the Old Bailey, New Scotland Yard and other targets in central London. One person died and more than 180 were injured by the explosions. Kelly was sentenced to life imprisonment, made constant efforts to escape and, in 1976, after going on hunger strike and enduring forced feeding for 205 days, won his demand to be returned to serve his sentence in Northern Ireland. He was far from a model prisoner. On one occasion he overpowered an armed police officer guarding him during a trip to an outside hospital but he did not get away. On another, while recovering from a collapsed lung in the secure wing of a hospital, he was apprehended while cutting a hole in the chain-link fence. He did get away in 1983, however, when he was one of the 38 IRA prisoners who escaped from the Maze prison, the largest jailbreak in British or Irish penal history. As one of the armed ringleaders, his role in subduing the prison officers was a notably violent one. He remained at large until 1986 when Dutch police recaptured him in an Amsterdam apartment along with Brendan 'Bik' McFarlane, another Maze fugitive. Their property included a large cache of cash, in several currencies, fake passports and the keys to a storage container packed with arms, ammunition, explosives and bomb-making equipment. The Dutch courts initially refused to hand them over because the Old Bailey bombings were 'political offences' exempting them from the provisions of the extradition treaty, but relented when the British government agreed to remit their life sentences – McFarlane had murdered five people in a sectarian gun and bomb attack on a bar. Back in Belfast, they were sentenced to five years for offences connected with the escape. Kelly was finally freed in 1989 and ever since has played an active and influential role in the peace process. Soon afterwards, together with Martin McGuinness, another IRA leader from Londonderry, he conducted a top secret dialogue with the British government as a preliminary to the 1994 IRA ceasefire and thereafter was a member of the Sinn Fein negotiating team. He was elected to the Northern Ireland Assembly in 1998 – McFarlane was his election agent – and continues to play a highly prominent role in the new politics that are steadily transforming life in Northern Ireland.

Loyalist Assemblyman David Ervine, like his Republican counterpart, is also a great patriot or an iniquitous terrorist depending on standpoint. He was celebrating his nineteenth birthday with some friends on 21 July 1972 when the IRA launched a wave of eleven bombs throughout the city of Belfast, killing nine people and injuring 130 more. Ervine knew one of the dead, who was the same age and lived three streets away from him in east Belfast, where he had grown up. His father was an iron turner in the shipyard, his mother worked in a pram factory and he was the youngest of five children. Brimming with anger at this latest of a series of worsening IRA outrages, Ervine joined the outlawed UVF to help strike back. Two years later, on 2 November 1974, a police patrol spotted a stolen car travelling along the Holywood Road in Belfast and, when it halted at traffic lights, surrounded it. Ervine, who was driving, promptly admitted there was a bomb on board. A rope was tied around his waist and he was made to defuse and remove the 4.5 lb bomb by an Army bomb disposal unit. In May 1975, at Belfast City Commission, Lord Justice Jones sentenced him to eleven years imprisonment for possessing the bomb with intent. A relative shouted at the judge, 'You will make a terrorist of him,' and ended up in the cells for the rest of the day to cool off. But in prison Ervine, then aged 21, blossomed. Under the tutelage of the veteran Loyalist Gusty Spence (serving life for a sectarian bar murder in 1966) he picked up the pieces of the education he had abandoned at fourteen, achieved O Levels and commenced an Open University degree in arts and social sciences which he completed after his release from the Maze in 1980. Imprisonment had a profound effect on him. He remembers two young men, in for murder, arriving in the compound still in their school uniforms. He decided that he would not let prison beat him, and so used the time for observation and reflection. Free again, he earned a living as a milkman and newsagent, while carving out a role for himself as a Loyalist political spokesman. In 1994, when the ceasefire was called, the highly articulate, media-wise, pipe-smoking Ervine speedily emerged as an influential public figure. He was soon elected to the Northern Ireland Forum and, in 1997, to Belfast City Council. As a member of the Progressive Unionist Party delegation, he protected the UVF's interest in the negotiation of the Belfast Agreement in 1998 and was elected to the Northern Ireland Assembly the same year.

Ervine's closest political colleague, Billy Hutchinson, is another ex-prisoner who has played a significant part in creating the new politics. Jailed in May 1975 for life after pleading guilty to the double murder of two Catholic brothers walking to work, Hutchinson, who was then nineteen, was born in the fiercely Loyalist Shankill area of Belfast. His father was a bookmaker's clerk and his mother a home help and he was the youngest of their three children. In the Maze he became a fitness fanatic, endlessly running seven laps around Compound 21, which equalled a mile, and gaining a degree in politics and planning. After his release in 1988, he became a community development activist in west Belfast, forging a groundbreaking relationship across the peace line with Republicans to reduce sectarian tensions and tackle social deprivation on a joint basis. He was one of the prime movers behind the Loyalist ceasefire and soon built a powerful political base, winning a seat on Belfast City Council in 1997, becoming a delegate to the 1997–98 political negotiations and then securing election to the Assembly in 1998. That year he narrowly avoided assassination when he was warned by police not to go to the BBC in central Belfast for a live interview because the INLA, the extreme Republican group, was intending to ambush and kill him.

Further down the political ladder from the Assembly, many ex-prisoners are also making their political mark in the district councils. In June 2000, Cathal Crumley, who served four years for IRA membership, became the Mayor of Derry, the first Sinn Feiner to become the first citizen of an Irish city since 1922. In several of Northern Ireland's 26 district councils both Republican and Loyalist ex-prisoners are playing a full part in representing their communities, often joining forces, despite the considerable political differences that still stand between them, to push through policies and developments to benefit their people. In other community contexts, ex-prisoners are also highly active and influential. The peace process in Northern Ireland since the early 1990s has spawned hundreds of small groups and committees working to foster recon-ciliation and tolerance. In west Belfast, for instance, groups in which ex-prisoners are prominent, working on each side of the peace walls, control a network of monitors armed with portable telephones who keep in close touch with each other at times of tension to calm fears and smother clashes before they develop. Others are involved in work to regenerate communities where the effects of three decades of violence have left a legacy of unemployment, poverty, ill health and lack of self esteem. Among them are some 400 people who have served life sentences for murder, none of whom, remarkably, has ever killed again.

But while the alumni of the Maze and other Northern Ireland prisons are now playing a constructive role in society, it was not always so. For thirty violent years, men like Kelly, Ervine, Hutchinson and Crumley unleashed an awful onslaught. The violence was at first confined to Northern Ireland itself, but was soon exported to the Irish Republic and the British and European mainlands. According to figures compiled by the Royal Ulster Constabulary, there were 3271 deaths in Northern Ireland from 1969 until the end of March 2000 – that is, one every three days. In the same period, on average, a person was injured every six hours, there was a shooting incident every six hours and an explosion every fourteen hours. If a similar level of violence had taken place in Britain over the same period, there would have been 100,000 dead, one million shooting incidents and some half a million bombings.

Psychiatrists have found that those responsible for the killings were not mentally ill. 'I think society would like to think of these people as abnormal because the acts they commit are abhorrent. But when one comes to examine them that is not the case. These are not people who are psychiatrically abnormal,' said Dr H A Lyons, who, with Dr H J Harbinson, carried out a study of 106 killers in Northern Ireland between 1974 and 1984 – 59 non-political killers and 47 'politicals', both Loyalist and Republican.

The two eminent consultant psychiatrists concluded, 'The political killers tended to be normal in intelligence and mental stability, didn't have significant psychiatric problems or mental illness and didn't abuse alcohol. They didn't show remorse because they rationalised it very successfully, believing that they were fighting for a cause. The politicals, generally speaking, did not want to be seen by a psychiatrist; they feel there is nothing wrong with them, but they did co-operate. Some of them were probably quite bright, whereas among non-political killers you get more of limited intelligence, but that is common throughout the western world.' Dr Philip McGarry, another consultant psychiatrist, reached similar conclusions in 1993, after ten years work with paramilitary prisoners. 'The evidence is that in the main they are quite ordinary people. There are some suffering from personality disorders or some form of mental illness. But most paramilitary killers are not mentally ill.'

Based on anecdotal evidence, it is possible to profile the background and motivational influences on those who take up arms for the political cause they believe in. Republicans generally became active because of a family tradition of sympathy or in the aftermath of a brush with the security forces: the arrest of a parent, the searching of a house or vehicle or even being stopped on the street and aggressively questioned. Very often there was a complementary sense of grievance based on an historical perception of the Catholic/Nationalist/Republican being the underdog. This concept of a cause, reinforced through lectures, discussion and debate, and later formal education, was a major element in the Republican mindset and this sustained him or her through the travails of prison. The parallel concept of being a soldier fighting a just war was also an important one, erasing any sense of guilt or remorse and providing the commitment to fight on from behind bars. It was this strong sense of purpose which enabled so many IRA prisoners to endure the years of the blanket and 'dirty' protests and to engage in hunger strikes to the death.

Loyalists, on the other hand, were often motivated by no more than a sense of grievance about an IRA atrocity or just plain sectarian hatred. Many became actively involved in terrorism after being influenced by hardline Unionist political figures such as William Craig and the Reverend Ian Paisley, but rather than being inspired by a cause it was often out of frustration because the British government, the politicians, the security forces, the churches all seemed to be failing them. When Loyalists were apprehended they experienced a sense of shock, a feeling that they were being betrayed by those they were apparently defending. Many speak of the pain they felt that despite their 'Britishness' they were treated the same as Republicans by Her Majesty's Judges and police and prison officers wearing British Crown insignia on their uniforms. Loyalists tended to feel more guilty than Republicans and a very high proportion, especially those who had killed, found religion in prison. Other prisoners said it was a ruse to get early release, but a number who had born-again experiences became involved in religious activities after being freed. (At Easter 2000, in a public act of reconciliation, Tommy Kelly, a Republican who spent eight years in prison, washed the feet of Loyalist Jim Tate, also an ex-prisoner, with whom he now works for greater cross-community cooperation.)

Prison officers who had constant face-to-face contact with their charges for many years after they committed their crimes reckon that most of the Loyalists in custody over the years would have ended up there anyway, but that few of the Republicans would ever have seen the inside of a prison if it had not been for the troubles. Dealing with the men and women responsible for the 30-year line of milestones of massacre and destruction required superhuman restraint. 'You had to put their crimes, however awful, out of your mind,' said one long-serving officer. 'They may have slit someone's throat or blown someone's brain out but we still had to treat them as human beings.'

The way that the prison service performed this task, as the third arm of the security forces in Northern Ireland, is relatively unrecognised. Unlike the RUC and the army, its story, and its sacrifice and commitment in the face of unremitting intimidation and murder has been largely untold until now.

I would not have been able to write this book without the help and assistance of many people, some of whom wish to remain anonymous. I thank them all. In particular I should record my appreciation of the cooperation of Robin Halward, John Steele and Duncan McLaughlan, Gwyn Treharne and, later, Mark McCaffrey, together with Maureen Erne and Glenn Hughes at the Prison Service press office. Finlay Spratt and Sam Irwin were also invaluable and insightful sources. I must also thank Mgr Denis Faul, Paddy Joe McClean, Bob Rodwell, Bob Templeton, David Cook, Avila Kilmurray and Michael Hall for their help. I am especially grateful to Vincent Kearney for getting me access to the late Pat Creery's notes about the aftermath of the 1983 Maze escape which he campaigned to expose. Another trusted associate, Walter Macauley, who has an unrivalled encyclopaedic knowledge of the events and personalities of the troubles, was of invaluable assistance, as were Yvonne Murphy and her staff, who maintain and develop the political collection at the Linen Hall library in Belfast. Kelvin Boyes, a photographer of such skill that he has few peers, also helped in many ways as did my good friend Richard Ford. I also want to thank Sandra for transcribing interview tapes and Louise McElvanna for her help in sorting and organising research material.

I am also grateful to Anthony Goff and Georgia Glover at David Higham Associates, my agent; Max Eilenberg at Methuen for commissioning the book and Eleanor Rees, who so capably edited it. Above all, I wish to thank my wife, Genny, for her patience, support and encouragement while the book was being written.

Chris Ryder
Belfast
July 2000

List of illustrations

Chapter One

The warfare of the Red Indian

On 7 June 1921 the founder members of the newly-created Northern Ireland Parliament gathered for the first time at the imposing City Hall in Belfast to claim their seats. The same day, one hundred miles away in Dublin, Viscount FitzAlan of Derwent, the recently appointed Lord Lieutenant, signed an order transferring responsibility for prisons from the General Prisons Board for Ireland to the new Northern Ireland authorities in Belfast. The handover was virtually the first responsibility delegated to the new parliament and an early, tangible sign that the island of Ireland was on course to being partitioned in a bid to resolve the 'Irish question'.

For many years British administrations had been unable to reconcile the conflicting aspirations of Irish nationalists, who wanted an end to British rule in Ireland, and the Ulster Unionist minority, most of whom lived in the northern part of the island and who feared the consequences of ending the British link. As the campaign for Irish Home Rule from Britain gathered force in the late 1800's and the early years of the twentieth century, the Unionists in the north of Ireland became more and more determined in their opposition. 'Home Rule means Rome Rule,' they said, summing up their unwillingness to become a Protestant minority in what they feared would be an all-Ireland Catholic state run from Dublin. The backbone of their resistance became the Ulster Volunteer Force, an unofficial 100,000-strong militia formed by the leaders of the Unionist cause and financed by the landed gentry and business community. It was raised from 'reliable men' among the 218,206 who had signed the Ulster Covenant in September 1912, many with their own blood, as a sign of their opposition to severing the umbilical cord to Britain. The UVF was designed to demonstrate that the Protestants in the north of Ireland would resist Home Rule with force, and in April 1914, with the active connivance of Unionist political leaders, they defiantly imported 30,000 rifles and three million rounds of ammunition to underscore their determination not to be coerced into any links with Dublin.

The introduction of Home Rule was postponed with the outbreak of the First World War in 1914. Many members of the UVF then enlisted in the British forces where they formed the 36th Ulster Division. During the Battle of the Somme, fought across the poppy fields of northern France in the early days of July 1916, 5522 of them perished in a single day during which they took more than 500 prisoners and won four Victoria Crosses, Britain's highest gallantry award. Unionists regarded the sacrifice as the most telling demonstration there could be of their loyalty to Ulster, Empire and the British Crown. But their hopes that it would quench the Home Rule cause were in vain.

While many of those who fought and died at the Somme were volunteers from the southern counties of Ireland, there were other Irishmen who judged that 'England's difficulty was Ireland's opportunity' and used the British nation's preoccupation with the World War as a diversion for their own plans. A few months before the Somme, on Easter Sunday, 23 April 1916, in Dublin, a group of armed Irish Nationalists took over the main Post Office and displayed a proclamation declaring the formation of an independent Irish Republic. The Rising itself attracted little public support and was easily put down within a few days by the overwhelming superiority of the British Army. The rebel leaders were indeed jeered as they were arrested and marched away to prison. However, their speedy executions were deeply resented and the anti-British feeling stimulated by what was seen as their martyrdom was soon transformed into popular sympathy for the new Irish Republican Army and Sinn Fein ('Ourselves Alone'), its political wing. It was a telling indication of the way in which official policy and actions in the prisons could influence and even dictate the development of events beyond the walls. It was the first, but not the last time, in modern Irish history that this fateful interlock would have far-reaching political consequences.

On 19 January 1919 Sinn Fein emerged as a major political force, winning 73 of the 103 Irish seats in the election to the British Parliament. Instead of taking their seats in London, however, they announced the setting up of a new Irish parliament in Dublin. The same day, at Soloheadbag, a remote corner of County Tipperary, an eight-strong IRA 'flying column' ambushed two members of the all-Ireland police force, the Royal Irish Constabulary (RIC), who were escorting a horse-drawn cart delivering gelignite to a quarry. The constables were killed and their weapons and the explosives captured. The attack marked the beginning of a new style of hit-and-run guerrilla warfare and what is now generally regarded as Ireland's War of Independence.

At first the RIC, the eyes and ears of British power in turbulent Ireland, bore the brunt of the IRA violence. The guerrilla leaders calculated that if they could undermine the police they could easily take command of the administrative sinews of the country and, ultimately, control for in those days the police were not exclusively concerned with maintaining law and order. They also performed a wide range of important regulatory duties which included, for instance, checking weights and measures. In a poorly-educated society they were often called on to fill in forms and read or write letters, a service that contributed to an unrivalled intimate knowledge of the community they served. The resulting high grade, raw intelligence they obtained was filtered up the RIC organisation all the way back to the authorities at Dublin Castle, the seat of British power in Ireland, providing a clearly focused snapshot of the public mood at any given time.

But the initial ferocity of the IRA assault on the RIC was so effective that before long the police were on the run. The well-organised and unprecedented campaign of intimidation and assassination waged against the RIC is, in fact, now regarded as the forerunner and the inspiration of modern terrorism. In October 1920 Lord Curzon, the British Foreign Secretary, said the IRA campaign was not guerrilla warfare. 'It is the warfare of the Red Indian, of the Apache.' The IRA actions were given what was seen as political credence by the support of Dail Eireann, the rebel Parliament by then firmly established in Dublin. Policemen, and all too often their wives and children, who had been respected pillars of their communities were boycotted and harassed. RIC members often had to acquire their basic needs by forcibly serving themselves in the local shops and leaving the money on the counter. In many cases RIC officers were gunned down and murdered in carefully-laid ambushes, sprung on them both on and off duty. In the face of summary justice meted out to offenders by IRA 'courts', the authority of the police and British-led criminal justice system was steadily undermined. After ever more vicious attacks and killings the RIC were driven from their network of small barracks in villages and towns throughout Ireland and forced to regroup in heavily-guarded installations in the larger towns. With so many being killed or wounded, morale collapsed and there was a flood of resignations.

British plans to impose conscription in Ireland, which were hotly resisted by the increasingly nationalist-minded population, stoked up further resentment and were hastily dropped. In October 1919 an increasingly worried government in London posted General Sir Nevil Macready, the Commissioner of the Metropolitan Police and a veteran of the Boer War in South Africa, to Dublin to direct a campaign of repression against the IRA uprising to restore order and stabilise the situation. With the RIC demoralised and in disarray, the cutting edge of his force became 7000 ex-soldiers, most veterans of the First World War, recruited in 1920, who became known as the Black and Tans because of their mixed garb: khaki army trousers with dark green police jackets – a consequence of uniform shortages. Together with 1400 Auxiliaries, ex-officers formed into 100-strong companies and paid the then astronomical bounty of one pound a day, they imposed a reign of terror and reprisal throughout the country, but without much success. The IRA campaign was virtually unstoppable and was progressively eroding British authority in Ireland.

At the end of 1920, against this violent background, Parliament in London passed the Government of Ireland Act, but although it conceded partition, which satisfied the Unionists in the north by allowing them to remain under Britain's wing, its provisions for limited devolution to the new Dail in Dublin fell far short of the full-blooded independence for the whole of Ireland sought by Sinn Fein and the IRA. The proposals thus failed to reconcile the conflicting aspirations of either grouping and halt the violence, which intensified into a cycle of ever more ruthless reprisal and counter-reprisal. At the end of June 1921, scarcely six months after the Act's passage, with the island gripped in brutal turmoil and martial law in force over many counties, the British prime minister, David Lloyd George, decided to sue for peace.

In early July Lloyd George invited Irish Republican leaders to talks and participated in arranging a truce. By the time this came into force on 11 July, 418 RIC members and 146 British soldiers had been killed. After weeks of intensive negotiations, which began in London on 11 October, a controversial new Anglo-Irish Treaty was signed in the early hours of 6 December. It formally ratified the partition process, creating a southern Free State, with full Dominion status within the British Commonwealth of Nations, and a separate northern territory. The new northern parliament in Belfast would continue, subservient to the British parliament, and a Boundary Commission would be established to determine precisely where the Irish border should lie and what territory would remain under direct British jurisdiction.

While the British parliament overwhelmingly endorsed the new Treaty, it was not so enthusiastically received in Dublin, where it triggered off a major split within the IRA. The hardline Eamonn de Valera, who had conspicuously distanced himself from the London negotiations, condemned the Treaty as 'being in violent conflict with the wishes of the majority of this nation as expressed in successive elections during the past three years.' He became a focal point for uncompromising Republicans who wanted nothing of the London settlement and sought to restart the conflict with a view to annexing the separated northern territory. Before long the violence did resume but those who had so recently fought shoulder to shoulder for independence now engaged in an acrimonious civil war. The partition issue opened up such deep wounds in Irish society that the scars and effects would disfigure and divide the body politic for several generations, and would still influence and dictate political alignments and policies in the Irish Republic even some 75 years on.

Throughout the civil war period the most serious violence was confined to the southern and western counties of the island, but even so there was considerable IRA activity in the north which deeply alarmed the Unionists. While their earlier belligerence had persuaded the British government to abandon Home Rule and concede their demand for partition, they feared that if the IRA hardliners secured power in Dublin they would subsequently seek to annexe the north. There were acute fears that the war-weary British government might not come to the Unionists' assistance. Furthermore, the extent of partition and the exact line of the new north-south border had still not been finalised. Unionist uncertainty was also aggravated by the position of the one-third Nationalist minority in the north, who were far from content at being abandoned by the new Free State and exceptionally fearful as a result of the ugly sectarian violence they were suffering and the lack of any security force to effectively protect them. Against this background the Unionists of Ulster, this time with the decisive upper hand of being in government, decided that once again they must look to their own security and suppress the minority Nationalist community. London was encouraged to give them full control over law and order.

To the hard-pressed British government, preoccupied with containing the volatile situation in Ireland and finding it hard to obtain the money and manpower to do so, the Unionists' willingness to assume the law and order burden was most welcome. London showed little concern for the implications for the Nationalist minority. Consequently, on 22 November, even before the Treaty negotiations had been concluded, the necessary powers were transferred to Belfast. The task of implementing them was delegated to Dawson Bates, a Belfast solicitor and prominent Unionist, who had played a key role in the campaign against Home Rule. His reward was to be appointed as the Minister of Home Affairs. Bates was a small-minded, uncompromising hardliner of undoubtedly bigoted views, who regarded the entire Catholic nationalist minority in the north as a threat to the very existence of the state. He was also deeply wary of Catholics in the soon-to-be disbanded RIC.

Bates never recognised any need to create a law and order framework acceptable to both the Unionist and Nationalist traditions, and the highly partial outlook he pioneered dominated law and order policy long after he left office in 1943. His hardline views therefore set the tone and formed the cornerstone of a repressive security policy which was unashamedly enforced against the entire minority on the basis that all were potential IRA sympathisers. In stark contrast it was only selectively employed to curb the sectarian excesses of hardline Unionists. London, as it was to do for most of the next fifty years, turned a blind eye.

Within three months of gaining security responsibility Bates had supervised the drafting of the Civil Authorities (Special Powers) Act. This draconian piece of legislation was then pushed through the Belfast parliament in just over three weeks and came into force on 7 April 1922. (It was regularly renewed and remained on the statute book, virtually unchanged, for fifty years.) Its catch-all provisions enabled the authorities to detain and intern suspects without trial. Prisoners could be flogged or executed. Coroners' inquests could be dispensed with. Land and property could be commandeered for security purposes. Organisations, meetings, publications and gatherings could be prohibited by simple ministerial order. If any unforeseen security problem developed, the minister was empowered to take all such steps as may be necessary to preserve the peace and maintain order. The Act also made it an offence to commit any act prejudicial to peace and order whether specifically forbidden or not.

The Special Powers Act, as it became known, was the main instrument of law and order policy. The Special Constabulary, which was its principal cutting edge, was no less controversial. The Unionists had earlier persuaded the British authorities in Belfast and Dublin to permit the formation of a Special Constabulary, which, by drawing their most militant sympathisers into the fabric of the legitimate security forces, provided them with absolute control and, of course, intensified Nationalist fears. The Unionist administration was primarily concerned to have a well-equipped security force they could absolutely trust and directly control in the event of any British retreat from the promise of partition or, if the British would not come to their aid, to withstand any IRA attempt at taking the north.

By the time Bates came to power, the undisciplined behaviour of the

Specials – the 'B force' – was already a matter of serious concern. Indeed there were well-founded suspicions that many were taking the law into their own hands. A contemporary report by a police officer at the Belfast headquarters of the RIC summed it up: 'There can never be any possibility of establishing confidence and security so long as the B force, the ordinary Protestant countryman and, in many cases, corner boy, is supplied with arms and clothing by his government and authorised to "get on top," as it were, of his neighbour.' The report continued, 'In my own district there are B men who have confessed they committed a certain murder but evidence could not be gathered from the victim's relations or from the witnesses since all had been intimidated and warned that if they identified the B men, they would "go down" next.'

The influential *Manchester Guardian* communicated the fears about the Specials to a wider audience in March 1921 in a critical editorial. 'The Special Constabulary, drawn almost exclusively from the ranks of the Orange Lodges and the Unionist "Volunteers", was nominally raised to protect life and property and to maintain order, not to become a force of terrorists exercising powers of death over their Catholic neighbours, for in the Ulster Unionist mind Catholic and Sinn Feiner are synonymous. Ulster's case against a single parliament for Ireland has always rested on its alleged fear of persecution. It will be a bad beginning for the Ulster Parliament if its establishment coincides with the dragooning of the Catholic minority in the six counties by an armed Protestant force administering a sort of lynch law.'

Early in 1922, as the civil war raged in the south, it was agreed between the British government and representatives of the new administrations in Dublin and Belfast that the RIC would be speedily disbanded and replaced by two new police forces, one in each jurisdiction. The new Free State government, in a far-sighted bid to put law and order on a new footing, decided the southern police force was to be a civil unarmed organisation called the Garda Siochana ('Civic Guards' or 'Guardians of the Peace'), which came into existence after the RIC was formally disbanded on 4 April 1922.

In the north, RIC members were reprieved until a parliamentary committee considered the policing question. It began work in January and reported in March 1922 recommending a 3000-strong force, with one third of the places reserved for Catholics, the remainder to be recruited from the former members of the RIC and Specials. It was to be called the Ulster Constabulary. By the time it came into official existence on 1 June 1922, Buckingham Palace had been prevailed upon to allow the force to be called the Royal Ulster Constabulary (RUC). By imposing on the new force the dual responsibility for defending the state and maintaining law and order, the Unionist government blindly built a significant flaw into the RUC. Whilst it was to be tolerated by the Nationalist community and contain a small proportion of Catholic members over the years, it was never fully accepted, nor enjoyed the wholehearted consent it should have done, because it was long seen as nothing more than the instrument of Unionist repression.

Bates, who maintained a tight personal grip on the creation of the new police force, certainly saw it as the armed wing of Unionism. Although many of the officer-class in the RIC had Unionist sympathies, the rank and file, in hostile Unionist eyes, was predominantly comprised of southern Catholics who were at best sitting on the fence to see which way things would go, or, more probably, IRA sympathisers and no friends of Unionism. Small wonder then that there was little encouragement for them to join the new RUC. Of the 2000 RIC officers in and around Belfast who were paid off as the RUC came into existence only 250 were enlisted in the new force, a development that virtually removed what was already limited supervision of the unruly Specials when sectarian trouble was as bad as ever. In one three-week period in 1922, for instance, there were 138 killings: 96 Catholics and 42 Protestants. Despite this there was little urgency in getting the RUC operational. After three months in existence, only one third of its complement had been recruited. The RUC was actually built from the top down with priority being given to the command structure and the recruitment of officers who were suitable in Unionist eyes. This was a most important investment, for compliant officers were essential to the direct political control of the force which the Unionists forged from the outset.

The violence in Northern Ireland deeply concerned the new government in Dublin. They were put under great pressure by the Catholic Church and other representatives of the abandoned northern Catholics who were convinced that many of the grim murders and outrages continued to be carried out by the Specials. In one chilling incident eight members of a Catholic family were murdered in their Belfast home by five armed men, generally regarded as Specials, although this belief, which is maintained in Belfast folklore to this day, was never proved beyond doubt. Unionist insecurity was meanwhile exacerbated by a series of clashes with the IRA in disputed counties where a boundary commission was studying the fixing of the frontier between north and south. At first the proposal was to isolate the nine counties of the traditional province of Ulster but, after the Unionists did their electoral sums, they pushed, successfully as it turned out, for a more favourable split, taking only six counties which gave them a safe two-to-one majority over the Nationalists. (Final agreement that the border would enclose the six northern counties, Londonderry, Tyrone, Fermanagh, Armagh, Down and Antrim, was, however, not reached until December 1925.) Faced with this turmoil, London was terrified that the pro-settlement government in Dublin would collapse and be replaced by IRA hardliners who would overthrow the precarious deal and perhaps even march on the north. It therefore resisted Unionist calls for action against the IRA in the contentious border area, instead pushing representatives from both sides into discussions about ways to break the spiral of tension and violence. The result was a pact, agreed between leaders of the new administrations in the north and south, designed, with London's prodding, to create a cooperative relationship between them and draw the Catholics in the north, who had been boycotting the new parliament, wholeheartedly into the workings of the new government and administration in Belfast.

Winning Catholic confidence in the forces of law and order was seen as the priority in London and Dublin, so a new advisory committee was set up to oversee recruitment to fill the one-third quota reserved for Catholics in the RUC. Further confidence-building measures included a £500,000 relief scheme to aid the 10,000 workers and 23,000 homeless displaced during the sectarian pogroms. In a bid to take the heat out of the situation it was also agreed that police detachments in nationalist areas and search parties looking for arms would consist of both Protestant and Catholic officers.

Unionists did not really want a relationship with the south or anything more than nominal Catholic involvement in the running of the north. The hollowness of their commitment to the pact was exposed within days. After an RIC officer had been shot and murdered in Belfast, a party of Specials entered Arnon Street on the northern fringe of the city centre and shot two men dead in their homes. A third was beaten to death with a sledgehammer and his seven-year-old son was shot in the head and died a day later. These reprisals created further panic among Catholics and, under the terms of the pact, Dublin asked for more information about the incident. Repeated requests were ignored in Belfast, effectively ending the pact and breaking off the slim hope of formal relations between the two parts of Ireland. There was no substantial political dialogue between them again for forty years.

The last vestige of the pact was the police advisory committee which was urged into life by London, beginning to baulk at the cost of massaging Unionist insecurity by maintaining nearly 50,000 men under arms. It only met three times, never with its full complement of twelve present. The Belfast government had no desire to make it work, preferring instead to see as many of the 'loyal' Specials as possible fill the quota reserved for Catholics and thus ensure its control of the RUC. The Catholic members of the committee were equally half-hearted about their task, succumbing to intimidation and the mood of sullen non-cooperation with the Unionist government that was to dominate Nationalist and Catholic attitudes for the next four decades.

With the collapse of the pact, the Unionists stepped up their policy of repressing the Catholic minority to assert their own authority more decisively, albeit with some justification. Over the weekend of 20-22 May there were fourteen murders, and several houses belonging to the Unionist gentry, including those of the O'Neills and the Londonderrys, were put to the torch. On the Monday morning, William John Twaddell, a Unionist member of the northern parliament, was shot dead in the city centre of Belfast as he arrived at his tailoring shop. A crisis Cabinet meeting later in the day, ignoring advice from sympathisers in London about antagonising the government there, allowed the newly passed Special Powers Act to gather little dust. The Unionists decided to outlaw the IRA and other Republican groupings under the new Act, and to introduce internment without trial. In the early hours of the next day some 300 suspects were rounded up by Specials and the Army in dawn swoops and before long 400 were in indefinite custody. Few Unionist supporters were interned despite the fact that the violence was clearly being carried out by armed gangs in both communities.

It was against this turbulent security background that the Lord Lieutenant's order transferring responsibility for prisons to the northern authorities came into effect on 1 December 1921, after six months' preparation by a prisons branch established in the new Ministry of Home Affairs in Belfast. They thus assumed responsibility for implementing the provisions of the Prisons (Ireland) Acts of 1826 and 1877, the Private Lunatic Asylums (Ireland) Act 1842, the Central Criminal Lunatic Asylum (Ireland) Act 1845 and the Habitual Drunkards Act 1879. During the transitional period prisoners belonging to the southern part of the island were removed and on the handover date the northern authorities inherited responsibility for 460 male and 64 female prisoners, by then held in custody in the three northern prisons: Belfast, Armagh and Londonderry. There was ample accommodation at their disposal, 753 cells altogether. About 1400 prisoners remained in what was then known as the Free State.

With many of those in custody being held for offences connected with the political violence, regarding themselves as virtual prisoners of war and certainly not ordinary criminals, the authorities faced an immediate crisis. In the early hours of December 2, the day after the handover, a number of IRA prisoners overpowered and killed two Special Constables, part of the Derry jail guard, by asphyxiating them with chloroform. Assisted by a prison officer and accomplices outside, they then threw a rope over the wall and escaped but a police patrol outside fired on them and they were promptly recaptured. Later the two ringleaders and the prison officer were convicted of murder and sentenced to death, but the penalty was commuted and they were instead given lengthy terms of penal servitude.

The three prisons taken over by the northern authorities had been under the management of the General Prison Board since 1877, when the local provision and control of prisons in each county was centralised. They represented a ramshackle inheritance. Belfast prison, situated at Crumlin Road on the northern fringe of the city centre, was by far the largest with 586 cells. Its design can be traced back to 1837 when Lord John Russell, the Home Secretary, issued a circular letter to magistrates recommending a move from open to cellular confinement. A model prison was then constructed at Pentonville in London and opened in 1842. Its now classic design, with wings of cells radiating like spokes from a central building, was copied in 54 new prisons throughout the British Isles within six years.

In 1840, the Grand Jury in Belfast commissioned Sir Charles Lanyon, the county surveyor, to prepare plans for a new prison and courthouse to replace existing accommodation at Carrickfergus. Sussex-born Lanyon, who was responsible for designing such other enduring Belfast landmarks as the Custom House, Queen's College (now University) and the Presbyterian Theological College, travelled to London to see Pentonville and copy the design. Construction work began a year later after Lanyon reported to the Lent Assizes that he had obtained 'a most suitable site, containing ten statute acres. The ground was high, had a good fall for drainage and the means of obtaining a water supply.' The project, the first cellular prison in Ireland, which provided 320 cells and other accommodation, cost £60,000 and was designed with four three-storey wings radiating from a central building known as 'the circle'. When construction work on the chimney stack was completed, the hodsmen, masons and bricklayers stood at the top and waved and cheered to the crowds below. Afterwards they shared a celebratory quart of whisky.

The building was designated as the District Bridewell and House of Correction for Belfast and the first Governor was John Forbes, appointed in 1843. The first prisoners, 106 in all, were moved in during early 1845, having been marched from Carrickfergus in chains, and a report by the Commissioners, a body appointed by the Grand Jury to oversee the prison, stated, 'It is gratifying to know that crime has so much diminished since 1839, when our calculations were made, that at present the district of Belfast Quarter Sessions would not afford inmates for the 169 cells appropriated as a District Bridewell for the Belfast Division.' As a result of this, the Commissioners, 'with a view to economy' and 'keeping down the county rate,' recommended that the Lord Lieutenant direct that prisoners from all over County Antrim be allotted to the Belfast House of Correction. The Commissioners' fiscal rectitude even extended to the Governor. When Robert Auld was appointed in 1878, he had to sign 'A Bond for Performance of Duties,' which was witnessed by two sureties and three Justices of the Peace. It stated, 'The newly appointed Governor of Belfast (County Antrim) Gaol agrees to pay the sum of £500, with two sureties of £250 each, if he fails to carry out his duties diligently. The money is to be recovered from his successors if he fails to pay when he is alive. To cover the cost of any escape or wilful damage which, as Governor of the gaol, it is his responsibility to prevent.'

Apart from being one of the city's most prominent landmarks, the jail was listed in guides and directories and visitors to Belfast frequently went out of their way to see it. One such group were the British Medical Association, who in a guide to their 1884 meeting, were regaled with a whimsical description of the 'Crumlin Hotel, the managers being HM Ministers with boarders being taken by the week, month or year. Terms are in every case free, with all extras paid and clothing found.'

Later, in 1850, a courthouse was erected opposite the jail and linked to it with an underground passage across the Crumlin Road. In those early days it was paved with cobblestones until a prisoner secreted one in his clothing and flung it across a court, narrowly missing the Lord Chief Justice of Ireland. This courthouse and the adjacent prison were to play a central role in the affairs of Northern Ireland for many years to come.

There had been a prison in Derry as far back as 1620 but the prison inherited in 1921 was of more recent vintage, built in 1791, at a time when virtually every county had to provide its own prison, and later extended. Its original construction was criticised as being 'far too capacious for a district in which crime is comparatively rare'. Eight years later, Theobald Wolfe Tone, one of the leaders of the 1798 Rising, was initially held there after being captured aboard one of a fleet of French ships off the Donegal coast. He was later transported to Dublin where he cheated the hangman by committing suicide after his plea to be shot as a soldier was rejected by a court martial.

In 1820, Derry jail was considerably extended, notably by the addition of grandiose turrets constructed from locally cut Dungiven sandstone. Altogether £33,718 was spent creating 179 cells, 26 workrooms, a hospital and a residence for the Governor. Most of the inmates, whose number varied between 80 and 150 over the next ten years, were debtors or illegal distillers. There were usually about twenty women in custody, most of them prostitutes. During the construction period four members of the notorious Atcheson gang, highwaymen and sheep stealers, escaped from the jail by mingling with building labourers. Three were soon recaptured and publicly executed outside the prison in 1820.

Public executions ceased in 1860. After that, four executions by hanging took place inside the prison, the most recent in 1923, shortly after partition. During the 1930s and '40s part of the prison was used as a Criminal Lunatic Asylum, and from time to time it was also used to house internees, as those detained without trial were known. After the Second World War, the prison was used to house short-term prisoners, and although they worked breaking stones and sewing mailbags the regime was so relaxed that staff sent some prisoners on errands to the local shops. The prison closed in 1953 and was very briefly reopened to accommodate soldiers at the outset of the Troubles in 1969. It was finally demolished in 1971, save for one of its distinctive turrets, to make way for a housing scheme.

Armagh prison, opened in 1782, was the oldest of the three inherited establishments. It was designed by Francis Johnston, but behind the decorative Georgian façade, which provided a residence for the Governor and administrative offices, there lay a grim interior which included some dungeon cells. Until about 1850 prisoners who breached the harsh discipline were put on to a treadmill which required them to maintain a pace of 48 steps a minute for ten minutes before they were given a five-minute respite. An 1823 report underlined the toughness of the regime and the lack of facilities. There were eighteen cells and six debtors' rooms but no chapel or infirmary and the inmates, male and female, were crowded as many as four or five into a single cell. Things appeared to have improved over the next half century or so. In 1837 a hospital was added, the first of its type in the British Isles, and new wings with more cells. According to *The Book of County Armagh* by George Henry Bassett, published in 1888:

'At the south end of The Mall the front of the County Gaol occupies one side of the square to which it gives its name. It is a substantial, sightly structure, with large windows, and, in fact, is very much more like a benevolent than a penal institution. This is the "old part", three stories high. The Governor, Captain J. A. Chippindall, occupies a portion of it, and the rest is used for offices, officers' quarters, hospital ward, and cells, nine in number, for the reception of prisoners awaiting examination by the doctor, preparatory to classification. The new portion of the prison dates from 1846. Here there is the usual Central Hall, with which the male and female wards are in communication. The cells in both wards are maintained in perfect condition, the most sensitive nose failing to perceive the faintest trace of that odor expected to be found associated with bolts and bars. There are two tiers of cells, one at each side of the ward. An iron gallery surrounds the upper tier, and a substantial rope netting covers the open space, as a precaution against suicide. There are good bathing facilities, and the sanitary arrangements throughout are excellent. A well-filled bookcase in the central hall supplies material for improving the mind. During the first month of confinement the prisoner has an opportunity to become acquainted with the "plank bed" – a bare board. If he takes to it philosophically, he can earn two good conduct marks a day, and rise triumphant from the "plank" to a mattress in thirty days. The cells are each twelve feet by seven, and nine feet high, and are heated by hot-air flues. The buildings and premises include three and a half acres. Prisoners are received from the whole of Armagh, Cavan, and Monaghan, and from a portion of Down and a portion of Fermanagh.'

Public executions halted in Armagh after 1860. The last prisoner hanged, in 1904, was Joseph Fee, a Monaghan man who was known as the Clones murderer, whose last word was 'Guilty,' as he stood by the hangman on the scaffold. In 1924, after partition, Armagh was designated as a being a place of confinement solely for female convicts, but some male prisoners were detained there from time to time. They were kept busy making shirts, towels and bed linen for the prisons and the police. During the Second World War and subsequent periods of civil disorder, female internees were held there.

In 1922, all three establishments taken over were considered local prisons, suitable only for prisoners serving terms of less than two years. They were in a poor state of repair and had suffered wilful damage during the handover period. There was no provision for inmates sentenced to penal servitude or preventive detention. With the State Inebriate Reformatory and the Central Criminal Lunatic Asylum both located near Dublin, there was also no suitable accommodation available locally for what were then called Lunacy Administration and Inebriate Retreats.

A contemporary report for Bates records that 'many of the prisoners see themselves as "political" and are not amenable to prison rules and discipline.' None of them performed any work, and the report said that the unduly relaxed prison discipline was in danger of breaking down completely. Four years earlier, in 1918, a Special Commission appointed to investigate complaints of ill-treatment by Catholic prisoners held in Belfast for offences under the Defence of the Realm Act made its report. It provided an insight into the problem of dealing with such highly-motivated prisoners and the tensions and confrontational atmosphere they so skilfully created throughout this period on the assumption that their part in the fight for Irish freedom did not cease once they were put behind bars.

On 17 June one of those in custody, who was referred to as 'Commandant' McDonagh by the other inmates, had complained about the prison diet and submitted his own demands. In particular he asked that prisoners be allowed 21 ounces of butter a week, some four times more than the prescribed ration. The Prisons Board turned down the demand, triggering hostility between the Governor and the prisoners. Just over a week after making the request for more butter, the prisoners asked to be transferred to cells on the top floor of one of the blocks with a view out over the wall to the Crumlin Road beyond. The Head Warder agreed to the move when the prisoners gave an undertaking not to be noisy. Within hours, however, the prisoners opened ventilation panels in the cell windows and began a disturbance, shouting slogans, singing 'rebel' songs and exchanging insults with a hostile crowd which soon gathered on the road outside the jail.

McDonagh was interviewed by the Governor next day and warned that such conduct must stop, but that night the scenes were repeated, a larger crowd was attracted outside the prison and the Chief Commissioner of Police for Belfast warned the Governor that if the prisoners were not silenced he feared a serious breach of the peace. Warders were sent to re-seal the cell windows to prevent the prisoners seeing into and being seen from the Crumlin Road, but the action sparked violence with prisoners breaking cell doors and windows, digging holes in the walls, smashing furniture and resisting efforts to remove them from the cells. Nearly 50 police were called to assist the prison staff and, with the Governor and Doctor standing by, they used sledgehammers, crowbars and a fire hose to break down a barricade and restore order. Some of the ninety prisoners forcibly removed were handcuffed but after breaking the cuffs they were more effectively subdued by being cuffed with their arms behind their backs. The disturbances prompted complaints about harsh treatment from the prisoners who alleged 'wanton cruelty': specifically, being hand-cuffed, put in straitjackets, manacled with their hands behind their backs, fire-hosed and left to sleep in wet and fouled clothes as well as being handcuffed while attending mass and communion. They said the violence had been actuated by religious animosity and partisan and vindictive feelings by the Governor and Warders towards prisoners of a different faith from their own.

The Lord Lieutenant appointed the Rt Hon Mr Justice Dodd as Commissioner to enquire into and report on the complaints. He convened a hearing at the Four Courts in Dublin on 19 December 1918 stating in his opening remarks that 'in all matters of procedure the essentials of justice must be observed.' However, by the time he received the formal complaint and answer and reconvened on 9 January 1919 counsel for the prisoners had decided to absent themselves from the enquiry. Not surprisingly, as Dodd's eventual report records, 'the answer contained specific denials of most of the acts charged in the complaint, but as to some of them there was a justification, alleging concerted and combined acts of gross misconduct, insubordination and riot on the part of the prisoners, which made it essential to restrain them with an averment that what was done was done by the officials with all possible self-restraint and humanity.' Dodd went to considerable lengths in his report to show how carefully he had considered the allegations, even in the absence of any direct evidence from prisoners or their legal representatives. Great force is given to the fact that the head warder and the prison doctor were both Catholics. Citing the evidence of the doctor that no prisoner suffered abuse, Dodd says, 'He is a Catholic, a gentleman.' Dodd also reports how he was reassured about 'the matter that had been pressing on my mind' when the Solicitor-General for Ireland produced a communion cloth and showed how the sacrament 'could be reverently partaken of by the communicant, even in handcuffs.'

The report, which conceded nothing to the prisoners, concludes, 'The suggestion that the Governor was influenced by any vindictive design, any partisan motive, is clearly out of the question. Accordingly, as a matter of judicial inference from facts clearly proved, and it is hard to see how they could be controverted, I decide that the treatment of the prisoners in this respect by the Governor, though severe, was necessary and was salutary. I am of the opinion, therefore, that all the accusations up to this against the Governor and Officials are disproved.'

The Commissioner also notes how, a few weeks after the disturbances, the prisoners reacted to an offer by the Visiting Justices to 'restore ameliorations' including better food. Sir Robert Kennedy gave evidence that one of the prisoners told him they had no gratitude for the con-cession, and that they recognised no authority except that of their leaders. It was always thus. A 1920s poster in support of prisoners at the height of the War of Independence outlined the roll of honour of imprisoned Republican 'martyrs' since as far back as 1014 and asked, 'Why did they die?' The first name on the list was Brian Boru, a first century king of Ireland, followed in subsequent centuries by the Earl of Desmond (1467), Shane O'Neill (1567), Hugh Roe O'Donnell (1605), Owen Roe (1643), Bishop McMahon (1650) and Father Sheehy (1766). Archbishop O'Hurley, Fr John Murphy, Lord Edward Fitzgerald and, of course, Wolfe Tone are listed as victims of the 1798 Rising. In subsequent years others cited to inspire are Robert Emmet (1803), O'Neill Crowley (1867) and those involved in the 1916 Rising, Padraig Pearse and James Connolly, as well as Thomas Ashe (1917) and Richard Coleman (1918). 'They died to secure the liberation of the older political prisoner in the world – Ireland!' the poster text concluded.

Long-remembered and often long-winded Republican mythology and propaganda recounted the heroics of these martyrs in colourful language and often grim and gory detail. A 1970s pamphlet regurgitated some age-old Republican attitudes: 'Recognition of Republican prisoners as Political Prisoners-of-War is a problem which is certainly not new in Ireland. Since the days when the English first set foot on Irish soil, Irish men and women have doggedly fought their ever increasing control over the Irish nation. In many countries as far afield as America, Australia, Britain and, of course, here in Ireland itself, thousands of Irish patriots have struggled to wage the fight for the national liberation of our country, and for their efforts many have suffered imprisonment. Throughout those centuries imprisoned Irish Freedom Fighters resolutely refused to accept the classification of "criminal" despite the repressive and often inhuman measures imposed on them.' When it suited them Republicans would even quote Karl Marx, who, the pamphlet said, took a great interest in the Irish struggle and in particular the fate of Irish political prisoners. After the abortive Fenian Rising (1867), Marx wrote, 'One of the prisons where persons suspected of being Fenians were buried alive is Mountjoy Prison in Dublin. The Prison Inspector, Murray, is a despicable brute who maltreated the prisoners so cruelly that some of them went mad.'

In a pragmatic bid to bolster the uneasy peace in Ireland and bring an end to the perpetually confrontational environment in the prisons, the British government announced on 12 January 1922 that there would be an amnesty to mark the ratification of the Treaty, establishing the Irish Free State and partitioning Northern Ireland. Two days later, 26 prisoners under sentence of death had their sentences commuted to terms of penal servitude. In all 1008 prisoners convicted of politically motivated offences benefited. A special train was laid on to convey 130 Sinn Feiners from Crumlin Road prison to Mountjoy in Dublin, from where they were released.

The new Ministry of Home Affairs in Belfast then launched a crackdown to assert its control of the prisons and prisoners. A circular ordered the cancellation of any 'ameliorative treatment while undergoing imprisonment for political offences' and instructions were given rigorously enforcing prison rules and discipline. Over the next few months 191 prisoners, a third of the remaining prison population, were punished. At the same time all inmates were put to work, most sewing mailbags for the Post Office. By the end of the year, in a report to the Governor of Northern Ireland, Bates was able to write, 'Those in custody soon realised that they would be treated as ordinary prisoners and could not expect special privileges and by the close of the year 1922 the conduct and industry of the prisoners were quite satisfactory.'

The respite was only temporary, as unfolding events over the next eighty or so years would demonstrate. In the words of Dr Edward O'Dwyer, the pro-Republican Bishop of Limerick: 'Ireland will never be content as a province. God has made her a nation and while grass grows and water runs, there will be men in Ireland to dare and die for her.' As the penal history of Northern Ireland will also show, there were others from a Loyalist background, prepared to fight and die, and endure imprisonment, to see that Northern Ireland remained within the United Kingdom.

Chapter Two
Prisoners, lunatics and habitual drunkards

The crackdown and stabilising process in the prisons during the watershed year of 1922 reflected a settling in events outside. The Lord Mayor of Belfast succeeded in negotiating a ten-day truce which brought the sectarian shooting and killing to a halt, and before long the violence fizzled out altogether. At the same time the courts, implementing the Special Powers Act, had adopted a tough policy on offenders, imposing long terms of imprisonment and flogging. (Between December 1921 and May 1923, when the practice was abolished under pressure from the British government, 52 prisoners were sentenced to corporal punishment with the flogging carried out in 42 cases.) As a result, the average daily prison population had risen to 611 in 1922 from 479 the previous year. In addition there were around 600 internees, held indefinitely without charge or trial, to be accommodated.

In 1922 the partitioned province of Northern Ireland had a violent birth, with 231 murders in Belfast alone and another 295 murders elsewhere. As the violence subsided, the curfew was lifted and those interned without trial were gradually released, enabling the new province to come to terms with a precarious peace. Officials were meanwhile pressing ahead with arrangements for the government and administration of Northern Ireland, which was steadily being separated from the former all-Ireland institutions operated from Dublin. Great importance was attached to recruiting ex-service prison officers who could keep control and maintain discipline within the prisons. 'The post of prison officer is one calling for tact and judgment and the ministry have made it their aim to secure the best possible warders,'wrote Bates. Lord Polwarth, the Chairman of the Scottish Prison Commission, and Colonel Rogers, Surveyor of the English Prison Commission, were called in to carry out an inspection of the Northern Ireland prisons system and make recommendations for whatever alterations and additions were necessary. By then arrangements had been made for prisoners serving long terms, who were classified as convicts, to be detained in English and Scottish establishments. In 1923, for instance, 73 had been transferred to English prisons and another 62 to

Scotland because of the lack of suitable accommodation. This arrangement cost the financially hard-pressed Northern Ireland government £16,999 that year.

Over the next few years, reflecting the official judgment that things had settled down in the community and the prisons, gradual improvements were made to the facilities and running of the system. In 1925, what the ministry described as the 'public spectacle of the daily escort of women prisoners from the Belfast police court by train to Armagh' ceased when a motor van was acquired for the task. Work was commenced to install electric light in Belfast prison and provide married quarters for prison officers and workshops for the prisoners. One wing of the prison was converted, given its own workshops and designated to hold those convicts serving terms of preventive detention, and part of the prison in Derry was converted for use as a Criminal Lunatic Asylum, enabling the ministry to assume responsibility for eighteen male and four female inmates from the north and end its agency agreement with the Irish Asylum at Dundrum. Another gap in penal provision was closed in December 1926 with the opening of the Malone Training School, a Borstal for young offenders. During the next year fourteen youths were committed to Borstal, but two who 'proved of incorrigible character and were not amenable to discipline' were later transferred to Belfast prison.

Much of the work involved in renovating and converting the prison estate was carried out by prisoner labour, especially carpenters, joiners, labourers and whitewashers among the population. Other prisoners were put to work on cleaning, cooking, nursing, sick care and stoking the furnaces. A garden was established in Belfast prison to provide potatoes and vegetables and also a laundry to meet the needs of the prison and government departments. At the end of 1926, the ministry calculated the value of all this labour as being worth £9684 and recorded it as a significant contribution towards the total prison running costs of £49,557. 'The expense of maintaining prisons is being kept as low as possible without in any way lessening the efficiency of the service,' the ministry reported.

Then as now, Northern Ireland was a deeply religious, albeit divided, society and, while the public at large knew and cared little of what went on behind the forbidding walls around the prisons, there were elements who took a keen interest out of a sense of religious or charitable duty. Outside interest in the conduct of prisons had been legally recognised as far back as 1826 when the Prisons (Ireland) Act of that year had empowered Grand Juries to appoint Boards of Superintendence and Commissioners. The 1877 Prison Act reformed the system and Visiting

Committees were established for each prison, primarily with powers to impose additional sentences on prisoners found guilty of breaches of prison discipline. They fully subscribed to the theory that prison should be a forbidding place, a deterrent to wrongdoing. Reminiscing about his role as Chairman of the Visiting Committee and Board of Visitors to Convicts, in the *Belfast News Letter* on 9 July 1936, Mr Godfrey Ferguson, a Justice of the Peace and High Sheriff of County Antrim, said, 'If there be truth in the axiom that the architectural design of the exterior of a building should suggest its interior use, surely our own jail does not belie the axiom. No one could mistake what the building is. With its awe-inspiring portico and unclimbable walls, it suggests nothing but a prison. Those familiar with the interior know that it is as sombre inside as out – perhaps necessarily so. There is a depressing atmosphere which the visitor – even one with an easy conscience – feels the moment he enters the prison.'

Running parallel with this stern concept of deterrence was a softer, more philanthropic notion that prisoners were unfortunates who needed help. This was first given expression in 1923 with the formation of two discharge societies to aid ex-prisoners – one for the Catholics, another for Protestants. In 1927, for instance, Lord Justice Andrews revealed that 468 prisoners had been assisted on discharge, and made a broadcast appeal for funds to help the Prisoners Aid Society. But efforts to assist prisoners were not confined to the time after their release. An official was sent to Britain 'to study educational schemes and other means to restore to prisoners a sense of self-respect and make them useful citizens on release.' In its 1925 report to the Governor of Northern Ireland the Ministry noted that 'a break in the monotony of prison life by occasional lectures etc, attendance at which is dependent always on good behaviour, has been effective in preventing the dulling effect of imprisonment.'

In the 1920s an energetic prison welfare organisation, known as TocH, 'improved the education and brightened the outlook of prisoners' by providing classes in French, shorthand, drawing, arithmetic, geography, history, motor mechanics and book-keeping. It also organised lectures, concerts and debates. In 1931 the ministry records that two convicts were taught rug-making 'through the kindness of voluntary lady teachers'. Another contemporary reference has 'educational classes and concerts conducted under the guidance of ladies and gentlemen interested in the welfare of prisoners'.

By then the activities of the two discharge societies were on a considerable scale. That year 800 prisoners were interviewed prior to release, 300 discharged prisoners were aided with temporary board and lodging and

400 visits were made to give help to the wives and families of prisoners suffering 'want or privation'. In addition a large number of employers were interviewed and encouraged to give jobs to ex-prisoners. Sometimes representatives of the Societies intervened at the Police Courts offering to help 'men and boys make good' rather then be sent to prison. In their annual report they said, 'It is a matter of great satisfaction to the Societies that they hear regularly from ex-prisoners who, through the assistance of the Societies, have been able to make a fresh start and it is encouraging to learn that the great majority of them have taken full advantage of the chance which has been given them and have not again got into trouble.'

While there was an incorrigible criminal element who benefited from this apparently large amount of philanthropic and welfare work, Northern Ireland, regardless of its ongoing political divisions and periodic tension, was a relatively tranquil, law-abiding society. People remember life between the two World Wars as hard and spartan, but advances such as the steady spread of electric light and motorised transport gradually helped improve facilities and living standards. Although the RUC had not attracted the one-third Catholic quota outlined for it and was still an overwhelmingly Protestant force, it had fostered a good working relationship and was fully acceptable to both the Catholic and Protestant communities at local level. Police officers also acquired intimate knowledge of the areas and communities they served and lived among. By moving infrequently on transfer they got to know everybody and became known themselves, enjoying a high degree of respect and even fear. This enabled the RUC to keep a close grip on criminals in the community and apprehend them when necessary. People felt a strong sense of safety and security. In both urban and rural areas it was rare to find a locked house door. Families either left the door on the latch or the key was hung inside the letter box on a length of string.

Between 1922 and 1939, there were, for instance, only eight rapes recorded in Belfast and 43 elsewhere in Northern Ireland. From 1923 to 1939 the police recorded a total of 244 assaults in Belfast compared with 185 for the troubled year of 1922 alone. Outside the city there were 561 assaults compared with 365 in 1922. Robbery showed a similar decrease once the troubles subsided. In 1922 there were 843 robberies throughout Northern Ireland compared with a total of 636 over the next seventeen years.

The numbers of people in prison reflected this state of affairs. The average daily prison population rose from 278 in 1920 to peak at 611 a day in troubled 1922. After that it fell to, and hovered at, about half that number for several years. There were 353 in custody each day in 1926, for example. An analysis of the prison population for 1927 shows that there were 2661 people sentenced for offences: eleven were given terms of penal servitude, 2508 various sentences, and eighteen sent to Borstal. Of the other prisoners, one was sentenced by a court martial, 42 were debtors and another 81 surety defaulters. Of these offenders 143 were aged between sixteen and 21 years; 365 between 21 and 25; 433 between 25 and 30; 634 between 30 and 40; 578 between 40 and 50; 337 between 50 and 60; 145 between 60 and 70; and 26 were over 70 years of age. The trend was broken in the years between 1932 and 1935, the so-called 'hungry thirties'. Reporting that the prison population had increased from 2356 to 2622 in 1932, the Ministry of Home Affairs said the extra inmates were mostly minor offenders. 'The increase is due to the bad state of trade and lack of employment and to ordinary fluctuation which may be expected from year to year but a substantial proportion is due to sentences of imprisonment arising out of riotous disturbances of an exceptional character in Belfast and country districts.'

The murder rate also dropped dramatically once the 1922 troubles ceased. That year there were 231 killings in Belfast alone, while over the next seventeen years 23 people were murdered. Indeed there were six years when no murder was recorded in the city, and the total killings would have been even fewer if it had not been for fifteen victims in the years from 1933 to 1935 when sporadic sectarian trouble broke out again. Altogether there were 78 murders in the years between 1923, after the turbulent formation of the Northern Ireland state in 1922, and the outbreak of the Second World War in 1939. Over this period seven men were executed by hanging at Belfast prison, some for crimes which have since become notorious because the death penalty was implemented. At 8 am, the appointed hour of execution, large crowds would often gather outside the prison, the rare occasions when it became a focus of interest for anyone but the prisoners, their families and the staff.

The newspapers of the day recorded the crimes in the minutest detail, reflecting the macabre fascination with such cases and the high level of public reaction they prompted. Simon McGeown went to the gallows on 7 August 1922 for the murder of seven-year-old Maggie Fullerton, whose body was found in the grounds of Belfast Castle. Two years later, on 8 May 1924, Michael Pratley was hanged for a cold-blooded shooting during an armed robbery, described by the *Belfast Telegraph* as one of the foulest murders ever committed in the city. Four years after that, on 8 August 1928, farm labourer William Smylie went 'smiling to his doom' after being convicted of, and subsequently confessing to, the double murder of two sisters, Maggie and Sarah Macauley, who were shot dead during a robbery at their home in Mullaghduff, near Armoy, County Antrim. On 8 April 1930, Samuel Cushnan, 26, was hanged for the murder of James McCann, a postman, whom he killed with a shotgun near Toomebridge, County Antrim while stealing £60 which was being conveyed to a local post office to pay out pensions. The condemned man's mother, brother and other relatives were among the crowd gathered outside the prison in the rain on a dismal, grey morning. As the crowd recited the rosary and sang hymns, the mother clasped the prison bars and pressed her face between them, mouthing the words of the prayers. Another double murderer was hanged on 31 July 1931; Thomas Dornan had murdered the Aiken sisters from Ballymena.

The sixth hanging during these years followed one of the most bizarre murders ever to take place in Northern Ireland. In September 1931, Eddie Cullens, an American, and two Turks, Ahmed Musa and Assim Redvan, defected from a circus playing in Liverpool and caught a boat to Belfast apparently to see if they could create a better opportunity to exploit a Turk, known as Zara Agha, whom they were exhibiting as the oldest man in the world. They claimed he was 156 years of age. However, during the trip Cullens took Musa to a field near Carrickfergus where he shot him dead with an automatic pistol. When the body was discovered by a farm worker it was naked except for a blue female bathing cap on the head. The local police had no idea who the man was, and by the time the body had been found Cullens was back in Liverpool. However, members of the circus, which had moved on to Leeds, recognised the 'mystery' murder victim as Musa from photographs published in the national newspapers and contacted the police. Meanwhile two girls from Belfast, prostitutes who had been out on the town with Cullens, recognised the bathing cap and informed the police also. Cullens was eventually captured in London and returned to Belfast for trial. Police later discovered that he had rented a garage in Liverpool and was making preparations to murder Musa there and bury him under the floor. The motive was pure greed, to cut him out of the syndicate. Cullens was convicted and hanged in Belfast prison on 13 January 1932. Two years later, in Istanbul, Zara Agha himself went into rapid decline and died when doctors told him he was only 120 years old!

What was to be the last hanging for nine years took place on 7 April 1933. The titillating circumstances, in what were distinctly non-permissive times, ensured that the largest crowd for many years gathered outside the prison on the morning of the execution when Harold Courtney, a 23-year-old lorry driver, went to his death. He was convicted of murdering Minnie Reid, a young servant girl, at Derryane, County

Armagh in July 1932. The court heard that she was pregnant, having been intimate with Courtney. His defence was that she had committed suicide with a razor found near the body. After a five-day trial in Downpatrick the jury failed to reach a unanimous verdict, which was mandatory in those days, but after a second five-day trial in Armagh the jury convicted with a recommendation for mercy. However, Lord Chief Justice Andrews said that he profoundly disagreed with the jury's plea and imposed the death sentence. A number of Courtney's distressed relatives gathered outside the prison when the execution was taking place, and afterwards, as they walked away along the Crumlin Road, a section of the crowd followed them, staring morbidly from a distance.

The final hanging at Belfast prison took place on 20 December 1961, when Robert McGladdery, 26, was executed for the murder of nineteen-year-old Pearl Gamble, whose body was found in a field close to her home at Upper Damolly, on the outskirts of Newry, County Down. McGladdery, who had been seen dancing with her earlier that night, denied the murder but the police kept him under surveillance over the next few days while they tried to gather sufficient hard evidence to arrest and charge him. The breakthrough came when a sharp-eyed young police-man spotted that the earth around an old septic tank near McGladdery's home had been disturbed. At dawn on 9 February they moved in to search the tank and inside they uncovered a bag containing bloodstained clothes and the necktie, used to strangle the girl. McGladdery was promptly arrested. He maintained his innocence throughout his five-day trial at Downpatrick the following October, but the jury convicted him after an absence of only forty minutes. The death sentence was upheld on appeal and when moves to petition the House of Lords were rejected the hanging was set for 20 December. During his time in the condemned cell, McGladdery wrote a sixteen-page autobiography which was considered by the authorities before the death sentence was confirmed. On the day of the execution, he admitted his guilt and asked that it be made known. About 30 people gathered outside the prison when the sentence was being carried out and dispersed without incident a short time later when warders posted the official notification of death on the heavy main gates. A short time later McGladdery was buried in the prison grounds close to the wall, his grave marked only by his initials chiselled into the grimy stone. He was the seventeenth and, as it turned out, the last person to hang in Belfast prison.

Another aspect of prison life that attracted public attention and seriously embarrassed the authorities was the periodic escape of inmates from custody. The first escape after partition took place in 1924 from

Belfast, when a prisoner climbed over a wall which was being repaired. He was captured within a few hours. There were two escapes in 1927, the first by a prisoner working in the prison farm who buried himself under soil at the end of the working day. After dark he surfaced and scaled the prison wall but was recaptured within a few hours in what was said to be "an almost collapsed condition'. The second was a more serious affair. In the early hours of 9 May 1927, four prisoners overpowered and gagged two prison warders, taking possession of their keys and a revolver. Having gained access to the jail yard, they scaled the prison wall with ropes made of knotted sheets and blankets which had been thrown into the adjoining grounds of St Malachy's College, where a waiting accomplice secured them to railings. From there they made their way to the Crumlin Road and got away in a waiting high-powered car, evidence of a well-organised rather than an opportunistic escape.

The escapees were led by William Conlon, an American citizen, and included two Tyrone men, Frank O'Boyle of Beragh and Hugh Rodgers from Sixmilecross, all linked to the Republican movement and serving life sentences for the murder of William McDowell, a motor-car proprietor, at Gilford, County Down on 3 September 1920 during an armed robbery. The life terms of penal servitude were substituted after death sentences imposed by a military court martial, acting under the Restoration of Order in Ireland Act, were commuted. A jury had failed to reach a verdict at an earlier hearing. The fourth escapee, Edward Thornton, was serving a sentence of twelve years' penal servitude for slashing a girl in the throat with a razor while travelling in a train between Holywood and Belfast.

The authorities, clearly embarrassed by such a serious breach of prison security, immediately offered a reward of £500 for the recapture of the four convicts and widespread searches were mounted, especially after a suit of prison clothing was found at the Glen Road in Belfast. The search was even extended to London where members of Scotland Yard's famous Flying Squad carried out raids on the homes of Irish people suspected of giving refuge to the escapees. Six days after the break, a ten man police party set out on a planned dawn raid from the Springfield Road Barracks in Belfast and surrounded a small house at Leeson Street, in the Falls Road area. They found Conlon asleep upstairs and led him back to prison in handcuffs. A few days later Thornton was also recaptured after police, acting on another tip-off, went to a house at Donore Street in the New Lodge Road area of the city.

Nothing was heard of Rodgers or O'Boyle until 11 December 1928 when police in Dublin, acting on an RUC warrant endorsed by the

Commissioner of the Garda Siochana, made raids seeking out the two fugitives. In January 1929, both men made applications to the Free State High Court in Dublin seeking a declaration that the warrants were unenforceable. The applications succeeded and the two men were never returned to complete the balance of their sentences. (Although there was active cooperation between the police and courts in both parts of the island to deal with offenders of the criminal law, the concept of immunity, under the southern Irish system, for what were termed 'political' offences frequently strained relations.) The recaptured Conlon was finally released in December 1931 having completed his sentence.

For those serving time inside the prisons there was a tough regime. Discipline was tight, with irons, body belts, muffs and restraint jackets readily available to deal with unruly inmates. In 1931, 89 men and four women were given close confinement for breaches of prison rules, while another 90 men and four women were given dietary punishments. There was, however, a major concession in 1936 when untried prisoners and those serving penal servitude were permitted to smoke. The ministry reported that there had been no cases of misconduct arising out of the use of tobacco.

The outbreak of World War Two, if anything, compounded the austerity of prison life. The blackout forced the abandonment of the weekly concerts, with the sole exception of the Chaplains' Christmas Concert. Prisoners were put to work building air-raid shelters in the basement of their wings and drilled in firefighting arrangements. Otherwise prison labour was at least partially devoted to the war effort. In Belfast brass was recovered from discarded military equipment, while prisoners in Armagh provided a laundry service for the military. Belfast also continued to produce mailbags in large numbers, while prisoners in Derry cut firewood which was sold outside.

Although the city of Belfast suffered several major attacks the prison remained largely unscathed except for the night of 15/16 April 1941, during one of the three major attacks on the city, when a high-explosive bomb damaged part of the boundary wall and some buildings though without causing any casualties. The frequent air-raid warnings created difficult problems within the prisons. When alerts were sounded prisoners were supposed to be released from their cells and escorted to the shelters. However, with only a skeleton staff at night this presented security difficulties, and sometimes there were clashes as officers escorted prisoners from their cells to the air-raid shelters. After one such fracas, R Walker, an officer who was alleged to have vigorously batoned prisoners during an air-raid alert, was singled out for a revenge attack. He was shot and killed early on the morning of 6 February 1942 as he cycled along Durham Street in Belfast on his way from work. 'After that the screws tended to turn a deaf ear to the sirens,' recalls one war-time inmate. 'They just couldn't cope so we were simply left locked up in our darkened thirteen- by seven-foot cells.'

Paddy Devlin, who was interned during the war years, recalls the claustrophobic ordeal and the occasional episodes which relieved it:

'The steel-framed window was at the top of the nine feet high walls and you could just about see out if you climbed up and stood on the bed. When I first went into D wing my cell was on the inside of the building overlooking the exercise yard which was deserted when darkness fell. With the blackout there was no security lighting, so B Specials arrived every night to patrol the yard to foil anyone trying to escape. One of these guards used to whistle as he patrolled. Every couple of weeks I used to hear this beautiful sound which echoed round the walls in the absolute silence that pervaded the jail through the night. As the months went by new tunes were added to the whistler's repertoire. After the "Cuckoo Waltz" he moved on to Ravel's "Bolero" and John McCormack's lovely "Bantry Bay". I was not alone in enjoying the performances, and we eagerly awaited the nights when we knew the whistler was on the guard rota. One night he began whistling "Ireland Mother Ireland", which was a well-known McCormack recording, and one of my fellow inmates began duets with him, the two whistlers unseen by each other in the dark of the night. Suddenly he was gone. We never heard another tune. No matter how much whistling my friend did nightly from his window, our friend, the whistling B-man, never replied, but I still have the memory of him from the rare moonlit nights when there was a tall and a short B Special walking round the yard in step whistling lovely Irish airs. Only one of the two was the whistler. I never did find out which.'

By the end of the war in 1945 the prison population had fallen to the lowest levels then recorded. In 1939 there had been 2248 inmates, but in 1946 only 1422 people were in custody. The immediate post-war years also ushered in a notable process of reform of the conditions in the prisons and the privileges available to inmates. In 1947 the number of visits and letters was increased, cutlery replaced horn spoons and every inmate was given a personal hairbrush and a cell mirror. Bed-boards and trestles were replaced with wire-sprung beds and chairs replaced stools. A monthly cinema show was introduced and prisoners were allowed to have wirelesses. Longer evening association was introduced, lights-out time was put back and prisoners were provided with games and given access to the public library service. They were also allowed to make handicrafts for their friends and relatives. The allowance for luxury items from the prison tuck shop was increased from 2s 6d a month to 4s 6d. Refrigerators were also installed to store foodstuffs and facilitate changes to the prison diet. At the same time the working week for prison officers was reduced from 44 to 42 hours and they were given a substantial pay increase. In 1948, in a further significant liberalisation of the regime, short pre-release and Christmas parole schemes were introduced. In the first year 67 prisoners benefited and all returned on time. That year it cost the public purse £244 a year to keep each prisoner in custody.

The process of regime reform begun after the war was further progressed in 1953 when the Northern Ireland parliament passed two important Acts, one dealing with criminal justice, the other with prisons. It was the first time in its 30-year lifespan that parliament had taken more than a passing interest in the subject of penal policy, but even then it was a most cursory one. When the Prisons Bill was introduced and given its first reading on 26 February it took only ten lines to record the fact in Hansard. The Second Reading on 12 March takes four pages to record, virtually all of it the contribution by Brian Maginess, the Home Affairs minister. Pointing out that there had been many changes since the enactment of the Prisons (Ireland) Act 1826, he said, 'It is at times a matter of some difficulty to determine accurately what the law is and who, or what authority, has the power in any particular instance. Of even more importance is the fact that in this same century and a quarter the theory and practice of prison administration have fundamentally changed.'

Of all the MPs elected to the Northern Ireland parliament at that time only two had anything to say about the legislation or penal policy, and they had both been at one time interned, giving them first-hand experience of the system. On 19 March, speaking to a resolution to vote money for running the prisons, the South Fermanagh Nationalist MP Cahir Healy reminded the house that as an internee (from May 1922 to February 1924) he 'had seen the inside and outside of a prison', and said, 'I should like to see the officers or the warders recruited on a rather different basis to what has prevailed hitherto. Up till now the chief requisite of a warder was physique. He was always wanted as a man who would be in a position to administer punishment, if necessary. As a result many of these men were unpopular with inmates and they, therefore, had less control over the prisoners. If the warders had been selected on an entirely different basis, on humanitarian lines, they would have had greater control over the prisoners and would have been in a position to perform their duties in a far more satisfactory way, even from the point of view of the prison authorities.' Urging the minister to take his courage in his hands, demolish Belfast and Derry prisons and remove the prisoners, as a 'humanising factor', to the countryside where there was land for a farm, he added with poetic idealism, 'When men are permitted to plant and grow crops they somehow feel they are part of the creation.'

Harry Diamond, the Irish Labour MP for Belfast's Falls constituency, said he wanted to make it clear that his 'nightmare' stay in prison was not for burglary or larceny or any offence of that description but in defence of civil, religious and political liberty. He complained that no attempt was made to reform hardened criminals. 'They were thrown into prison and out of prison and the consequence was one conviction after another. The men became hardened and enemies of society.' Referring to prison officers, the MP said that 'a prisoner was released at the end of his term, whether it was long or short, but a prison officer spent his life in jail and this often had a morbid effect on him.' He said that prison life in England was far in advance of anything known in Northern Ireland and he called for reform. Wall-less prisons, he suggested, freed of the whole atmosphere of iron bars and officers armed with batons, would be better for the prison staff as well as the prisoners.

The Committee stage of the bill on 24 March is marked by a five-page entry in Hansard and it takes all of five lines to record the Third Reading in the Commons on 26 March and the reference of the Bill to the Senate. On 28 April five lines marks its return from the Senate with a minor amendment and on 7 May a full column was all that was needed to record that the Senate amendment was accepted without debate or discussion. The Bill received the Royal Assent and became law on 19 May, codifying a range of statutes going back for 125 years. Among its innovations was the creation of a Board of Visitors for the prisons, consisting of Justices of the Peace.

The associated Criminal Justice Act also attracted little attention despite the post-war rise in crime and its far-reaching implications for the running of prisons. It too simplified things for the prisons by abolishing penal servitude, hard labour and other divisions between different classes of prisoner, substituting a common regime for all with the only distinction being drawn for those untried, who remained innocent in the eyes of the law until convicted. The courts were however empowered to impose terms of preventive detention for habitual offenders. At this time the emphasis of imprisonment changed fundamentally, moving away from the long-standing concept of punishment, confinement and labour to the more liberal one of employment and training for a life afterwards. As a further incentive to what the Ministry described as 'earnest endeavour and good behaviour' an earnings scheme was introduced. It has to be said that the rates of pay – 1s 3d a week then 2s 6d after six months – were probably not even good by pocket money standards at the time but with the simultaneous lifting of all prohibition on tobacco, chocolate and knitting material the value of the earnings was no doubt enhanced. The real prison economy, however, continued to run underground with tobacco as the principal currency.

Cumulatively the new legislation and these concessions marked a watershed in penal policy. They were firm evidence that, despite the strictures of the two Catholic MPs, the official attitude to the prison population was fundamentally changing. This was articulated in the first full revision of the 1925 Prison Rules in which it was laid down that from then on warders were to be called prison officers. (The following year they were awarded a pay rise bringing them parity with their counterparts in Great Britain.) The new emphasis was to be on rehabilitation and training, not punishment. But, with the majority of the staff coming from a background in the armed services, the emphasis on spit and polish, respect for the officers, strict discipline and institutional routine continued. By the end of 1955 the prison population numbered 1443, including 191 women. That Christmas 135 prisoners were released on parole and those who remained in custody were, for the first time, given roast goose with all the trimmings for the traditional Christmas lunch.

In January 1956, Belfast scored a first in British prison history when a groundbreaking, hour-long radio programme about life behind bars was broadcast throughout the United Kingdom. The Ministry allowed a BBC radio interviewer and a sound recordist unprecedented access, over a five-day period, to both staff and inmates who volunteered to take part. Never before had a broadcast been recorded inside a jail. Bethyn Stoodley Thomas, the interviewer, later wrote that it had been an unforgettable experience. 'Over a score of prisoners, in turn, sat with me in a prison cell and talked of their life and work inside, of the meals and the exercise, the recreation and the routine, the good things and the bad. They spoke freely. They were volunteers and they spoke their minds about everything from parole leave to porridge. With me still are the impressions of life inside – the cleanliness and order, the humanity that lies behind even the strictest discipline, the contrast between the Victorian view of a house of correction and the modern idea of a prison as a place of rehabilitation. As I was often told, the only real punishment in a prison sentence today is the loss of liberty – but how great that loss is, only a prisoner can tell.'

Later, in another progressive move to relieve what the Ministry called 'the tedium of Sunday inactivity', a series of evening lectures were given by prominent figures from Northern Ireland society. They were a mix of the populist and worthy. Clearly talks on boxing, cricket, world football (by Billy Drennan of the Northern Ireland Football Association), and even lifeboats and the Post Office would have some appeal to a prison audience. On the other hand, whatever the attraction of spending a Sunday evening out of their cells, the majority of prisoners must have found it demanding to sit through experiences of Soviet Russia by Professor Sir Eric Ashby of Queen's University, Belfast, the Middle Eastern military exploits of Brigadier Ronald Broadhurst or the contents of 'An Editor's Postbag' by Jack Sayers, the distinguished, liberal editor of the *Belfast Telegraph*. Another notable contributor was Brian Faulkner, the future prime minister of Northern Ireland, who gave a talk entitled 'Around the world in five weeks', a report on one of his successful globetrotting sales missions to attract inward investment and provide employment in Northern Ireland. At the end of the series the prisoners were polled on their preferences and talks about travel came top of the list followed by sport. During the summer months a series of open-air concerts were given by musicians who included the Temple Quartet from Belfast and the bands of the Salvation Army and the Irish Guards. Christmas pantomimes, performed by inmates, were also instituted after the Presbyterian chaplain to the prison came up with the idea and enlisted the help and advice of the professionals at the city's famous Grand Opera House, who willingly loaned props and costumes.

The liberalising regime was all the more remarkable given the surge in crime after the war. Speaking on the BBC's Home Service, in June 1954, Dr J L J Edwards, Reader in Criminal Law at Queen's University, Belfast, said that in 1953 there had been nearly one crime committed every hour, an average of twenty serious crimes a day compared with seven a day before the war. Pointing out that one in three of these serious offences – stealing, swindling and burglary and violence – was committed by a person aged between eight and seventeen, he said, 'Northern Ireland seems to be breeding a hive of young Fagins.'

Yet further reform of the prison regime took place in 1957. Reporting that there had only been one breach of the parole scheme, and then only for a few hours, since it was introduced in 1948, the Ministry said that long-term prisoners with good records could now qualify for a week of summer leave as well as Christmas parole. Alderman Cooper, chairman of the Board of Visitors, praised the success of the scheme at the Board's annual luncheon in October 1959 and revealed that the one breach of the scheme had been caused by a prisoner who had arrived back late and 'under the weather', brandishing a bottle to stand a drink to the Governor and his Deputy. A new pre-release leave scheme was also introduced enabling prisoners to make arrangements for life after prison and seek employment. Remission was also improved with prisoners serving less than two-year terms getting a one-third 'discount' and those serving longer sentences being able to earn a quarter off. By the end of 1959, with a population of 1270 in custody, the Ministry was able to report: 'The inmates, as a whole, appear to be quite content and accept their terms of imprisonment without demonstration against authority save in the case of corrective trainees who usually settle down later. Complaints are rare and on interview by the Governor prior to release many prisoners pay tribute to the prison staff for the humane and understanding treatment they have received.' Alderman Cooper, chairman of the Board of Visitors, echoed these sentiments. 'Some people think we are making the place too comfortable but our aim is not to break a wrong-doer but to make him into a man fit to take his place in the law-abiding community and to become a good and worthy citizen.'

One repeat offender who conspicuously failed to respond to the new, more liberal regime was 'the great escaper' Alfie Hinds, who passed through Crumlin Road, albeit briefly, in 1960. Hinds escaped from custody in British prisons three times in the 1950s, skilfully conducted his own case in seventeen appearances before the highest judges in the land and even suffered the rigours of force feeding to end a hunger strike as part of a twelve-year campaign to overturn what he claimed was a wrongful conviction for robbery. In doing so he captured the public imagination for his cheeky confrontations with the authorities and the law, earned a unique place in criminal folklore as the most successful escaper in British penal history and won the grudging admiration of many in the legal profession. Although he was a self-taught, unqualified advocate, they flatteringly regarded him as one of the shrewdest legal minds never to have been called to the Bar.

Both of Hinds' parents had served prison sentences and his own record dated back to when he was seven years old. First imprisoned in 1953 for his part in a robbery at the furniture store of Maple & Co in central London, and having lost an appeal and had a petition to the Home Secretary to reopen the case turned down, Hinds decided that his only hope was to escape from prison, flee to the Irish Republic and campaign for a pardon from there. But that proposition presented its own problem. 'The golden thread which ran through all my years of imprisonment was that I must not commit one crime in order to prove that I was innocent of another,' he said. However, Hinds had worked out a legal loophole. 'My idea was this: to let some other prisoner make the breach.' By following on, Hinds could only be charged with escaping from lawful custody, which is not a criminal offence, only a violation of prison rules. He had equally to be careful that no one knew he was planning to escape, which could have invited the criminal charge of conspiracy.

Hinds' first escape took place in 1955 from Nottingham jail. Despite his self-imposed restrictions he cooperated with another inmate to copy a prison workshop key and make door frames which were convertible into a ladder for scaling the prison wall. Both escaped to London concealed in a lorryload of orange boxes driven by an accomplice. After dispatching letters to newspapers protesting his innocence, Hinds travelled to Dublin by ferry, began his legal researches in the reading room of the National Library and was smuggled into criminal law lectures at Trinity College by a friendly porter. After eight months of freedom he was recaptured on 31 July 1956 at Greystones, County Wicklow, where he was living in a cottage bought for £750 in the name of Patrick Joseph Flynn.

Back in prison, Hinds continued his campaign for justice. His wife Peg was sent to the Reading Room at the British Museum to follow up his legal research. 'I go there to follow up points of law which Alfred passes on to me from prison. Further references he wants expanding. But, oh dear, I find it all very difficult. Laws going back to 1742, George the Second, and all that, and the language with those double ff's instead of s's,' she said. Hinds himself continued his efforts. In June 1957 he was taken to the Law Courts in London for a hearing. He asked to go to the lavatory, and when his handcuffs were removed ducked between his guards and, with the help of a friend who was in on the plot, locked them in the toilet cubicle. By the time they were discovered he was well on the way to Bristol Airport, 110 miles away by car. There, however, a British European Airways employee raised the alarm after Hinds' brother Bert bought a one-way ticket to Dublin. Police arrested the brother, thinking he was Hinds, and took Alfie off the plane before it departed, thinking he was the accomplice. They were taken back to London: Bert in handcuffs as the real fugitive, surrounded by police; Alfie as a material witness. It was only when the Yard men, who knew Alfie, turned up that the mistake was recognised.

Returned to Pentonville, Hinds immediately embarked on a hunger strike. After refusing to eat meals such as roast beef, vegetables and semolina, placed every day in the cell in front of him, he was pinioned by warders and forcibly fed with a pint of glucose from the sixth day of the protest, which lasted for 25 days before he relented. 31 MPs tabled a House of Commons motion calling for an enquiry into the case but their plea was rejected.

On 1 June 1958, Hinds was free again. This time he escaped over the wall from Chelmsford Prison, and cheekily wrote to the governor at Chelmsford authorising him to hand over to his wife property he left behind: his law books, a portable radio, a suit, a miniature chess set and £3 wages owed for making brushes in the prison workshop. At the same time, in a letter to the *Daily Mail* on prison notepaper, he reaffirmed his innocence and called for a Select Committee of the House of Commons to investigate his conviction and sentence. 'Offer me justice and I will return at once,' he wrote. No concessions were forthcoming and this time Hinds disappeared for some eighteen months. He had one narrow escape, however. The 'Whizz Mob', a team of pickpockets working one of the London stations, spotted Peg and the Hinds children catching the Irish boat train and tipped off the police, who followed the family to Dun Laoghaire. Alfie spotted the trap, gave them the slip and joined his family later in time for Christmas.

On 13 January 1960 a man calling himself William Herbert Bishop was arrested by customs officers near the railway station in Great Victoria Street, Belfast and accused of smuggling cars across the border from the Irish Republic. While being questioned at the Customs headquarters at Albertbridge Road, the man made a run for the door, but was caught and treated for cuts and bruises. After a court appearance, charged with Customs offences, 'Bishop' was remanded in custody to Crumlin Road prison.

'I decided that my best policy was to play the innocent,' [Hinds related afterwards] 'so when I was taken in on reception, I made out that I had never seen the inside of a prison before. I kept up the same act when I went before the Governor, Mr Lance Thompson, a little fellow known to the prisoners as "the wee man". To him I was a well-dressed, quiet-mannered Dublin businessman, naïve to the point of stupidity. I went in with my hand heavily bandaged and in a sling and explained that I hadn't tried to escape from the Customs office. I said that I had been threatened with twenty years by the Customs officials, which was true, and that I had tried to kill myself by diving through a plate glass window.

'Thompson took pity on me and explained in a patient, almost fatherly, way that the threat was groundless and that I was not to worry. He took my story so seriously that I was transferred to the prison hospital as a potential suicide where I was well looked after. In Crumlin any professional or business man was treated very humanely and was even allowed home after sentence for a few days to settle his affairs. On the other hand, the hooligans who made up the large part of the prison population were robustly handled by the prison officers; yet they did not receive crippling sentences, as in England.

'The jail was a forbidding place with a double wall on three sides and a machine-gun tower in each corner. Though it was proof against armed attack from outside, the boast that it was the maximum security prison in the British Isles was sheer nonsense. Two escape-minded English criminals could have broken out in five minutes. One of my fellow-prisoners was a fly Belfaster by the name of McKee, who had received six months for bouncing cheques. We got talking and I told him that I was very anxious to escape. He asked me how much I would be prepared to pay and I said I'd gladly give £500. His jaw dropped. I don't suppose he'd ever had five hundred pence. From then on, he kept coming to me every few minutes with suggestions for getting out.'

At his next court appearance, the prosecutor asked for Bishop's finger-prints to be taken. It was clear that suspicions had been aroused during follow-up investigations into the car-smuggling operation in Dublin. He did not object but instead disfigured his fingertips with sandpaper and a razor blade in a bid to thwart the check. The ploy failed. On a Saturday morning, while he was in the exercise yard with some of the IRA prisoners, the Governor appeared. Hinds recalled:

'The look on his face left me in no doubt that he knew who I was. By the time exercise was over, every prison officer in the yard was staring at me open-mouthed. As I walked off, one of them came up to me warily, as if I were an escaped animal, and told me I was being transferred from the hospital to the prison.

'When I arrived at the hospital, everyone was very distant, even hostile. As I was packing my things, McKee, who had licence to roam wherever he liked, sidled up to me and whispered in my ear: "They've captured that chap Hinds."

' "Have they?" I said. "Who is he?"

' "He's the famous escaper. He gets out of everywhere. But he won't get out of here. They've got him down on chokey and they're kicking the living daylights out of him."

'I was escorted to the main prison and locked in a cell. Soon after, I was taken out to see the Medical Officer, who compared my teeth with

my dental record. He nodded to the P.O. beside me. "That's him, all
right," he said. I was brought before the "wee man", who was attended
by two Belfast CID men, one a high-ranking officer and the other an
inspector. I knew the inspector because I had got into conversation with
him at Great Victoria Street station shortly before Christmas about a
model of a church on one of the platforms. Since then we had been on
nodding terms. The high-ranking officer asked me my name.

' "I won't beat about the bush," he said, pointing to a document he
was holding. "That's your police record."

' "Then there's no point in keeping the farce up any longer," I
replied.

'The inspector chipped in. "I'd have known him anywhere," he said,
but I wasn't spiteful enough to remind him that we had already met.'

At the end of a two-day hearing, Hinds was sentenced to six months'
imprisonment for 55 smuggling offences and fined £400 – later
increased, without Hinds being informed, to £1150 – or a consecutive six
months in custody. Lord McDermott, the Lord Chief Justice of Northern
Ireland, refused to let the now notorious Hinds out on bail pending
appeal. In the Belfast High Court Hinds argued that the smuggling convictions should be quashed because he had not been informed of his right
to trial by jury. Mr Justice Sheil refused but, clearly captivated by the way
that Hinds cockily argued his own case, said, 'I regret the result.'

Hinds changed legal tack, claiming immediate freedom on the grounds
that the £400 fine had been increased without him being informed, but the
High Court in Belfast refused his habeas corpus application. On 18
November, in an attempt to wrong-foot Scotland Yard officers who were
waiting to take him back to Britain, Peg promptly paid £13 in lieu of one
day's imprisonment for failing to pay £1150 fines for smuggling, thus
triggering Hinds' immediate release. Before he could flee he was held in
court and handed over to the Yard. However, after clinging on to the
aircraft boarding steps at Belfast airport and threatening to make trouble
during the flight, he was returned to Belfast prison. Peg had by then
lodged evidence that the fine was paid and an affidavit seeking habeas
corpus. The Ministry of Home Affairs ordered that Hinds stay in
Northern Ireland, but after hearing the case the next day the court ordered
him to be handed over to Scotland Yard for return to Chelmsford prison.

On 22 December Hinds was moved to the top security prison at
Parkhurst, Isle of Wight. His car was escorted across country by police
cars and motorcycle outriders. With him were no less than four warders,
two on each side. As they transferred to the island by ferry, twenty police

and plain-clothes detectives and dogs were deployed at Portsmouth Harbour station. As the ferry crossed the Solent a naval launch escorted it. 'We're taking no chances. He's as slippery as an eel,' said a detective.

Parkhurst's Governor was paranoid about the responsibility of preventing another escape. Orders were issued that Hinds was to sleep with his bed in view of the cell peep-hole with his hands outside the blankets all the time. A warder was ordered to check he was still there every half hour. Hinds spent weeks playing cat-and-mouse with his guards, enlisting other inmates to kick up a din every night in protest at the level of surveillance. Meanwhile he appealed the decision of the Northern Ireland Court to five Law Lords, and lost. Although he continued from his cell to contest his conviction by every means, each and every avenue proved to be a dead end.

In 1962, Detective Superintendent Herbert 'The Iron Man' Sparks, who had originally put Hinds behind bars for the Maple's robbery, wrote a series of articles in the *Sunday Pictorial*. One of them stated that Hinds was guilty and should take his medicine like a man. Hinds at once commenced libel proceedings. In July 1964, after a lengthy hearing at the Law Courts in London, he won the libel action and £1300 damages against Sparks, who had gone on to head the Flying Squad. As a result of the verdict, which he interpreted as overturning the Maple's conviction, Hinds applied for a free pardon. The following October he was released from Pentonville on licence, but in November 1965 the Court of Criminal Appeal rejected a new appeal against the original conviction and refused leave to apply to House of Lords. Hinds was by now a free man, having served his sentence for the Maple's robbery, but the conviction stood. Although he had satisfied the standard of proof in the civil courts 'on the balance of probabilities', he failed to establish that his case was 'beyond reasonable doubt' in the criminal courts.

Despite the libel victory and the damages from the top Scotland Yard detective who put him behind bars, Hinds never secured the pardon or the ringing endorsement of his innocence for which he had so thoroughly campaigned. In 1966 he published an autobiography, *Contempt of Court*, in which he argued his innocence in minute detail. By then his exploits had earned him sympathetic notoriety and he was much in demand as a speaker and lecturer. 'The law in England is quite good in itself but I believe its administration leaves much to be desired,' was the common theme of what he said on such occasions. He settled in Jersey where he dabbled in property development, and his IQ of 150 propelled him to the position of Secretary in the Channel Islands branch of Mensa. Until his dying day he railed against the policemen and legal practitioners who were all, he insisted, guilty of contempt of court for the way they had manipulated the system against him, not least because if he had succeeded an avalanche of self-styled lawyers would have flowed from the prisons behind him. Hinds died in January 1991, aged 73, full of respect for British justice but unrelentingly scornful of those who implemented it.

The 1960s were essentially years of tranquillity for both Northern Ireland and its prison system. Although the number of indictable offences doubled from 7500 in 1952 to more than 15,000 in 1966, crime remained at a level well below that elsewhere in the United Kingdom, and the RUC's detection rate was by far the highest in the United Kingdom at between 54 and 60 per cent. There were only a dozen lifers convicted of murder among the prison population. Most of those in custody were men in their twenties, most commonly convicted of an offence involving theft or violence. Once inside Crumlin Road, the prisoners were rigidly segregated into three categories: young offenders, and either short-term or long-term inmates. It was strict policy to prevent the categories from mixing.

There was also a continuing tide of improvements to the regime and facilities. At Belfast prison 35mm cinema-standard shows were started after projection equipment from the city's old Imperial Picture House was donated and installed in the gymnasium. An all-weather sports pitch was built and there were improvements to the gardens. There was still a heavy official emphasis on using prison labour profitably. In 1952, for instance, outside sales contributed £13,000 to the £140,000 cost of running the prisons. Hospitals and residential homes for the elderly and infirm paid handsomely for the prison laundry to deal with soiled linen. The cost of postage was kept down by the continued sale of mailbags to the Post Office at a price which private manufacturers were unable to match and logs, railway sleepers and other timber were cut into firewood by young prisoners and sold outside, the deliveries also being carried out by prisoners, distinctively clad in their brown or blue prison overalls. From time to time squads of prisoners were taken out by bus to carry out construction projects at government installations at a considerable saving to the public purse. Among the facilities they provided were a garage, lecture rooms and offices for the Northern Ireland Fire Authority at Whiteabbey, accommodation for the Civil Defence organisation in Londonderry and a drill hall for the Special Constabulary in Belfast.

Prison labour, especially the skills of incarcerated tradesmen, was also put to good use in expanding and maintaining facilities inside the 30-acre prisons complex. By 1968, after expanding the greenhouses, the prison was making an annual profit of £1000 from selling its tomato crop outside. Inmates made uniforms for the prison officers and clothing for themselves in the tailoring workshop. Others were deployed in constructing a new two-storey dining hall and kitchens. When the building was completed association at meal times was permitted and cafeteria-style service introduced. The regular breakfast of porridge, bread and butter and tea was replaced on Sunday mornings by the staple 'Ulster fry' – egg, bacon and soda bread. An Alcoholics Anonymous group, with twenty members, was established inside the prison. 400 Gideon Bibles were also donated for the use of those prisoners who felt in need of spiritual uplift. Major Albert Mullin, the Governor, said there would be many who would not even open them but there might also be as many who would find comfort and consolation in their pages. Many of the prisoners did help the charity Oxfam make its annual postal appeal for funds that year by helping lick and stick about 200,000 address labels to envelopes.

When Derry prison finally closed down in 1953, the entire prison population was confined in Belfast except for women, who were detained in Armagh. In addition, at the Borstal, the Malone Training School, 191 male officers and 21 females were responsible for looking after young offenders. Major Mullin summed up current penal policy: 'Prison will never be a pleasant place, nor should it be, but we do try to make it as humane as possible and to see that offenders are not just punished but are also set on the road to the recovery of their personal pride and given a certain amount of new hope.' Despite this he did admit that about one in six of the prisoners under his control were beyond reform, being either habitual criminals or just plain dangerous. In 1965 the average daily population was 403, housed one to a cell, reflecting the fact that the available accomodation was usually only half full. But by the end of 1968, when the civil rights marches got under way and the first waves of civil disorder ensued, it had already risen by about a third to 614, a stark pointer to the then unthinkably troubled times that lay ahead.

Chapter Three
John Bull's political slum

The great turning points in Ireland's volatile history have usually been massacres, sieges, battles or rebellions. By these grandiose precedents there could not have been a more unlikely starting point for a renewed phase of the Irish conflict than a pair of humble council houses in a picturesque rural village. Towards the end of 1967 builders had put the finishing touches to numbers nine and eleven, Kinnard Park, in Caledon, a village with some 1600 residents, set in the Tyrone countryside about 45 miles south-west of Belfast. Even the most pessimistic observer would not have dared forecast the grim sequence of events that would follow after Emily Beattie, a nineteen-year-old unmarried secretary and a Protestant, took possession of one of them on 13 June 1968.

During the afternoon of 18 June, five days after Miss Beattie acquired number nine, a cadre of bailiffs acting for the Dungannon Rural District Council, which had built the houses, evicted the Goodfellow family from number eleven, next door. The Goodfellows, Catholics with three small children, the youngest just nine weeks old, had been illegally squatting for the previous eight months. They were among 269 desperate people on the local waiting list for a home. With only twelve houses under construction, and given the anti-Catholic track record of the diehard Unionist councillors who allocated them, their hopes of being housed legitimately were regarded as non-existent. Austin Currie, the local Nationalist member of the Northern Ireland Parliament was deeply disturbed at what was, by any humane standards, a major housing crisis. The next afternoon, speaking during an acrimonious adjournment debate in the House of Commons at Stormont, he complained bitterly about a situation where an unmarried teenage woman could be given a house ahead of obviously needy families who had been waiting for years.

Currie, a graduate of Queen's University, Belfast and the youngest ever MP when he was elected to Stormont four years earlier aged only 24, delivered a speech fired with anger and passion, not least because he had established that Miss Beattie's tenancy seemed to be the fruits of political pull. Her employer was a prosperous Armagh solicitor, Brian McRoberts, at the time the prospective Unionist parliamentary candidate for West Belfast and legal adviser to the Council. Throwing his notes across the floor of the parliamentary chamber in exasperation, Currie stormed out. The following morning, 20 June, he entered Miss Beattie's proposed dwelling and commenced a sit-in. It did not last long. Within a few hours a party of Royal Ulster Constabulary officers, including Miss Beattie's brother, manhandled him out. The incident was to have far-reaching consequences.

Before the events at Caledon, Northern Ireland had enjoyed just over four decades of relative tranquility following the partition settlement in 1921. The people in the southern 26 counties formed first their own Free State and then a Republic, severing their formal links with Britain. In the six northern counties a devolved parliament, subsidiary to the British parliament at Westminster, was allowed to rule unhindered by any interest or interference from London. With the turmoil of the early part of the century settled and the island divided, the overwhelming majority of people on both sides of the border were content to let their deep wounds heal.

The outlawed Irish Republican Army (IRA) periodically tried to re-open the Irish question but its limited violence was quickly extinguished by public apathy and unofficially coordinated security action north and south of the border. Extradition was frequently enacted in both directions by police officers exchanging prisoners in dark country border roads to bypass the legal complications which effectively offered IRA activists immunity. Despite the political differences between north and south, practical necessity forced cross-border cooperation and pragmatism in other areas of clear mutual interest such as fisheries, railways and drainage.

The 1960s had in fact ushered in a period of prosperity and stability previously unknown in Northern Ireland. Inward investment created new jobs in modern industries and unemployment reached record lows. There were even signs of non-sectarian issue politics with the development of a Northern Ireland Labour Party drawing members from both religious denominations. The collapse of the well-planned IRA campaign in 1962 firmly pushed partition off the active agenda and for the first time liberal Unionists talked of admitting Catholics to the party. Nationalists too exuded a whiff of compromise and began to play a part in public life for the first time. The emergence of the liberal Unionist Captain Terence O'Neill as prime minister stimulated the mood of change, especially when he brought Irish prime minister Sean Lemass north for talks at Stormont, the first such contact after forty years of silence.

The time was ripe for fundamental reform and change, but on both sides the dark forces of extremism were already mustering again to undermine it. The IRA had embarked on a course of subversive political action, infiltrating groups campaigning on civil rights, social and economic issues. This reflected the influence of what is best described as a communist element. Years later, after the collapse of the Soviet empire in the early 1990s, it transpired that they had in fact been in touch with the Eastern bloc unsuccessfully seeking huge funds for their activities.

Unionist extremists were simultaneously undermining the standing of O'Neill, thwarting his efforts to achieve equality between Catholics and Protestants, improve relations with the South and generally modernise Northern Ireland. Gunmen from an organisation styling itself the Ulster Volunteer Force had carried out several acts of anti-Catholic violence, including the brutal murder of a young Catholic barman, forcing O'Neill to outlaw them. Street disorder over the flying of the Irish tricolour had taken place during an election campaign marking a slide towards confrontation and a resurgence of the old religious tensions.

Ever since 1925, when the partition settlement had been finalised, successive governments in London had turned a blind eye to the conduct of affairs in Belfast. By convention they were never raised at Westminster, where all twelve MPs from Northern Ireland were Unionists with no inclination to do so. However, in 1966, Gerry Fitt, a colourful nationalist leader with socialist leanings, broke the Unionist monopoly by becoming the West Belfast MP. Helped by sympathetic British Labour MPs who steered him through the parliamentary procedures, he led the cry for the government in London to force O'Neill to deliver on the reforms he admitted were necessary.

Fitt's tactics were closely in tune with contemporary Catholic opinion in Northern Ireland. Although they were a permanent one-third minority of the 1.5 million population, most of them, especially the older ones who had lived through the partition crisis, still felt that the southerners had selfishly abandoned them to the uncertainties of partition and that they had accordingly suffered at the hands of the Protestant/Unionist majority. But among the younger elements like Austin Currie, whose memories were not first-hand, there was a new pragmatism emerging, helped by the fact that they enjoyed an altogether higher standard of living than their compatriots in the south. Thanks to the hefty British subsidy all the people in Northern Ireland enjoyed parity with the rest of the United Kingdom in the levels of social and welfare payments, a high standard of education and the benefits of the free National Health Service. However, a fully justified sense of grievance remained, for the Unionists were riddled with insecurity about a Catholic/Nationalist takeover. So they gerrymandered and discriminated to prevent Catholics getting any share of real political power.

Thus the franchise and electoral boundaries were rigged to ensure permanent Unionist dominance in the parliament at Stormont and the local councils. Catholics were discriminated against at every turn, particularly when it came to jobs and houses. Prominent Unionists made no secret of their feelings. On 12 July 1933, for instance, Basil Brooke, the future prime minister of Northern Ireland (1943–63) who ran an extensive estate in Fermanagh, boasted at an Orange demonstration that he 'had not a Roman Catholic about his own place'. Roman Catholics, he told his audience, were endeavouring to get in everywhere and were out with all their force and might to destroy the power and constitution of Ulster. There was a definite plot to overpower the vote of Unionists in the north. Wherever possible, he appealed to Loyalists, they should employ 'good Protestant lads and lasses'. Speaking at another rally the same day, John Miller Andrews, who also was to serve as prime minister from 1940 to 43, challenged the allegation that 28 out of the 31 porters employed at Stormont were Catholics. 'I have investigated the matter and I have found that there are thirty Protestants and only one Roman Catholic, there only temporarily.' A year later, James Craig, the prime minister from 1921 to 1940, boasted that 'we are a Protestant Parliament and a Protestant state.'

Unionists' behaviour and fears were all too easily exacerbated by equally bigoted attitudes in the south which appeared to underline their worries about the undue influence of the Catholic church. In a revealing incident in 1931, Monsignor E A D'Alton, the Dean of Tuam, supported Mayo County Council's decision not to give a Protestant woman a post as a librarian. 'We are not appointing a washerwoman or a mechanic, but an educated girl who ought to know what books to put into the hands of the Catholic boys and girls of this country. Is it safe to entrust a girl who is not a Catholic, and is not in sympathy with Catholic views, with their handling?' When the hardline Republican leader Eamonn de Valera implemented a new Constitution declaring Ireland a Republic in 1937, Unionist hostility was compounded, for its provisions heavily reflected Catholic teaching, such as prohibiting divorce, and even recognised the special position of the church as that of the majority of the population.

These mould-setting sentiments had helped to solidify the divisions in Ireland, both across the border and between Unionists and Nationalists in the north, but the failure of Unionist leaders to see the definite mood change among Catholics in the early 1960s was a major error. By attempting to stifle rather than meet, even at that late hour, the growing clamour for reform after the events at Caledon, they condemned Northern Ireland to its subsequent tragedy.

The changing mood coincided with events of momentous historical significance elsewhere: the Russian invasion of Czechoslovakia; the assassinations of Martin Luther King and Robert Kennedy; the student riots in Paris and the worldwide protests against the United States' involvement in the Vietnam war. But the greatest inspiration for people in Northern Ireland, strongly wedded as they were to the concepts of struggle and martyrdom, was undoubtedly provided by the black Civil Rights campaign in the United States. By early 1968 a Northern Ireland Civil Rights movement was under way, campaigning for peaceful reform within the existing Northern Ireland set-up by achieving equality between Catholics and Protestants. It contained a broad church of Republicans, Liberals, Socialists, Catholics, Protestants, Unionists, Nationalists and even a prominent Communist. After Caledon, which provided a perfect focus for its activities, it took to the streets and organised a protest march in nearby Dungannon which was prevented by the police from entering the town centre. Its first major venture was a march in Londonderry on 5 October 1968, the venue pointedly chosen because the city manifested many of the shortcomings in Northern Ireland society they were campaigning to rectify. Religious discrimination was evident; bad housing conditions were compounded by unfair allocation procedures; electoral boundaries were unequally drawn and the franchise was unfair, with businessmen, usually Unionists, having extra votes and many people, most of them Catholics, having none at all. No wonder then that 'one man, one vote' was the Civil Rights campaigners' most fundamental objective.

The other major reforms they demanded were the disbanding of the all-Protestant reserve police, the 'B' Specials, and the repeal of the Special Powers Act. In 1936 the National Council for Civil Liberties said that through this Act the Unionists had created a permanent machine of dictatorship under the shadow of the British constitution. Its draconian potency was quickly demonstrated when the march was announced. The government promptly utilised the legislation to ban it.

On the Saturday afternoon the Civil Rights marchers formed up as planned at the Waterside railway station and began to walk along Duke Street towards Craigavon Bridge. Gerry Fitt, the Nationalist MP who sat at both Stormont and Westminster, was in the front rank, flanked on either side by Austin Currie and Eddie McAteer, the veteran leader of the Nationalist party. Ahead of them the police had positioned a couple of tenders to block the narrow street and were grouped in front of it to halt the marchers. As the protesters advanced slowly toward the cordon they ignored loudhailer warnings about the illegality of the demonstration.

Fitt vividly recalls that as they came within a few yards of the police he noticed they had drawn their batons.

> 'Suddenly there was a big push from behind and we were propelled forward. A sergeant grabbed me and pulled my overcoat down over my shoulders to prevent me raising my arms. Two other policemen held me and I was batoned twice on the head. A stinging pins-and-needles feeling followed and I could feel the blood coursing down my neck on to my shirt. As I fell to my knees I was roughly grabbed and thrown into a police van. At the police station I was shown into a room with a filthy wash basin and told to clean up. But I was not interested in that. I wanted the outside world to see the blood, which had dried all over my face. The police were confused about what to do with me and eventually I was driven to Altnagelvin hospital where my wound was stitched but the police would not let the doctors put a bandage around my head in case it provoked the crowds who had gathered. By then others who had been injured after me had arrived at the hospital and I heard the full details of the clash.'

Fitt gave a succession of television and radio interviews, still dressed in the bloodstained shirt, and by the time he got back home to Belfast later that evening his telephone was red hot. Fleet Street had suddenly discovered 'the Northern Ireland problem' in a big way, and radio and television too were on to the story, forcing rigorous examination of the the state of affairs in Northern Ireland into the national spotlight for the first time. By then most people realised that a watershed had been crossed but few comprehended just how dangerously the smouldering embers of Ireland's turbulent history had again been fanned.

Harold Wilson, the British prime minister, moved swiftly in the aftermath of the march to defuse the escalating disorder by pushing through the most comprehensive reform package since partition. Over the next year or so a Development Commission was set up to help improve the quality of life in Londonderry. A new centralised housing body, with a scrupulously fair system for determining housing needs and allocating dwellings accordingly, was also created. Electoral reform was quickly introduced, giving everyone the vote at both council and parliamentary elections. The 'B' Specials were eventually stood down and a new framework to distance the police force from direct political control was also put in place.

As far as many Catholics were concerned these overdue reforms provided the basis for long-term peaceful coexistence between both sections of the divided community in Northern Ireland. There was still no significant demand for Irish unity despite the strength with which many Catholics cherished the long term aspiration. What was remarkable was that, for the first time, a significant number of Catholics and moderate Protestants worked together in the civil rights movement to create a better state of affairs in Northern Ireland.

Hardline Unionists opposed any concession whatever to the Catholic minority and in the upper echelons of the Unionist Party there was turmoil as the reformers fought, increasingly in vain, to maintain forward momentum. The Reverend Ian Paisley, an uncompromising, fiery fundamentalist preacher, rapidly emerged as a street leader and his bellicose activities played a significant part in raising tension. On the other side, an equally subversive minority of Republicans and radical student hardliners, committed to a united Ireland, refused to settle for any compromise short of that and, agitating under cover of the civil rights banner, provoked more and more serious riots and confrontations between themselves, hardline Unionists and the RUC.

Between October 1968 and the summer of 1969 the RUC fought vainly to control the rising tide of public disorder. Civil Rights marches were invariably met by counter-demonstrations by extreme Unionists, normally led by the voluble Paisley. The force was unprepared for the onslaught. Manpower was inadequate to cope; there had been no coordinated public order training, and protective equipment, such as shields and helmets, was outdated and in short supply. The RUC and the people of Northern Ireland were to pay a heavy price for the lack of investment in training, manpower and equipment and the failure to divorce the police from day-to-day political control. In dealing with the disorder the RUC and the Ulster government were further forced to operate in the unprecedented glare of the international media spotlight for the first time, as the bones of fifty years of unchallenged Unionist hegemony were picked over ever more critically by amazed outsiders. The London *Sunday Times* presented a penetrating analysis of the discrimination, political corruption and gerrymandering under the headline 'John Bull's political slum'. There was particular criticism from these onlookers that on the frequent occasions when the RUC were caught in a confrontation between opposing crowds they invariably turned their backs on the Protestants and faced the Catholics.

By July 1969, with the start of the traditional summer marching season, the seams that held the beleaguered RUC together were coming apart.

The force, only 3000 strong, had been overwhelmed and exhausted by the almost constant running battles throughout Northern Ireland for eight months and the political process was once more overshadowed by the gun and bomb. In the spring, British soldiers had been called out to guard strategic installations after extremists, who turned out to be Unionists and not, as thought, the IRA, blew up water and electricity installations serving Belfast. Militant Loyalism had been stirred by fears that the liberal drift in Unionism would lead to some rapprochement with the south and open up once more the possibility of a united Ireland. As the level of trouble inexorably increased throughout Northern Ireland, all attention was focused on a customary Protestant march in Londonderry on 12 August which the government decided not to ban. It was no surprise when, late in the afternoon, trouble broke out after stones were hurled at the procession by Catholic youths.

Several days of intensive rioting, now known as the 'Battle of the Bogside', got under way. Barricades were thrown up around the area as petrol bombs and other missiles picked off the exhausted and ill-protected police like tenpins in a bowling alley. Over the next twenty-four hours, despite CS gas being used against the rioters for the first time in the United Kingdom, the trouble worsened and spread throughout the Catholic areas of Northern Ireland. Late in the afternoon of 14 August, with the entire six counties in a state of what a senior RUC man later described as 'incipient civil war', the government in London was forced to intervene directly and commit British troops to maintain law and order. As the British Home Secretary, James Callaghan, remarked at the time to Gerry Fitt, 'It is the easiest thing in the world to put the troops in but it will be the devil of a job to get them out again.'

The killing had started even before the first soldiers went into Londonderry, then Belfast twenty-four hours later. Overnight on the 14/15 August a joint party of 25 RUC and twenty 'B' Specials was trying to deal with a riot involving several hundred Catholics and Protestants in the city of Armagh. Seventeen more armed Specials, from the Tynan area near the border, arrived in four private cars to reinforce the party and were delegated by a senior RUC officer to deal with a section of the crowd at Cathedral Road. As they arrived they found a blazing car, an angry crowd and the road strewn with items, including a garden seat, to form a barricade. The officers, completely untrained in riot control, opened fire and shot dead John Gallagher, a 30-year-old Catholic. His is now the first name on a list of victims that climbed without respite for 25 years, reaching the 3000 mark in August 1992 and only slowing, a further 170 victims later, when the Republican and Loyalist terrorist organisations declared unilateral ceasefires, ushering in a fragile peace in the autumn of 1994. By the turn of the century, the death toll totalled 3296.

The escalation of civil disorder and violence in the turbulent aftermath of the October 1968 march had a swift effect on the process of justice and triggered what were to be far-reaching changes to the prison system and the character of the prison population. Many Civil Rights marchers, prosecuted for breaches of the government prohibition on demonstrations and offences arising from the ensuing clashes with the police, opted to serve prison terms instead of paying fines imposed by the courts. The majority of them were people who would never have seen the inside of a jail in any other circumstances. One of the most prominent persons to be imprisoned at the time was the Rev Ian Paisley. On 27 January 1969 he and his right-hand-man Major Ronald Bunting were sentenced to three months' imprisonment for unlawful assembly the previous November, when they had mounted an ugly counter-demonstration to a Civil Rights march through the city of Armagh. After the hearing they announced there would be no appeal and they were taken off to Belfast prison to serve their sentences. It was the not the first time Paisley had been imprisoned. On 19 June 1966 he and two of the ministers from his Free Presbyterian church, the Reverend John Wylie and the Reverend Ivan Foster, were fined £30 for unlawful assembly after leading, and clashing with the police during, a noisy demonstration outside the headquarters of the mainstream Presbyterian Church in Belfast two weeks earlier – an event which had caused O'Neill to apologise to the Governor of Northern Ireland, Lord Erskine, and his wife. After refusing to pay the fines the three men were arrested in Belfast city centre on 20 June and lodged in Belfast prison. On 22 June, while they were in custody, a 2000-strong crowd gathered outside and sixteen arrests were made during scuffles with the police. During Paisley's second incarceration a crowd again gathered outside the prison and attacked the police with stones and bottles.

However, the swiftly changing political events outside the prison interfered with Paisley's plans for martyrdom. O'Neill, in terminal political trouble inside the Unionist party, called a general election. After less than a week inside, Paisley lodged an appeal against his sentence, signed a bail bond and was released on 30 January to fight the election. Five days later he went back to the Crumlin Road and signed Bunting out. Paisley stood against O'Neill and was defeated. On 25 March the appeals against the conviction and sentence were rejected at Armagh County Court, and Paisley and Bunting went back to Belfast prison to serve the remainder of their sentences. But their stay was again cut short. O'Neill was overthrown and replaced as prime minister by Major James Chichester-Clark, whose first action on 6 May, five days after taking over, was to declare an amnesty for all offences (except sabotage) committed after 5 October 1968. It was a bid to halt the growing crisis and make a fresh start, and his officials in the Ministry of Home Affairs had been put to work combing through the archives to establish whether any precedents or legal powers might prevent the initiative. Among the beneficiaries were Paisley and Bunting, released from jail; MPs Gerry Fitt, Austin Currie and Ivan Cooper, who had charges already laid against them dropped; and Bernadette Devlin and the Nationalist party leader Eddie McAteer, who were facing charges. In all 133 cases were dropped and the people concerned released from prison or the threat of it. However, the gesture failed to halt the slide into turmoil and even after the Army was deployed in August 1969 the disorder continued, taking on an ever more sinister dimension.

On 10 February 1970 a bomb exploded at the wall of Belfast prison causing little damage. The police said it was not thought to be connected with an escape attempt. A week later there was a second explosion in the courthouse across the road, while a jury was considering its verdict against five Loyalists accused of blowing up the northern water main for Belfast at Dunadry, County Antrim in April 1969, in the days before O'Neill was finally brought down. Not surprisingly, after the intimidatory explosions, the five suspects were acquitted.

In June that year the prison system accommodated another public figure, this time the fiery Bernadette Devlin, who had become the Westminster MP for Mid Ulster on the back of the Civil Rights campaign. She was given a six-month prison sentence for her part in the August 1969 riots in Londonderry and was held in the women's prison at Armagh. There she wore the regulation brown dress, blue cardigan and black shoes and worked sewing shirts, pillowcases and sheets. She earned about 3s 6d a week, enough to buy her about 25 cigarettes, which was substantially less than she usually smoked. Later she would bemoan the fact that she was not very good at rolling her own cigarettes, a skill quickly acquired by most prisoners who smoked because their scant remuneration would buy more loose tobacco. On 6 July, during her stay in Armagh, 100 male prisoners were moved from Belfast to Armagh to make room for the increasing number of offenders detained as a result of the widespread and sustained rioting, especially in Belfast and Londonderry.

Another MP was imprisoned in January 1971. Frank McManus, a man of Republican views who represented Fermanagh and South Tyrone at

Westminster, was jailed for six months for failing to comply with an order banning marches when he organised a Civil Rights march in Enniskillen the previous November. By the beginning of 1971 the prison population had soared from 727 in 1968 to a record 944. In the early months of the year the security situation continued to spiral out of control. Gun attacks and fatal no-warning bombings were taking place with growing frequency. Thirteen people had died as a result of the violence in 1969 and another 25 perished in 1970. As the level of disorder inexorably increased the Stormont government demonstrated its impotence by offering the substantial sum of £50,000 as a reward for information about who was responsible for the wave of terror. At the same time the Firearms Act was amended to impose a six-month mandatory sentence for discharging a firearm in a public place. The courts responded to the disorder by taking a tough line. In June 1971 Judge Topping, at Belfast Recorders Court, refused an appeal brought by a man who had shouted 'Up the IRA' during an Orange parade in the city. He was sent to prison for twelve months for disorderly behaviour and conduct likely to lead to a breach of the peace. The judge said he could easily have caused a riot. A month earlier the BBC Television journalist Bernard Falk was sent to Belfast Prison for four days for contempt after he refused to give the authorities the identity of a masked IRA interviewee who had appeared on a news programme.

As a result of the steadily deteriorating law and order situation, the prison population increased from a daily average of 602 men and twelve women in 1968 to 803 men and thirteen women in 1970. Those going to prison by then faced longer sentences for more serious offences, stretching the available prison accommodation to breaking point. After just one weekend of rioting in July 1970, for instance, there were some 250 people arrested and remanded in custody until they could be dealt with by the courts. Robert Mitchell, the Unionist MP for Armagh, suggested in parliament at Stormont that long-term prisoners should be transferred to remote parts of Canada, where there would be no possibility of escape, to help them return eventually to a useful life. Another MP, Joss Cardwell, called for the use of the birch, although corporal punishment in the prison system had finally been abolished a year earlier, not least because of the difficulty in finding someone to carry it out when it had last been imposed in 1961.

A more feasible and practical bid to ease the overcrowding problem was already under way. In August 1969 about 100 short-term male prisoners were moved to Armagh, which then housed both female prisoners and some 60 young male inmates who were transferred to other

Borstal accommodation at Woburn House, on the County Down coast at Millisle. A new open prison, the first of its type in Northern Ireland, was then established at Castle Dillon, County Armagh, a once stately mansion recently acquired by the Northern Ireland government. Perched on a hill overlooking a large fishing lake, and surrounded by open farmland, it was an idyllic setting to rectify the lack of such a facility, which was then at the height of progressive penal fashion. Work parties drawn from the short-term prisoners sent to Armagh began to travel the short distance to Castle Dillon early in 1970 to begin converting the mansion into dormitories and living accommodation for prisoners. There was room for a maximum of 80 prisoners, in two-tier bunks, at any one time. They also created visiting and dining areas, while accommodation for staff was provided in portable buildings positioned at the rear of the site. One Castle Dillon work party constructed a public access roadway leading from the shore of the fishing lake to the adjacent main road, which was promptly nicknamed the 'Burma Road'. Other parties were employed on the many farms and agricultural facilities dotted around the nearby countryside, including a husbandry farm in Loughgall, a chicken farm in Gosford and the nearby Castle Dillon Agricultural College.

The prisoners selected for the new open regime had to meet strict criteria before being transferred from closed conditions. In a circular to Governors, dated 12 November 1970, the Ministry of Home Affairs set them out in detail. Escapers and potential absconders, former Borstal inmates, homosexuals and prisoners suffering from abnormal or mental conditions should never be allocated to an open prison. Those eligible had to be serving sentences of less than four years and to have been at least one month in Belfast Prison before transfer. Particular care was to be taken with other categories of inmate: those under the age of 25 or with more than four previous convictions; former inmates who had served a period in a Training or Approved School, Special Care Institution or Mental Hospital; prisoners sentenced for offences connected with community strife or previously sentenced for more than six months for violence; and inmates normally resident in the Republic of Ireland. To distinguish the prisoners from category to category, adult 'Star Class' prisoners wore a brown prison uniform with a red star on the right sleeve. Young prisoners wore two white bars on their right sleeve of the brown uniform, though sometimes this was replaced by a red 'Y'. All wore overalls with the same markings for work.

The relationship between the staff and the inmates at Castle Dillon was a good one and very relaxed. That Christmas Eve the Governor, Bob Truesdale, who was later to serve at the Maze, was able to send his 100 inmates home for leave and lock up for the holidays. But the experiment was short-lived. With the civil unrest in the community constantly surging to new heights and scarce prison staff resources already stretched to the limit, the groundbreaking establishment was abruptly closed on 15 August 1971. Inmates who had less than six weeks of their sentences to serve were given early release on licence. The rest went back to Belfast Prison. Soon afterwards the Army, hard-pressed for accommodation as its role in the growing conflict steadily escalated, occupied the complex, where troops remained for another decade.

The Stormont government, whose exclusive control of security policy had been diluted once the British Army had taken to the streets in 1969, was now seriously frustrated by the rising tide of disorder and the inability of the army and the police to isolate the ringleaders, bring them to justice and restore what was fondly referred to as normality. There were constant embarrassments for the government and the prison service during this period. In March, James McCann escaped from the Crumlin Road jail, only the third person to do so since 1945, and in June a seventeen-year-old Provisional, wounded while carrying out a bomb attack on an Army patrol, was taken away from armed police guards at Belfast's Royal Victoria Hospital by four gun-toting terrorists clad in the white coats usually worn by doctors. These provocations were the last straw for Brian Faulkner who had replaced Chichester-Clark as prime minister a few months earlier. Throughout the early summer of 1971 his view hardened that it was necessary to introduce internment without trial to bring the situation under control. With the British Army by then playing the major role in trying to maintain law and order, such a fundamental change of policy could not be introduced without the approval of the British prime minister, Edward Heath. At first the British were sceptical, but, swayed by Faulkner's argument, they eventually gave the go-ahead and Operation Demetrius was launched with dawn raids on some 450 addresses in the early hours of 9 August 1971. The decision was to have very far-reaching consequences indeed.

Chapter Four

An element of martyrdom

On the strength of the historical evidence Faulkner's faith in the effectiveness of internment to bring a fast-deteriorating situation under control appeared to be fully justified. Internment had indeed neutralised Republican militancy in both the north and south on several previous occasions. During the War of Independence in the south, detention without trial, together with martial law and authorised reprisals, had been implemented by the British administration in some of the most troubled counties. Although the IRA broke the primary rule of conventional warfare by fighting in civilian clothes it nevertheless claimed prisoner-of-war status for its captive members. Sir Hamar Greenwood, the lawyer despatched to Ireland in April 1920 as Chief Secretary by the prime minister, David Lloyd George, to put down the IRA campaign, conceded that they would be treated as such but not formally given the status, a problem of definition that would recur at difficult moments in the years ahead with increasingly potent implications. This left his forces free to execute combatants captured in arms, a central element in his strategy to meet force with force. Although at least twenty inquests found against the British forces and laid charges, Greenwood ignored them and finally abolished the holding of inquests at all. By January 1921, when a general power to intern was introduced, there were already 1463 civilians in custody, many of them in a major detention facility at Ballykinler, a windswept military base on the County Down coast near Newcastle. There was little for the inmates to do, and after the Red Cross supplied a job lot of fiddles Martin Walton, who was an award-winning player, formed a camp orchestra. (He later went on to found a major business in Dublin specialising in traditional Irish instruments and music.)

After the War of Independence was brought to an end by the truce in July 1921, the British released all interned IRA members on 9 December, forty-eight hours after the signing of the Treaty which provided for the partitioning of the island of Ireland. This political solution split the IRA into two opposing factions and quickly triggered off a brutal civil war. Those in favour of the Treaty, and Partition, who formed the new Free

State government in Dublin ruthlessly used both internment and execution to establish their new administration and to suppress their former comrades who wanted to fight on for an all-Ireland solution. 'We are not going to treat rebels as prisoners of war,' said William T Cosgrave, the President of the National government, in September 1922, unconsciously defining the ideological ground on which rounds of prison struggles, north and south, would be fought out for the next 75 years.

By 1 July 1923, soon after the anti-Treaty forces led by Eamonn de Valera called a halt to the Civil War, the new government was holding 11,316 prisoners. Before they were eventually released the government stood firm in the face of a mass hunger strike in which two prisoners died before it was called off. Tough tactics had been used to suppress the anti-Treaty forces and their defeat contributed to a lasting belief, on both sides of the border, that internment, at least, was a valuable and essential tool to smother subversion. Not surprisingly, the right to intern was one of the core powers already taken in the 1922 Special Powers Act, passed on 7 April immediately after the formation of the separate government in Northern Ireland. (It was renewed annually until 1933, when its provisions became indefinite.) Regulation 12 enabled the Minister of Home Affairs to order indefinite house arrest or internment (in both cases without trial) where it appeared to him on the recommendation of an officer of the RUC, not below the rank of County Inspector, that a person was 'suspected of acting or having acted or being about to act in a manner prejudicial to the preservation of the peace or the maintenance of order'.

Against a background of serious sectarian violence and reprisal throughout the newly-partitioned north, these draconian powers were quickly implemented. After a particularly violent weekend over 20-22 May, the security forces were ordered to round up several hundred IRA activists and sympathisers. There was inadequate conventional prison accommodation available to hold them so the authorities acquired a steamship, the SS *Argenta*, to provide accommodation. The vessel was docked at the Musgrave Channel in the port of Belfast, and at the end of June, having taken on board 450 inmates, it set sail for a point off Carrickfergus at the mouth of Belfast Lough, where it dropped anchor. Later it was moved to a more sheltered location in Larne Lough where, together with the Larne Workhouse which had been commandeered for the purpose in September 1922, there were places for nearly 600 internees.

The 4000-ton wooden vessel was of recent construction, with electric light throughout and a modern wireless room, having been built in the United States in 1919. While she was at anchor one of her two boilers was kept in steam to provide the ship's services. A Governor and twelve prison officers were on board to supervise the inmates and a party of Special Constables was also present to ensure the security of the vessel. There was a hospital bay and a doctor and priest assigned to the ship. Solicitors were given access to their clients on request. The *Northern Whig* reported on 21 June:

> 'If the prisoners will not have exactly a pleasure picnic, they will, provided their conduct is good, be housed under extremely comfortable, airy and healthy conditions. In fact, apart from the inevitable restraint, their lot will be even better than that of the average third-class passenger crossing the Atlantic or other ocean. They will be accommodated in a large, flush deck running more than half the length of the ship, this being divided into eight compartments by means of steel wire-netting. This, in addition to other facilities, provides that air and light will circulate with utmost freedom. Air renewal is arranged for by means of powerful fans and everything in this respect is on a more generous scale than laid down in the Board of Trade regulations for third-class passengers. There are also three large skylights, two companion hatches and ample electric lighting. Sleeping accommodation is provided by iron bunks in fours, with wire mattresses and straw palliasses. Each man is provided with a life-jacket which folded up forms a pillow, while as a precautionary measure the ship carries a full complement of lifeboats and rails.'

Showers, washing basins and laundry tubs were also provided. The upper deck above the living accommodation was wired off and the prisoners were allowed two 90-minute periods of exercise in the open air each day where they were also allowed to smoke. Books were available and postcards could be sent ashore to friends and relatives. The internees had to rise at 7 am and observe lights-out at 10 pm. They were given three meals a day: breakfast at 8 am consisted of porridge, tea and bread; dinner at 1 pm started with pea soup or broth on alternate days, then six ounces of meat, or fish on Fridays; and supper at 6 pm was tea, bread, butter and cheese. Families ashore were not allowed to send any extra food but they were allowed to provide additional clothing. The Ministry of Home Affairs said the internees were allowed free association in comfortable quarters, clothing was renewed when required and the scale of the dietary provision was liberal. 'Despite mendacious propaganda the internees have been well-treated and their own private letters to friends, which are necessarily censored, give the best evidence of this truth.'

The number of internees peaked at 575 during May 1923. Over the year 369 were released although 132 were taken into custody. By then the level of violence had subsided and there were demands for the unconditional release of the internees. A hunger strike was begun by 269 men on the ship on 25 October 1923, which spread to other internees in custody at Belfast and Derry prisons. However, when the hunger strike collapsed on 11 November the Belfast government had made no concessions nor authorised any releases. It was with good reason that Bates later bragged that 'the old familiar hunger strike was grappled with and the prisoners quickly learnt its inefficiency when in Northern Ireland prisons.'

Nevertheless, by January 1924 numbers had been reduced to the point where the *Argenta* was closed down and the remaining 297 detainees were held in the Larne Workhouse and at Belfast and Londonderry prisons. A single female detainee, one of seven held during this period, was accommodated in Armagh. During the year the remaining detainees were gradually released with the last going free on 23 December in time for Christmas. Larne Workhouse was restored to the Board of Guardians. Altogether it had cost the authorities £94 a year to keep each internee and £11,512 to charter the *Argenta* and her captain and crew. Between 1922 and 1924 a total of almost 500 people were detained.

The use of internment had undoubtedly contributed to the swift end to the violence in the north by removing the activists from circulation. Given the lawless environment and the problems the police consequently faced in gathering evidence, finding witnesses and bringing charges through the courts, internment enabled the troublemakers to be expeditiously rounded up and isolated where they could pose no further challenge to public safety. There is no doubt that the notion of its effectiveness was well and truly grounded in the official and political mind at this stage, and the Unionist government, riddled with fear and insecurity about the permanence and stability of Partition, from this point on came to regard it as one of its most important and potent weapons.

After the turbulence of the early 1920s Northern Ireland settled into a period of comparative tranquillity. The tensions and hatreds were still evident but apart from sporadic clashes with the police, including serious rioting in 1935, the situation remained under control. Unionist anxieties were not seriously stimulated again until 1938 when internment was reintroduced on 22 December amidst growing fears of a major new IRA campaign, prompted by sporadic signs of an IRA resurgence over the previous five years. In 1933 there had been raids on public houses and a train during which barrels of English-brewed ale had been poured away. Two years later a police officer was wounded when he encountered an

IRA group trying to steal arms from the Officer Training Corps depot at Campbell College in Belfast. A few months afterwards the police broke up an IRA 'court martial' being held in a pub in Crown Entry, off High Street, Belfast, and arrested eleven 'subversives'. Two men with IRA connections were subsequently murdered for being police informers. Customs posts along the border were attacked by gangs with bombs, three men dying in a premature explosion during one such incident. The police advised the government that IRA violence was intended to continue, and so in a pre-emptive swoop internment was brought back and 34 suspects taken into custody on 23 December 1938.

A more serious threat materialised on 12 January 1939 when the IRA issued a four-day ultimatum to the British government to remove its troops and withdraw from the six counties. When the deadline was ignored, the IRA implemented its so-called 'S-plan' and bombs began going off throughout mainland Britain. By July, when Parliament rushed through legislation to impose controls on Irish residents, two people had been killed in almost 130 explosions. The campaign effectively ended on 25 August, a few days before the outbreak of the Second World War, when a bomb attached to a bicycle exploded in Coventry, killing five people. Although there were some explosions in 1940, at the same time as two men were hanged for causing the deaths in Coventry, the campaign in Britain was effectively over.

But back in Northern Ireland, where it was judged that England's difficulty was, as in 1916, Ireland's opportunity, the IRA was planning for trouble. Charles Wickham, Inspector-General of the RUC, warned the government that the IRA was setting up outrages and advised that the Specials be mobilised and the internment camp at Ballykinler, County Down be made ready again. The main fear of the government and the police was a nationalist uprising in the north, inspired or not by the IRA, in the wake of German parachute troops leading an invasion of the Free State. Some of the captured IRA material outlining sabotage tactics, on which these fears were based, was subsequently revealed to the Stormont parliament in March 1943 by the Attorney-General for Northern Ireland, John McDermott. Air-raid warning sirens were to be stolen and operated in different districts to disrupt the war effort and harass the fire and civil defence organisations. Armed attacks were to be made on them and the police and water and electricity supplies were to be sabotaged. If this had been a matter of froth and bubble, the Attorney-General told the House of Commons, he would not take up the time of the House in reciting from the documents. Unfortunately, he said, it was quite clear this was not froth and bubble but preparations for a campaign of violence. This scenario never materialised, and there is every likelihood that when the Unionist government rounded up the first 34 of the many detainees who were held during the war years it was engaging in one of its regular IRA scares, intended to keep its supporters fired up and deflect criticism of the serious shortcomings in its emergency planning. It later emerged there was complacency about procuring firefighting equipment and anti-aircraft weapons and planning to deal with Luftwaffe air raids, despite the fact that Belfast's large shipyards, aircraft factories and engineering industry made it an important contributor to the war effort and consequently a prime target. The myth that Nationalists had defied the blackout and shown lights to guide the bombers is now regarded as a piece of black propaganda stimulated for the same purpose. In reality, while the IRA had recognised the opportunity, it was too weak to pose a serious threat, lacking individually dynamic leaders and sufficient weapons, although some incidents, more notable for recklessness as opposed to cold-bloodedness, did demonstrate its continuing capacity to make trouble.

By far the most serious action of the time was the murder, on Easter Sunday 1942, of RUC officer Constable Thomas Murphy. That afternoon the police were on full alert to thwart planned Republican marches defying a ban on any commemoration of the 1916 Rising. To distract police attention a number of gunmen took up positions behind an air-raid shelter at Kashmir Road in the Falls area and waited for a target. Soon afterwards they opened fire on a police patrol car. Constable Murphy alighted from the vehicle and gave chase, pursuing the gunmen into the rear of a house at Cawnpore Street. By now most of the gunmen had dropped their weapons into a shopping bag to be whisked away by two girls waiting nearby, but one, Tom Williams, had retained his gun and now opened fire. When police colleagues caught up with Murphy he was lying dead in the scullery of the house and Williams, a nineteen-year-old house repairer, was lying wounded on a bed upstairs. The rest of the gang quickly surrendered. A few months later all six concerned were sentenced to death at the end of a murder trial in Belfast. It was the first time the death sentence had been passed on any IRA prisoner, despite the violent history of the organisation and the repressive instincts of the government.

The IRA's martyr-making propaganda machine was trundled into place, but cooler heads intervened, recognising the enormous boost that would be provided to the Republican cause by six executions. As George Bernard Shaw had warned about the pending execution of Sir Roger Casement in 1916, 'In Ireland he will be regarded as a national hero if he is executed . . . but Ireland has enough heroes and martyrs already . . . manufactured by England in fits of temper.' So although the Appeal

Court had confirmed both the convictions and sentences, all but one of the hangings set for 2 September 1942 were called off. Williams, regarded as the ringleader, was put to death, the only subversive actually to have been executed by the Unionist administration. The IRA planned a major protest to coincide with the hanging, but pre-emptive police action thwarted any serious reaction although rival crowds sang hymns and exchanged insults outside Belfast prison while the hanging was being carried out.

The authorities once more ensured the impotence of the IRA by interning its key members. The wartime detainees were held in Belfast and Londonderry prisons for the duration of the conflict, making up a large proportion of the prison population which peaked at 2559 in 1942 but fell to 1422 in 1946, a year after the last internees were freed at the end of the conflict. For a time, from September 1940, some internees were also held on the SS *Al Rawdah*, which was moored in Strangford Lough, three miles off Killyleagh, County Down. However, the scheme was not successful and the men were transferred to Belfast prison in 1941. Seven lunatics had been moved from Derry prison to the local Public Mental Hospital to make room for them. One of the perks enjoyed by the Derry detainees was a billiard table originally provided for the lunatics. When word of this privilege filtered back to Belfast, Fr McAllister, the Catholic chaplain, raised funds to provide a table there which was eventually handed over to the prison authorities for the use of ordinary convicts at the end of the war.

One of those interned in Belfast prison during the Second World War was Paddy Devlin, then a young IRA activist, who was ultimately to become a prominent Nationalist politician and a minister in the short-lived power-sharing Executive in 1974. In his award-winning autobiography *Straight Left* (1993) he vividly recalls life as an internee after his arrest in 1942.

'The police van was backed into the main gates of the prison and when the doors were opened I got my first view of the inside of Crumlin Road Prison, whitewashed walls and tall, barred gates. I was handcuffed and taken through another gate, across a yard, then up steps into the reception hall where I had my pockets emptied of three shillings in cash and four or five religious medals. After they were scrutinised I received them back again. The next stop was at what is called the circle, to wait on someone coming to assign me to a cell. The circle is the hub of the prison from which the four wings of cells radiate like the spokes of a wheel. This enables the warders to see along each of the wings, which were designated by a letter of the alphabet. The sentenced criminal prisoners accounted for the bulk of the inmates. "A" and "D" wings held the long-term political inmates, who were always referred to as "the internees". Part of "C" wing was also occupied by detainees, who fell into two categories.

'These were those, like me, recently arrested and waiting the statutory twenty-one days for internment orders to be confirmed. The others were known as "the signees". They were long-term internees seeking release who had signed an application for a hearing by the Appeal Tribunal. It had power to free them if they co-operated with the police beforehand and signed an undertaking to sever their links with the IRA. They were ostracised by the main body of internees who stubbornly refused to concede the legitimacy of the Unionist administration by recognising the appeal mechanism. They were also regarded as traitors for everybody recognised they could not be released without giving the police information, such co-operation being evidence of their reformation. Despite accepting this stigma as an informer, in the eyes of their comrades, the men, many of whom were forced to sign for the tribunal by pressing family circumstances, received little sympathy from the authorities. Once they applied for a hearing they immediately had to face interviews with detectives on their activities prior to internment. They were, of course, presumed to be active members of the IRA. But it was not uncommon for them to be knocked back four or five times by the tribunal for failing to co-operate. Many of them spent a further eighteen months inside before regaining their freedom.'

Devlin became a fully fledged internee on schedule after three weeks when his internment order was formally signed by Bates. After a time he was transferred to what he describes as the 'paradise' of D Wing, where he was shown to an allocated cell on the second of the three floors, not by a scowling warder but by another internee. D Wing, surrounded by barbed wire, was set aside from the other wings with only one door through to the prison circle. An elected 'staff' of internees ran the wing. They decided who would be admitted and administered the allocation of all equipment and food to each internee. They even controlled a separate cookhouse. Good order and discipline in the wing was the responsibility of the internees and the staff negotiated direct with the prison governor, an ex-army captain, on any points of dispute. Although the prison officers were supposed to maintain their distance from their charges many ignored the regime and acted in an intimidating and often bullying manner. Devlin recalls the 'Beating-Up' gang, a group of burly officers who amused themselves during the night by cruelly assaulting in their lonely cells any prisoners who may have crossed them during the day.

Stories of such beatings had a cautionary effect on the conduct of prisoners but it failed to cow all of them, especially one particular inmate who used his irreverent sense of humour to bait the warders. One morning, suffering from influenza, he was waiting outside his cell for the prison officers to say that the doctor was on the way. The doctor was regarded as next to useless by the internees, says Devlin, for whatever the ailment, inside or outside, his sole remedy was 'M&B' tablets.

After a time the call came. 'D1, D2 and D3, the doctor is in,' shouted the principal officer.

The prisoner leaned over the landing railings and shouted down at the officer, 'Sure the doctor is only a fucker.'

The officer was aghast and scanned the landings for the heckler. 'Up there, up there,' he said. 'Who called the doctor a fucker?'

'Down there, down there,' replied the prisoner. 'Who called the fucker a doctor?'

Although they did not have to work, as convicted prisoners did, the internees were not spared the privations and hardship of prison life at the time. The day began with the degrading experience of 'slopping out', emptying the bucket which served as an overnight toilet in spartan cells devoid of all but a chair, table and bed. Food was brought to the cell by other prisoners. Breakfast invariably consisted of eight ounces of hard bread, a small square of margarine and a tin beaker of tea. The main meal consisted of two large potatoes and usually tasteless, unrecognisable vegetables. Between mealtimes many inmates spent the the time endlessly marching around the exercise yard. From time to time the monotony would be broken by the mounting of a hunger strike to remedy some grievance or other. This meant the men staying in their cells and existing on hot water laced with salt and pepper. These protests often reflected antagonisms between various factions among the prisoners and usually faded out after a few days of hardship with no negotiation or concessions coming from the prison Governor.

The internees were, however, given much more latitude than convicted prisoners, such arrangements reflecting the fact that none of them had been charged, tried or sentenced for any offence. It also satisfied their own perception of themselves as prisoners of war or political prisoners. So they enjoyed social association from 7.30 am until 8.30 pm each evening before lock-up for the night. The exercise yard was open three times each day except in winter. Outdoor sports like Gaelic football and general athletics were also ongoing. Inside, in the dining areas, where the meals were eaten rather than in cells, all sorts of recreation took place: Irish language classes, nightly Rosary, meetings and parades, Sunday Mass, concerts, sometimes choir practices, bridge and chess. Above all, the prisoners wore their own clothes and not prison uniform, a factor which visibly distinguished them from the 'criminal' prisoners. They also maintained their own command structure to preserve discipline and decide who should cook the food, wash the utensils, clean the cells and corridors and organise the recreation programme.

Against this semi-autonomous background, the warders generally maintained their distance. They saw their job as being mainly concerned with keeping the detainees in custody through constant head-counting of the internees from the opening of the cells each morning to lock-up every evening. There was long-standing official paranoia about escapes, but although some of the internees constantly sought the opportunity, few succeeded. In 1941, however, five did manage to get out of Belfast, by going over the wall at night at a time when the blitz was taking place and air-raid alerts were constant. About 100 prisoners were said to have been involved in the plot. One of those who got away was Gerry 'The Bird' Doherty, who had scrawled 'The Bird has flown' on his cell wall before the escape. By far the most embarrassing escape episode took place in January 1943 when the IRA leader Hugh McAteer and three others got out of Crumlin Road prison. The government offered a £3000 reward for their recapture amidst a row about the effectiveness of security at the prison. Their embarrassment was compounded that March when Jimmy Steele, one of the escapees, helped coordinate a breakout by 21 internees from Derry jail. They had been digging for months down a twelve-foot shaft from a ground floor cell and disposed of the five tons of spoil by flushing it into the sewers. Eventually their 50-yard tunnel reached the coalhouse of a house in nearby Harding Street. On the night of the escape, the prisoners dashed through the house and into a furniture van, hired by Steele in Belfast, which quickly got them across the border. The escape was financed with the £1500 proceeds of a raid on a horse-drawn mail van held up at Strabane railway station two months earlier. The IRA's provocative activity then reached another plateau when the fugitive McAteer read the 1916 proclamation from the stage of the Clonard cinema in Belfast on Easter Sunday after armed men had halted the film and forced the projectionist to put on the house lights. After that however there was a security clampdown at the prisons and Devlin remembers that for the rest of the war all but the most dedicated had given up any thought of trying to break out:

'The majority were thoroughly bored with being in prison and were so completely fed up with each other's faces, habits and ideas that they had fragmented into disparate factions on the numerous issues of the day. Talks on strategy had been abandoned and gun lectures discontinued. These developments were clear evidence of the low morale. At the time some of the men had been there for five years, since the start of the S-plan bombing campaign in Britain in 1938. Others were interned in 1939 on the outbreak of war. These were very long sentences for men who had never faced a judge or jury. Worse still was the likelihood of being kept in custody until the war was over. In 1942 that looked a very distant prospect. This was perhaps the most agonising aspect for them. You could not count the days to release because each of us was detained for an indefinite period.

'The older, more mature men and some of the friendlier warders had a saying, a piece of advice. for those troubled by their indefinite imprisonment. "Dean do hoil (do your time)," they were exhorted, meaning put up with it, stop moaning and complaining.'

The Irish wartime government had also cracked down on the IRA to prevent any serious challenge emerging to its own authority and thwart any potential cooperation with the Nazis. While their strategy was to remain neutral in the World War, de Valera was anxious not to give Britain any pretext for threatening Ireland by invading or, more likely, seizing strategically important ports or points along Ireland's extensive Atlantic coast. Some hardline Irish Republicans believed or hoped that the Germans would invade Ireland to lay siege to the British mainland and, in so doing, present them with the prize of the British occupiers being driven from the north into the Irish Sea, leaving a fully united Ireland to emerge in their absence. Although this was no more than romantic Republican nonsense shared by a small cadre of hotheads, its adherents had a proven ability to upset the fragile stability of the fledgling state. The government therefore passed a tough Offences Against the State Act in June 1939 and activated the internment provisions in August. Two days later it set up Special Criminal Courts consisting of five Army officers. However, when one of the detainees challenged the consitutionality of the Act, de Valera was forced to release 53 prisoners arrested under its provisions. A few days later, two days before Christmas, the IRA carried out a highly provocative raid in Dublin by removing almost one million rounds of ammunition from the headquarters of the legitimate Irish Army in a convoy of thirteen lorries. De Valera moved swiftly to remedy the flaw by reinforcing the wartime emergency powers his government had already assumed. Early in January he took open-ended powers to detain IRA members for the duration of the war. Those who challenged his authority further were either executed by firing squad or in one case hanged, in a grim irony by a British hangman specially imported for the purpose.

The simultaneous use of internment throughout Ireland during the war years clearly shattered IRA morale and prevented any exploitation of the war with subsequent embarrassment for either the Dublin or Belfast administrations. The enthusiasm with which both governments regarded its effectiveness against the IRA, which was by now widely seen as a common enemy throughout the partitioned island, was underlined by the fact that emergency legislation, including the power to intern without trial, was made permanent and maintained in a state of immediate readiness in both jurisdictions.

Altogether the Belfast government locked up about 800 people without charge or trial during the 1939-45 period, some for as long as five years. Once all these were freed, the IRA appeared to go into hibernation for seven or eight years, but it was not entirely dormant. There was a flurry of threats and small explosions at the time of the coronation of Queen Elizabeth in 1953, mostly aimed at cinemas showing newsreels of the ceremony at a time when television was in its infancy and only available to a privileged few. A sign of a more serious preparation for hostilities came on 12 June 1954 when fifteen men, in a cattle lorry borrowed from its owner, entered the British Army's Gough Barracks in Armagh, overpowered the sentries and emptied the armoury, getting away with 670 rifles, 27 Sten guns and nine Bren guns. Later in the year, on the Saturday night of 17 October, the IRA tried to repeat the success. A party of nineteen young men alighted from the Londonderry-Belfast train at Omagh, County Tyrone. They all had single tickets and no baggage. At 3.15 am they forced their way into the town's military barracks but the guard force, clearly more alert in the aftermath of the Armagh raid, responded and a gun battle ensued. The attackers fled in a waiting lorry, leaving behind four wounded soldiers and a fifth who had been beaten about the head with a revolver butt. Eight of them were quickly apprehended by the RUC and later sentenced to long terms of imprisonment.

These preparations clearly pointed to to a new IRA offensive, but before it could be launched a militant breakaway group called Saor Uladh ('Free Ulster') attacked a border police station and several customs posts, losing a member shot dead by the RUC in the process. The full IRA offensive, Operation Harvest, followed on 11 December 1956. That night there were ten attacks on targets throughout Northern Ireland and along the border. They included the bombing of a BBC transmitter at Londonderry, the burning of a courthouse at Magherafelt and a 'B' Special drill hall in Newry, and another bombing at an Army barracks in Enniskillen. Several bridges were also severed. The next night two police stations at Lisnaskea and Derrylin endured gun and bomb attacks. On 30 December the attackers returned to Derrylin, opened fire from across the border and murdered one of the RUC officers on duty. Two nights later two IRA members were killed during a similar attack on the police barracks at Brookeborough.

By then Brian Faulkner, the Minister of Home Affairs at Stormont, had invoked the Special Powers Act and internment had begun. Within a few months 343 people had been apprehended and held for various periods. Three years later at the beginning of 1960 there were 166 still in custody, all in Belfast prison. At that stage the IRA campaign was clearly fizzling out, crippled by tough action by the authorities on both sides of the border, including internment, and by a marked lack of any significant public support for the IRA's activities, especially in Belfast. The Catholic Church's denunciation of the organisation had undoubtedly helped. There was thus little sympathetic interest in the cause of the prisoners beyond the dwindling colony of committed Republican families and the political representatives of the Catholic population felt safe in taking only a cursory interest in their plight. Nationalist leader Eddie McAteer was told in a parliamentary exchange in April 1957 that the internees' conditions were the same as those for people awaiting trial and that they were given a superior diet to that of ordinary prisoners – 4750 calories a day, described as a quarter more than the amount required for a manual worker. W B Topping, the Minister of Home Affairs, also said the men were imprisoned as a precaution to ensure the public safety and not as a punishment. In line with this policy he had extended their hours of exercise and association on Sundays from four to six and a half. This gave rise to an adjournment debate at Stormont during which Norman Porter, an Independent Unionist who was noted for his extreme religious views, protested about them being allowed to play football on Sundays 'in breach of Protestant teaching and opinion regarding the Sabbath day'. Topping replied that there would no change to the arrangements.

Internment continued until 1961 with the progressive release of the hard core of 33 inmates, one of whom had been held continuously since 1957. In April, five and then seven of the last dozen were quietly freed in the space of a weekend.

When the IRA campaign was launched in 1956 the Irish government in Dublin threatened stern action if it continued, although a minister at the Foreign Office in London recorded that the Irish ambassador was 'more voluble than convincing' when called in to discuss the situation. Nevertheless on 8 July 1957 the Irish government invoked the Offences Against the State Act and began detaining IRA suspects in the Curragh military camp, County Kildare. By the time the campaign was twelve months old there had been 366 incidents with seven IRA deaths and three RUC officers murdered. The effect of simultaneous internment on both sides of the border was clearly crucial in slowing down the pace of violence after that. By the time the IRA called it off unilaterally on 26 February 1962 there had been a total of 605 outrages since 1956, leaving sixteen dead: six RUC and ten IRA. The way the campaign had been so speedily and effectively suppressed was heavily credited, by Faulkner and the Unionist establishment, to the effectiveness of internment.

Its importance, from the unchanging Unionist perspective, was vigorously defended in 1968 by the prime minister, Captain Terence O'Neill. The statement came at a time when the storm clouds were clearly gathering over Northern Ireland and there was heavy pressure from both sides of the Irish Sea on the British Labour prime minister, Harold Wilson, to force the Unionist administration into a comprehensive reform package, including the total repeal of the Special Powers Act. Speaking to the Stormont House of Commons on 25 July in defence of the Act, O'Neill said:

'We deprecate and deplore the circumstances which, over so many years, have necessitated such powers and we have always been conscious of the need to be sparing in their exercise. It goes without saying that questions such as this are under continual review. But those of us who sit on these benches have a grave responsibility. We are charged, in the solemn wording of the Government of Ireland Act itself, with the "peace, order and good government" of Northern Ireland. This is our responsibility and we cannot shirk or evade it. It is a responsibility we must place before all other considerations.

'Now some honourable Members opposite, who clamour for change without having to weigh all the other factors involved, will say of the special powers – sweep them away, they are no longer necessary. That is attractive until one wakes up one morning, as I did very recently, to hear that an RUC car had been lured into a grenade attack which, but for a faulty fuse, could have had most grave results. An isolated incident, some will say, but is it not another nasty and squalid example in a long history of violence stretching back over the years?

'Special powers are used for many people and many times. I do not say that a time will not come when we can relax our guard. But it is our responsibility on these Benches, and no one else's, to judge this in a sober way and not as a response to public or parliamentary clamour. People's lives and freedom are at stake here.'

A more outspoken contribution, reflecting the view from the grassroots of Unionism, came from Joe Burns, the Unionist Whip, who had become a Special at the age of fourteen and was a senior and prominent figure in the Orange and Black Orders and the Apprentice Boys of Londonderry.

'I think that we would all like to see that Act put away in the files for ever. At the same time how would it be possible for that Act to be shelved if we are going to have incidents now and again such as the one that we had the other day? How would it be possible for the Special Powers Act to be shelved if we know very well that the IRA is recruiting, drilling and preparing for what it hopes will be another all-out campaign? Sometimes it is not a bad thing to look at past history because by looking at it we can get some idea of what is going to happen in future. We find on looking at history that every ten years or so there is a blow up.

'I am quite certain that my right honourable friend, the Minister of Home Affairs and my right honourable and gallant friend the Prime Minister would be very glad to look at the Special Powers Act if they were given assurances that there would be no more incidents and that the IRA and Sinn Fein were dead horses. They would also be glad to do this if they were assured that all the rifles and ammunition, which are numbered in their tens and thousands all over Northern Ireland, were handed in to the proper authorities.'

As the disorder and violence in Northern Ireland progressively escalated throughout 1969 and 1970 there is no doubt that many in the RUC and the Unionist administration favoured the introduction of internment to combat the disorder. However, there was never much likelihood that Wilson would agree to such a draconian step, given the close interest that his Labour government was taking in the pace of reform in Northern Ireland and the pressure from Civil Rights campaigners to do away with the Special Powers Act. Security policy promptly hardened after Wilson lost the British general election in June 1970 and a Conservative government, led by Edward Heath, took office. Reginald Maudling, as Home Secretary, assumed primary responsibility for handling the worsening situation, but, with a languid approach to life and politics and questions about his financial propriety beginning to engulf him, he would far rather have been somewhere more congenial. When he got on board the RAF aircraft to return to London after his first visit to learn about the situation, Maudling said, 'What a bloody awful country. Get me a large Scotch.'

Within days, however, another 3000 troops were drafted in, bringing the garrison to 10,500. The Army General Officer Commanding (GOC) announced that anyone carrying firearms would be shot on sight and troops were issued with rubber bullets to be fired at rioters. A number of Mercedes water-cannon vehicles were acquired in Germany and flown to Northern Ireland by the RAF. On 1 July, after an eighteen-hour sitting at Stormont, mandatory prison sentences of between one month and five years for rioters, looters and bombers were introduced. At the same time the Army started to carry out major search operations hunting for weapons and explosives, in one case imposing a curfew on the Lower Falls area of Belfast over a weekend. While the searches were not confined to Catholic areas, these places bore the brunt of them, prompting anger from public representatives. Paddy Devlin, the Stormont MP for the Falls area, declared, 'The Army are deliberately provoking trouble in certain selected areas where Catholics live to justify their saturation of these areas by troops. The British Army are now behaving like a conquering army of mediaeval times. With the restraining hand of Mr James Callaghan gone from the Home Office, General Freeland is reverting to the type of General that Irish people read about in their history books.'

With the change of government and the military crackdown there were clear indications for the first time that internment was now on the active security agenda. Three Nationalist MPs, including Devlin, stormed out of an angry meeting with Maudling on 30 June when he refused to give them an unequivocal denial of a newspaper report that morning forecasting the imminent introduction of internment. As hardline Unionists called for its introduction, the Joint Security Committee (chaired by the Northern Ireland prime minister and consisting of other ministers, the GOC, the Chief Constable of the RUC and the United Kingdom government representative at Stormont) revealed on 5 August that it had decided not to invoke immediately the internment provisions of the Special Powers Act. A few months later, on 2 November, Major-General Anthony Farrar Hockley, Commander Land Forces, the second-in-command of the Army in Northern Ireland, said the Army was geared to face a possibly prolonged terrorist campaign by the IRA and gave the first hard indication of intelligence gathering to support internment when he claimed that the

Army and police had considerable knowledge of internal terrorism within Catholic areas.

The internment cause was given a sensational boost from a southern perspective on 4 December when the Irish prime minister Jack Lynch and his Justice minister Des O'Malley ordered places of detention to be prepared immediately and moved to inform the Secretary-General of the Council of Europe that Ireland might have to enter derogations from the European Convention on Human Rights. The government was reacting to police reports of a secret armed conspiracy by subversives who were planning to mount large-scale bank robberies and kidnap diplomats. The threats were given such official credence because a month earlier two former government ministers, one of whom was the future prime minister Charles Haughey, had been acquitted by a Dublin jury after a trial which heard how they had allegedly conspired with members of the emerging Provisional IRA to illegally import arms for use in Northern Ireland.

The Dublin announcement, which was soon forgotten, served to renew pressure for internment in the north and nourish hopes that the south would follow suit, thus ensuring, as in the past, its swift effectiveness against the newly rampant Provisional IRA. Asked about the possibility, prime minister James Chichester-Clark pointedly refused to rule it out: 'I reserve the right to do whatever may be necessary to protect the security of Northern Ireland.' By then shooting and bomb attacks were daily occurrences and hardly a night passed without serious rioting erupting at one or more of Belfast's many sectarian flashpoints. At the end of 1970 the number of murders had gone up from five to fourteen, including two police officers; shooting incidents had increased from 73 to 213 and explosions from nine to 153. Another grim statistic was added on 6 February 1971 when Gunner Robert Curtis became the first soldier to die in the conflict, killed by a gunman while on patrol in Belfast's New Lodge Road area.

As the security situation continued to deteriorate, hardline Unionists naïvely maintained their calls for internment to be implemented, as if it, rather than genuine and long overdue political and social reform, would miraculously retrieve the situation. Nationalists, especially the newly-formed SDLP (Social Democratic and Labour Party), equally strongly opposed it. On 4 March the party leader, Gerry Fitt, said, 'All reasonable people realise that internment would be the final step in the tragedy that has been played out here within recent years.' Fitt knew that there was no immediate security solution, and as the indications grew that internment was indeed being actively planned he toured the bars and tea rooms at Westminster urging everyone to realise just what a disaster it would be.

The Reverend Ian Paisley, who had become an MP at both Stormont and Westminster, broke ranks with other Unionists and, the same month, told a rally in Newtownards, County Down that the government should not be given the power to intern. With declared self-interest he forecast that if it were one Protestant would be interned for every Catholic. 'I would be the first to be put inside,' he said.

Chichester-Clark's position as prime minister was inexorably weakened by the ongoing violence, with up to a dozen explosions taking place each night and almost constant rioting and disorder throughout Northern Ireland. Criticism of his security policies came to a head in mid March when three young off-duty Scottish soldiers were abducted from a public house in downtown Belfast, taken to the hills above the city at Ligoniel and murdered. After crisis talks at Downing Street, Chichester-Clark failed to get backing for tough new security measures, including internment, and, having had enough, resigned on 20 March because he saw 'no other way of bringing home to all concerned the realities of the present constitutional, political and security situation'. A few days later Brian Faulkner became prime minister and, in a bid to establish cross-community credibility and make a new start, promised he had no plans to 'get tough with Catholics'. As well as leading the government he retained the Home Affairs portfolio for himself, a signal that he was personally going to handle the security problem. His strategy, outlined a few days earlier in the Stormont parliament, was already clear.

'Our aim is not just to defeat the present vicious conspiracy but to create conditions in which such men and such activities can never prosper again. This aim makes it necessary that any measures taken by the security forces should be firm but not repressive, tough but not needlessly harsh, aimed at the real enemies of this country and not indiscriminate.

'There may even have to be – if on the basis of cool judgement it is considered essential – a curtailment of ordinary liberties through the use of the power of internment. I do not rule it out. I will certainly not be prevented from taking this step, if I deem it to be for the good of the country, by any political clamour against it. Nor will I be pushed into it against the advice of the security experts by any political clamour in favour of it. I will not deal with such a question on a political basis. It is much too serious an issue for that. The yardstick will be: will such a step at any particular point of time help or hinder our return to peace, not just immediately but in the longer term as well?'

On 31 March 1971, Maudling indicated the British government's increasingly pragmatic position on the issue. 'Internment is a very ugly thing but political murder is even uglier,' he said, adding that it would only be introduced if a strong and convincing argument could be put forward. Behind the scenes, in conditions of necessarily strict secrecy, that argument had already been put forward by Faulkner – and won.

The RUC Special Branch was ordered to compile lists of suspects to be arrested and detained. Planning to accommodate large numbers of internees was put in hand. In April, officers from the British government's special forces arrived in Northern Ireland to teach RUC officers controversial interrogation techniques, which had never been written down but had been used and developed during the twilight of Empire counter-insurgency campaigns in Palestine, Malaya, Kenya, Cyprus, the Cameroons, Brunei, British Guyana, Aden, Borneo and the Persian Gulf. The aim was to improve intelligence by filling in more of the specific detail in the general picture of IRA activity and personnel then available to the RUC from Special Branch activity. All that remained to be decided was the precise timing of the operation, and that would depend on events.

Meanwhile the security environment steadily continued to deteriorate. At the beginning of May the number of explosions since the start of the year reached 136. A dozen detectives from Scotland Yard were brought in to help the hopelessly overstretched RUC cope with the escalating murder rate. Rewards of up to £50,000 were offered for information about those responsible for murdering police officers and soldiers. In a remark which hindsight would invest with some significance, Faulkner told Fitt that intelligence reports indicated no group other than one with Republican aims was responsible.

As the preparations for internment continued and the violence intensified, Nationalist opinion remained solidly opposed to any round-up. Speaking in the Northern Ireland House of Commons on 19 May, in response to yet another Unionist member calling for immediate internment, the SDLP MP Ivan Cooper said, 'I want to make it clear that in my constituency – and I believe in the majority of constituencies in this province – people want to see an end to the use of the gun. By introducing internment one brings in an element of martyrdom: in other words, potential support for the lunatics and maniacs who engage in the use of the gun is increased and I believe internment would be a retrograde step which could only hinder the programme of reform. I would warn the government against this step because it will be opposed by the opposition in every possible way.' John Taylor, who was Faulkner's junior minister at the Home Affairs department, replied, 'There is no question of introducing internment without the advice of the security forces and such advice is not forthcoming. References to internment are not the least bit helpful at this stage. It is a deterrent which we hold up our sleeve.'

A week later, on 26 May, the growing impotence of the Army and police was underlined when Taylor revealed that 2000 pounds of gelignite had been detonated since August 1969 with only nine prosecutions resulting. The crisis finally came to a head in mid July when continued IRA attacks, including ten bombs strung along the route of the Orange march through Belfast on 12 July, exacerbated the traditional sectarian tensions of the marching season. The final provocations were the rescue of the wounded seventeen-year-old gunman from Belfast's Royal Victoria Hospital by terrorists dressed in doctors' coats, and the destruction of the *Daily Mirror* printing plant on the western outskirts of the city. Maudling reacted by stating that a state of open war now existed between the IRA and the British Army. On the back of that admission the Army was ordered into action. In dawn raids in Belfast and nine other towns on 23 July, 48 persons were detained for questioning. The operation, the first full-scale rehearsal for the introduction of internment, was followed by daily early-morning swoops in towns and villages throughout Northern Ireland including Belfast, Strabane, Coalisland, Dungannon, Londonderry, Lurgan and Portadown. Little useful intelligence was gained from the operations and those arrested were released after 48 hours, the maximum legal period of short-term detention, having remained silent and refused to answer questions. Discord between the Army and the Catholic community reached new levels after two youths were shot dead by soldiers during rioting in Londonderry, provoking the SDLP to walk out of the Stormont parliament in protest, but by then the security forces were locked on to a course that could only end in the introduction of widespread internment.

The final go-ahead for the major arrest operation, codenamed Demetrius, was given by the Heath government at the end of a crucial meeting with Faulkner at Downing Street in London on Thursday 5 August which the GOC, Harry Tuzo, also attended. During the discussion Faulkner skilfully used supposed 'intelligence' material and statistics to persuade Heath finally that the IRA was solely responsible for the most serious terrorist activity and that active Loyalists were largely hooligan elements and rabble-rousers who did not pose a serious threat at that time. He argued that the IRA was mounting a highly-organised, politically motivated campaign, whereas Protestant activity was being carried out on a significantly less organised basis. At the end of the meeting Maudling lamely urged Faulkner to 'lift some Protestants if you can' to forestall the inevitable criticism there would be from the Catholic and Nationalist communities about the one-sided nature of the coming operation.

As the politician and the soldier flew back to Belfast to order the arrest teams into action, another 1000 troops were mobilised to reinforce the Northern Ireland garrison and bring its strength up to 11,900. While they arrived in Northern Ireland over the weekend there was yet more violence as final preparations were made for the largest planned security operation since the outbreak of what had then come to be universally known as 'the Troubles'. An Army post in Belfast came under machine-gun fire from the top deck of a hijacked bus. Explosions damaged several police and Army posts, an employment exchange in Belfast, an electricity power station at Larne and the home of a Resident Magistrate in Omagh, County Tyrone. On Saturday 7 August a van driver was shot dead by soldiers outside a Belfast police station, an incident which triggered widespread rioting throughout the city. Overnight a solider was killed by gunfire in the Ardoyne area. Tension was still running high in the early hours of Monday 9 August as police and military arrest teams took up positions throughout Northern Ireland in readiness for the coordinated 4.30 am swoops.

The wanted lists had been compiled by the RUC Special Branch and the increasing number of Army intelligence personnel who had been tasked to assist them. Ever since the Army had first been deployed in August 1969 it had, on the direct orders of the British government in London, taken the lead from the beleaguered RUC in implementing security policy and maintaining law and order. This had stimulated considerable rivalries and tensions between the two organisations. These had their origins in a visit to Northern Ireland at that time by the head of the army, General Sir Geoffrey Baker. According to contemporary secret documents, on his return he reported to Denis Healey, the Secretary of State for Defence, 'There is no doubt that the RUC is behind the times, poorly led and administered and with a sadly inefficient Special Branch . . . speculation and guesswork largely replace intelligence.' Healey in turn complained that the government had 'no intelligence sources independent of the RUC by which to evaluate the threat of terrorist movement across the border. We are at present working almost entirely in the dark.' A special group was then set up by Whitehall to establish an independent network of sources in Northern Ireland. A heavily censored report among these papers from the period, released at the Public Records Office in London, records that in September 1969 the Home Secretary, James Callaghan, 'over the past few days has had a number of contacts with (passage deleted)'. This was clearly a reference to MI5, the British agency responsible for the internal security of the state, which, other files reveal, was already carefully monitoring the civil rights movement in Northern Ireland and other groups interested in events there. The documents also show that from the start of the civil rights demonstrations in 1968 the government was expressing concern about what the Home Office described as 'the increasing difficulty of reconciling the situation in Northern Ireland with our international obligations on human rights'.

The issue of internment without trial therefore cut to the very heart of these concerns in London and the dominant Army influence over the scope and style of the internment operation was clearly visible. Soldiers were to carry out all the arrests and bring their quarries to a nearby rendezvous point for identification by RUC officers. The arrest teams were ordered to work at speed to avoid becoming tangled with the hostile crowds that were expected to gather as soon as news of the detentions spread. As it turned out crowds of women took to the streets in Belfast when the arrests started and gave what had become the traditional warning, clattering metal dustbin lids on the pavements. In some remote country areas RUC guides were assigned to lead the military arrest parties to the right addresses, but in every case the suspects were hauled from their beds by soldiers who read a prescribed form of words advising that they were being arrested under the provisions of the Special Powers Act.

The plan was to take the arrested persons to one of three holding centres, specially created inside military installations at Girdwood Park, Belfast; Ballykinler, Co Down; and Magilligan, Co Londonderry. There they would be screened and, under Regulation 10 of the Special Powers Act, could be held for preliminary interrogation for 48 hours. After that the Act enabled them to be arrested and held for an initial period of 21 days' detention before being interned indefinitely under Regulation 12. The Girdwood Park contingent were to be walked through a gate in the wall to the adjoining Crumlin Road prison, while helicopters were to be deployed to ferry prisoners from Ballykinler and Magilligan to Belfast where the vintage HMS *Maidstone*, moored in Belfast Harbour, had already been designated as a prison ship. The *Maidstone* was built at Clydebank and laid down on 30 August 1936. She went into service in May 1938 and for the next six years was stationed in the Mediterranean and north Atlantic. In 1944 she was sent to the Far East and for a time was the support vessel to the 8th Submarine Flotilla. She ultimately returned and was laid up at Rosyth in 1968. With the rapidly increasing numbers of troops deployed in Northern Ireland through the late summer of 1969 having to camp out in a string of spartan, cramped schools, church halls, overcrowded police stations, and even a bus station, at flashpoints throughout the city, the *Maidstone* was pressed into service again. The ship arrived in Belfast in October 1969, and was moored at the Musgrave Channel, to provide more comfortable living quarters for 1500 soldiers.

Faced with the prospect of hundreds of additional prisoners coming into indefinite custody as a result of the internment decision, the prison authorities took over the stern part of the *Maidstone* to hold them, while soldiers continued to occupy the rest. Inmates were to be contained in two decks of dormitory accommodation in tiers of bunks, two or three high. These were in the lower part of the ship on decks three and four. Two messes, formerly used by the Naval crew of the ship, were set aside for them, one with BBC Television, the other with ITV. There was an Army guard force on board ship and the meals were prepared by Royal Naval cooks. The prison staff of the ship consisted of a Governor, two Assistant Governors, a Chief Officer, two Principal Officers, two Senior Officers and thirty Prison Officers. They were housed above the detainees, on deck two, and there was a screened-off exercise area in the open air on deck one.

Visits to the ship were conducted in a specially-constructed complex on the quayside and visitors were transported by an Army van which picked them up at the then Queens Quay railway station, close to the main gate of the harbour and shipyard estate. An old black-painted ambulance brought parcels to the ship, where they were security checked and loaded on board by another gangway. Security was clearly a preoccupation and the Army had a quick reaction force on standby at all times. There was an emergency entry access from the bulkhead leading to the Army quarters. If an incident occurred on any of the decks, the prison staff had no way out, so as they moved from deck to deck they always kept in line of sight of each other.

By breakfast time on the morning of the swoops, as the prisoners were being brought in, a head count showed that 354 of the 452 on the original wanted list had been detained. The largest number, 185, were at Girdwood, while 89 were held at Ballykinler and 68 at Magilligan. Within 48 hours 104 were freed and the remainder lodged in either Belfast prison or the *Maidstone*. However, twelve of those captured had been singled out for special treatment and were handed over to the teams of police and Army interrogators who had been specially trained the previous April. In the words of the subsequent official report by Sir Edmund Compton into allegations against the security forces of physical brutality arising from the events of 9 August, 'they were believed to possess information of a kind which it was operationally necessary to obtain as rapidly as possible in the interest of saving lives.'

Over the five days from 11 to 17 August these men, clad in boiler suits, were subjected to five interrogation-in-depth techniques involving degrees of physical and psychological deprivation. Apart from periods of interrogation and when they were placed in a room on their own they were kept hooded. They were subjected to continuous and monotonous 'white noise' designed to disorientate and isolate them from communication. During the early days of the process they were deprived of sleep and sustenance, being given only a round of bread and a pint of water at six-hourly intervals. They were also made to stand against a wall in a required posture, with legs apart and hands raised above the head against the wall. If they attempted to rest or sleep by propping their heads against the wall they were prevented from doing so, and if they collapsed on the floor they were picked up by the armpits and forced to resume the posture. The detainees were each subjected to this regime for periods totalling from nine to 43 hours during the five days. (In a second episode, two men were later subjected to similar treatment between 11 and 18 October.) Some of those involved later claimed that they had been denied toilet facilities, suffered assaults and other abuse and experienced hallucinations, thirst and blood circulation problems.

In the immediate aftermath of the internment operation, the authorities maintained it had been an overwhelming success. Seven hours after the swoops, Faulkner presided at a news conference in the main hall of the Stormont Parliament building where he gave the first official confirmation that the powers to intern had been activated.

'The outrages to which we have been subjected now threaten our economic life and create every day deeper divisions and antagonism within our community. These, indeed, are the clear objects of those who carry them out.

'Every means has been tried to make terrorists amenable to the law. Nor have such methods been without success, because a substantial number of the most prominent leaders of the IRA are now serving ordinary prison sentences. But the terrorist campaign continues at an unacceptable level, and I have had to conclude that the ordinary law cannot deal comprehensively or quickly enough with such ruthless viciousness.

'I have therefore decided, after weighing all the relevant considerations, including the views of the security authorities and after consultation with Her Majesty's Government in the United Kingdom last Thursday, to exercise where necessary the powers of detention and internment vested in me as Minister of Home Affairs.

'I have taken this serious step solely for the protection of life and the security of property. At all times I have consistently emphasised that it was not a step towards which I would be moved by any political clamour. Equally, I cannot now allow the prospect of any misrepresentation to deflect me from my duty to act.

'This is not action taken against any responsible and law abiding section of the community. Nor is it in any way punitive or indiscriminate. Its benefits should be felt not least in those areas where violent men have exercised a certain say by threat and intimidation over decent and responsible men and women.

'The main target of the present operation is the Irish Republican Army which has been responsible for recent acts of terrorism and whose victims have included Roman Catholic and Protestant alike. They are the present threat; but we will not hesitate to take strong action against any other individual or organisations who may present such a threat in future.'

The security forces quickly embellished Faulkner's bullish tone about the success of their operation, declaring that a high proportion of the IRA leadership had been picked up. They were later to justify the move, and especially the in-depth interrogations, by saying that for the first time they were able to gain new detailed information about the IRA. The Parker report into the efficacy of the interrogation procedures, published in March 1972, said that as a direct result of them they had identified a further 700 IRA members and their positions in the organisation, gleaned 40 pages of information about organisation and structure, uncovered details of possible operations, arms caches, safe houses, communication and supply routes and locations of wanted persons, obtained details of morale, operational directives, propaganda techniques and future plans, and, finally, discovered responsibility for 85 incidents recorded on police files which had previously been unexplained. The report also contained figures for increased seizures of munitions and explosives after internment. Between 1 January and 8 August 1971, 193 weapons, 41 rounds of ammunition and 1194 lbs of explosive were captured, compared with 413 weapons, 55 rockets, 115,000 rounds and 2541 lbs of explosive between internment and the end of the year.

Whatever the accuracy of the figures and the validity of the case made on their back, hopes that internment would quell the trouble were speedily dashed. Thirteen people were killed in the first 24 hours afterwards as widespread rioting, shooting, arson and disorder erupted on a previously unseen scale throughout Northern Ireland. Families were driven from their homes on both sides of the recently-erected Army peace lines and within a week 7000 refugees fled over the border from the north to Irish Army camps which were hopelessly incapable of accommodating them.

The IRA leadership in Belfast dealt a devastating propaganda blow when the veteran Republican Joe Cahill, who had been reprieved from a death sentence in 1942 for his part in the murder of Constable Murphy, held a news conference in a Belfast school and boasted that because of a tip-off about the impending arrests only 30 of their members had been captured. Two days later an IRA statement from Dublin admitted that 56 members were being held.

During the year the number of explosions had steadily risen from sixteen in January to 86 in the month of July alone, a pre-internment total of 245. Up to that time 27 people had lost their lives: two policemen, ten soldiers, and fifteen civilians of whom four had been shot by the security forces. Injuries had been inflicted on 454 civilians, 71 policemen and 110 soldiers. In the remaining months of 1971, after internment, the death toll for the year jumped from 27 to 173; explosions increased to 131 in August, 196 in September and 117 in October before reaching a total of 1022 at the end of the year. Shooting incidents soared from 213 in 1970 to 1756 in 1971. The following year was even worse. The death toll reached 467 over the twelve months, in what turned out to be the worst single year of the conflict. Shooting incidents reached 10,628 while 1382 bombs exploded and another 471 were defused. Some of them were car bombs, packed with explosives and often left to explode without warning in city streets or town centres. People close by were slaughtered or maimed indiscriminately, and damage to property by blast and fire was invariably devastating. The campaign of violence was substantially fuelled by the proceeds of armed robberies which increased fourfold in a year to 19,031, raising a sum almost certainly understated by the authorities at £800,000.

Far from taking the IRA activists and leaders out of circulation, the devastating escalation of violence after internment exposed the abysmal quality of the intelligence on which the arrests were based. Many of the persons detained were arrested on the basis of inadequate and inaccurate information. In some cases fathers and sons with the same names had been confused. Many of those lifted were traditional, well-known Republicans who were no longer active in the movement. The identity of the cadres of new, younger activists, who had first taken to the streets and then become involved in more sinister and threatening violence, would take the authorities several more years to identify with any certainty and in any number. Indeed, there is ample evidence that many people became directly and indirectly involved with the IRA after internment. In particular, its one-sided implementation, with no Loyalists or Protestants arrested in response to Faulkner's flawed analysis of the threat posed by each side, justified the claim by Nationalist critics that internment was the best recruiting sergeant the IRA could ever have hoped for.

Internment turned out to be a disastrous and defining episode with far-reaching political and security consequences. The whole exercise, including powers of arrest, and indeed all the Army's actions in Northern Ireland since August 1969, was later deemed to be illegal by the courts, forcing the London parliament to rush through unprecedented legislation retrospectively legalising the Army's entire activities. Britain ended up in the dock at the European Court of Human Rights after the internment and interrogation operations, facing complaints of torture made by those affected but brought with the active support of the Irish government. More importantly, the introduction of internment sowed the seeds for an even more debilitating conflict that would turn the prisons into universities of terrorism and heavily influence the turbulent events of the next quarter of a century.

Chapter Five

The men behind the wire

When the Second World War broke out in 1939, Britain had a pressing need for airfields as far west as possible to enable land-based aircraft to operate at the limits of their fuel range out over the Atlantic. With powerful German warships and especially U-Boats marauding along the north-western approaches, it was essential to provide aerial protection for the incessant shuttle of convoys bringing vital food and war material from North America. There were also fears of a German invasion, with the first strike from airborne troops coming in by parachute and glider. As the Irish Republic was firmly neutral in the conflict, and had rejected overtures from Winston Churchill to exchange partition for the use of some ports and airfields, Northern Ireland's geographical location became a highly valuable strategic asset within the technical and communications constraints of the time. In the early years of the war, therefore, large tracts of flat land, especially along the coast, were promptly commandeered and concreted over to provide runways and marshalling aprons.

The Lagan Valley, to the west of Belfast and Lisburn, where the urban sprawl gave way to flat farmland, was ideal for the purpose, and so in November 1941 the townland of Long Kesh, 'long meadow' in Irish, gave its name to a hastily-constructed military airfield. In common with many other aspects of Northern Ireland's war effort it appears, according to a contemporary report cited in David J Smith's *Britain's Military Airfields 1939–45*, to have been a rather ramshackle facility:

'January 3–4: Exercise Bella for defence of RAF Long Kesh. Number of personnel required to effectively defend station is 1,000. The Battle headquarters is not sufficiently large, at least two more rooms are required to accommodate 12 to 14. The Battle HQ and all Flight Commanders' posts must be supplied with heat and telephone, also, four-inch ducts are required for heat, light, telephone and tannoy. Arrangements must be made to drain all localities, in fact the whole aerodrome requires draining. The north and north-west sides of the aerodrome are unprotected and give the enemy covered approach to the aerodrome, bomb stores and Short and Harland. The north-east corner is blind and requires pillboxes. Newport Bridge, main line of approach for counter-attacking troops, and the technical area require pillboxes. The transmitting and direction finding station is outside the defensive area and cannot be defended by the RAF. Can arrangements be made for the Home Guard to defend? There is no defence work at Maghaberry [the nearby satellite] except for defensive localities in varying stages of completion. There are no Home Guard localities. All work done by civilian contract is very slow and requires constant Royal Engineers supervision.'

The aircraft which flew in and out of Long Kesh during the war were mainly fighters, either carrying out defence patrols or training with the Army for joint combat in other operational zones. Since Short Brothers and Harland's aircraft factory, ten miles away in Belfast, was an important contributor to the war effort, Long Kesh was also used from August 1942 for the assembly and flight testing of Stirling bombers. There were 56 serious accidents and many fatalities involving the ill-fated Beaufort aircraft operating from the base. All were grounded to have modified oil pipes fitted after one serious accident in 1943, and the type was phased out soon afterwards.

In 1942, when US forces began to muster and train in Northern Ireland in preparation for D-Day, the invasion of mainland Europe which eventually took place in 1944, Long Kesh was inspected as a potential base for them but then rejected. However, it did play a part in the preparations for D-Day when a series of proving, towed-glider flights from Netheravon in Wiltshire came over the shortest sea crossing from Stranraer in Scotland to Long Kesh. The object was to test the aircraft and equipment and to train crews over long distances for their part in the big operation.

Commencing in August 1942, the US Navy operated a thrice-weekly air service between Hendon, north of London, Eglinton, near Londonderry, and Long Kesh. In March 1944, in the final run-up to the invasion of France, nearly 60 fighters were posted to Long Kesh for battle training with other aircraft and ships off the Irish coast. At the end of the war, Long Kesh earned a footnote in the history of the British Royal family when King George VI and the Queen, together with Princess Elizabeth, made their first visit to Northern Ireland by air in July 1945, landing there in a DC3 Dakota. Another VIP visitor, General Dwight D Eisenhower, the US military commander in charge of the D-Day landings, passed through Long Kesh a month later. However, with war at an end, Long Kesh was closed in 1946 but remained in military hands. The British Army continued to use its hangars and workshops as a storage and maintenance facility and for years lines of lorries and other vehicles were parked along one of the now disused runways.

In the halcyon days of the 1950s and '60s, when Northern Ireland enjoyed a generally peaceful period, a coveted posting to the Army's headquarters at Thiepval Barracks in Lisburn was a sinecure for people about to retire. With no more than routine staff work to carry out, the military personnel had plenty of time for the huntin', shootin', fishin' and flyin' that abounded in the area, and, indeed, across the border. There was also scope and encouragement for other sporting and leisure activity. Thanks to the influence of a woman Lieutenant-Colonel serving at Thiepval, a couple of miles away, who was a glider enthusiast, the Ulster Gliding Club obtained the use of a hangar and the old airfield for the peppercorn rent of £30 a year. However, one Wednesday evening in the early summer of 1971, the Club officials were suddenly given notice to quit – by the following Saturday. The members, mostly local civilians from a range of backgrounds, were not surprised. Ever since the previous May they had watched a combat construction team of troops building rows of Nissen huts along the concrete of the old storage pans and runways. With the rapid escalation of the British Army deployment in Northern Ireland over the previous couple of years as the troubles intensified, and troops having to sleep in schools, church halls and even buses parked overnight, they assumed that what they could see taking shape was much-needed military living accommodation. They could not have been more wrong. What was in fact under secret construction was what would soon become officially known as the Long Kesh internment centre, or to its inmates, the Long Kesh concentration camp.

When the first internment swoop took place on 9 August, it was planned that those arrested would first be held on the *Maidstone* or at Belfast prison for up to 28 days and then either be released or transferred to Long Kesh, if they were deemed a sufficient threat to society to merit longer-term detention. The first internees to occupy the centre arrived by air from the *Maidstone* and Belfast prison on Sunday 19 September 1971. In an operation that began shortly after dawn and lasted well into the afternoon, some 200 detainees were flown to Long Kesh in groups of ten, in a fleet of Wessex military helicopters. As the aircraft clattered into the sky above the harbour and skirted 'Samson and Goliath', the giant yellow cranes at the Harland and Wolff shipyard, they were shadowed out over the city's southern suburbs and down the line of the River Lagan, by other guard helicopters. At one point, over the *Maidstone*, a light aircraft containing news cameramen was 'buzzed' to prevent pictures being taken. On the ground a web of checkpoints was set up to keep sightseers away from the country roads around the now heavily guarded former airfield. Overnight the detainees on the *Maidstone* had rendered it uninhabitable by setting fire to their mattresses, bedding and any other combustible material. The scale of subsequent repairs was so extensive that the ship was not ready again for occupation by prisoners until 14 December.

Anyone stepping into the Long Kesh internment centre in the winter of 1971/72 would easily have been forgiven for thinking they had stepped back some thirty years into a Second World War POW camp. Long Kesh had barbed wire compounds, corrugated iron huts, armed soldiers, watch-towers on stilts, floodlights, barking guard dogs, searchlights – all the elements so familiar from the numerous books, newsreels and films of that period. Inside the reinforced airfield perimeter was another heavily guarded compound, surrounded by a corrugated iron wall with watch-towers every 50 yards or so. Inside that again was a series of compounds, or cages, as the inmates preferred to call them, with barbed wire fencing. Each contained three living huts, a communal hut used as a classroom, recreation centre, church and canteen, and a wash-block. The Ministry of Home Affairs issued an official description of the accommodation:

'There are a number of buildings of the Nissen-type design, each of which accommodates a group of internees. The buildings are fitted with two-tier bunks and with lockers for personal effects and each group of internees have their own television and radio sets. There are adjoining dining areas which are separate from the living accommodation and internees receive four meals daily – breakfast, lunch, tea and supper. Separate toilet blocks are equipped with hot showers, wash-hand basins and lavatories. The buildings are heated. Quarters are set aside for visits by relatives and for legal consultations, where required, and there are facilities for medical treatment. Internees are given facilities for recreation and exercise throughout the day. Library and educational facilities are being provided at the camp.'

The reality was quite different. In summer, former inmates remember, the huts became sweltering ovens, and in winter they acted like cold chambers. They were also far from weatherproof. When it rained the water seeped in and ran down the walls, and when it was windy draughts of cold air whistled in the windows and through the cracks in the wooden walls at each end. One former inmate remembers two Belfast internees huddling under blankets one particularly cold and stormy night.

'You know, I worked for one of the sub-contractors building these huts,' said one.

'Well, you didn't do a very good job,' said the other, shivering.

'No. They're jerry-built. You see we thought they were for the Brit soldiers, so we didn't go much trouble. If I'd thought for a minute I was ever going to end up here myself, I'd have done a far better job.'

From the outset, the prisoners were only deprived of their liberty and not subjected to any formal prison regime. Like their interned predecessors over the years, they were not obliged to work and were allowed to wear their own clothes instead of prison uniform. They were also entitled to a more liberal quota of visits, letters and parcels than convicted prisoners. Each compound elected its own 'officers' and they in turn formed the Camp Council, which maintained contact with the prison authorities. Eventually the prison consisted of 22 compounds and the population peaked at almost 2000 inmates. At their own request, they were segregated by faction. After the convulsions of 1969, the IRA had split into two: the original or 'Officials' and the breakaway 'Provisionals'. Later another splinter group, the Irish Republican Socialist Party and Irish National Liberation Army, would emerge. When Loyalists were rounded up in due couse, they too resisted official efforts to keep them together. Instead they unilaterally imposed their own segregation, creating exclusive compounds for affiliates of the Ulster Defence Association, Ulster Volunteer Force, Ulster Freedom Fighters and Red Hand Commando.

The Army was responsible for perimeter security of the prison establishment while prison officers carried out headcounts and supervised the virtually autonomous internal prison regime. Four officers were assigned to each compound. One occupied a sentry box at the gate, two patrolled the perimeter fences in a no-man's-land between the compounds and the fourth stood by in reserve. By this time, although the number of locally recruited prison staff had increased dramatically from 292 in 1969, the service was severely overstretched and officers virtually untrained. At the same time a similar internment centre had been opened at Magilligan in County Londonderry, inside a bleak military training area and firing range, with views across Lough Foyle to the hills of Donegal. To help relieve the pressure, a scheme had been set up to enable prison officers from the British mainland to serve in Northern Ireland on detached duty. At the end of 1971, 75 officers had volunteered for temporary secondment. Five were assigned to the *Maidstone* in August 1971 and others to Long Kesh, where they lived for a time in notably poor accommodation including a number of caravans. Eventually portable buildings, with individual rooms and separate shower, washing and toilet facilities were provided. This residential area within the prison complex became known as 'Silver City' because of the aluminium ablution buildings. At first the detached officers only came from England and Wales. The Scottish Prison Officers' Association initially prevented its members from going – 200 volunteered – to Northern Ireland because of under-staffing and recruitment difficulties in Scottish prisons, but they eventually relented. Before the scheme was scaled down in the late 1970s, the number of detached officers climbed from 377 in 1973 and peaked at about 490 during 1974.

One of the original inmates at Long Kesh was Phil McCullough, who had been arrested in the August 1971 swoops. In 'Behind the Wire', a pamphlet published by the left-wing, Republican-socialist party People's Democracy, he gives an account of life in Long Kesh from a prisoner's perspective.

'A typical day's routine would begin at 7.30 a.m. Lying on one's bunk the rattle of keys are heard outside the hut doors and those awake check with their watches and, with a sigh of relief, find that it is 7.30 and not 5.30 as this would mean a dose of harassment by the British Raiding Party who call at that time. A few stir at the familiar metallic noise grinding as the duty screw makes a racket opening the badly fitted doors and rusting padlocks. One, two, three, four, all the way up the hut, stomp the four duty screws pulling a blanket from a covered face here and there, to reassure himself that the bulk in the bunk is actually a body and not just pillows. He then assures the chief screw that everyone is accounted for. Out they march with a slam of the door and back to sleep for us until rising time, usually for most men about 10 a.m. "Is the boiler full?" someone would shout in between a puff of a Park Drive. If the answer is in the affirmative, a sweet tone and friendly air is put on as a mug of tea is requested. Lying there, mug in hand and Army blankets pulled well over our bodies, our eyes zero on to that all too familiar hut and its inhabitants. They were newly built by the British Army when we first arrived at Long Kesh but now signs of wear and rust are appearing. The constant stripping of the huts by the Raiding Parties have left them just a bundle of tatty corrugated scrap iron. A wet day like today is hated by all here, as this means constant dripping of rain and large puddles of water on the floor. The rainy days also mean confinement indoors because the cage is usually under water.

'Gulping the tea down the day really begins in earnest. Into the wooden locker, soap and towel over the arm, out the door for a wash, but back again to put on a pair of boots and an anorak because of the rain. Out the door again, hopping and dodging the puddles right up to the washroom, fifty yards away. The place, as expected, is crammed tight with bodies queuing for a sink. As the toilets are also contained within the washroom complex, the odour of excrement and Palmolive soap make an extremely unpleasant smell. Blocked drains mean that the washroom is under several inches of soapy water so we have to stand on duckboards to keep our feet dry. Someone down the line breaks into the well worn strains of "The Boys of the Old Brigade", but is told from all directions just how much his singing is appreciated at that time in the morning. But the guy continues amidst the insults. He has a visit today and nothing, just nothing in the world could annoy him. Lucky him, as he carefully shaves and preens himself to perfection. Someone swears and utters threats to an unknown previous sink user for leaving "an F'n razor blade" in the sink.

'Back in the hut finds everyone up making their beds. A mop, mop-bucket and brush are produced and the Internee on duty fatigues starts his daily task of cleaning out the hut. No one bothers going round for breakfast, we know for sure that will be the usual trash. On the hour every hour, just as the newscaster says, a little group huddles round the radio listening with anticipation for last nights incidents or "sceal" [news] as it is commonly called in Long Kesh. A cheer goes up as the newscaster, in the solemn tone usually reserved for deaths and disasters, announces the death of a British soldier killed by a "terrorist's" booby trap bomb. The good news is rapidly transmitted from bedspace to bedspace. I suppose it is morally wrong to cheer such an incident as a death, but it is understandable. Plastic buckets and containers are strategically placed under the leaking holes and beds are re-positioned to avoid the rain pouring in through the badly fitted corrugated sheets. This makes the hut look extremely untidy, but it is necessary.

'How to get the day in, is a problem faced by all. There is absolutely nothing to do except a bit of woodwork or read a book but after a year or two, this gets extremely boring.

'Boredom can be very dangerous and some men have ended up as vegetables because they were unable to combat it. These guys usually took to their beds as an easy means of escape, but this was too easy a way out for the next day and the next. Soon one is seen to deteriorate and to be existing day to day with the aid of sleeping drugs which are freely administered by the Camp Doctor. After a very short period a person becomes a complete mental wreck. To keep sane we must always keep busy pottering around doing something to pass away the hours. To attempt any serious study is impossible because neither the facilities or the privacy are available to do so. Privacy I believe is very important and the lack of such slowly whittles away at one's nerves. It is impossible to get away from it all, even for a few minutes. If only there was a sound-proof room, or someplace with a door to lock behind you to escape from it all for a few minutes. Even the toilet door is a half one.

'I find that everyone is highly strung, nervous and wound up like a tense spring. Hardly anyone talks anymore, but shouts, even in normal conversation. With the immense frustrations and emotions at such a level, it is surprising that the men have not had more flare-ups. There is the occasional fisticuffs, but thankfully no grudge is ever held, and the incident is soon forgotten.

'Twice a week two cage teams are permitted the use of the heavily guarded football field, but I would not term this as sport or as a means to work out frustrations, as the two teams concerned have been playing against each other for two years now and no matter how much we re-arrange, chop or change the teams, every move is predictable as well as the score. Inter-cage matches are not permitted on security grounds. Some guys pass away an hour or two walking round and round the small Cage, but this is sometimes like walking down Royal Avenue on a Saturday, before the bombing of course.

'When talking about frustrations it would be wrong not to include sex or should I correctly say, the lack of sex. The absence of this very vital function adds to the frustration of healthy men, but it is an angle never talked about. Unfortunately some of the Catholic population and even some Republicans, term sex as porn and a thing not to be talked about but the lack of it plays a significant role, not only with Internees but with every man political and non-political. To mention conjugal rights for prisoners is looked on with disgust by most. Surprisingly, homosexuality is non-existent within Long Kesh.

'At mid-day the cry "grub up" is shouted in through the door by an Internee, but as usual during grub call, there is no clamour. Our plastic plate, plastic knife, plastic fork and plastic spoon are not the best to eat grub with anyway. Fifteen or sixteen guys go round anyway and queue before the aluminium containers containing a hash the establishment call stew. It is again dumped into the dustbin and men filter away uttering threats regarding the tyrant Commandant Truesdale. Even the cooks' parenthood comes into question again, for the millionth time.

Our Camp representative has just arrived back from Commandant Truesdale's Office. He goes almost daily with the usual list of grievances looking for a change of attitude from the Commandant, but today just like the past has been in vain. Promises, promises and more promises is all we receive from him. The list of grievances is the same today as it was last year and the year before i.e. draughty huts, leaky huts, vermin ridden huts, flooded cages, blocked drains, lack of recreational facilities, lack of educational facilities, military harassment, etc. etc. etc. The list is enormous.

'The middle of the day I would guess to be the "five to one" Ulster news. Everyone and everything stops. The usual post-mortem is in progress after the news. By early afternoon news begins to filter through from guys just back from their visits and from this news is pieced together and an accurate "State of the Nation" report for the day is built up. One is always "keyed" up during visiting days and the half-hour with one's loved ones is cherished more than gold. To hear the screw read one's name from the pink coloured permit card is like music to your ears. The screw picks up the Internees' Identity card which contains a photo, description and security classification of the Internee i.e. high security risk, low security risk etc. The screw accompanies the Internee to the visits precinct. Here we take off our boots in the search area provided and are intimately searched before being given box numbers. Seeing our children, wife and family walking towards the box down the corridor is a real deep and heart-warming feeling, but the miserable 30 minutes passes very, very quickly. Goodbyes are made and children weep, but we have to go just the same, sometimes with a lump in our throat, as we watch a weeping child being led away by its mother sobbing "why can't my daddy come too?"

'On the way back to the Cage it is noticed that the inhabitants of the cage are standing outside the huts in the rain. It is discovered that it is our weekly screws raid. As well as the frequent British Army raid, the screws come into the cages every week, tapping every single inch of the floor with a hammer, checking for that hollow note which would mean a tunnel and ultimately promotion for the lucky screw. Nothing found they tramp out and everyone goes back into the huts again. Four thirty brings what the cook calls supper, but once again our stomachs go empty because supper consists of what is known as "riot roll," a round piece of vegetable roll, approximately three inches in circumference and is usually either badly burned or uncooked.

'Bad news occasionally brings its gloom to the cage such as the death of a loved one or a close relation. One very sad case in particular

I recall was concerning a new Internee. Two weeks after his arrest and internment he received the joyous news of the birth of a baby son to his wife. Parole was refused when requested because of a sudden illness of the child. Three weeks later a priest came into the cage and informed him of the tragic death of his young newborn son whom he had never seen. The only time he saw the child was when he was released for four hours to attend its funeral. A tragic case. Another Internee, whilst listening to the RTE news, heard of the shooting to death of his young son one hour before in the Ardoyne area. Tragic news and grief is shared by one and all here at Long Kesh camp. Every Sunday at 2 pm all cages form up in military fashion facing each other for a two minutes silence which is observed in respect for all who have died during the previous week in the struggle for Liberation. During this parade, the screws discreetly hide themselves.

'Nine-thirty has everyone outdoors walking in little groups round and round the small Cage. This is pretty monotonous because of the size of the cage. Every one walks in the same direction because of the lack of space. Just twelve miles away, one can spot the red warning light on top of the TV aerial on the Black Mountain and Colin Glen mountain silhouetted against the fading daylight brings a string of nostalgic memories of bygone days. At night even the barbed wire and guard towers adopt a strange picturesque beauty outlined against the deep flaming orange and gold sunset.

'Goodnights are exchanged and all retire to their respective huts. The screws padlock the doors quickly in an attempt to catch a quick pint in the NAAFI canteen within the camp. Some men indulge in a quiet game of chess whilst others are content to read. There is a laziness hanging over the camp at this time of night. Not a physical tiredness but more of a mental one. Soon all turn into bed, but not to sleep, no, not just yet until the late night news has spewed out its final propaganda for the night. One by one sleep overtakes the hut and men escape for the night into wild fantastic dreams. One or two guys are still awake writing a few words to their loved ones. I bet everyone writes almost identical letters, as only certain things are permitted to be written by the establishment.

'But all is just not quite over for the night. A mouse has been observed by the men trying to gain entrance to an Internees' food supply in his locker. All hell breaks loose and the whole hut is soon awake once more, armed to the teeth with both offensive and defensive weaponry. The unfortunate mouse is soon cornered and beaten to death. Debate rages over whether it was a rat or just a large mouse. It is disposed of down the loo and peace reigns once more. Lights out tell us that it is 1.30 a.m. The quietness is overpowering. Not a noise. Well almost. Somewhere mice can be heard scraping at the corrugated iron and a war dog howls eerily somewhere. The stillness is wonderful and it is the only time of day that is relatively noiseless. The red glow of the cigarettes are extinguished one by one and minds stray to better days.'

By the middle of November 1971, official figures revealed that since the initial August swoops a total of 882 people had been arrested and 476 released. 278 had been interned and 128 held temporarily. An Advisory Committee had been established to review the cases of every prisoner and ten had been quickly released. However, they were required to give an undertaking in the following terms: 'I swear by Almighty God that, for the remainder of my life, I will not join or assist any illegal organisation, nor counsel nor encourage others so to do.' Many Republicans refused to do so on principle and remained imprisoned. That the crackdown was almost exclusively against people from the minority community, suspected of active involvement in violence, fired anew the sense of injustice that had brought Civil Rights marchers on to the streets in the first place. Against a background of intense media coverage of the ills and discrimination in Northern Ireland society for the first time and the fact that extreme Loyalists had actually exploded the first bombs and killed the first police officer to die in 1969, there was general incredulity that it was so one-sided.

Faulkner's image as an outright hardliner was confirmed, but Catholics and Nationalists despaired because, after all that had been promised from Westminster about reform, what they were seeing was a typical Unionist-inspired, one-sided crackdown. Because it was so indiscriminate in many areas, and clearly based on dubious intelligence, it only served to draw many people into sympathetic, if not direct, support for active Republicans. The IRA and its cherished cause of a united Ireland were thus each given a new lease of life.

The Army's heavy-handed, often brutal, tactics also contributed to this process of revitalisation. Families who watched as a father or brother was pulled from his bed at dawn, manhandled into an armoured vehicle and driven off to detention soon became active themselves, joining the street protests, contributing to the growing disorder and violence. The military raiding parties were often serenaded by the song 'The Men Behind the Wire', which had been written by one of the internees, Pat McGuigan, and went on to become a standard in the Republican musical repertoire:

> 'Armoured cars and tanks and guns
> Came to take away our sons,
> But every man will stand behind
> The men behind the wire."

Internment actually prompted the major surge in violence that was feared and which it was supposed to thwart. In line with longstanding Republican tradition, those who had been imprisoned continued to agitate from custody. Within a month of taking up residence in Long Kesh, the internees began what was to be a sustained campaign of 'continuing resistance behind the wire'. In doing so they were inspired by a long list of Republican martyrs, but none more so than Terence MacSwiney. In March 1920, when taking office as Lord Mayor of Cork at the height of the War of Independence, he said, 'This contest of ours is not, on our side, a rivalry of vengeance, but one of endurance – it is not they who can inflict most, but they who can suffer most, will conquer.' These words would echo again and again in the coming years.

The first serious trouble erupted on 25 October, when a full-scale riot developed after the prison authorities refused to meet a prisoners' deputation to discuss a range of grievances, especially about the quality of the food being served. The centrepiece of the meal that day was vegetable roll, sausage meat flavoured with spices and coloured with parsley. After it was distributed to the compounds, the prisoners flung it over the wire in the direction of the cookhouse. (Ever since they have referred to vegetable roll as 'riot roll', as Phil McCullough called it in *Behind the Wire*.) In one compound, four warders were taken hostage and a hut was set on fire. Troops arrived in force and were forced to fire CS gas before they could bring the disturbances to an end. Afterwards many prisoners had to be treated in the prison hospital and five were temporarily removed to the Musgrave Park hospital in Belfast. The prisoners also mounted a hunger strike for 48 hours to underline their discontent. Soon afterwards, following a critical report by the International Red Cross, the Faulkner government announced that conditions for internees would be improved.

Again, in keeping with Republican tradition, some prisoners set out to escape from custody. On 16 November nine prisoners, all awaiting trial on arms and explosives charges, who were afterwards known as the 'Crumlin Kangaroos', got away from Belfast Prison. In a carefully coordinated plan, helpers outside threw rope ladders over the prison wall during a football match and the nine men got away. Cars were waiting for them outside with a change of clothes. Two were recaptured two days later as they tried to cross the border into the Irish Republic dressed as priests. The next day two Cistercian monks, who were arrested during a follow-up search of their monastery at Portglenone, Co Antrim, appeared in court charged with aiding and abetting the fugitives. They were later fined £250 and £500 separately for the offence. The hue and cry after that escape had barely subsided when there was an equally daring breakout from the same prison.

During the afternoon of 2 December three men, Martin Meehan, Anthony 'Dutch' Doherty and Hugh McCann, concealed themselves in a drain during an exercise period. Other prisoners caused a mêlée on their way back to the cells and frustrated the routine headcount by prison officers. When the prison fell silent after lock-up, the three fugitives got away from the prison. Well before their absence was discovered, they were safely across the Irish border, their families had been told and there were celebratory bonfires burning in the Ardoyne area of the city where they had recently been captured. Soldiers on patrol asked why the fires were burning and reported back the reason. The embarrassed authorities immediately ordered a massive seal and search operation to recapture the prisoners, and for the next 48 hours traffic throughout Belfast and on the main cross-border routes was brought to a standstill as police and soldiers vainly searched virtually every vehicle. A couple of days later, as Brian Faulkner, the prime minister, announced that Sir Charles Cunningham was being called in to conduct a review of the security arrangements at the prison, the escapees were conducting a news conference in Dublin. At the time, fugitives from Northern Ireland enjoyed virtual immunity in the Irish Republic, as long as the Irish courts accepted that there had been a 'political' motivation for their offences in Northern Ireland.

In an immediate bid to ease the overcrowding at Belfast prison and beef up security there, it was decided to reopen the *Maidstone* as a primary detention centre. The idea was to hold arrestees there while it was decided if they should be charged through the courts, interned or released. So in mid December about 100 prisoners were airlifted on to the ship by helicopter. A *Daily Mail* article at the time reported that the move had been ordered by security chiefs after the Belfast prison escapes. They said its isolated position in the harbour and special security screen, involving radar and electronic detectors on the dockside and underwater, made it virtually escape-proof.

It was a dangerously foolhardy boast, for an escape committee among the prisoners was already at work. Long before Cunningham reported, they succeeded in prompting a further outcry about the effectiveness of prison security when seven of them escaped from the heavily guarded vessel. About 6 pm on the evening of 17 January, after the bar on a porthole had been severed with a fretsaw smuggled on board for the purpose, the prisoners waited for a headcount to be completed. While planning the escape they had thrown scraps of food to a seal, tempting it to come close to test the ship's security measures and the alertness of the sentries. They also threw plastic bottles and containers into the water to see the way the currents flowed around the vessel. Then, dressed only in underpants, they squeezed through and climbed down an anchoring cable into the waters of the Musgrave Channel below. It was a bitterly cold winter evening and they had smeared themselves with butter and black polish in preparation for swimming some 400 yards across the harbour to the adjacent Queen's Island. The 20-minute swim proved to be exhausting and one of the escapers said he had nearly given up hope. 'I prayed so hard I even invented a few new saints,' he said afterwards. When they eventually clambered ashore on a pier, they rested for a time near the power station and then hijacked a bus waiting to take shipyard workers into the city centre. They ordered the driver off before going to the Markets area, close to the exit from the Belfast harbour and shipyard complex. There they obtained warm clothes and were driven to safe hide-outs before the alert was raised. Again the authorities mounted an intensive hunt for the escapers, already cast in Republican escape folklore as the 'Magnificent Seven', who proved they had evaded it by appearing to tell their story at a triumphant news conference in Dublin a few days later.

On 7 February, there was another uncomfortable blow for the prison authorities. During the evening a Belfast newspaper received a call that Francis McGuigan, a prisoner interned in Long Kesh, had escaped the previous day and was safe. At first the authorities insisted he was still in the prison and it was only after organising a roll-call that they finally conceded he was missing. Official reports of the incident tell the inside story.

On 9 February the Principal Officer received the stiff memorandum, 'Please explain for the Governor's information why, that you on Sunday 6 February 1972, when in charge of evening duty, did report Internees' numbers correct at 502, when it now appears there were only 501 when you handed over charge at 9.30 to the night guard.' Alongside it, in handwriting, the Officer replied, 'The reason I gave the numbers as 502 to the night guard instead of 501, was that apparently, there is no way that I had of knowing that the figure was incorrect. I accepted the figure of 502 on taking over from the day staff and had no way of checking same unless I used Army personnel, which I had no reason to do, as I assumed the numbers were correct. On going off duty, I gave the numbers to the PO night guard assuming them to be correct.'

Another report reveals how McGuigan's escape was belatedly discovered and the extent of the subsequent inquest.

'A number check was completed at 2.30pm on Sunday 6 February of Compound No. 3. Because there were no visits on a Sunday it was assumed that a ruse had taken place and an inspection of the gate-book record, together with interviews with Prison Officers, confirmed that McGuigan left the Camp at 5.55 pm on Sunday under the name of Father Park, and appropriately dressed as a priest. Six priests entered the Camp to celebrate Mass that day, seven priests had left the Camp. The report, attached leaves no doubt that the person leaving the Camp at 5.55 pm stated he was Father Park, and further reports by officers indicated that the genuine Father Park left the Camp in the company of another priest at 7.00pm. There is no definite evidence as to how McGuigan gained exit from Compound 3. Searches of the food trolleys and the tea urns did not raise any suspicions but, by demonstration, it was proved this method of getting through the gates was possible. I feel certain he could not have climbed out over the compound perimeter fence unnoticed and the absence of any cuts leads me to believe the trolley method was used. Having come through the compound gates, the trolley is taken to the kitchen area for unloading. McGuigan could then have dropped off the trolley and concealed himself between buildings sufficiently enough to tidy himself and make his approach to the guard room gate exit.

'Attached reports answer the question – Why was McGuigan not missed on number check at 10.00 pm on Sunday 6 February and again at 7.30 am on Monday 7 February? If number checks are 100% foolproof on all occasions, particularly on occasions when internees have good reason, such as covering up an escape, then it would be absolutely necessary that we admittedly support an Order to have all internees formed up for counting. My staff would never have been numerically sufficient to carry out such an operation and if they did such an operation would become involved in violence.'

By the time all this had been established by the prison authorities six days later, McGuigan had received rapturous applause when he appeared on the platform at a rally in support of the Provisional IRA outside the General Post Office in Dublin, scene of the 1916 Rising. Within a few more weeks he had been paraded in Washington and Paris promoting the

IRA cause.

Two further escape attempts from Belfast prison, however, were foiled. On 12 February three men sawed through the bars of a cell window and shinned down a rope into the yard below. They were spotted by a patrolling prison officer and, after a brief scuffle, the men climbed back up the rope into their cell. After the alarm was raised the police and troops mounted a search of the area surrounding the prison. In the grounds of St Malachy's College, next door, they apprehended a number of co-conspirators who were in possession of docker's hooks and knotted ropes to help the escapees climb the main prison perimeter wall. A month later guns were produced during another escape attempt but it too was thwarted.

An account of life on the *Maidstone* after the escape, from the inmates' perspective, was given in a letter to the *Belfast Irish News* on 16 February. Describing the 'soul-destroying' situation on the ship, the Internees' Committee wrote:

> 'We are subject to so-called "counts", morning, noon and night. This entails being herded into the so-called dining hall, with a steel wire-meshed door bolted behind us, for long periods until the wardens have finally convinced each other that none of us has gone missing.
>
> 'These "counts" are the big events of our day, since there is absolutely nothing else with which to occupy our time, except get on each other's nerves-which seems to be part of the plan. This is only thwarted by the rigid discipline of the Internees' Committee and our own unbroken spirits.
>
> 'Now, only this morning (Sunday, February 13), we had 200 troops to awaken us and herd us, with whatever clothes we could snatch, into the dining hall. The purpose of this exercise was to raid our lockers, toss our beds and write "God save the Queen" etc., where it could be read by us, and search each of us personally and rip up painted hankies (our only pastime to try and combat boredom).
>
> 'Remembering our enforced captivity in a confined space, the uneatable food, the monotonous days and nights, the hopelessness of complaining to the governor, the uncertainty of how long we may be here, lack of privacy etc., our complaints are valid.'

At this time the detainees were refusing prison food most days and relying on the contents of food parcels provided by their families. They claimed hair and other foreign bodies had been discovered in prison food and that a prisoner had been injured eating a potato into which a piece of glass had been inserted. The on-board tensions finally erupted at the end of March when the detainees barricaded themselves into Number 3 Deck and refused to cooperate in the headcount. Troops stormed into the area to break up the protest and a prisoner was taken to hospital after he fell down stairs and broke an arm during the disturbance. In a subsequent search the troops uncovered hacksaws, blades and other potential escape implements concealed in the prisoners' quarters. After the clash, the delivery of food parcels was halted while, the Army said, damage to the ship and accommodation, was being made good. The 132 prisoners retaliated by launching a hunger strike which lasted for over a week during which the Committee for the Release of Internees held a series of pickets and rallies in their support.

The protest coincided with a highly significant political turning point: the prorogation of the Northern Ireland parliament and the introduction of direct rule from London on 24 March. Ever since the introduction of internment, the rising tide of violence in the community, the inability of the Northern Ireland authorities to stem it even with the help of the British Army and finally the escape debacles had caused the Government in London, led by Edward Heath, to become increasingly exasperated over Northern Ireland. The international disapproval after the events of Bloody Sunday, 30 January 1972, when soldiers shot dead thirteen unarmed civilians during an illegal Civil Rights march, finally persuaded them of the need for a change of policy. When the Belfast administration would not agree to relinquish control of security they were relieved of all power and stood down. In their place came William Whitelaw, the first Secretary of State for Northern Ireland, and the creation of the Northern Ireland Office to provide more effective government.

Whitelaw flew to Belfast on the morning of Saturday 25 March and established a base in Stormont Castle. After a preliminary meeting with the heads of the RUC and British Army, he signalled that he would personally review the case of every one of the 800 internees then in custody. Within two weeks, as a sign of good faith, he ordered the unconditional release of 47 internees and 26 detainees and the closure of the *Maidstone* as a prison ship. (The elderly vessel continued to house soldiers until the end of 1976. In January the following year, it was towed to Scotland and finally broken up.) Whitelaw's conciliatory stance was evident again on 26 April when he freed another ten prisoners. One of them was Charles McSheffrey, from the Bogside area of Londonderry, who had been in custody for six months. A week earlier his wife, Elizabeth, had confronted Whitelaw during a visit to the city and pleaded for her husband's freedom. He took a note of her name and address and promised to look into the case. On 1 May, 40 internees were transferred to Long Kesh from Magilligan, and although it continued as a prison, it too ceased to be an internment centre. At this point some 700 internees remained in custody.

Although Whitelaw had publicly rejected peace overtures from the Provisional IRA upon his arrival in Belfast, in private, he used two Stormont MPs, John Hume and the former internee Paddy Devlin, as go-betweens to explore the prospects for a ceasefire and talks leading to a lasting peace. Indeed he was to go to extraordinary lengths in his bid to end the violence.

The terms laid down by the 'Provos' for a permanent ceasefire were publicly spelled out by Sean Mac Stiofain, the chief of staff, at a news conference behind the barricades in Free Derry on 13 June. In essence the Provos wanted the British to withdraw from Northern Ireland and let the Irish people decide how they would then be governed. He offered a seven-day ceasefire if the British Army ended arrests, halted searches and stopped 'harassing' the civilian population. Mac Stiofain, who was, ironically, English-born, invited Whitelaw to Derry to discuss the proposals face to face. Whitelaw promptly replied that he would not respond to what he called an ultimatum from terrorists, but Hume and Devlin sensed the Provos were serious and that 'we should try to pick up the ball and run with it'. They reached a private understanding with Whitelaw at an undisclosed meeting in London two days later. Whitelaw indicated that the total ending of internment could follow after two weeks clear of violence. With the release of about 150 internees in the week before the meeting, there were by now only some 400 men still in custody. A future amnesty for those convicted of offences arising from the Troubles, people who would not have been in jail under other circumstances, was also discussed at length and, significantly, not ruled out. The question of granting these prisoners political status in the meantime, to distinguish them from ordinary criminals, was raised, especially in the light of the hunger strike to back this demand which had started at the Crumlin Road prison in mid May and was causing ever-increasing ripples on the streets. A wave of riots had followed a false report that one of the hunger strikers had died.

Republicans had initiated their campaign for political status in the time-honoured way by refusing to undertake prison work or share cells. This was an especially aggravating factor for the authorities, who were already hard-pressed to accommodate the rapidly escalating number of prisoners. With their demand falling on deaf ears, they then started a phased hunger strike with five men joining in every week. Whitelaw also indicated that he was prepared to meet the Provos to discuss their policies, but not while their campaign of violence was still being waged. None of this detail was revealed in the fairly bald joint statement which followed the two-hour meeting. By way of amplification, Whitelaw merely said that if violence ceased the possibility that existed for long-term peace would be greatly extended and that he and the security forces would respond to any genuine end of violence.

Confident that they had the makings of a ceasefire in their hands, Hume and Devlin flew immediately to Dublin to contact the Provo leaders. After going first to a pub in Donegal town and then to Hume's house in Derry, they eventually met Daithi O'Conaill and Mac Stiofain. The latter was a volatile, unpredictable individual, but O'Conaill, who had been badly wounded in a gun battle with the RUC during the 1956–62 campaign, was altogether shrewder and more able. After explaining Whitelaw's words and assurances, the two went back to Belfast to report to Whitelaw on the talks. The unpublicised meeting was highly successful. He agreed to create a 'special category' section for convicted prisoners at Long Kesh, to release a young internee called Gerry Adams from Belfast prison temporarily into Devlin's custody, and to provide personally signed letters of safe conduct to enable the Provos to make arrangements for a ceasefire. Most dramatically of all, Whitelaw confirmed that he was indeed prepared to meet the Provos face to face to discuss their policies.

Over the weekend, in an estate car provided by the Provos, Devlin rounded up a number of men who were either 'wanted', as the British Army would have said, or 'on the run', as the Provos would have put it, and brought them to Belfast under the protection of the letters of safe conduct provided and personally signed by Whitelaw. There was another meeting with Whitelaw that Monday afternoon at which more details of the ceasefire package were discussed, including the immediate introduction of 'special category' status in the prisons with separate accommodation for Republicans and Loyalists. (After a previous series of violent brawls between prisoners from both sides, their leaders concluded a pact to avoid conflict and to cooperate on obtaining political status and segregation. This was a highly significant turning point, for it was an unprecedented joint pact and the first time that Loyalists had ever sought political recognition in prison.)

Adams was one of fourteen internees released that day, the others freed to obscure the significance of his release. That evening, staying in Devlin's house at Shaw's Road, Belfast, there were Adams and Frank McGuigan, the man who had escaped from Long Kesh dressed as a priest.

Later that night the whole deal very nearly unravelled when Devlin was told that Billy McKee, the leader of the convicted IRA prisoners in Belfast prison who had been on a 30-day hunger strike for political status, had been taken to hospital. He discovered that the governor and staff at the prison were standing by with hot soup and milk for the striking prisoners, 80 Republicans and 40 Loyalists, waiting to be told officially of the details of the agreement reached with Whitelaw. With Devlin's own character-forming experience of the frustrations of internment always dominant in his mind, he was furious to discover that Whitelaw's deputy, Lord Windlesham, whom Devlin accused of 'an appalling degree of callousness', had not promptly communicated the information to the governor or the prisoners. He started what he later described as 'a telephonic bombardment' of the Northern Ireland Office, finally getting Whitelaw himself out of bed in the early hours after failing to get Windlesham to take immediate action to end the strike. Whitelaw gave the required order and medical staff moved in to feed and examine the strikers. With what amounted to political status safely achieved – the convicted prisoners could, in future, wear their own clothes and receive more privileges than conventional criminals – the ceasefire effort was fully back on course.

Some 48 hours later, in a statement issued in Dublin, the IRA announced a ceasefire with effect from midnight, Monday 26 June. Whitelaw promised to reciprocate once offensive operations by the IRA ceased. Brian Faulkner, who had once more aligned himself with the more extreme Unionists after direct rule, remarked that the ceasefire had come 379 lives, 11,682 explosions and 7,258 injuries too late.

Although the violence stopped and IRA leaders in Belfast pledged the ceasefire would be observed, all was not well within the ranks in the city. The old-guard leaders like Seamus Twomey and his friends in Andersonstown were critical from the outset and felt affronted that Dublin had gone over their heads by bringing in Gerry Adams. They felt that they were older, wiser and had more experience than Adams, who they believed had lost his rank by being interned and should not have been included. This rampant jealousy amongst the Belfast leaders was ill-concealed when Whitelaw laid on an RAF aircraft and flew the entire leadership to London for his promised face-to-face meeting on Friday 7 July. With breaches of the ceasefire already being reported in Belfast it was clear the Belfast faction was waiting to destroy the hard-won truce at the earliest suitable opportunity. While the leaders were in London, events that would bring it to an end were already gathering pace back at home.

For the previous week there had been growing tension at Horn Drive, which marked the boundary between the Protestant Suffolk area and the Catholic Lenadoon estate in the IRA's west Belfast heartland. A dispute had arisen over the re-allocation of a number of empty houses earlier abandoned by Protestants, who had either been intimidated into leaving or had fled after being pinned down in the regular crossfire between Provo snipers and their military targets. Plans to move Catholic families in were halted by the Army after the Loyalist UDA threatened to burn out the new occupants. The Provos said that if the Army did not back down they would move the families in themselves on Sunday 9 July. The issue was put on hold while Twomey went off to London, but upon his return on the Saturday he and his functionaries resumed the brinkmanship. The Army refused to budge, so the next afternoon the Provos provoked a confrontation. As soon as soldiers halted a quarry lorry piled up with the furniture of one of the Catholic families, stones began to fly and within minutes gunshots rang out, bringing the short-lived ceasefire to a violent end. That evening ten people lost their lives. But special category remained. In his 1989 memoirs, Whitelaw was later to admit the concession had been a mistake: 'In the circumstances of that moment the decision seemed a fairly innocuous concession, although I was clearly warned by my officials of its dangers vis-a-vis the prison system throughout the United Kingdom. Alas, though, it did establish a practice which caused my successors considerable trouble. I conclude today that its immediate impact was limited and it was later found to have been a misguided decision.'

Chapter Six

Not an ordinary prison

The introduction of special category status – political status in all but name – in June 1972, was matched by another piece of equally creative ambiguity: the renaming of the Long Kesh internment centre as Her Majesty's Prison, Maze. In the same way that the RAF had appropriated the Long Kesh name in 1941, this time the Northern Ireland Office commandeered the name of the small hamlet alongside the perimeter of the complex, which was much more widely known for its nearby racecourse.

The redesignation was to clear the way for the accommodation of the growing number of 'politically motivated' prisoners conventionally charged, tried and convicted by the courts. Over the preceding year or so, with their agitation for political status, they had seriously aggravated the overcrowding and the overstretched facilities in Belfast prison by refusing to conform to the statutory regime. Now these prisoners were to be held in the Maze compounds, well away from the general prison population, or 'ordinary decent criminals' as they were soon unofficially categorised by the prison staff and authorities. To qualify for special category status the new inmate had to have been sentenced to serve more than nine months and had to be 'claimed' by one of the paramilitary compound leaders. In effect, the so-called 'Officer Commanding' in each compound, elected by fellow-prisoners, dictated who would be held there. Although the internees and special category prisoners were kept apart, they enjoyed similar privileges and conditions. There was no organised work. They wore their own clothes, not prison uniform, and could receive one food parcel from home a week as well as a weekly, half-hour visit. Detainees held without trial had the same rights, but they got an extra weekly visit and could receive unlimited food parcels.

The introduction of special category status marked a crucial and remarkable turning point in penal policy in Northern Ireland. It triggered off what would be a lengthy and often turbulent process and, in the end, would lead to the authorities settling for little more than depriving convicted prisoners of their liberty. More than a quarter of a century later, after a full inspection of the Maze, Sir David Ramsbotham, Her Majesty's Inspector of Prisons, wrote, 'It was the first step towards official acknowledgement that the institution was not an ordinary prison performing an ordinary function. These special category prisoners held within the compounds were neither supervised nor controlled to what, in any other prison in the United Kingdom, would be accepted as a satisfactory standard by prison staff.' Sir David had first-hand knowledge of the Maze. As he put it, he had first stood on the ground of Long Kesh Detention Centre in September 1971, and he had spent a considerable part of his Army career (1969–93) involved in all aspects of military operations in Northern Ireland. He concluded, 'The Maze is unique within the prison system in the United Kingdom, and probably the world, in that it holds the bulk of the paramilitary prisoners, from all factions, who have been convicted, or are awaiting trial, for crimes committed in the course of a campaign of violence against the State. In the eyes of those prisoners, they remain part of the campaign, and their imprisonment has been the catalyst for a variety of incidents over the years.'

Following the introduction of internment, the rapid build up of internee numbers to almost 1000 led to consecutive extensions at Long Kesh and the opening of a smaller internment centre at Magilligan. In 1972 the release of some 700 detainees in the period following the introduction of Direct Rule made it possible not only to close the Magilligan internee accommodation but to use some newly constructed compounds at Long Kesh for ordinary prisoners and so relieve overcrowding at Belfast Prison. The increasing violence and disorder throughout Northern Ireland at this time led to substantial increases in the numbers of both detainees and prisoners, including the newly created special category prisoners. Magilligan was therefore renamed and reopened in May 1972 as Her Majesty's Prison, Magilligan, and was initially used to house low-risk prisoners.

Such was the growth in demand for prison accommodation in 1972 that speed of construction was paramount. The only way in which accommodation could be provided in time was in the form of more of the original compounds built by the Army to house the first internees. At the Maze, accommodation was rapidly increased from five compounds at the beginning of 1972 to 22 at the end of 1974 when the number of inmates had reached about 1800. The compounds, or 'cages', as the occupants insisted on calling them, were strung out side by side along the concreted lines of the old wartime runways. As the number of compounds expanded so too did the length of the high concrete-grey perimeter wall of the prison, the number of sentry towers and the intensity of the yellow glow from the searchlights and the extensive security floodlighting which at night threw a reflection into the clouds above and could be seen for miles. On clear nights the Maze glow, as commercial airline pilots came to describe it, was actually visible from as far away as the airspace over the Scottish coast and the Isle of Man. During often clandestine night operations, military helicopter pilots all over Northern Ireland would use it as a failsafe navigational beacon, climbing vertically from the ground until they could see it and confirm their instrument checks.

Although it was never said in public, the government was by this time actively seeking a way out of the internment maze, which was a massive political embarrassment for them because it required a formal derogation from international agreed human rights standards and conventions. But the appalling acts of indiscriminate terrorism and loss of life (472 casualties in 1972) and the urgent need to thwart violence and protect the community as much as possible dictated that, far from releasing all those in this unsatisfactory form of custody, the swoops and detentions had to continue. Early in 1973 there were two notable milestones. On 1 January, nineteen-year-old Elizabeth McKee became the first woman to be interned and was sent to Armagh jail where she was joined a month later by a seventeen-year-old girl. On 5 February the first two Loyalist internees were imprisoned, causing the United Loyalist Council to call a one-day general strike. In the ensuing disturbances a Catholic Church was ransacked, there were widespread riots, 35 malicious fires and eight explosions, and five people, including a firefighter, lost their lives. It was yet another chilling reminder for the prison authorities and their political masters of how events in the prison could all too easily be manipulated to influence what went on outside in the community. With a circle of family and friends directly interested in the well-being of each inmate, the prisoners' constituency, especially when Republicans and Loyalists combined, was a powerful one.

In a bid to underpin the internment process with at least a quasi-judicial credibility a panel of three Commissioners was established to consider the case of every prisoner and enable him or her to challenge the reasons given for detention or make representations for release. But the farcical way these quasi-judicial tribunals were conducted stripped them of any credibility and fuelled the widespread sense of injustice stimulated by internment. The Commissioners were minor legal figures brought in from Britain, as were the Crown Prosecutors. All worked and lived within the secure confines of Long Kesh while they were in session. They conducted their hearings in the carpeted room of a hut hung with drapes and a British coat of arms to cover the bare walls. The Commissioner sat on a high-backed, upholstered chair behind a desk. In front of him there was a clerk and a stenographer. On his right there was another desk for the Crown Prosecutor. The internee, guarded by a prison officer, sat on a chair in the centre of the room. The 'witnesses' were RUC Special Branch officers, who entered through a separate door and gave evidence from behind a curtain so that they could not be seen or identified. The case they made would be based on hearsay or what informers had told them, and would be heavily censored in case anything betrayed the identity of the informer. The entire process was such a charade that the inmates and legal profession largely boycotted it.

At the same time another, higher-powered Commission, chaired by Lord Diplock, was tasked to lay the longer-term foundations for a more defensible form of justice, in which the executive act of detention on suspicion alone could eventually be replaced by a conviction obtained in the courts after a fair trial in which evidence was the test of guilt. Diplock reported in December 1972 and recommended that non-jury trials should be introduced for a wide range of terrorist offences with just a single judge on the bench to decide guilt or innocence. There had already been instances of explosions outside court houses, threats to jurors and the murders of witnesses, which had often forced the authorities to intern, rather than charge, some suspected offenders. The commission also held it should be easier to admit self-incriminating confessions in court to help secure convictions. These proposals were endorsed by the Government, incorporated into new legislation (the Emergency Provisions Act) which replaced the Special Powers Act, and brought into operation in 1973. The courts became known as Diplock courts.

In a highly significant addition to the Act, on 12 April while it was in the final stages of its passage through Parliament, the death penalty for murder was abolished. Six days earlier, Whitelaw had ordered a life sentence instead of execution for Albert Browne, 29, a member of the Loyalist UDA. On 17 October 1972, one of the occupants of a stolen car stopped by police on the M2 motorway near Belfast opened fire, wounding RUC Constable Andrew Harron, who died four days later. Browne was subsequently convicted and sentenced to the mandatory death penalty for the murder of a police officer on duty. An appeal was turned down on 3 April and an execution date of 25 April was set, but well in advance, on 6 April, Whitelaw moved to silence the growing clamour both for and against the death penalty by intervening with a reprieve. Browne was the first person to be sentenced to death in Northern Ireland since 1961 and indeed the last. At Belfast prison, the double-size condemned cell and gallows on the ground floor of C Wing were afterwards kept in place for a number of years. In due course, the condemned cell became an office, and in the execution cell next door, where seventeen murderers had met their own deaths, the gallows trapdoor was tiled over and the space converted into a toilet and washroom.

As ever in Republican prison history, there was unremitting confrontation between prisoners and staff and unrelenting efforts to escape, especially from the Maze. During the period from 1972 to 1974 a persistent series of attempts and escapes underlined the increasingly ruthless nature of those coming into custody and the uncompromising way in which they continued to promote their cause from captivity. On 20 April 1972 four IRA prisoners, sentenced to terms of eight to ten years for causing an explosion, overpowered an armed policeman and three prison officers inside Armagh jail on their return from an appearance at court. At one point, during the four-hour siege that ensued, the policeman, held at the point of his own gun, was forced to falsely shout from a window at news cameras that one of the prison officers had been killed because the Governor, Stanley Hilditch, would not meet their demand for a van to drive ten prisoners to the Irish border, some dozen miles away. The incident was brought to an end when troops and police fired CS gas and freed the hostages. When the prisoners again appeared in court, one of them, aged nineteen, said that they were an IRA active service unit within the prison and felt morally justified in using force in order to carry out political demands on behalf of themselves and their people. 'The forces of this Fascist Orange State and British Imperialism in the north have used violence for the last fifty years against our people.' All four were given consecutive sentences of three to five years for their part in the hostage-taking.

Suspicious soldiers charged with guarding the area immediately around Belfast prison thwarted a potentially major escape in December 1972. The plot was unusual in that the tunnellers were not prisoners but helpers outside digging into the prison. They had taken over a house in Landscape Terrace, which runs along the perimeter wall, sunk a shaft from a cupboard underneath the stairs and excavated a 40-yard stretch, which was 2.5 feet square and shored up with wood. There were two rooms full of the earth that had been taken out. In January 1973, an IRA prisoner on remand awaiting trial walked free from Belfast Prison by impersonating another inmate, who was being released on bail. He was the sixteenth escapee since 1969. Security procedures were then tightened up and a similar effort was foiled a few weeks later. This time an alert warder rubbed tattoos on the prisoners arm and found they were false. The prisoners were not deterred. Around the same time, three remand prisoners cut through the bars of their cell window with hacksaw blades and shinned down a rope into the yard below. However, they were quickly spotted by warders on patrol and, after a scuffle, they climbed back into the cell. On 22 February 1973, James Bryson, one of the *Maidstone* escapers who had earlier been recaptured in Belfast, got away again while he was being taken through the underground tunnel from Belfast prison to the courthouse opposite. (Bryson was fatally wounded the following September during a gun battle with troops in the city.) During an intensive search of the prison over the next few days, a tunnel was uncovered after troops found bags of soil and an imitation handgun. The three-foot shaft had been sunk from under the linoleum in a cell in a wing occupied by Republican remand prisoners. In August, a group of prisoners broke away from a recreation group and tried to get over the prison wall with a grappling hook and a rope made from strips of blanket.

Later in the month, again during a recreation period, a 25-strong group of Loyalist prisoners tried to form a human pyramid against the prison wall to enable the top two or three to clamber over. Both attempts were doomed from the start. Ever since the 'Crumlin Kangaroos' incident the fortifications along the wall had been strengthened, and electronic beams were instantly activated, alerting the staff. The second incident triggered off serious trouble in the prison which lasted several hours. Prisoners ripped off cell doors and had to be forced back by troops who fired rubber bullets to bring one man from the roof of the cell block. A prisoner and two warders were injured. Magilligan also experienced escape attempts and, in one of the more unusual efforts, two short-term prisoners got away. The men, serving sentences for petty crimes (motoring offences and theft) seized a mini-van while they were outside the prison with a work party and drove off at high speed. The van was discovered a few miles away where the men were either picked up or stole a boat and made their getaway by sea.

The first two women interned, who had been lodged in Armagh prison, also figured in an escape attempt. In the early hours of 4 March 1973 Elizabeth McKee and Teresa Holland, together with three other young women serving sentences for arms and explosives offences, cut through the ventilation flaps of their cells and the window bars with smuggled saw blades before slithering to the ground on makeshift ropes made from plaited wool. Other prisoners played their radios loudly and made noise while preparations for the breakout were under way. During the routine half-hourly cell check, a prison officer spotted the damaged windows and discovered dummies had been left in the prisoners' beds. The alarm was raised and staff discovered the five women at the Army look-out post on the prison wall. Some were inside the post and Holland was entangled in the coils of barbed wire surrounding it. She had to be cut free by an Army officer. When the five later appeared in court charged with attempting to escape they came to attention in response to a military-style command by McKee. She told Judge Rory Conaghan, who was murdered by the IRA less than twelve months later, 'As prisoners of war we have a duty to ourselves and our country to make a bid for freedom. As Irish women we refuse to recognise this illegal assembly.' Later she gave the 'at ease' command and the five women sat down.

There was an equally regular occurrence of escape-related activity at the Maze. In December 1972 the authorities claimed to have foiled an escape attempt from the prison when parts of a prison officer's uniform and other unauthorised articles were uncovered during one of the constant searches by the Army. Staff at the Maze grew increasingly alert to the impersonation route to freedom. They detected two attempts on consecutive days of the same month, bringing their successes to nine, but there were other embarrassing failures. On Sunday 9 September 1973 another priest-impersonator, John Francis Greene, escaped from the Maze dressed in clerical clothing. Later his brother, a genuine priest who had been visiting the prison, was found in his underwear, tied up in one of the compounds. (Greene was later found murdered at a farmhouse across the border in Co Monaghan.) In September, six Republicans overpowered two doctors and six warders in the prison hospital after producing what appeared to be handguns. They then tied up their captives and changed into the warder's uniforms but they were recaptured before reaching the main gate of the prison after the alarm was raised. In a follow-up security sweep, two tunnels, on which digging had started, were discovered and an imitation handgun like those used in the escape was seized. The third successful escape from the Maze took place on 8 December 1973 when Brendan Hughes, 25, reputed to be one of the key IRA leaders, got out concealed in a mattress dumped in a refuse lorry. Forty-eight hours later, James Burns, 25, swapped clothes with a visitor and walked to freedom. On Christmas Eve, Gerry Adams was one of three prisoners who were apprehended by warders while trying to cut their way through the perimeter fencing.

There was a rare insight into the way impostor escapes were set up in March 1973. The Northern Ireland Winter Assizes heard how a young man had been approached the night before visiting a friend at the Maze. When he got to the prison, he was wearing clothes identical to the prisoner and changed places. At the end of the visit, the prisoner headed for the exit while the real visitor was being escorted back to the compound. The ruse was quickly exposed by routine checks and the prisoner was apprehended again while sitting on a bus waiting to leave the visits area. He was given a two-year sentence and an accomplice one year, and the visitor, a juvenile whom the court accepted had been subjected to pressure, was given a conditional discharge.

The same year a prison officer working in the Maze ended up behind bars himself after being given a five-year sentence when he admitted passing a document with intent to facilitate the escape of a prisoner. The officer was on duty with two others at Compound 12 on 16 January 1973 when he was approached by a prisoner he knew through a former acquaintance with his sister. The officer agreed to take a letter to her and add a sketch map of parts of the prison and the compounds. He also accepted a second letter from another prisoner. When he was going off duty he was challenged and the letters were discovered. He later said that he had foolishly agreed to take the letters only because he feared for his life, both inside and outside the prison. The Judge said he had committed the most serious offence a member of the Prison Service could commit. 'The whole working of the system of imprisonment in any country depends absolutely on the trust placed in them and this was broken in a most despicable way.' The case highlighted the general inexperience and lack of training of the large number of officers who had been rapidly recruited to help cope with the vast surge in prisoner numbers after 1969.

Up to that point, the 292-strong prison service staff had largely consisted of mature officers, many of them with a military service background, who had considerable experience in maintaining discipline in an institutional environment, a good background for handling the variety of flawed and often difficult people encountered in any prison. The urgent need for extra help forced the authorities to introduce an almost permanent recruiting drive for a new grade of temporary officer, who was initially paid £22.54 a week with either rent-free housing or a £5 weekly allowance. Single men received half that allowance or rent-free quarters. Established officers, who were eligible for promotion, earned a basic £30.62 weekly. Specialist officers, with trade skills such as bricklaying, plumbing, painting or electrical work or who were qualified as nurses, caterers or physical training instructors could earn another £3.10. Recruitment advertisements at the time stated that people who wore spectacles or contact lenses for close work were not ruled out. A constant element in the recruiting campaign during these years was the regular quarter and half-page advertisements in the magazine *Soldier*, which enjoyed a wide circulation and readership throughout the British

Army, offering ex-servicemen a good salary and a bright future in the Northern Ireland Prison Service.

They would have felt quite at home, for the Prison Service was run on authoritative, quasi-military lines with a lot of rigid formality and 'Yes Sir,' 'No Sir.' The bottom of the hierarchical ladder was the BGO (Basic Grade Officer, the term Warder having already been officially phased out in 1940), who could rise on promotion to Senior Officer, Principal Officer and Chief Officer, the most senior uniformed post. (This level was abolished in 1989.) After that came the Governors, who did not wear uniform and could work up from a lowly Governor Five level to Governor One, the qualification to take control of a top security prison like the Maze or run one of the administrative or policy divisions at the Prisons Branch of the Northern Ireland Office, which was based at Dundonald House, close to the Parliament Buildings in the Stormont estate in east Belfast.

In the early days of the rapid expansion there was little opportunity for formal training but in May 1973 a two-week training course was introduced for recruits. In March 1975, a new Prison Officers' Training School was opened at Millisle and all recruits started with a two-week period of familiarisation at Belfast prison followed by a four-week training course at the School. Additional courses of one week's duration were also provided at the School for in-service officers. Although they were only scheduled to work a five-day, 40-hour week, in practice many officers worked twice that and earned very considerable sums of money. Indeed it was not uncommon to find men working seven consecutive days without a break, and officers serving at the time now recall that without such intensive overtime working the entire prison service could well have broken down.

> 'You didn't have any choice,' [one said.] 'I was often working a seven-day week and it was really like you were the one who was serving time. I hardly ever got an opportunity to spend proper time with my wife and kids and it destroyed my social life. But there was no way of getting out of working the long hours, which were often pretty boring. They would not accept any excuses. One weekend there was trouble in one of the prisons and when that happened you were expected to stay on duty on standby. Now one of the officers, who had promised to take his wife out for a special occasion, refused. The following day the Governor sent for him and told him he would have to put in his resignation. You soon learnt that if you were in the Prison Service you did as you were told. If not you had to leave.'

An official report reviewing the administration of the Prison Service during this period, which was published in 1976, described the conditions faced by prison officers:

'At times during the period under review discipline and control have been difficult to enforce particularly in the compound prisons of Maze and Magilligan. There are several reasons for this. Firstly, the lack of cellular accommodation has limited the ability of the Prison Service to isolate troublemakers or segregate prisoners into manageable groups. Secondly, the compound design allows free association of large numbers of men within each compound. Thirdly, segregation into factions has enabled para-military groups to preserve their organisational structure and influence within prisons. Fourthly, large numbers of prisoners convicted of violence are still committed jointly to a cause which they believe justifies the use of violence. A fifth factor was the combination of a high turnover of seconded staff and the inexperience of the large number of newly-recruited prison officers which militated against a settled and stable environment in which worthwhile relationships could be formed between prisoners and staff.'

Many prison officers did not entirely consent to the prison regime they were employed to implement. One dissatisfied officer, who left the service in the early 1970s, said at the time:

'If they continue to get their demands met then the prisoners will soon be running the prisons. Either you have a prison or you don't. There should be no half measures. When the ordinary criminal gets caught he accepts the fact that he is going to be deprived of his freedom as a form of punishment. Special category prisoners believe they have the right to engage in violence and yet not be responsible for their actions. [. . .]

'The prisons in Northern Ireland are housing people who have shot people, who have been responsible for bombing buildings causing death, as well as millions of pounds worth of damage to this country. Some of these people would shoot you as quick as they would look at you simply because you happen to belong to a particular religious sect. Yet how do we treat them? They are given food parcels from outside, their own clothes, clean shirts, their day is their own. Then you have some poor critter who is inside for a bit of thieving. He has to go to the workshop, has to wear prison clothes, has few rights as far as being a prisoner goes. No one gives a damn about his conditions. What has he to do then? Go out and kill someone and say he did it for his country or cause, so that he is given the better facilities? Is that justice?

In the prisons, Republican and Loyalist prisoners were rigidly segregated by internal faction. There was at least one compound each for the Provisional IRA, Official IRA and the Irish Republican Socialist Party (later to spawn the Irish National Liberation Army). On the Loyalist side the Ulster Defence Association (including the Ulster Freedom Fighters) and the Ulster Volunteer Force (who accepted the Red Hand Commandos) also had at least one compound. The outside enmities that had so inflamed the communal disorder were imported into the prison undiluted, and the two sides very rarely mixed or met except to gang up against the prison authorities to push jointly for their latest demands. Contact within the prison, both between the two sides and from compound to compound, was maintained in different ways. Tennis balls cut in half to hold a written message were hurled from one point to another. Sometimes Loyalists would climb on the hut roofs and use semaphore flags for signalling around the prison. Contacts between prisoners also took place at the visits area, where greetings and messages could be exchanged. Over the years, ever more sophisticated means were developed to carry secret communications, known as 'comms', in and out of the prison undetected by the searches carried out by prison staff. One of the most durable methods was for a note, written in small handwriting on a sheet of toilet paper, to be concealed in a prisoner's anus before going to a visit. After being searched, the note, which was also wrapped in kitchen clingfilm, was retrieved and passed to the visitor, sometimes mouth to mouth during a kiss. Again it would be intimately concealed by the visitor to avoid searches on leaving the prison.

There was also ample opportunity for contact between the prisoners because of the pseudo-military structure they had adopted. By now the Provisional IRA Maze prisoners had styled themselves the Fourth Battalion of the Belfast Brigade of the Provisional IRA. The other 'battalions' covered different areas of the city. Every compound was ruled by an elected 'Officer Commanding' (OC) who was supported by a 'staff' consisting of a leader in every hut, a 'Quartermaster', 'Adjutant' and other 'officers' responsible for welfare, education and administration. There was also an OC for the entire prison, elected by the compound commanders, and a subsidiary 'Battalion Staff' answerable to him for a range of functions: education, finance, welfare, training, Quartermaster's responsibilities and public relations.

The Loyalist groups had similar command arrangements and designations with the UVF differing in that it had a 'Commanding Officer', an 'Adjutant', a 'Regimental Sergeant Major', 'Sergeant Majors' and 'Hut Sergeants', and maintained a rigid military-style hierarchy which was appointed rather then elected. The UDA prisoners elected their representatives.

The commanding officer in each compound was the pivotal figure who enforced the policy of his own terrorist organisation and liaised with the prison authorities. His authority was absolute within the compound. He decided if a prisoner could be lodged there, and the men needed his permission to go for visits, have interviews with the governor or even receive parcels from their families. These leaders ensured that discipline was enforced when necessary. One man had his nipples badly burnt with a cigarette lighter, another had tram-lines burnt on his back with the bars of an electric fire and another received severe body and head bruising when he was beaten with a wet, knotted towel. One Loyalist, nineteen-year-old George Hyde from Portadown, was one of nine prisoners locked up in Compound Nine on Christmas night, 1973. At 3 am the next morning, six hours later, his body was found with severe head injuries after warders were called. It was later put about on the Loyalist grapevine that the dead man had been an informer who had betrayed an escape plan. Every new arrival to the prison, especially if on remand to await trial, was interrogated to ensure he had not talked to the security forces and, if so, to assess what damage limitation was necessary for the terrorist organisation. The Compound Intelligence Officers' who carried out this task were also anxious to learn of any new techniques or tactics being employed against their activists so that others arrested in the future could be alerted and trained to deal with them.

The nature of the unique and highly unorthodox special category regime, especially at the Maze, was characterised by constant confrontation, where the staff merely contained the prisoners, routinely with the help of military muscle. In a memoir, a UVF prisoner described life for prison officers as 'a monotonous series of routine and mundane tasks. Locking and unlocking gates and doors, taking a morning and evening count of the inmate population and generally carrying out the minor duties of delivering mail or escorting prisoners from point to point in the giant complex of compounds and roadways inside the camp perimeter. For them life is a thankless task . . .'

An IRA prisoner's scornful and more colourful view of the 'screws' and their daily role is contained in an contemporary IRA propaganda pamphlet, entitled 'Prison Struggle – the story of continuing resistance behind the wire'. The pseudo-military argot and culture they cultivated peppers the language they use.

'First of all the Screws come into the Cage at 7.30 a.m. There is usually no contact here between us and them as most of us are fast asleep. This is the only time the Screws are permitted into the huts apart from searches when we are locked in the canteen. Any other time they conduct their business through the Cage Staff. Next would come the search. The Screws wait outside the Cage until the O.C. (Officer Commanding) is informed that they wish to make a search. By the time we get up, get washed, make a cup of tea and filter down to the canteen it is about 9.30 a.m. The P.O. (Principle Officer) [*sic*] then commences the search on word from the Cage Adjutant that all our men our out of the huts. The search usually lasts from half an hour to one and a half hours. When it is over the P.O. informs the Adjutant who tells us to return to the huts. There is a body-search before we go into the huts again. The Adjutant watches over this procedure to make sure that there is no unnecessary friction or aggro. The body-search is usually a quick frisk. The search party then leave the Cage and we check our belongings to see if anything is broken or missing.

'By this time the milk and bread ration will have arrived and the Q.M. (Quartermaster) distributes it to each hut. If the bread ration is short or if the Q.M. thinks it might not last the day, he informs the Screws on duty to send for more before tea-time. At around 10 a.m. the Cage Adjutant goes out to negotiate with the Assistant Governor on some issue which has arisen. This sometimes ends up in a row or each trying to get the better of the other and then the continual conning exercise is over for another day. These meetings of our Cage staff and the Prison Governors take place usually when we need something replaced in the Cage – radio, sheets or blankets – or when something more serious arises, like an application for compassionate parole for a family bereavement. As you can well imagine, the Governors don't get the same respect here as they would in an English Jail, but at the same time they get the respect they deserve.

'Shortly after 10.00 a.m. the Q.M. will give the Screws a list of cleaning stores needed for the week. Usually what is supplied is not sufficient so the Screw on duty will shuttle back and forth until the list is supplied and the Q.M. is satisfied he has enough to last the week. Next we have a laundry change (sheets and towels once a fortnight). Each hut O.C. collects and leaves the dirty laundry from his hut at the gates of the Cage until they are exchanged for the "clean" ones. Out of 76 pairs of "clean" sheets on one occasion, 34 had to be returned as unacceptable. When the 34 were exchanged 11 of these had to be returned as they were in some cases dirtier than the ones we had left out. Again it is the screws who get the job of running to and fro until the Staff are satisfied with the exchanges.

'By about this time the dinner will have arrived. Anyone with a weak stomach is advised not to read on! It is said on TV and in the papers that the meals in here are on the same par as would be served in the Europa Hotel. Maybe that is why it has been bombed so many times. The food is delivered in aluminium containers, pulled into the Cage on a wooden cart. An indication of the quality of the food can be taken from the fact that about 20% of the men eat it. What is not eaten must be thrown out. If it was sent back to the cook-house more than likely it would be "doctored-up" and served to us the next day. It wouldn't be the first time that it has happened.

'At around 2.00 p.m. the dry-food stores arrive (tea, sugar, margarine, salt etc). These stores are for 76 men, to last a week. The Screws on the stores can make a profit if they can manage to give each Cage less than their entitlement. They seem to manage this very, very well. The week's ration usually runs out after about 3 days. This develops into a row between the Screws and the Q.M.; it is the Screws on Cage duty who must take all the stick as the Store Screws do not come in direct contact with us therefore there is no come-back on them.

'The afternoon is usually quiet; the tea arrives at about 4.30p.m. This consists of soggy underdone chips with burnt bacon. Makes your mouth water, doesn't it? The screws send up any medicine or tablets for those men on the Cage sick list. The Company Staff supervise the distribution of the tablets. The next great event is lock-up. This entails the men parading in front of the huts, they are "fell out" and are counted by the Screws on their way into the huts.' [Night-time lock-up initially lasted from 9 pm to 8 am but prisoner pressure eventually got it revised to start at 10 pm and end at 7.30 am.]

The prisoner leaders constantly sought to demean, undermine and demoralise the uniformed grades. They insisted on negotiating any of their demands with Governor grades, contemptuously regarding the officers as 'Imperialist slaves. There is a constant struggle between us and the Camp Administration over basic necessities. The Screw is the fall-guy the stooge in the middle. He must put up with the balling-off from both sides, it is our only outlet for getting things done. We do not want to live in unhealthy huts or sleep in dirty bed-linen. He must see that we are satisfied.'

The prisoner said that 'anyone with experience as a message-boy or cinema commissionaire will find himself at home' as a prison officer. He summed their role up like this: 'COMPOUND DUTY – You stand outside the Cage in a sentry box and do the running and see to the prisoners complaints. LOOK-OUT DUTY – You stand in a watch-tower all day long on your own and watch the wee men walking around the cage. VISIT-DUTY – You take the prisoners to their visit, stand outside the visit cubicle and return the prisoners when the visit is over. You also take part in search parties to search the Cages.'

The prisoners also waged constant psychological warfare against the officers, alternatively threatening or being friendly to them. 'The screw must always be on his toes so that he does not compromise his position as guard and be seen to come under the influence of prisoners; authority must be maintained,' wrote the IRA prisoner. Officers who served in the prison at the time point out that even the apparently friendly conversations had sinister undertones. 'They were always trying to get personal information to use against you or one of your colleagues. The more inexperienced or talkative officers would be pumped about getting a new car or moving house or going on holiday or even just the locality they lived. In due course this information would be dropped back at them by somebody else, with a threatening tone. In some cases the information had clearly been passed outside the prison for more details to be obtained. It was very unnerving and you soon learned to keep quiet about yourself or where you came from although that was difficult for local people from Northern Ireland where everybody knows everybody else,' said one. Another officer was quite fatalistic about the constant threats. 'They were part of the job and you just learned to put up with them.'

This extraordinary prison regime provided the inmates with a great deal of independence within the compounds which was exploited to the full and not only to plan escapes. The Maze prison effectively became an academy of terrorism with captive, but fully committed, students subjected to military-style discipline. Just as conventional military units would be regulated by a series of directives, standing orders and routine taskings, so too were the prisoners by their respective organisations. Indeed their days were tightly regulated from reveille – 9 am on weekdays and 10 am on Sundays for the Provisionals, and 9 am daily for the Loyalists – to lights out, normally 30 minutes after midnight for the Provos and midnight for the Loyalists. Drowsy Provos were given fifteen minutes' leeway to get up in the morning before being put on charge, while the Loyalists were specifically obliged to wash and shave daily. Both sides laid down exhaustive rules and regulations about maintaining the tidiness and cleanliness of their accommodation and there were rotas and responsibilities for everything from cleaning the toilets to distributing post and library books. The Compound OC's maintained a rigid grip on their underlings who were not allowed to communicate directly with prison staff about welfare matters, compassionate leave, visits or any other matter. UVF inmates were required to have black cord trousers, jacket, polo-neck, boots and woollen cap for formal parades, while the Provos designated some of their huts as 'gaeltacht' areas, where Irish only was spoken and radio and television in English banned. In time these areas became known as 'jailtachts' and the unique Irish dialect that developed was similarly described as Maze 'jailic'.

Martin Snoddon, writing in the *Journal of Prisoners on Prisons* in 1996, provides a Loyalist perspective:

'The level of cleanliness and maintenance varied between the factions depending on the policy adopted by them. Loyalists, on one hand, chose to make their conditions as habitable as possible, and in the process had to haggle with the prison administrators in order to obtain the basic resources of paint (allocated once per week and saved until enough was available to cover the job in hand), disinfectant, soap, and wire wool (used to remove unwanted marks on tiled floors and for the scrubbing of ovens and cookers, brushes, mops and even the very rubbish bins). All were a source of dispute at one time or another. Daily work parties were organised and cleaning and maintenance duties were strictly carried out. Each man was responsible for the cleanliness in his own cubicle, a 6.5-foot high, sectioned-off area from the middle of the Nissan hut measuring 9.7 foot in floor space but restricted in volume by the curve of the hut. All areas were inspected by an officer during the work detail and extra duties often resulted for below standard conditions. On the other hand, Republican prisoners had a policy of not alleviating the conditions in which they found themselves incarcerated by their sworn enemies the British. They did, however, carry out basic cleaning of facilities in their cages, and each man kept himself clean. This led to great dismay amongst the prison officers and prison administrators, who often pointed an accusing finger (while still denying the Loyalists their sought-after cleaning resources!), when in embarrassment, they tried to explain to some outside visitor the contrast between Loyalist and Republican conditions.

'Discipline was an ever-present factor in the daily life of the prisoner, with their officers exercising complete control over their lives, indoctrinating them with their meaning for life, while on occasion training them for death. In the 1970s, military parades were fashionable, some factions held a weekly muster parade with their volunteers turning out in uniform; however, all factions held annual parades. In the Loyalist cages, these took place in July and on

Remembrance Day, while the Republicans commemorated the Easter Rising in 1916. Patriots of both traditions, from all over the six countries, (Benny from Londonderry, tragically killed while making a desperate bid for freedom; Ironjaw from Antrim; the Horse from Fermanagh; Alarm Clock from Tyrone; Ralph from Armagh; Zeb from Down), and some even from Scotland (Jock and Big Bill), England (English Bob), and Southern Ireland (Tipperary Tim), gathered for their traditional parades. Flags and uniforms were prohibited by the prison officials who searched all year round for them. Union and Ulster flags, Starry Ploughs, and Tricolours were confiscated and often found their way to the prison's black museum of memorabilia. But come a parade day, men in uniform with flags blowing in the breeze turned out in full view and in defiance of the prison authorities, taking solace and pride in their comradeship as an oration was read by some charismatic authoritarian leader of either a green or orange hue.'

In 1979, for instance, Mr J M Mahood, Commanding Officer, Ulster Volunteer Force political prisoners, Long Kesh Camp, delivered the following speech to the Officers assembled on parade:

'Once again we the imprisoned patriots of Ulster parade in full military uniform with colours flying, as we celebrate the 289th anniversary of the Williamite crossing of the Boyne Water. Throughout the length and breadth of our beloved province, thousands of our fellow officers, men and women will be marching in demonstration of their continued loyalty to the historical principles of our protestant loyalist heritage and it is only but right that we, who have been imprisoned for these very principles, should demonstrate in a similar fashion. We do not have the music that blasts forth from the instruments of mass bands or that lisps gently from the softly flopping silken banners that wafts sweetly in the zephyr breezes. We do not march to the regimented cheers of the Belfast or provincial citizenry that line the streets and lanes of Ulster to encourage our be-sashed brethren on their way to the field. Outside of what we see on television the only semblance of normality for us will be the cane grapple of the Lambegs, returning to the Lodge rooms at the Maze and Broomhedge [*two Orange Halls within earshot of the prison*], but in spite of these deprivations we can still march proudly and honourable as volunteers of Ulster. We need no music but the music of marching feet. We need no beat but the beat of loyal hearts. We need no cheer but the cheering sight of the England flag that still floats defiantly over Ulster. In the midst of our incarceration, from the heart of this maximum security encampment, we are proud to demonstrate again our loyalty to the cause of Ulster and to proclaim again our eternal opposition to the endeavours of the Provisional IRA and similar bodies that would seek to undermine and destroy our distinctive Protestant heritage and British way of life.'

During each afternoon, but especially in the evening between lock-up and lights-out, when the prison officers and soldiers were least likely to come in, the Maze Republican and Loyalist compounds became the lecture theatres and tutorial centres of the university of terrorism. The training and instruction that took place was far from theoretical. Wood and other material, permitted into the prison for handicraft work, was often fashioned into realistic, life-size replica firearms which could be used as lecture aids as well as in escape attempts. Over the years an accumulation of such weapons, general purpose machine guns, Sterling sub-machine guns, FN, Armalite and AK47 Kalashnikov rifles, as well as a range of handguns, were unearthed in hut searches. 'If one of them had been pointed at you, it would have been impossible to tell if it was the real thing or not,' recalls a prison officer who regularly took part in the searches. Detailed notes listing the specifications, weight, calibre, rate of fire, type of fire, feed, muzzle velocity and range of each weapons had also been compiled. There were detailed working instructions and 'exploded' drawings listing the components and parts of the weapons and how they fitted together, along with firing instructions.

Other terrorist training material discovered contained drawings and instructions about the manufacture and siting of improvised explosive devices such as pressure plates and micro-switches for booby-traps. Actual incidents over the years, in which people were killed, maimed and injured, underline the deadly tactics that were developed and perfected by terrorists while in prisons. Anti-personnel mines, often concealed in derelict buildings, were a regular hazard for the security forces. Bombs concealed in lamp posts were used to ambush police and army patrols on the streets. Spent rounds wired to concealed explosive devices were planted to kill or maim bomb disposal officers called to deal with them. The positioning of landmines, containing up to three thousands pounds of explosive, by roadsides and in culverts, and the location of effective firing points from which to attack security force vehicles were also extensively covered in training material. More basic training in fieldcraft, the care and maintenance of weapons and first aid is also outlined. Prisoners had access to typewriters and many of the extensive haul of documents are closely typed on foolscap paper, indicating that at least some of them were written in the prison. Other documents, originating from both sides, cover a range of other topics: position papers on IRA policy and intelligence gathering and an analysis of the war situation in Northern Ireland as seen by UVF Prisoners of War.

An instruction book entitled 'A handbook of Republican public relations and propaganda' provides a telling insight into their view of an aspect of the conflict they constantly exploited to full effect.

'We should not fear the use of propaganda for contrary to the widely held view it need not be a distortion of the truth. The word itself derives from Latin and means to extend, to spread an idea. The raw material of propaganda is information. To be effective, it must arouse interest and maintain that interest. Tried and trusted facts and figures on their own cannot do this, so they are dressed up and made attractive or startling and the end result is what we call propaganda. The Republican movement over the years has gained a reputation for being truthful in its propaganda and it is essential that this reputation be guarded by all members and Public Relations officers in particular, for it hinges on our credibility. Extravagant claims and cliches should be avoided in all our propaganda material and activities.'

Another document, 'Police and Army procedure security – Lecture No 1', shows how the terrorists were constantly reviewing the tactics being used against them and seeking ways to beat or circumvent them.

'Arrest and interrogation – interrogation techniques, physical abuse, solitary confinement, water-tight case, accomplices, memory depriv- ation, degradation, deal, the trickery and deception summary. This is a lecture on Police and Army procedure. It explains the methods they use and why they use them. The information it contains and the methods it purposes [*sic*] to combat these techniques is based on very careful analysis of the experiences of over 250 people, most of them members of this movement who have been questioned about alleged offences by the RUC or screened by the British Army. The people whose experiences have helped make up this lecture are in many ways different, they range from experienced men and women, young boys and girls, interrogated for the first time, members of the Cumann na mBan [the women's branch of the IRA], members of the IRA, civilians and members of the Provisionals. The one thing they all have in common is that they have all been interrogated by the RUC or the Brits and they have all contributed to give us a clear picture of how the interrogation methods work and interrogation methods can then be beaten.'

Within the Republican and Loyalist compounds, there was also a considerable amount of political debate. Prisoners on both sides were convinced that out of an ultimate victory and political settlement would come an amnesty and that they would be hailed as the returning heroes. This is what kept them going and was the key factor in their blind belief in the violent campaigns they had supported. They were so convinced of the rightness and justice of their cause, especially the Provisional IRA prisoners, that it was easy for them to turn a blind eye and a deaf ear to the torrents of condemnation and pleas for peace that poured out daily and reached rip-tide pace in the aftermath of the succession of multiple murders and atrocities that punctuated these years of violence. In his pamphlet 'Behind the Wire', Phil McCullough observes:

> 'Political prisons, camps and places of detention during an upheaval are sometimes regarded as Universities of Revolutionary thought. I would not exactly call Long Kesh a University, but it most certainly is a school of political thought and a school of human experience. Political activities shared between two groups Sinn Fein (Provos) and a group known as the Political Debating Group which is of a pretty leftish type but this activity is not always consistent and fluctuates up and down, dies and revives, but political consciousness has been raised if only slightly. Debate and discussions around individuals bed space areas are very common during evening time and the Ulster situation has been solved many times over by our budding politicians. I find this informal approach to political discussion more rewarding than, the organised debates.'

Against this background it is not surprising that Tam Dalyell, the outspoken Labour MP, should tell the House of Commons, in June 1974, that Long Kesh and Armagh were breeding grounds for a loathing of English politicians among the next generation. 'Here is where the terrorists of the 1980s are being trained.'

Throughout the first half of the 1970s the sectarian violence in Northern Ireland soared and peaked, not least on account of the intellectual and practical contribution made by the prisoners. After direct rule in 1972, and despite the collapse of the short-lived IRA ceasefire that year, intensive efforts to create a political solution were continued by an ever-patient Whitelaw, who succeeded in drawing the Unionists,

Nationalists and Irish government into round table talks and a ground-breaking accord at Sunningdale in December 1973. He was recalled to London immediately afterwards to help the prime minister, Edward Heath, break a mid-winter industrial confrontation with the powerful miners. The Conservative government took the issue to the country in February 1974 and lost. A new Labour administration, headed by Harold Wilson, then came into office and Merlyn Rees, was appointed Northern Ireland Secretary.

Rees, a Welshman, former teacher and university lecturer who had represented south Leeds as a Labour MP since 1963, had prepared for his time in Northern Ireland by reading *Gladstone and the Irish Nation*, a scholarly study of a period in the island's history as turbulent as the one he now faced. Within a few months of arriving in Belfast, in the face of a crippling general strike mounted by the Loyalists, Whitelaw's hard-won political initiative foundered and the historic power-sharing Executive, in which Unionists and Nationalists worked together in government for the first time, collapsed. The concept of an Irish dimension, expressed through a Council of Ireland, improving practical relations between Belfast and Dublin, was simply too much for the hardliners to accept. In this context of a barren political landscape and continued violence, Rees was to have a profound effect on the shaping of penal policy.

Chapter Seven
Protests, rocket fuel and escapes

By the mid 1970s the tensions inside the Maze were every bit as bad as those outside in the community. Their origins could be traced back to 3 June 1973, a Sunday afternoon, when the body of an interned prisoner, Patrick Crawford, 22, was found hanged in a compound. In his account of life in Long Kesh, Phil McCullough described how every Sunday at 2 pm all cages would form up in military fashion for a two minutes silence, observed in respect for all who had died during the previous week in what he called 'the struggle for Liberation. During this parade, the screws discretely [*sic*] hide themselves. It was after one of these parades that the body of young Pat Crawford was found hanging from one of the huts. The emotion felt by one and all was undescribable. The tension was so thick one could almost see it. As Pat's body was carried out on a stretcher and placed into the grey prison wagon we all once more formed up and came to attention as a final mark of respect for a comrade.'

Although Crawford was subsequently denied an entry in the 'The Last Post', the IRA's official roll of honour, the next day the Belfast Brigade of the Provisional IRA issued a statement warning that 'unless all forms of brutality, whether physical or mental, ceased forthwith, male and female prison officers in Northern Ireland would now be regarded as legitimate targets.' A few weeks later, on 13 July, a woman in Londonderry received serious hand injuries when she opened a letter bomb addressed to her son, a warder at the Maze prison. Following the threat and this incident, it was clear that prison officers were now directly in the terrorist firing line along with the police and soldiers. Worries about the vulnerability of prison officers to attack increased further after a bomb exploded at the home of a Maze officer in Hillsborough, County Down the following February.

A particular source of grievance between the Republican prisoners and the authorities was the often long delay in responding to sick calls at night and the resultant deaths of a number of prisoners. The system was that if anyone should take sick after night lock-up, the prison officers responded to an electric bell rung from the cage. On some occasions, because of delays in responding, prisoners forced open hut doors and left the sick man at the compound gate. In this context the IRA's roll of honour lists Francis Dodds, aged 31, who died in Compound 18 on 9 September, 1973 'because of medical neglect'. Shortly after his internment in Long Kesh he was beaten by soldiers during a riot. He had often complained of pains in his feet and legs, and had been treated at the Royal Victoria Hospital for 'athlete's foot'. The cause of his death was later diagnosed as a circulatory disease. Patrick Teer died in hospital of an ear virus on 2 July 1974, a few days after being moved there from the prison. He had been in constant pain from 26 June until his death. Eamonn Campbell and Sean McKenna both died shortly after being released from Long Kesh after suffering severe illnesses while there. The authorities had moved to improve the prison medical service in January 1974, when it became the direct responsibility of the Department of Health and Social Services, with the aim of ensuring the service was of a similar standard to that provided in the community and that prisoners had access to the full range of available treatments and services.

The prisoners' sense of grievance was heightened by the incessant raids and searches by prison officers and soldiers, which were designed to frustrate the planning of escapes and to uncover imitation weapons and other items which could be used to facilitate an escape attempt or to train terrorists. In the eyes of the authorities the raids were fully justified, for there was a relentless ongoing campaign on the part of the prisoners to disrupt the orderly running of the prisons and to escape. On 13 February 1974 one of 40 part-time lecturers who visited the prison every week was taken captive. A Republican serving five years for arms offences tried to get free by impersonating him, but was stopped at the tally lodge at the main gate of the prison and detected. A Loyalist prisoner concealed himself under soiled laundry and remained in a storage hut for two days in March 1974. However, when a work party had difficulty lifting the trolley on to a lorry, prison officers became suspicious and he was discovered. In June 1974 six prisoners dressed as soldiers and marching in formation, were challenged by a warder and halted when they tried to leave their compound. They were wearing false uniforms fashioned from blankets, and carrying replica firearms modelled from wood permitted into the prison to make handicrafts, such as shields, statues and harps.

Barely a month later, at the end of July, the 26-year-old Gerry Adams was involved in a carefully planned escape plot to switch places with a look-alike visitor. Adams, the young internee whom Whitelaw had released to take part in his London meeting with the Provisional IRA leadership and who would later become a prominent political figurehead, had shaved off his own distinctive bushy beard and put on a false beard and wig before his visit. However, on his way into the visit area, warders became suspicious because the beard was coming away at the side. During the visit with the look-alike and three females, who had all given false names, Adams took off the false beard and wig and exchanged jackets. When the visit was over, the lookalike embraced one of the women and they and Adams then sought to leave but they were immediately challenged and arrested.

A couple of weeks later the senior prison officer involved was set upon in one of the IRA compounds. (The prisoner who so violently assaulted him later became Gerry Adams' constant bodyguard and subsequently also served a prison sentence for his prominent part in the horrific crowd attack on two British Army corporals in 1988, who were dragged from their car, stripped, beaten and then shot dead on nearby wasteground.) The prison officer was so severely assaulted, with two iron bars taken from a piece of gym weight-lifting equipment, that he was rushed to hospital, where he lay critically ill, in a coma, at the point of death for several days.

'I didn't know what had happened then for many days after that,' he recalls. But the IRA did not leave it there. Within a few weeks, some days after he came home from hospital to convalesce, a bomb was left outside the bathroom window, exploded and demolished the house. His two young children, a boy and a girl, were asleep. 'They were in the one bedroom upstairs, in separate beds, and actually the whole floorboards lifted up and dropped down again. I don't quite know how but my daughter got her arm broke. My wife had just left the bathroom, she was in the kitchen. She had gone to have a bath. The bathroom was on the ground floor and they set the bomb just where the light was for the bathroom and it blew the car into the hedge, blew the wall down between the bathroom and the lounge where I was lying on the couch. It actually fell over on top of me, and some blocks fell on my legs, but the wife wasn't in the bathroom. Had she been in the bathroom she'd have been killed. I was just scratched. I was on a stick for a day or two after it, because, it was only bruising, because this wall had actually come down, and fortunately seemed to fall away out over the far side of the room. But the house was demolished. We could only sell it for site value.'

Failure did not deter other prisoners. Although a fellow-prisoner had earlier been seriously injured while trying to escape the Maze concealed in a refuse lorry, a Republican prisoner succeeded in getting outside the prison in July 1974. He was apprehended when a police patrol spotted him running away from the refuse dump at nearby Dromara and returned him to the prison.

An Army officer who served with the prison guard force at this time summed the situation up in a handover note to an incoming colleague: 'It follows that there is a need for frequent searches within the prison, and a startling amount of home-made escape equipment and contraband has been recovered in recent years including grappling hooks, rope (made from sheets and volley-ball netting), detachable ladder parts (made from metal bed-ends), wire and bolt cutters, false uniforms (complete with badges and buttons fashioned from silver paper), keys, crowbars, files, spanners, knives, clubs, daggers, hatchets, imitation firearms (pistols, rifles and revolvers with working wooden parts), ammunition, weapon magazines, electrical and mercury tilt switches, batteries, modified watches, field-craft, weapon and explosives manuals.'

Several prison officers said that there was hardly a single item of material or equipment within the prison that had not been adapted or misused for some unintended purpose. Some of the most ingenious invention took place in support of the almost constant tunnelling operations. One set of tunnelling hardware and equipment, seized in Long Kesh in 1971, illustrates the extent of the improvisation that went on. Food scoops and other kitchen utensils were flattened or reshaped to become digging implements. A trolley to convey spoil along the tunnel was made from a food tray with wheels fashioned from wood, and a chain was made to pull it in and out. Knives, chisels, wedges and lathes, supposed to be used for wood and leather crafts, also found their way into the tunnelling operations. Digging at the tunnel face was a tough proposition in what was a dark, airless, confined space. Ventilation came by way of an electric motor removed from a heater and a propeller-shaped from the metal lid of a Fray Bentos steak and kidney pie tin. Light and power came through coils of wire, plug boxes and plugs, stripped out of the huts or cell accommodation to use in tunnelling. Over the years full-size and miniature cameras, mini-guns and cigarette lighters were smuggled in and out to facilitate escape attempts. Platform shoes, training shoes with thick soles, radios and all sorts of items which could be hollowed out were used to smuggle material such as detonators, bullets, small guns and money in and out of the prison. There were even attempts to train homing pigeons to carry messages.

Against this background, as in the Second World War prisoner-of-war camps, the topic of escape was therefore a constant one and many prisoners spent a lot of time and mustered a great deal of ingenuity seeking ways to beat the prison security, which was under constant review and was continually being upgraded in the light of escapes and attempts and in line with the ever improving range and technological quality of detector devices. Towards the end of 1974 I visited the Maze Prison, only the third time a journalist had been allowed to do so. As I reported later for the *Sunday Times*:

'The Maze prison lies in the centre of a heavily-guarded military camp 10 miles south-west of Belfast, alongside the M1 motorway. Having entered the army post, presented my press identification, waited while my appointment was confirmed by telephone with the prison gate-house and had my car searched by soldiers, I was given a pass. This allowed me to drive to the outside of the prison where three armoured water cannon vehicles were parked adjacent to the main gate. The Army mans the perimeter towers and guards the limits of the prison. Security inside falls on the shoulders of 500 prison officers, two-thirds of whom are local. The remainder are on secondment from mainland prisons. They get a disturbance allowance for their tour of duty in Ulster. a minimum of three months, although most officers do longer.

'The outside wall is fifteen feet high and made of corrugated iron. Inside this are four parallel chain-link fences about five feet apart, with coils of barbed wire strung between. There are many electronic devices, some underground. Entry to the prison is through a gatehouse, where my pass was checked and my escort issued with a small metal disc called a tally. People returning through the gatehouse are checked against a gallery of photographs on the wall of prisoners who have either tried to escape or are considered to be high escape risks.

'One with me,' said my escort as we squeezed through a creaking green turnstile into the prison proper – a cry I was to hear repeated each time we passed from one section of the prison to another. In the main reception area, green painted prefab huts contain the administration and governor's offices. A solitary rose-bed provides the only contrast to the drab colours. Dark green sentry boxes are placed on each gate, at the entrance to each compound and along the central pathway of the triangular-shaped prison. In the boxes, prison officers, keys dangling from their waists, sheltered from the rain, the collars of their dark blue greatcoats turned up. I was driven around the nineteen compounds, the minibus splashing through the mud and puddles of the network of access roads which criss-cross the compounds. I saw the kennels where the Army's guard dogs are kept. My escort pointed out the compounds as we passed: "UDA there, UVF there." (Ulster Defence Association and Ulster Volunteer Force.) He indicated compounds where there were Provisional IRA prisoners, others where they were Officials. It was like a tour of a human safari park. Behind the chain-link fences which seal off the compounds I saw prisoners walking up and down or chatting in groups. Through the open doors of some huts others could be seen lying on their bunks reading. Radio One blared out.'

The aftermath of the regular escapes and attempts and the regular prison searches were now characterised by increasingly violent clashes between the inmates and the searchers and gave rise to a sustained propaganda war between the two sides, which was, at first, mainly fought out in the columns of the local newspapers. There was controversy in April, after four Unionist MPs carrying a letter of authorisation from Lord Donaldson, one of the ministers at the Northern Ireland Office, to see conditions for themselves, were refused entry in 'unparliamentary language' by an Army sergeant. The Adams incident prompted further controversial accusations that a guard dog had been set on two women and that soldiers had destroyed or eaten the contents of food parcels destined for prisoners that day.

An incident in May 1974, as recorded in a prisoner's statement in a contemporary pamphlet campaigning for an end to internment, was a typical example:

'On Tuesday, 14 May 1974, I was awakened by soldiers running into the hut, screaming and throwing lockers on the floor. They then told us to stay in our beds and to put our arms out from the blankets and to hold them straight down by our sides. Then they told us not to move a muscle. One at a time they told us to get up, dress, and then to lie straight down on our backs and to keep our eyes on the corrugated sheeting above us.

'I was lying fully dressed and following this procedure. I heard a commotion going on down the hut. I looked down and saw a soldier beating my brother on the legs and shouting to him to keep his legs straight. My brother answered him, telling him they were as straight as a stick. The soldier then started to baton him more furiously on the legs and three more soldiers started pulling him off the bed. At this stage my vision was obstructed owing to a few lockers which were situated beside my bed, so I made a move to get off my bed because I was concerned for the welfare of my brother. When I jumped off the bed I was immediately batoned by a soldier, so I hit him back. (I must state that the blow I struck him was just a reflex action on my behalf.) As soon as I had hit the soldier I was attacked by about eight more soldiers, who continually batoned and kicked me about the back, head and neck. I was dragged out by the hair of my head and once outside the hut I was run off my feet by two British soldiers and rammed head first against the wire which surrounds the compound. There I saw my brother, who was standing naked except for underpants. They told us to get up against the wire. As I turned round I felt myself going faint and I must have gone unconscious for I woke up later in the small canteen. I was lying on the flat of my back on a table. The British soldiers were standing over me. Then the officer in charge brought in a medical officer. After seeing me the medical officer went out and came back with two other prison warders and a stretcher. They then carried me down to the camp hospital. I was laid out on the flat hardback couch in the 'surgery'. There I lay for four full hours in pain without any medical assistance. The only treatment I was offered was two pain killers, which I refused.'

Prison officers adopted an air of weary resignation to the issue.

'Let's put it this way,' [one recalled]. 'If you were a prisoner and I was a prison officer and I asked you to do something and you refused and took a swing at me, I would hit back. Too bloody right I would. Everybody heard plenty about the so-called ill-treatment of prisoners but we were having to cope at close-quarters with people who have killed and maimed men, women and children. Some of them were multiple killers or had killed more than once. Yet when we carried out searches or told them to turn out their pockets after a visit from a relative, in fact just do our job efficiently to make sure they were not planning a breakout, then there were often fisticuffs, or worse, all round and a major outcry from politicians and the public about us. In fact, they managed to con everybody into believing that all sorts of monstrosities were being inflicted upon them. I mean we are talking about bombers and killers. They are experts at propaganda and they certainly made good use of it. Let's face it; they had nothing to lose and everything to gain so it's only natural that they tried every trick in the book to get outside support.'

From time to time to time, though, the civil courts appeared to endorse the claims that prisoners were indeed being ill-treated. In June 1974, a nineteen-year-old detainee won £100 agreed damages from the Ministry of Defence for personal injuries sustained during an encounter with soldiers in his compound in May the previous year.

Although the prisoners strongly preserved the factional allegiances and the political and sectarian rivalries that had put them on opposite sides of the communal conflict, while they were in prison a common interest in improving their lot and removing shared grievances brought the faction leaders into periodic contact in common parts of the jail, such as the visiting, administration or welfare areas. Other contact points were the 'tuck shop', the gymnasium and the football pitches. At first such exchanges in the Maze were pretty cursory and the underlying tensions remained high. However, after hand-to-hand fighting between Provisional and Official IRA prisoners on 22 March 1974, in which six of the latter group were injured, two seriously, a mutual non-aggression pact was speedily concluded between all the factions. But the major catalyst for this action was a security crackdown imposed after an IRA prisoner escaped on 15 April by impersonating another prisoner being paroled to get married. The authorities were more than usually embarrassed by the escape for the prisoner concerned was Ivor Bell, who was considered to be the commander of the Belfast Brigade and one of the most influential leaders of the Provisional IRA. (He was recaptured after just two weeks.)

Up to that point prisoners could receive their visitors in a cubicle with a small table and two doors, which were closed, although officers could observe through glass panels. There was, however, sufficient privacy and enough fear or discretion, on the part of most officers, for them generally to look the other way on the regular occasions when sexual intercourse took place. On one occasion a prison officer who intervened to stop a sexual encounter was later so seriously assaulted with an iron bar while in one of the compounds that he was off work for three months. Another officer, from a strict religious background, resigned from the service weeks after being posted to the Maze when he realised what was taking place and refused to condone it. Indeed, apart from wives and girlfriends, who often brought blankets to the visits to mask the fumblings, what could be called 'comfort women' were sometimes recruited to visit prisoners. A prison officer recalls seeing girls going from cubicle to cubicle. 'They were bold as brass about it and didn't even stop if you looked into the cubicle.' A prominent politician recalls a young woman coming to him in desperation after being threatened with tarring and feathering and having her hair shorn if she refused to go to Long Kesh. Ex-prisoners boast that there were even 'war babies' conceived in the prison. On this topic, the Army officer's hand-over note says: 'The open visit system permitting physical contact between prisoners and visitors has always proved a security headache. Apart from some grotesque attempts at physical intimacy, evidently culled from the more obscure chapters of the Kama Sutra, the open visits have yielded an interesting array of contraband including ammunition, alcoholic spirits, cameras, film cassettes, transistor radios, chisels, saws, files, knives, tobacco, drugs, letters, photographs, homing pigeons and meteorological balloons. These items have been secreted in bread, cakes, cheese, soap, butter, toothpaste, books, pens, shoes, contraceptives and crucifixes, to mention but a few, and, on one memorable occasion, 22 smuggled letters were recovered from the rear end of one stoical prisoner.'

In a bid to improve security, halt this tide of contraband and deter escape plots, the doors of the cubicles were removed and new tables were installed to prevent physical contact, and the prison officers were ordered to mount a much greater degree of surveillance over visits. For the first time the Republicans and Loyalists joined forces and launched a 'visits strike' refusing to see friends and family until the facilities were restored. The protest lasted over three months and was reinforced by regular street disturbances in both Republican and Loyalist strongholds. It was the British government that blinked first in the trial of strength by announcing in the House of Commons on 16 May that open visiting was to be restored although the visiting cubicle doors were to remain removed. What was not publicly revealed, at that point, was that the Compound OCs, by now formed into a Camp Council, had been consulted about the new plans and approved them. On 27 June it was disclosed in Parliament in London that there had been discussions between ministers and 'Mr D Morley and Mr Quigley of the Provisional IRA, Mr P O'Hare of the Official IRA, and Mr Jim Craig and Mr Gusty Spence of the Loyalists' about prison issues but, although the precise details were not given, it was clear that a political, and not an administrative, decision had been taken.

The move set a precedent which the prisoners readily accepted as a sign that further gains could be made if they kept up the pressure but it was all the more extraordinary for it appeared to fly in the face of the long overdue strategic prisons policy which Merlyn Rees was then beginning to fashion. With the Wilson government now publicly committed to ending internment without trial as soon as security conditions permitted and, at this point only privately, to replacing special category ('a grave mistake,' according to Rees), a seven-strong committee chaired by Lord Gardiner was appointed to map out the route. Gerald Gardiner was one of the leading lawyers of his day and had served as Lord Chancellor in Harold Wilson's Labour government from 1964 until 1970. Such was his professional dedication that he listed law reform as his recreation in *Who's Who*. His committee met for the first time on 19 June to 'consider, in the context of civil liberties and human rights, measures to deal with terrorism in Northern Ireland.' As they got down to work, Rees's officials were working on a coordinated basis to put in place the physical measures and accommodation necessary to hold a swollen prison population – at the time there were 1500 special category prisoners – which was put to the British Cabinet on 6 September for policy and financial approval.

More immediately Rees was grappling with the threat of a strike by 1900 prison officers and the discovery that if it went ahead the Army, in a classic instance of Whitehall warrior syndrome, was not prepared to become involved in running the prisons, merely to maintain its role as a perimeter guard force. The strike threat soon receded, and in due course the Ministry backed down. With a British general election scheduled for October the newly emboldened prisoners decided to pursue their demands more militantly. From mid 1974 both Republicans and Loyalists had further submerged their enmities and joined forces through the Camp Council to remedy a shared, lengthy and, in their eyes, worsening list of wide-ranging grievances.

Their first demand was for an officially recognised Camp Council to meet with the Governor at least monthly and which would have day-to-day contact with Northern Ireland Office officials to deal with grievances. They also wanted the compound leaders and members of the Council to have the freedom of the prison complex to move around, meet their 'constituents' and maintain contact with each other. Earlier in the year the detainees had rejected the terms of a compassionate parole scheme enabling a prisoner to have a minimum period of home leave following the death of a close relative. They wanted a scheme to apply to all prisoners permitting them leave from prison to visit sick close relatives and attend to urgent domestic problems. There were also demands for better visiting arrangements and waiting rooms for visitors, the provision of vocational training and educational equipment such as tape recorders and a projector, which could also be used for showing feature films. The inmates also wanted improvements to facilities in the prison hospital and the laundry service and more attention to maintenance work throughout the complex, where flooding was a serious problem. The prison authorities had, understandably, clamped down on allowing tools and handicraft materials to prisoners because of their potential to contribute further to the plethora of escape plots and attempts that were a constant feature of the daily prison routine. Similarly, to curb the curriculum of the 'university of terrorism', the authorities had imposed restrictions on books and literature permitted to prisoners, and on the import of black clothing and personal effects, which were central to the pseudo-military parades and drilling that were daily features of life in the prisons. These displays reached a crescendo at Easter in the Republican compounds and around the Twelfth of July in those occupied by Loyalists.

These high season festivities were customarily marked by boisterous parties at which smuggled spirits, or poteen made in improvised stills inside the prison, flowed. 'We had everything from vodka being injected into oranges to the actual making of alcohol,' recalls one Maze officer. 'The UVF made the best stuff. I'll tell you how good it was. I remember being on duty one Twelfth of July and there'd been a skirmish in Compound 21 the night before, and one of the staff said "Well, I've never seen this stuff," and he went and he came back with a spoon. You know if you burn methylated spirits it will leave a ring on the spoon. This stuff was that good it didn't even leave a ring. It was pure alcohol. Yeah. Rocket fuel it was.' Among the methods employed to import alcohol into the prison was to put vodka, brandy and whiskey into bottles of Coca Cola and other soft drinks or cartons of orange juice or milk. Down the years over 1000 gallons of home-made poteen have been seized in the Maze and many more drunk, in the words of ex-prisoner Martin Snoddon, leading to 'a night to remember and a morning after to forget'.

There was a startling example of how strong prisoner power had become in July. After disputes between elements of the UVF and UDA in parts of Belfast and elsewhere, ripples of tension reached into the prison, causing demands for segregation which the prison authorities resisted. However, a few days later, in a coordinated move, the Loyalist prisoners broke out of the three compounds they jointly occupied and segregated themselves. The UDA prisoners took two compounds, the UVF a third. The authorities, fearing the inevitable clashes in the prison and collateral trouble on the streets outside if they tried to retrieve the situation, pragmatically accepted what had taken place, but it marked yet another milestone in the increasingly extraordinary course of events in the prison.

Shortly after this episode the Camp Council, articulating general dissatisfaction with the insufficient quantity and inedible quality of food and the infrequency and standard of the laundry service, launched its first united campaign against the prison authorities. A press release from the Northern Ireland Office, on 26 July 1976, explained what happened:

"Special category prisoners at Maze prison professing membership of the Provisional IRA, IRSP, and the UDA joined together today in throwing their lunch meal over the fences of their compounds. The lunch menu today at the Maze was: Lancashire Beef Hotpot, carrots, boiled new potatoes; creamed rice. A total of 673 lunches were destroyed at a cost of hundreds of pounds. In addition, prisoners in one compound later burnt their bedding, beds and mattresses. The cost of equipping one prisoner with all these items is approximately £50. Total damage in the compound is about £3500. In addition 66 insulated food containers, costing about £30 each, were also damaged, and many are likely to have to be replaced. Because of the prisoners' actions, visiting had to be temporarily suspended this afternoon. It was later resumed for all prisoners except those in the compound where the bedding was destroyed.'

By the beginning of September the protest was intensifying. In every special category compound the prisoners took to stripping their beds and tying the sheets and pillowcases to the surrounding chain-link fencing. At the same time, when the food lorry delivered meals in heated trolleys to the compounds, the food was now regularly being thrown over the wire fencing on to the service roads which criss-crossed the complex. The Northern Ireland Office waited over a week and then tried to retaliate on 9 September by banning the prisoners' regular food parcels except for toilet requisites and cigarettes. The prison tuck shop was also closed down. Rees calculated that it would not be so easy for the prisoners to throw away an average £6.64 worth of food a day for each prisoner if there were no other sources of nourishment available. The Governor said that the prisoners were served food on a par with that available at Belfast's Europa Hotel. Rees's decision was answered by widespread Loyalist street protests and hijackings 24 hours later, which brought the already bomb-battered city of Belfast to a standstill. The food and laundry protest was also extended to Magilligan. Over succeeding days both Republican and Loyalist supporters took to the streets in significant numbers causing widepread disruption by their actions.

Back at the Maze, the 550 inmates still detained without trial (now being steadily released at the rate of fifteen to twenty a week), who were not involved in the protest and were still receiving food parcels from outside, now launched a defiant act of solidarity with the special category protestors. While the prison staff looked on, a network of ropes, wires and pulleys was strung up from the top of huts and poles from compound to compound around the prison complex. Over the next few days it was used to ferry supplies from the internees to the special category prisoners. Rees then offered to build a new laundry, increase the supply of sheets and speed up the delivery of food from the central prison kitchen to the compounds. But the prisoners jointly rejected the plan, presented their own 36-point alternative to improve conditions at both the Maze and Magilligan, and renewed their demands for a more liberal compassionate home leave scheme.

At the height of these exchanges, two men went to the front door of a house at Hillmount Gardens in the south Belfast suburb of Finaghy at about 10 pm on the evening of 22 September. When the door was answered, they opened fire, hitting 58-year-old William McCully twice in the head and wounding his wife in the leg. McCully was rushed to hospital but was declared dead on arrival. Although he was working as a school caretaker at the time of his death, he had retired in 1971 after serving as a prison officer for 23 years, initially as a physical training instructor and later as a hospital officer. A telephone caller to a Belfast newspaper office claimed the murder for the Provisional IRA. McCully was the first victim of the Troubles to be connected to the prison service and the timing of his death, during a period of tension in the prisons, underlined that the periodic terrorist threats to prison staff as 'legitimate targets' could not safely be ignored.

The ongoing protests simmered consistently for weeks, but at the end of the month were overshadowed by the interception of a smuggled letter making the prison authorities aware of a far more sinister protest plot: the Provisional IRA was planning simultaneously to burn down the Maze, Magilligan and Armagh prisons. Prison officers had already reported the unusual fact that many Republicans had sent prized possessions out of the prison to their families. These developments sparked fears that the fire would be the cover for a mass escape or would be used to force the government to release a large number of prisoners because there was nowhere to else to hold them.

The spark which ignited the flames came on 23 September when two warders foiled an apparent escape attempt by two Republican prisoners. As was now routine in the wake of escapes or attempts, the Army went into the compounds to carry out a search. The next day, in a statement smuggled out of the prison, the Republican prisoners publicly warned that the three prisons would be burned down imminently if their demands about food were not met and if the Army did not cease beating Republican prisoners. Outside, the street protests continued with vehicles being hijacked and burned and inside the food protests went on stoking up further resentment and tension. Even a statement from the Northern Ireland Office that they were now going to review the compassionate home leave scheme failed to defuse the growing crisis. On 9 October, in another conciliatory move, the Northern Ireland Office conceded that in future offences by a single prisoner would not mean punishment measures for an entire compound. The next day, Thursday, the Labour Party won the British general election, returning Harold Wilson to power. Rees resumed his duties as Northern Ireland Secretary and returned to Stormont Castle where the prison crisis was steadily coming to a head.

It finally exploded at 6 pm the following Tuesday after a clash between three warders and Republican prisoners in Compound 13. According to Republican accounts, when the OC asked for one of the warders, who had allegedly made insulting remarks about the wife of one of the prisoners, to be pulled out because he could not guarantee his safety, the officer refused to go and the prisoners then assaulted him. They claimed that there was 'a long-standing procedure whereby an undesirable prison officer can be asked to leave by a Compound OC'. In his history of the Northern Ireland Prison Service from 1920 to 1990, Jim Challis, a member of the service, gives a different explanation for the incident. 'During the early evening an almost insignificant incident took place in Compound 12, a republican compound. Staff were refused entry to the compound, which happened quite frequently. This did not raise any undue suspicion. However the Governor was determined that staff would carry out their duties and two staff volunteered to enter the compound to carry out their regular patrol. The staff were not long in the compound when they were set upon by the prisoners.'

Other accounts of the original incident indicate the assaulted officer was rescued and taken to hospital but his two colleagues only received minor injuries. Whatever the precise circumstances of this original incident, it provoked a major confrontation and troops were called to surround the compound and back-up a demand from the prison authorities that the prisoners responsible for the assault should be handed over for punishment. Inside the compound, prisoners could be seen armed with table and chair legs and padded clothing. David Morley, the overall leader of the Provisional IRA prisoners, serving ten years for explosives and firearms offences, who was in nearby Cage 16, became aware of the trouble through the prison grapevine and asked to visit his OC in Compound 13. He was angered that troops had been deployed before he had the chance to resolve the dispute and became even more furious when he was refused permission to visit. After a second refusal, and an unsuccessful plea to leave the situation overnight until tempers had cooled all round, he warned that the prison would be burned down if troops were used against the inmates. At about 7.15 pm he put all compounds on standby to set the prison alight. When the prison authorities refused his request for the third time, in breach of an understanding he believed had been reached with the recent creation of the Camp Council, he issued orders for the prison to be burned down at 9 pm.

The special category prisoners ripped huts apart and started the flames in their compounds, followed by both the Provisional and Official IRA detainees. Gusty Spence and Jim Craig, the leaders of the Loyalist prisoners, decided not to join in the destruction and ordered the Loyalist prisoners to break out of their five compounds and gather together in Compounds 14 and 19 for strength of numbers. Despite the cooperation of recent weeks, tit-for-tat sectarian assassinations were taking place throughout Northern Ireland on a nightly basis and neither Republicans or Loyalists completely trusted each other. The Loyalists also raided the medical centre and seized supplies.

Jim Challis gives this account of what then happened and the officers' side of the story: 'After extracting themselves from the prisoners staff were able to get out of the compound. The prisoners then set about wrecking their huts and setting fire to the compound. This set off a chain reaction around the whole prison amongst the republican prisoners and eventually the republican detainees, held in the lower end of the prison. An orgy of rioting and wrecking took place in which several members of staff were trapped and unable to escape from their various posts: some were trapped in observation towers, others in observation posts at the rear of republican compounds. However, all the staff. after some tough negotiating managed to extricate themselves safely from their various predicaments. Most of the staff made their way out of the prison and were organised into squads for the retaking of the prison.'

During the late evening, as the uncontrolled flames spread from compound to compound, and a column of thick smoke rose miles into the night sky, the distinctive Maze glow was brighter than ever before or since. Rees rushed from Stormont Castle to the Army headquarters at Lisburn, where he watched as troops were hastily called in from all over Northern Ireland to secure the perimeter of the prison and prevent the feared mass breakout. Inside the prison complex, staff were overwhelmed by the enormity of the breakdown that had taken place. They repulsed an attempt to rush the main gate and some risked their own lives to rescue four prisoners from the punishment cell block.

According to Challis: "Some sixty staff, under the leadership of a Principal Officer, found themselves unable to get out of the prison and decided to stay and prevent any attempt to escape through the main gate of the prison. The front gate area of the prison was funnel-shaped, with a gate fourteen feet wide at its narrowest end. This funnel area was where the staff took their stand. Despite the repeated attacks by the detainees, the sentenced republican prisoners were unable to breach a gate separating them from the detainees, the staff stood firm and held their position. Several staff were injured with food container lids being thrown like frisbees at them, and rocks and many other missiles were hurled at their position. The staff even managed to baton charge the detainees several times, when the detainees were getting too close to the gate area, always returning to their original position and preventing any escape. This episode was endured by the staff for several hours while the Army and prison staff were being re-grouped and prepared to re-enter the prison.'

Other accounts say that at this point, in line with a decision not to further endanger soldiers, prison staff or the outside fire service, they were pulled back to the perimeter as prisoners armed with a variety of makeshift weapons gathered in groups on the football field adjacent to Compound 13 to await the operation to re-take the prison. Challis says, 'The Army were first into the prison followed by prison staff; and they quickly and efficiently set about their task of regaining control of the prison, with the aid of armoured vehicles and helicopters. One incident was reported of a Trades Officer, William Fulton, joining a line of eight soldiers advancing towards Compound 21 which housed Official IRA prisoners. These prisoners, numbering about 40, marched out of their compound in formation, armed with iron bars, cudgels, and various other weapons and advanced on Officer Fulton and the eight Army personnel. Seeing the line of nine men standing abreast and not moving, the prisoners stopped their advance, dropped their weapons and hurried back to their compound. The Army and prison staff eventually regained control of the prison some 18 hours after the first fire was struck. There were inevitably injuries to both prisoners and staff, but none were life threatening and all injured parties received immediate medical treatment.'

Other accounts, including those of eyewitnesses outside the prison, police and military sources and both Republican and Loyalist prisoners say that at dawn Army observation helicopters swooped low over the complex dropping CS gas, and soldiers wearing gas masks poured in on the ground, firing both CS smoke and baton rounds. At first there was some hand-to-hand fighting among the still smouldering buildings, but after Gusty Spence intervened and mediated between Morley and the Army commander the prisoners accepted assurances that there would be no reprisals, agreed to drop their weapons and returned to their compound areas. However, the prisoners later claimed that the Army broke its word and that, during the subsequent headcount, they were made to stand along the wire fences for five hours, some enduring beatings, and that soldiers let guard dogs loose to bite them. Unofficial pictures taken inside the prison that day by a military photographer appear to confirm these claims and lists of injuries which emerged from the prison over the next couple of days added veracity to them.

In all eighteen of the 21 compounds were destroyed or damaged beyond repair as well as the hospital, kitchen, shop, visiting centre and internal watchtowers. Nine prisoners had been taken to hospital and others treated at the scene, some by the Loyalists using the supplies taken from the hospital before it was burned. Fifteen prison officers had been injured and sixteen soldiers, but none seriously. (Later, in an amendment which called the credibility of the Northern Ireland Office into question, it was admitted that 29 prisoners, 23 soldiers and fourteen prison officers had been hurt. Further doubt was cast on the accuracy of official information when it was admitted that prisoners had not sadistically burned guard dogs in their kennels, as Rees originally claimed.) Official sensitivity to the event was such that the award of the George medal for bravery to two prison officers has never been publicly disclosed until now.

As news of the conflagration spread the next day and rumours that the Army were taking violent reprisals on the prisoners gathered force, violent trouble erupted throughout Northern Ireland. Vehicles were hijacked and main roads blocked, and many shops and businesses closed early because of the extensive disruption. During the afternoon visiting period at Belfast prison, remand prisoners barricaded themselves in the canteen and cells of A wing and proceeded to wreck furniture and fittings. Order was restored after some hours when a strong force of troops, backed by police and warders, fired baton rounds and CS gas. Again there were convincing allegations that the prisoners had been made to run a gauntlet of security force members who assaulted them with truncheons. In all 131 received injuries.

Potentially the most serious incident developed at Armagh where the Governor, Hugh Cunningham, and three female prison officers were taken hostage during their morning round and bundled into a cell by a small group from among the 110 women prisoners demanding assurances that there would be no ill-treatment of prisoners at the Maze. Many had friends and relatives detained there. Troops and police surrounded the prison in the centre of Armagh and as the siege continued into the night of 16/17 October prisoners at Magilligan, where 300 Republicans and Loyalists were being held, set fire to a number of huts, the cookhouse and the prison shop. Some hours later, at 1 am, fourteen hours after the siege began, the Armagh prisoners released their hostages unharmed after a Catholic priest and a Protestant clergyman visited the prison and sat on the stairs for some 40 minutes passing on assurances about the safety of 'their men' in the Maze. That night, after a government decision to keep them on site, the 1500 prisoners in the Maze, who now possessed only the clothes they stood up in, were sleeping in makeshift shelters constructed from the remnants of their huts, wrapped in additional clothes rushed in by prisoner support groups like Green Cross and blankets issued late in the afternoon by the prison authorities. The first night after the fire was wet and stormy and many of the flimsy shelters blew down. A priest who visited the prison said the prisoners were like the 'slum dwellers of Sao Paolo'. The prison officers trying to restore order and control were marginally more comfortable. During the day the entire stock of a caravan dealer near the prison had been hastily acquired, transferred to the prison and positioned to replace their burned-down accommodation.

For the first couple of days the prisoners had to live on bread, margarine and cartons of milk, but after 48 hours the Army set up a field kitchen and hot food was provided. 'We got stew at dinner time and soup in the evening and never was a bowl of hot grub so welcome,' one prisoner wrote to his family. Over the next week, conditions steadily improved. Plastic sheeting was used to cover the frames of the least damaged huts and provide shelter and portable buildings were hired and positioned by Army construction teams. Older prisoners and those who were sick or injured were given priority in being allocated places in them. To facilitate the urgent reconstruction work 107 special category prisoners were temporarily airlifted by helicopter to Magilligan on 27 October. Altogether the cost of repairing the damage caused during the October riots was calculated at approximately £2m.

But the trouble in the Maze was far from over. Taking advantage of the chaotic situation following the fire, a group of Republican prisoners set about completing work on a partly finished tunnel from Hut 27 in Compound 5. With so much repair work going on in the ruins of the prison they had little trouble disposing of the excavated soil unnoticed. Prison officers uncovered looted uniforms and prison plans on 1 November as well as a cache of imitation weapons but failed to uncover any signs of the tunnelling. The prisoners were also helped by the fact that the regular military overflights of the prison, during which infra-red photography was used to check for signs of fresh soil disturbance, had been temporarily interrupted. (Previous diggings had been monitored by such photography and then been 'discovered' by searchers in time to foil an escape.)

In the early hours of 6 November the prisoners made their move when

33 crawled along the completed 134-foot tunnel, which ran under several layers of security fencing and the two tarmac roads which encircled the prison, and made a run for the M1 motorway along the southern edge of the complex. As the succession of figures emerged into the darkness just beyond the perimeter wire, they were spotted by three soldiers, troopers in the Royal Hussars travelling in a Land Rover, part of the military guard force patrolling outside the prison. The soldiers later testified that they had challenged the prisoners and ordered them to standstill. According to the evidence of one, he saw an object glinting and opened fire after shouting several warnings. One of the escapees, Hugh Gerard ('George') Coney, aged 24 and an internee for eighteen months, was shot dead about twenty yards from the perimeter wire. The Army said that he had been shot after being challenged by soldiers who thought he was carrying a weapon. The Northern Ireland Office admitted no weapon was found at the scene and, the next day, in response to allegations that there had been no warning, Rees told the House of Commons that a full investigation was already underway by the Army's Special Investigation Branch and the RUC and that a report would eventually go to the Director of Public Prosecutions. In the event none of the soldiers was ever charged, and at a subsequent inquest the Coroner said that it could well have been that the soldier believed he was faced with at least one armed man. Of the other escapees, 29 were rounded up in the vicinity of the prison within a few hours and the other three were recaptured on the western outskirts of Belfast the next day. There was some rioting inside the prison after the escape when the internees learned that one of their number had been shot and saw the recaptured prisoners being forced to run a gauntlet. Several of them suffered guard dog bites and all were assaulted by troops and prison officers in riot gear, who used CS gas and rubber bullets to subdue the remaining prisoners. In follow-up search activity a second tunnel, almost ready for use, was uncovered.

That evening the Provisional IRA lured the security forces to an electricity installation near Stewartstown, County Tyrone where a booby-trapped landmine had been placed. As two members of an Army bomb disposal team worked at the device, it exploded killing them instantly and wounding five soldiers, a policeman and two civilians. The Provisional IRA acknowledged responsibility for the murders, which, it said, were carried out as a reprisal for the death of Coney, who came from nearby Coalisland. Coming so soon after the fire, the latest Maze escape and fatal shooting stoked up renewed political tension about the continued use of internment. The Social Democratic and Labour Party, the main party representing the Catholic community, was bitterly opposed to the policy and after a meeting at Stormont in the aftermath of the incidents said there was now a 'rising urgency' to settle the whole unsatisfactory issue.

Chapter Eight
An aimless existence

The turbulent events in the prisons in autumn 1974 forced Rees to accelerate his game plan to create, for the first time since the outbreak of the Troubles, a strategic policy framework for the hugely expanded prison service in Northern Ireland. Staff numbers had soared from 292 in 1969 to 2184 by the mid 1970s. The prison population too had risen inexorably since 1968, when there were 727 inmates. The biggest surge came between 1971 and 1972, with the introduction of internment, when it almost doubled from 944 to 1752. It increased to 2359 during 1973, and by November 1974 there were 2848 persons in custody, 540 of them internees. By far the largest group was made up of the 1119 special category prisoners, over 100 serving life sentences and many others facing lengthy terms for their part in the inventory of violence and disorder that had then disfigured Northern Ireland for six bloody years. By the end of 1974, 1145 people had lost their lives and there had been almost 21,000 shooting incidents and some 6500 bomb attacks.

The prison strategy was an integral part of a longer-term 'Ulsterisation' policy to expand and prepare the locally recruited security forces, the RUC and UDR, to take prime responsibility for maintaining law and order and to get back to the point where the courts, and not executive detention without charge or trial, were the principal avenues of justice. There were two central strands to Rees's emerging prison policy: to build a new top security prison on a greenfield site, with traditional cellular accommodation and a conventional prison regime, and to bring an end to internment as swiftly as possible. 'I wanted especially to get away from Long Kesh/The Maze and all that was associated with it,' he wrote in his 1985 autobiography, *Northern Ireland: A Personal Perspective*. A month after the Maze fire, on 18 November 1974, he outlined the first stage of his ambitious prison strategy and building plans in a written answer to a question in the House of Commons. There would be a new £12 million prison constructed at Maghaberry with accommodation in cells for up to 500 male prisoners and a separate women's prison incorporating a young offenders' centre, which opened five years later and would ultimately lead to the closing of Armagh prison. More immediately, Rees announced that there would be an advance prison built on the site to house 700 men in cellular accommodation from early 1976, intended to replace the Maze.

Within weeks he had to make an embarrassing retreat and abandon the advance prison plan. Officials had to admit that the proposed timescale could not be met because of legal and planning processes. Instead, despite Rees's deep misgivings and opposition, there would have to be a new short-term prison in yet another expansion of the Maze site. From that point on there were two prison establishments: HMP Maze (Compound) and HMP Maze (Cellular), each with its own Governor and staff. The cellular phase would be constructed at high speed by the teams of Royal Engineers and other Army specialists who had already provided habitable accommodation for all the prisoners affected by the Maze fire. As an incentive to the soldiers they would be able to earn additional leave for meeting the tight deadlines set for the project. The four new cellular blocks, each containing 100 cells, were to be built in the shape of an H. They would, in time, through the medium of an unprecedented hunger strike, leave an indelible mark on the history of Northern Ireland and its prisons.

While these developments were taking place the Provisional IRA carried out what proved to be one of the most calculated acts of indiscriminate violence of its entire terrorist campaign. In the early evening of 21 November bombs exploded in two public houses in the centre of Birmingham, one of Britain's major provincial cities, killing nineteen people and injuring around 200 more, many very seriously. The Provisional IRA had given a coded warning to the telephone switchboard operator at a local newspaper office but far too late for the emergency services to take any effective action. Daithi O'Conaill, one of the terrorist organisation's most influential leaders, gave a rare television interview a few days later and admitted for the first time that the IRA had been responsible for a sequence of bomb outrages in Britain dating back to a series of explosions in London in April 1973. Although it was not spelt out publicly at that point, the IRA leader was reinforcing a message that was simultaneously being conveyed to the British government and Rees by a series of aspiring ceasefire brokers: the bombings would continue and worsen unless there was a British withdrawal from Northern Ireland, but movement on internment and a declaration of intent about eventual withdrawal could unlock a more gradual approach to meeting the aims of the IRA.

Although the British government's judgement was that the

Provisionals were still far too politically inept and impotent to contribute to a lasting political settlement, they sensed that there was a real whiff of change in the air and that they had a duty to attempt to save life by encouraging a ceasefire to see what, if any, progress could be made. Rees was anyway increasingly anxious to find a way out of the internment maze and put prisons policy on a more conventional, long-term footing, so he was not opposed to carefully using the issue as a bargaining chip in any exchanges. He had long been personally opposed to internment and, when in opposition, had indicated Labour would end it as soon as they came to power. Since taking over at Stormont Castle in February 1974 he had supported a policy of phased releases, although he continued to authorise detentions where the police advised that an individual presented a serious threat to life or property and there was not enough evidence to charge him and seek a conviction through the courts. The British government was also growing ever more anxious about the damage the existence of detention without trial was doing to its international humanitarian credentials. At the time the Irish government was pushing a formal complaint to the European Commission on Human Rights about the interrogation and treatment of a number of IRA suspects in August 1971. It was already clear that when the Commission reported, as it eventually did in September 1976, that Britain would be accused of breaching the rules by subjecting the prisoners to inhuman and degrading treatment and torture.

There were also concerns about a series of cautionary reports from the highly respected and influential International Red Cross, whose inspectors had been granted regular and unrestricted access to the prisons. In October 1971 they reported: 'The constant presence of the British Army around the internment camp seemed to be a factor making for tension which could not but increase in time . . . and could in the long run constitute an explosive mixture.' Another report, in December 1972, stated: 'It must be admitted, however, that during this visit the delegates found that the atmosphere in the camp and the morale of the internees had suffered a grave deterioration. In the opinion of the International Red Cross delegates, this deterioration may be traced to two causes. The first must be sought among the internees themselves. Each man lives in a state of mental stress, convinced that he has been wrongly deprived of his liberty. He preys on the mental distress generated by his uncertainty as to what is in store for him, and by the anguish he feels at the thought of his family. Morally weakened, such a person slumps gradually into a state of neurosis, and his decline is all the more rapid as all those around him are in a similar condition of mental anguish. The delegates have many times observed this phenomenon in various places of detention in different parts of the world, including now at Long Kesh.'

The July 1973 report made equally grim reading for the British Government. 'The delegates were of the opinion that the security measures were at least partly responsible for the noticeably increased psychological tension among detainees and prison officers which seemed to aggravate the stress of prolonged detention.' A report on their visit to the Northern Ireland prisons in May 1974, published the following November, noted that 'as the delegates had become increasingly familiar with the situation in Northern Ireland and with the resulting tensions and, as their understanding of the diametrically opposed points of view deepened, they were increasingly discouraged by the intractable character of the problems involved.' The report questioned the entire process of detention and whether the Army was the appropriate instrument for prison searches. It also expressed concerned about the long-term psychological effects of detention on all detainees, whose average age was around twenty, and especially on young females. 'While fully appreciating the difficulties and the problems with which the authorities and the Army are faced,' the report stated, 'the delegates feel very deeply that greater efforts should be made, if not to phase out or abolish detention, at least to avoid its being counter-productive, sterile and even destructive.' The delegates said they once again wished to encourage the authorities to persevere in their constant endeavours to ameliorate the general conditions of detention, notably by refurbishing those compounds which urgently require it, introducing the cubicle system in the new or refurbished huts, reducing overcrowding, reducing time spent waiting by visiting families, recruiting more staff for education, handicrafts and instruction in artisan trades, providing better sports, games and leisure facilities, improving electricity and water supplies and installing a better sewage system. They added that it should not be inferred that many important measures recommended by the delegates to the authorities in the past had not been put into effect. The delegates commended the attitude of the Governor and his staff in this and in other respects and the attention with which the authorities listened to their preliminary verbal reports.

Rees received this report a few days after the Birmingham bombings and, as he records in his autobiography, it 'confirmed my need to act on detention'. Rees knew there had already been private IRA overtures that there could be a ceasefire if there was movement on the issue, and so a multi-denominational group of Protestant clergymen, who intimated to government officials that they would shortly be secretly meeting the IRA leadership at Feakle, County Clare to urge an end to violence on them, unwittingly found themselves cast as the postmen of peace.

Over the next few weeks, through a series of indirect public and more important private exchanges between the government and the IRA, the groundwork was laid for an IRA ceasefire. At first it was only to last over the Christmas 1974 period, but early in 1975 it was made open-ended until it withered and died later in the year without ever being formally called off. As Rees and his advisers anticipated, the Provisionals had no sense of *realpolitik* and were unable to decipher and move in tandem with the customary creative ambiguities and coded signals buried in private exchanges, messages through intermediaries and public and parliamentary speeches from the government side. Given the need to take account of the one million Unionist majority in Northern Ireland, who wanted to remain within the United Kingdom, there was no way any British government could have announced its intention to pull out its troops and withdraw from the place, as the Provisionals were naïvely demanding. The most tangible public gain for the IRA was the achievement of face-to-face meetings with British officials, which gave it a much-coveted whiff of legitimacy, and the consolidation of an unpublicised back-channel link with the British Secret Intelligence Services. This would eventually bear great political fruit, but not until many more tragic years later.

More immediately and significantly, internal differences over the wisdom of the ceasefire prompted a generational change in the leadership of the Provisional IRA. Out went the veteran 'armchair generals', most of them of southern Irish origin who had been involved in the unsuccessful 1956–62 campaign of violence along the border. In came a new layer of street battle-hardened young leaders like Gerry Adams and Martin McGuinness, many of them graduates of the 'university of terrorism' at the Maze. Under their command the IRA settled down for what it now calculated would be 'the long war' to finally drive the British out of Northern Ireland. At Stormont Castle, one of Rees's most senior advisers shared their analysis. 'This is only round two or three of what is going to be a very long fight indeed.'

Rees did, however, use the hiatus created by the ceasefire to progressively run down the entire internee population. He was given further stimulus to do so by the publication of the Gardiner report in January 1975. After an exhaustive six-month study of the administration of justice in Northern Ireland, the commission concluded:

'Detention cannot remain as a long-term policy. In the short term, it may be an effective means of containing violence, but the prolonged effects of the use of detention are ultimately inimical to community life, fan a widespread sense of grievance and injustice, and obstruct those elements in Northern Ireland society which could lead to reconciliation. Detention can only be tolerated in a democratic society in the most extreme circumstances; it must be used with the utmost restraint and retained only as long as it is strictly necessary. We would like to be able to recommend that the time has come to abolish detention; but the present level of violence, the risks of increased violence, and the difficulty of predicting events even a few months ahead make it impossible to put forward a precise recommendation on the timing. We think that this grave decision can only be made by the Government.'

Rees did not shirk the clear political risks and pressed on. The last eight female detainees were released from Armagh on 28 April 1975, and on 24 July he publicly announced he would end internment by Christmas. Despite the resumption of IRA violence in the latter half of the year, he took a deep breath on 5 December and freed the last remaining 46 internees, the terrorist suspects the Army referred to as 'the hard core'. During the four years and four months internment had been in use, 1981 people had been imprisoned without trial, all but 107 of them Republicans. The policy was generally reckoned to have been a disastrous one in every respect, and although the power remained on the statute book and there were regular calls for its re-introduction, especially after major terrorist atrocities, it was never used again and is most unlikely ever to be introduced again in the future. (The power to intern without trial was, in fact, finally removed from the emergency legislation in 1998.)

Meanwhile life in the Maze and the other prisons was characterised by the usual round of protests and escapes. In June 1975 two UVF prisoners disguised themselves as prison officers and were only a couple of steps from freedom when they were apprehended at the main gate of Magilligan. Another prisoner, impersonating a priest, managed to get out of the Maze in July. The real priest, a Canadian, was overpowered and stripped to his underclothes after saying Mass in one of the compounds. Twenty-year-old Patrick Joseph Campbell, wearing the priest's outer garments and impersonating his Canadian accent, got to the main tally lodge at the front gate and asked prison officers to call a taxi to take him to Belfast. But while he was waiting, a prison officer spotted another priest leaving the prison by car and arranged for the bogus priest to get a lift instead. When he reached

Belfast, Campbell, who was serving eight years for IRA membership, possession of an Armalite rifle and plotting to murder soldiers, made off into the city. Both priests were later cleared of any role in the escape. Lord Donaldson, the minister responsible for prisons, admitted there had been a security slip-up. One of the measures taken to halt the spate of 'impersonation' escapes had been the introduction of a procedure requiring visitors to give a specimen signature on arrival for comparison on departure. In this case, the signatures had not been checked. At that point there had been some 29 successful escapes from Belfast prison, 56 from the Maze, eight from Magilligan and seven from the *Maidstone* as well as many more foiled by a mixture of luck and the vigilance of the staff.

By the beginning of 1975 practical preparations were going ahead for the radical transformation of prison policy that Rees had set in train just over a year earlier, but the Gardiner Report, in a scathing, hard-hitting, outspoken chapter entitled 'Prison Accommodation and Special Category Prisoners', expressed the fear that even what had already been set in motion might not be enough to cope. The landmark report provided a penetrating and critical analysis of all that had gone before and proposed some urgent, far-reaching and fundamental changes.

> 'The prison system in Northern Ireland has a most important role to play in the maintenance of law and order. We do not believe that it is fulfilling that role adequately at present and, to be blunt, we were appalled at certain aspects of the prison situation. The influence of the terrorist leaders must be reduced and rehabilitation work started. The failure of successive administrations to take earlier action has significantly reduced the effectiveness of the penal system. This situation must not be allowed to continue.

> 'The present situation of Northern Ireland's prisons is so serious that the provision of adequate prison accommodation demands that priority be given to it by the Government in terms of money, materials and skilled labour such as has been accorded to no public project since the Second World War. Specifically we recommend that the Government find suitable sites on which building can start immediately on both the proposed temporary cellular prison for 700 and the permanent prison for 490-500. We believe that they could at once evacuate a camp or barracks on Government land and begin building or adaptation within a few days if the will was there. If no Government sites are available, emergency legislation should be passed to give the Secretary of State general powers to acquire suitable sites at once without the delays consequent on normal compulsory purchase and planning procedure.'

Pointing out that the prison population was up by 50 per cent in 1973, and by a further 21 per cent in 1974, and with increases of this order likely to continue, the report expressed the fear that 'the recently announced programme is scarcely adequate and, even if speeded up, may well fall far behind what is needed.' But the Commission focused its strongest criticism on the compound-style accommodation and the existence of special category. Expressing concern that 71 per cent of male prisoners – 1881 out of 2648 – were held in temporary prisons of the compound type rather than cellular accommodation, the report continued: 'We believe that the prison staff, who are in charge of the prisoners, do their best with the limited manpower available, but the layout and construction of the compounds make close and continued supervision impossible. The dormitories are locked at night, but otherwise the prisoners in each compound are very much left to their own devices. There are no facilities for organised employment. Each compound is virtually a self-contained community which keeps the premises it occupies to such standard as it finds acceptable and engages, if it so wishes, in military drills or lectures on military subjects.' It goes on to describe the origins and implications of special category: 'In practice this has meant that any convicted criminal sentenced to more than nine months imprisonment who claims political motivation and who is acceptable to a compound leader at the Maze or Magilligan Prisons is accorded special status.' The Commission said the housing of male special category prisoners in compounds meant that they were not as closely controlled as they would be in a normal cellular prison, and that discipline within compounds was in practice exercised by compound leaders. Prisoners, they believed, were more likely to emerge with an increased commitment to terrorism than as reformed citizens:

'The special category prisoners regard themselves in much the same light as detainees, expecting that an amnesty will result in them not having to serve in full the sentences imposed on them by the courts, and the paramilitary organisations find it easy to encourage this misunderstanding in the public mind for propaganda purposes. The result of this is that the sentences passed in the courts for murder and other serious crimes have lost much of their deterrent effect.

'Although recognising the pressures on those responsible at the time,' [the Commission concluded,] 'we have come to the conclusion that the introduction of special category status was a serious mistake; we even have some doubt as to whether its introduction administratively by a surprisingly liberal interpretation of Prison Rules was legal. It should be made absolutely clear that special category prisoners can expect no amnesty and will have to serve their sentences. We can see no justification for granting privileges to a large number of criminals convicted of very serious crimes, in many cases murder, merely because they claim political motivation. it supports their own view, which society must reject, that their political motivation in some way justifies their crimes. Finally, it is unfair to ordinary criminals, often guilty of far less serious crimes, who are subject to normal prison discipline.

'We recognise that to remove the privileges from existing special category prisoners would cause trouble within the prisons, not least because of the low level of control afforded by the compound type of accommodation. We also recognise the difficulty facing the authorities in the present state of prison accommodation in providing work and proper prison discipline for these prisoners. On present plans it does not seem that it will be feasible to begin to phase out special category status on any scale until the new temporary cellular prison accommodation, recently announced by the Secretary of State, is ready in early 1976. This date must be brought forward, either by urgently adapting part of the Maze Prison if our recommendation for moving detainees to a separate prison is accepted, or by completing the new cellular accommodation earlier as we also recommend. Any necessary preparatory steps, such as the equipment of the necessary workshops and recruitment of appropriate staff, should be planned now and taken in good time. Nevertheless we recommend that the earliest practicable opportunity should be taken to end the special category. The first priority should be to stop admitting new prisoners.'

The serious crisis in the prisons had been heavily overshadowed by the succession and extent of murders and atrocities in the community outside and the hard-pressed prison officers, the third arm of the security forces after the police and army, were very much overlooked. The Commission, however, recognised their vital contribution in the battle against anarchy and paid them an appropriate tribute. 'Long before the demands of the present emergency, and when [the Prison Service's] numbers were relatively small, it had gained a deserved reputation for its devotion to duty and its high standards. Despite a rapid expansion over the last few years and a lower proportion of experienced officers, it has maintained these qualities and has continued to discharge its difficult and hazardous tasks in a manner that has earned the thanks and respect of the community.'

The Commission, however, pointed to the relative inexperience of the service – out of a total of 700 basic grade officers, 635 had under five years' service – and said that as the shortage of prison staff exacerbated the defects in the prison system even greater efforts must be made to find prison officers and staff to assist in education, prison employment and rehabilitation. While fully recognising the difficulty of attracting suitable people to undertake work which it described as 'always arduous and demanding and involving long hours and danger', it called for the rates of pay and allowances to be reviewed with a view to attracting more recruits. 'The pay of prison staff, although high because of large amounts of overtime did not take sufficient account of the arduous and dangerous nature of the work.' (At this time prison officers were earning £40 to £50 a week on average, but intensive overtime working increased it substantially.)

In the short term Gardiner called for additional efforts to be made to recruit staff from Great Britain, and suggested that the possibility of attracting staff from Commonwealth countries such as Canada, Australia and New Zealand should be examined. 'Special grants and allowances are already used to attract officers from Great Britain on a temporary basis; we recommend that these inducements should be raised, and if necessary widened in scope, to attract greater numbers of experienced staff. The efforts and sacrifices already made by the English and Scottish prison authorities are considerable and have played an important part in maintaining the prison system in Northern Ireland. The present prison situation in Northern Ireland is so serious that the prison authorities in the remainder of the United Kingdom, despite their own recruitment difficulties, must make even greater efforts to help the Northern Ireland prisons.'

The thrust of the Gardiner report was very much in line with his own thinking and the policy priorities he had already articulated, so Rees had little difficulty in accepting it. A first hint of what was intended came in the House of Lords in July when Lord Donaldson, the minister responsible for the prisons, said it was hoped to reach a stage when the government could say that special category would not be given to prisoners after a certain date. However, there was also an early indication of the strength of the opposition to the move that the government had already encountered in its private soundings. Saying that special category was greatly resented by ordinary criminals, the minister continued, 'The problem is that it is not easy to get rid of something which is so highly valued by the offender and his friends. Northern Ireland has roughly three times as many people in prison in proportion to its population as any other European country. As a result there are a large number of citizens outside the prison walls who actively oppose the government for shutting up their friends and relations in spite of the frightful nature of many of the crimes committed.'

The switch from detention without trial to arrests and charges, leading to convictions in the courts, was now in full swing, and on 4 November 1975 Rees was able to give the House of Commons details of its effect. During the previous ten months, the number of detainees had fallen from 545 to 175 while the number of convicted offenders going into the special category compounds had soared from 1095 to 1465, an increase of 35 per cent. More than 1000 people were also awaiting trial on a range of charges, including 118 with murder and 77 with attempted murder.

Affirming that there would be no amnesty for those convicted, Rees said, 'Those who purport to believe that murder and bombing with a convenient political label means that they will receive an amnesty tragically mislead themselves. Let there be no misunderstanding of this.' Going on to decry special category, he said, 'I want to end this system but the hard facts of life are that it cannot be ended while so many prisoners have to serve their sentences in compounds.' So in an initiative to phase it out, he announced that with effect from 1 March 1976 any persons committing offences would not be able to claim special category status, although those already in prison, or convicted of crimes carried out before the cut-off date, would still be entitled to it. As an incentive to accepting the new cellular-based prison regime, where prisoners would be required to wear uniform and to work and would not be segregated by faction, he also signalled that there would be more generous rates of remission. From that point too, it would be increased from one-third to one-half of sentence. Officials using the channels open to the paramilitary leaders outside through the Camp Council had already privately offered further sweeteners in an effort to get the new prison regime accepted without protest. They said that the wearing of prison uniform could be confined to work hours and that work could include vocational training and some educational activity. At other times the prisoners could wear their own clothes. Concessions on the frequency of visits, writing letters and the receipt of parcels were also offered. The Northern Ireland Office, where officials took to calling the non-terrorist prisoners 'ordinary decent criminals', described the new prison policy as 'normalisation', but Republicans and Loyalists were uncompromising. They both saw it as 'criminalisation' and vowed to resist it to the bitter end.

By then the military construction teams had completed the refurbishment of what was to be called Maze Compound, significantly improving the quality of accommodation for the special category prisoners. The wooden ends of the Nissen huts had been replaced by bricks, providing better insulation, and, in response to the Red Cross comments about the lack of privacy for prisoners, the open dormitory layout was abandoned in favour of individual partitioned cubicles. The soldiers immediately moved on to start work on a series of blocks to provide cellular accommodation.

For ease and speed of construction the blocks were just single-storey, with flat roofs, grey concrete walls and barred windows. They were H-shaped, with 25 cells, a dining area and association room in each leg of the H. There was a security and administration control and common storage, classroom and medical facilities in the central bar, or 'circle', as it was more commonly called. Each cell was kept at a constant 65 degrees Fahrenheit by oil-fired central heating. The four wings, designated A-D, were isolated from each other by barred grilles – 'like in a Yankee jail,' one early Loyalist inmate exclaimed. Each block was surrounded by a double layer of chain-link fencing and entered through a double airlock gate – the inside and outside gates, controlled by prison officers, were never supposed to be open at the same time. The enclosed area was used as an exercise yard and for sports such as volleyball. Elsewhere in the expanded complex there were all-weather sports pitches, a vast indoor sports hall and gymnasium, a well-equipped hospital and a series of workshops where it was intended the prisoners would learn trades like motor maintenance, bricklaying and plastering or choose to better themselves by taking one of a wide range of study courses. The first block, completed in October 1976, was designated H1, the second, when it was finished a month later became H2, and so on. Eventually there were eight H-blocks, each having cost about £1 million to construct, and by day, like the Maze glow at night, their sharp white outlines could be seen for miles from the air, like pieces of a giant alphabet set dotted on the predominantly green landscape. Three identical H-blocks were also constructed in an expansion of the Magilligan prison site.

As special category had been introduced by Whitelaw by sleight of hand within the existing prison rules, there was no need for specific legislation to bring it to an end. But Rees underpinned his prison regime initiative with the Treatment of Offenders Order, pushed through early in 1976, which contained a number of 'good housekeeping' provisions, including the formal abolition of what he described as the 'largely obsolete powers to impose corporal punishment in prisons'. (However, the use of corporal punishment, with a cane rather than the birch, continued at the Millisle Borstal for some years and was finally phased out after the medical officer fainted while supervising a caning.) In common with all Northern Ireland legislation made under direct rule, Parliament could only briefly discuss the measure and not debate or amend it as with a bill. On 16 February 1976, during this discussion, Rees confirmed to the House of Commons that special category status was being ended because 'the aimless existence followed by special category prisoners in compounds is no preparation for a return to normal living.' He went on to outline how prisoners would benefit from the increased remission scale but be subject to serving the remainder of their original sentence, if they were convicted of any further offences, with any additional sentence only coming into consecutive effect. 'This is a real and important sanction,' he said.

Rees added, however, that instead of simply releasing prisoners in this way, unsupervised on licence, he would have preferred to bring in a parole scheme, similar to that already operating in England and Wales. However, given the requirement to collect comprehensive information about a prisoner prior to sentence, his behaviour during sentence, his plans for the future and the circumstances in which he will live on release, Rees admitted that in the prevailing circumstances in Northern Ireland parole was not a practical possibility. 'With the compound conditions in which the majority of Northern Ireland prisoners are housed, it would not be feasible to make the kind of assessment of readiness for release which is a feature of the parole scheme. Nor is it realistic to expect probation officers to supervise prisoners on parole who may be motivated by influences which probation officers are neither qualified or trained to control.'

What Rees did not say was that the Probation Service had refused point blank to operate any scheme involving ex-paramilitary prisoners, although they would work with prisoners who voluntarily requested their help. The decision was hardly surprising for their potential clients came from the hard areas where the troubles were at their most acute. At that time lawlessness was rife in Northern Ireland. Rent collectors and tradesmen were routinely robbed. Civil process servers were unable to function in many areas. Enforcement of civil matters like television licensing was virtually impossible, with detection teams being threatened and chased. Belfast was a city under virtual gang rule, where protection payments and racketeering had become endemic. Indeed the police could not maintain a presence and carry out their duties in many areas without the support of heavily armed soldiers. As one police officer put it at the time, human life had become so cheap in parts of Northern Ireland that you could have had any score settled for the price of a pint of Guinness!

Among the other provisions in the Order was one empowering Prison Governors to double from two weeks to periods of up to one month, loss of remission for breaches of prison rules although the tariff of up to six months, which could be imposed by Boards of Visitors, remained unchanged. Rees also advised the House of Commons that the new remission rules would be retrospectively applied to the existing special category inmates which would mean 450 going free earlier than originally anticipated, over the four months from 1 March to 30 June. This concessionary element in an otherwise draconian package did nothing to mitigate the opposition that was gathering force in both the Republican and Loyalist heartlands to the abolition of 'prisoner-of-war status'. Even a guided tour of the new H-blocks failed to persuade the Loyalist paramilitary leaders from outside the prison to change their mind. In the compounds, UVF prisoners were ordered to step up their physical training in preparation for the protests to come. An order issued to UDA members awaiting trial warned: 'In no way will you wear prison clothes. In no way will you work for the prison. Always remember that you are political prisoners and no one can take this from you. Any man who wears prison clothes will automatically be disowned by us, the political prisoners of the UDA. You have full backing from your comrades here in Long Kesh.'

While the countdown to abolition day continued, a range of reaction from violence to international propaganda was being planned. Meanwhile the prison authorities and the inmates remained still embroiled in confrontation and sporadic clashes over the extent of compassionate parole, the quality of food and laundry and, a new issue, strip searching – the sometimes intimate body searches which were vigorously opposed by prisoners. During August 1976 there were three incidents at Magilligan prison when prisoners overpowered prison officers in the compounds and stripped them naked. In a statement smuggled out afterwards, they said the officers 'were not ill-treated or intimidated, merely informed that the action taken was not directed at them personally but at the whole corrupt prison system which they represented.' The intention was not to degrade the officers but to have them experience the unpleasantness of the strip-search procedure, the prisoners added.

But at the heart of the tension was the looming end to special category. There was, predictably, serious and destructive rioting in the Republican and Loyalist heartlands of Belfast and elsewhere overnight on 29 February/1 March when the ending of special category eligibility for new offenders actually came into force. In a major escalation of the protests, Edward Truesdale, whose brother Robert was then governor of Belfast prison, was taken at gunpoint from the car showroom where he worked and held for eight hours with a bag over his head. The Ulster Freedom Fighters said he had been well looked after, but that 'this may not always be the case for future kidnap victims if political status is ended.' At the same time the IRA's Belfast Brigade issued another warning that prison officers and their families were 'legitimate targets. From today all those involved in the imposition of the British de-politicisation policy in prisons here will have to bear the consequences of their actions. Only prison welfare workers, chaplains and medical staff are exempt from IRA action.' The warning came as a determined war of intimidation against named individual officers was being waged in Provo publications, notably the weekly newspaper *Republican News*. The warning and the campaign did not create undue alarm at first, but just over five weeks later the threat was fulfilled when the Provisional IRA violently propelled prison officers into the front line of the conflict by murdering two of them in quick succession.

On 8 April, Pacelli Dillon, 36, a Basic Grade Officer who had only been in the service for seven months and worked at Magilligan prison, was shot dead outside his home in Loughmacrory Park, Mountfield Road, Carrickmore, County Tyrone. He had left the house at about 2.15 pm that afternoon to travel to nearby Omagh to make arrangements about a new house he was intending to buy in the town. Moments after he went outside, he was confronted by two gunmen who fired at close range, hitting him twice in the head and neck and twice in the body. His wife Teresa, mother of their five children who were aged from one year to eight (one of them crippled and blind from birth), heard the shots and thought they were a vehicle backfiring. She ran outside and found her husband slumped dead by the side of the car. Later that afternoon, the burned-out shell of a white van, earlier hijacked at gunpoint to convey the killers, was found near Carrickmore, a strongly Republican village. In paying tribute to the dead man, Rees said his murder was 'a tragic example of blind gangsterism. The men and women of the prison service perform an invaluable service for society against criminality; to attack them is to attack the community as a whole.' For a few days after the murder, colleagues of the dead man restricted parcels and visits to Provisional IRA inmates at Magilligan prison.

The Provisional IRA was undeterred by the widespread condemnation of the killing. Eleven days later they struck again. About 8 pm on 19 April, John Cummings, 55, a clerical officer who had prepared staff wages at Belfast's Crumlin Road prison for eleven years, did not wear uniform and had no contact with prisoners, was watching the Morecambe and Wise comedy show on television at his home on the fourth floor of a block of flats in the suburb of Dunmurry, on the southern outskirts of Belfast. His wife later described how he was laughing as he went to the front door to answer a knock and how she heard a scuffle as he was rushed by two teenage gunmen. When she went to see what was happening, one put his hand over her mouth and held her while the other forced her husband into their bedroom and fired three shots. After they fled, she found him lying in a pool of blood and he died almost immediately in her arms. The same evening, when the shifts at Belfast prison were changing over, three gunmen fired a hail of shots at departing officers from a parked car which was then driven off at speed. A police patrol gave chase and an officer on foot tried to intercept the getaway car by firing a shot at it but he had to jump clear when it was driven at him. Outside the prison one officer lay on the ground, seriously wounded. Fortunately he was the only casualty.

When news of the killing was broadcast later that evening, prisoners in the Maze cheered loudly. The 1900 prison officers, shocked by the violent turn of events, immediately imposed a ban on visits and the receipt of food parcels for Provisional IRA prisoners in all prisons. Speaking at the funeral a few days later, the Reverend G Temple Lundie, Moderator of the Presbyterian Church, who had been a prison chaplain for over 25 years, said, 'The work of a prison officer is never an easy or pleasant task. He has to deal with those who have rebelled against society, who have broken the laws by which society exists, and who have ruthlessly followed their own violent and selfish purposes. It would be natural that in such circumstances, prison officers should become hardened and harsh with those who are committed under them.'

Ken Daniels, the national leader of the Prison Officers Association, had travelled to Belfast for the funeral and he later visited Belfast prison and the Maze, where he met his local officials and talked to members of the staff. Feelings were still running extraordinarily high, and especially among some of the younger, more militant short service officers the restrictions had escalated into a totally unrealistic demand that the government abolish special category status altogether. At the Maze 400 out of the 600 officers were reported to be in favour of this position.

There was also an overwhelming demand that, like the police and members of the locally recruited Ulster Defence Regiment, they should be issued with permits to carry firearms for personal protection when off duty. The protest solidified throughout the prison system and even spread to the secure ward in the heavily guarded military wing at the Musgrave Park hospital in Belfast, where prisoners undergoing medical treatment were confined. Branch votes in each of the prison establishments defied the advice of their leaders and formidable official pressure to restore the visits and food parcels for IRA prisoners. At the height of the protest, which brought Republican demonstrators on to the streets calling for a restoration of prison privileges, lawyers acting for a remand prisoner in Belfast invoked a twelve-year-old Act to force the Governor to comply with prison rules and allow the prisoner his statutory one hour of exercise a day. At the Maze a number of women visitors staged a sit-in and had to be forcibly removed after being denied access to relatives. Another attack on a prison officer at this time – shots were fired through the front door and window of his home but nobody was injured because the family were all out – underlined the direct danger prison staff now faced. Indeed some officers from Catholic backgrounds, living in isolated rural areas, moved away from their homes as a precaution and temporary 'safe houses' for threatened staff were established at a couple of locations, including the training complex at Millisle, County Down.

After three weeks of negotiations between the Northern Ireland Office and the national leaders of the Prison Officers Association, the rank and file officers in each of the prisons finally voted to end the sanctions against prisoners. The government reiterated that special category was to be phased out and there were no public assurances about their safety but it was agreed privately that those who felt at risk could apply for a firearm in the normal way and that, subject to a police assessment of the risk, approval would be given. However, it very firmly remained official policy that personal protection weapons could only be carried off duty and armouries were soon established in the prisons for the safekeeping of firearms while officers were on duty. Later in the year, after a complaint about the prison officers action by Frank Maguire, the MP for Fermanagh and South Tyrone, the Ombudsman – the Commissioner for Complaints – ruled that there were 'mitigating circumstances' for the protest although special category prisoners were denied their rights.

There was new controversy after yet another serious escape on 5 May when nine prisoners, from the breakaway group the Irish Republican Socialist Party, escaped from the Maze by crawling along a fifteen-yard tunnel, cutting through a security fence and climbing over the newly-built twenty-foot perimeter wall, using ropes made from sheets and blankets. The men had been counted and locked up at 9.30 pm the previous evening and were only discovered missing after the roll-call early the next morning. Although one escapee was recaptured promptly in the fields between the M1 motorway and the A1, the main Belfast-Dublin cross-border road a short distance away, the others were thought to be long gone by the time the alarm was raised. In response to questions from MPs, Rees was forced to admit that disciplinary action was being taken against some members of staff on duty that night. Although he did not confirm it publicly, the shaft used to facilitate the escape had been discovered earlier during routine army searches, but while the ends of it had been sealed the tunnel itself had not been filled in.

By the standards of what had been going in the prison system in recent years, the summer of 1976 was comparatively uneventful. The Republican and Loyalist organisations engaged in an intensified propaganda broadside to highlight the inadequacies of their conditions in the Maze and their case for retaining full prisoner-of-war status. Their argument ran that, because of special legislation, the emergency powers and interrogation procedures available to the police, and the special courts, where a single judge presided without a jury, they were entitled to special status when convicted and sent to prison. In July, at the Maze, there was a potentially murderous incident when UDA prisoners broke out of their compounds and attacked a prison van carrying UVF inmates back from the visiting centre. The targets of the attack were two prisoners, awaiting trial for their alleged involvement in the murder of UDA members during feuding between the two organisations the previous year, but they were not in the van. Although the confrontation quickly subsided, the prison authorities said the Army was going to carry out a strip search of all those involved. The prisoners immediately threatened 'a riot to end all riots' and, again underlining the full extent of the prisoner power that then existed, the authorities backed down although, at a strategic level, there remained unyielding commitment to the phasing out of special category.

The same month, Rees escaped assassination in Dublin when the IRA detonated a massive landmine in the path of a car carrying Christopher Ewart-Biggs, the British ambassador to the Irish Republic, who had only been in the post for a short time. The ambassador and a female private secretary, Judith Cook, were killed instantly and Brian Cubbon, the most senior civil servant at the Northern Ireland Office, was seriously injured. If it had not been for the necessity to stay in London for a parliamentary vote, Rees himself would have been with them. The attack, and the fact that the Provisional IRA had clearly expected Rees to be in the vehicle, pointed to the high stakes that were now in play over the coming prisons confrontation.

Throughout that summer a number of people captured after the cut-off date were on remand in custody awaiting trial. Once one of them was convicted he would be denied special category, and instead of being consigned to one of the 21 Maze compounds he would instead become the first inhabitant of H1 in what had been designated Maze Cellular, a prison within a prison, with its own Governor and staff and its own rules. But before events came to a head, Rees left Belfast on transfer to become Home Secretary on 10 September and was replaced by Roy Mason, a pugnacious former miner from Barnsley in South Yorkshire, who had some first-hand knowledge of the situation in Northern Ireland from his former job as the Minister of Defence. Four days later, on 14 September, after a hearing at the Belfast City Commission, eighteen-year-old Kieran Pius Nugent was sentenced to three years' imprisonment for an offence committed on 12 March, twelve days after the special category cut-off date, thus making him the first convicted prisoner to be ineligible for special category. Sinn Fein and the Relatives Action Committee, set up to spearhead the campaign to retain political status, promptly promoted his coming fight as being not 'the sacrifice of a criminal but the dedication of an Irish patriot'.

Nugent, easily recognisable with his distinctive bright ginger hair and moustache, was hardly a first-division patriot or even terrorist. If anything he was a merely an unfortunate child of the troubles. He lived with his parents in a terraced house at Leeson Street in the Lower Falls area of Belfast, one of a family of ten, and had been unemployed since leaving school in 1973. In February that year he was convicted for disorderly behaviour and given a conditional discharge for two years. Shortly before he had been wounded in a shooting incident on the Grosvenor Road, sustaining gunshot wounds in the chest, arms and back when fired on from a car whose occupants had first stopped to ask directions. His friend, Bernard McErlean, aged sixteen, was killed. The gunmen were almost certainly Loyalists, probably UDA, and it is probable that Nugent and his friend may have been acting as IRA lookouts or vigilantes. Whatever the exact truth, and it has never been conclusively established, the incident brought Nugent to the notice of the security forces and his home was raided and searched on a number of occasions. Early in 1975 he was arrested and eventually interned until 12 November that year. On 12 March 1976, a plumber was loading his green Commer van at a scrapyard on Cullingtree Road, a few streets away from Nugent's home, when it was hijacked and driven away. Soldiers recovered the abandoned van later that afternoon. Nugent was arrested and charged after a chase through the Divis Flats complex during which he jumped from a fifth-floor level, breaking both legs, which left him with permanent injuries. According to Sinn Fein's evasive version of his life and times, he was unable to wear shoes or boots, and was always shod in sandals until his death (apparently as a result of alcohol poisoning) in May 2000. When he was convicted in 1976, Lord Justice McGonigal, sentencing him, said that while hijacking may not in itself be a serious crime, it should be remembered that terrorists often required some preparation before committing serious crimes, and stealing a car was often part of this.

In 1979, in an interview with the Revolutionary Communist Group's publication 'Hands off Ireland' after his release, Nugent recalled what happened when he was taken from the court in Belfast to the Maze prison.

'On remand in Crumlin Road jail we decided among ourselves that something was going to have to be done. It was a very funny thing too because it was the screws who stripped us of our clothes and it was them who gave us the blankets, so effectively they set off the blanket protest – they gave us what is now the symbol of the H-Blocks.

'It all started when I went into the [Maze] reception and the screw asked me: "What size clothes do you take?" I refused to answer. I said: "I'm not wearing your gear." He said: "You can't do this here." He was astonished. So he went to get the Principal Officer. I was manhandled a bit and then he put the prison clothes in a brown bag and said: "Right, carry it." I refused to lift it so he had to carry it himself. They drove us up to H1 Block. When we arrived in the H-Block there were about nine or ten screws there. This was in the main administration part of H-Block. They stood me against the wall and punched me about a bit, and then they grabbed me and ran me about twenty or thirty yards into one of the wings – D Wing. They pushed me into one of the cells and told me to put the uniform on. I said: "No, I'm not putting that gear on." So they said "Right, take your own clothes off." I refused, so then they jumped on me and forcibly removed my clothes, and held me down and punched me about. One of them then threw a blanket at me – so in fact he started the protest.

'The cell at that time had nothing in it at all. I got a wee bit of food and water at night about five o'clock. That was all until five o'clock the next night. They kept up a barrage of banging and kicking the doors the whole night. Then they came up with a new idea. I was the only man in this block, which had approximately a hundred cells. They decided that they would have two cells for me – a day-time cell and a night-time cell. So at 7.30 or 8 o'clock at night they put me in a cell with a bed and a mattress and blankets in it. There was no furniture in the other cell – it was an empty cell. So every morning at 7.30 or 8 o'clock they took me to this empty cell, and at 8 o'clock at night they took me back to the cell with the bed in it. It happened on two or three occasions that I ended up not getting a bed at all – I had to stay on the floor all night. While I was in the cell with nothing in it they patrolled the place all the time and every time I sat on the floor they opened the door and got me off the floor, standing between two of them. This continued for a very long time.

'Then a P.O. said I could be his number one orderly and offered me concessions if I would put the prison clothes on. I just refused to answer him. This went on for weeks and weeks. At that time too – in September and October – it was pretty cold. You're entitled to an hour's exercise a day, so I said that I would go out because two of the screws had to go out with me. It was just to take them out with me because they hated it. So I used to go out with only a blanket on and walk round for about an hour in the mornings. It was often raining pretty hard but they were out with me. This went on for about six to eight weeks, then they stopped it. They said: 'We won't exercise you until you wear a prison uniform.' I refused to do this.

'The protest went on and other men kept joining in. At this time I was in H1. Then they moved myself and three others to H2. I got moved there about November. All this time the food was very bad. They would give you just one slice of bread a day. Sometimes you got tea, sometimes you didn't. It all depended on whether they wanted to give it to you or not. You ate every meal with a spoon: they wouldn't give you a knife and fork – not that there was any need for a knife and fork. They wouldn't give you salt, sugar or sauce which every prisoner is entitled to. They kept up a steady barrage of brutal attacks on prisoners. Prisoners were assaulted daily – maybe two or three times a day. They were dragged out naked and indecently searched and subjected to degrading treatment. But as time went on more and more prisoners joined the protest.'

What would turn out to be years of protest had begun. The scene was set for what was to become one of the most enduring and acrimonious confrontations between terrorism and government in the entire history of the twentieth century.

Chapter Nine
The slums of Calcutta

Two days after he was imprisoned in the Maze, Nugent put on the dreaded grey prison uniform, blouson-style jacket and trousers, so that he could receive a visit from his mother. During the encounter he apparently said that the British would have to 'nail the uniform to his back' to keep it on. The phrase was promptly added to the Sinn Fein database of emotion-stirring propaganda. After that, they said in a newspaper advertisement, he was confined to a cell 24 hours a day, stripped naked save for a rough prison blanket, deprived of his mattress by day, forcing him to sit on the cell floor, and denied letters, visits and parcels, with the Bible, one to each cell, his only reading.

The preparatory protests that had begun well before Nugent reached the Maze now intensified. While the central focus was on the ending of political status, there were subsidiary concerns, shared by Republicans and Loyalists, that the new era of criminalisation also involved a gen-erally tougher regime being introduced. They were right. Strip searching, for instance, was increasingly being used as part of a crackdown to impose more control over the special category prisoners and their activities and to tighten security to curb the incessant wave of escape planning, although most of it was spectacularly unsuccessful. Prison officers believed that it was only the certainty that some of them would be shot by the armed military sentries in the watchtowers dotted around the prison and at intervals along the perimeter walls, that inhibited the increasingly difficult inmates from staging more escapes, even a mass breakout.

At Belfast prison, in line with the new cellular regime prohibiting factional segregation, Republican and Loyalist prisoners awaiting trial were being held in the same remand accommodation. The new policy also benefited the hard-pressed police and army. Every day they had to form guards to escort convoys, moving an average 100 prisoners, between the prisons and the courts. The task was all the more complicated because prisoners from opposing factions could not be placed in the open-plan prison vehicles used to transport them. But with the first of a new fleet of purpose-built vans, each with eighteen individual cubicles, going on the road, the number of daily convoys was quickly cut, reducing the constant risk of an ambush designed to free prisoners, and enabling some police and soldiers to be redeployed to other duties.

These developments were all fully exploited by both factions in an attempt to create a sense of crisis over the prisons issue, reflecting the high degree of cooperation between the two apparently warring sides. An incident a few days before Nugent arrived in the Maze prompted the Ulster Freedom Fighters, a Loyalist grouping associated with the UDA, to echo the IRA by issuing a specific threat that prison officers and their families were legitimate targets unless there was an independent inquiry established. They claimed that masked prison officers with riot shields and batons invaded the compounds to remove prisoners by force, who were not armed and who then suffered brutal treatment. According to the Northern Ireland office, UDA prisoners violently attacked prison officers who moved into three compounds to transfer prisoners. In one of the compounds, prisoners armed with wooden and metal clubs attacked the officers and in subsequent clashes 32 prisoners and six prison officers were injured. Trouble immediately flared outside. 21 vehicles were hijacked and fifteen, including nine buses, were set on fire. In addition there were four arson attacks on business premises and six incidents where petrol bombs were thrown. There were ugly clashes at the Maze when about 100 Loyalist protestors, mostly women, arrived outside the prison in buses, took over the gate giving access to the visiting centre and prevented visitors going in to see Republican inmates. But the most sinister element of the outburst was a concerted series of attacks on prison staff. Shots were fired at the home of one officer, hoax bombs were left outside the dwellings of six others and two more officers were taken from their homes at gunpoint during the night and warned not to report back to work at the Maze.

As part of its crackdown to regain proper control of the prison institutions, the Northern Ireland Office had also recently decided to fight fire with fire by taking a then unprecedented proactive stance in explaining and defending penal policy, which thanks to the growing agitation was assuming equal importance with the more established battlegrounds in the Northern Ireland conflict. So, for the first time, it entered forcefully into the propaganda war which the prisoners and their support groups had hitherto monopolised. Photographs of weapons seized in the compounds were published to 'illustrate the lengths to which some prisoners are prepared to go' and the conduct of staff was strongly defended as being 'disciplined and proper in all circumstances'.

For the first time, too, a statement was made on behalf of the prison officers stressing their commitment to carrying out their duties impartially and in strict accordance with prison rules. 'Threats have been made by various factions against prison staff and in some cases carried out. However, we would like to make it clear that we shall not and cannot be deflected from the responsibility placed on us by the community. Prison officers do a difficult task on behalf of the community. They deserve the wholehearted support of the community.'

Shortly afterwards, on 8 October, the Provisional IRA murdered the third prison officer that year. That evening, just after 7 pm, Roy Hamilton, 29, a bachelor, who worked at Magilligan, pulled his car up outside his mother's home at Grosvenor Road in Londonderry. As he got out of the vehicle his three IRA killers shot him six times in the chest before escaping in a stolen car. He was declared dead on arrival at the Altnagelvin Hospital. As a mark of their outrage, prison officers at all four institutions again banned visits, parcels and letters until after his funeral. A month later the IRA again attacked prison officers. This time four officers were collecting goods for the prison tuck shops from a cash and carry warehouse at Dunmurry, south Belfast, when two men emerged from a car and opened fire on them. The gunmen escaped at speed in a car driven by a third man, which had been hijacked a short time earlier from a bar in the IRA's west Belfast heartland. One of the officers and a security guard at the warehouse were shot and seriously wounded.

With another dozen Republican prisoners having quickly followed Nugent into the new H-blocks and 'on the blanket' because of their refusal to wear prison clothing, and more coming down the pipeline behind them every week, the IRA renewed its threat against prison staff in the front page story of its weekly *Republican News* on 27 November. 'It is they who have forced the men into naked solitary confinement, forced them to live as caged animals. It is they who shall presently pay while they remain a party to this agreement. If need be, the Belfast Brigade will instruct its units for a mobilisation and concentration on this one issue.'

With their sense of grievance being so menacingly fostered by Republicans and Loyalists, the growing confrontation between the government and the paramilitaries was aired in many different ways through the autumn and winter. Prisoners appearing in the Belfast courts regularly shouted protests about conditions at the magistrates or judges. One morning after fighting between prisoners and police in the dock, the magistrate had to adjourn proceedings for two hours. Another morning there were undignified scuffles when police were ordered to remove a pregnant woman from the courtroom after she applauded protesting prisoners and shouted obscenities. Later a Republican prisoner, in the dock to face a charge of armed robbery, set his clothing alight and shouted, 'This is a protest against the withdrawal of political status.'

There were more instances of prison officers being stripped and humiliated. In one case, fourteen women, relatives of Loyalist inmates, overpowered two officers supervising visits at the Maze. Their clothes were pulled off and then a man stepped forward and photographed them in their underpants. After one of the stripping clashes at Magilligan prison, for which members of the Board of Visitors used their powers to discipline a prisoner, two visitors were later assaulted and forced to remove some items of their own clothing.

During the period between June and August, as part of their wider protest, 94 Republican prisoners refused the offer of a week's summer parole. The scheme, unique to Northern Ireland, had been introduced in 1955 to enable prisoners temporary leave in the summer and at Christmas to re-establish family contacts and deal with domestic problems. It also helped to prevent longer term prisoners becoming institutionalised. The terms of the parole had always been respected and, over the years only one young offender had failed to return on time. In 1975, 202 inmates, including 122 special category prisoners, had taken summer parole but in 1976 only Loyalists and ordinary criminals among the 220 eligible prisoners had benefited.

As the turning-point year of 1976 drew to a close, there was only stalemate in the prisons and every sign that, with both sides uncompromisingly committed to their positions, the confrontation would only worsen. Not surprisingly the Republican prisoners turned down Christmas parole, although Loyalist special category inmates numbered about half of the 98 temporarily freed. Shortly before Christmas a large number of 'Republican prisoners of war' at 'Long Kesh concentration camp' were listed in an advertisement in the Belfast morning newspaper, the *Irish News*: 'We the undersigned wish to express our unswerving determination to ensure that the political status which is ours by right will be retained for all Republican POWs. We express our total condemnation of those politicians and organisations attempting to bolster up this illegal, sectarian and undemocratic system. We pledge our undying opposition to the presence of British Imperialism in Ireland. We wish to extend our sincere gratitude to all those organisations and individuals who have during the past year supported Republican POWs everywhere. We wish you all a happy and holy Christmas.'

There followed lists of prisoners and their sentences, grouped by Cage and H-block. The Northern Ireland Office swiftly replied with its own advertisement: 'Prisoners of War? Who are they kidding? Of the convicted criminals whose names appeared in a newspaper advertisement on Wednesday 22 December 1976, 29 were convicted of murder, 31 of attempted murder, 71 of firearms offences, 134 of explosives offences, 29 of robbery and 31 of other offences. These men want special status for their friends. No way: they'll pay and they'll stay.'

The same day, underlining what it professed to be its humane approach to the situation, the Northern Ireland Office published the Christmas Day menus for each of the four prisons. At the Maze breakfast was Weetabix and milk, bacon, fried potato bread, fried egg, bread, margarine and tea or coffee. Lunch was tomato soup followed by roast turkey and stuffing, grilled sausages, roast and creamed potatoes, sprouts, diced carrot and gravy, followed by Christmas pudding with rum sauce. Orange juice was also served. For tea there were assorted cold meats (cooked ham, ox tongue and corned beef) with cheese, mixed pickles, bread, margarine, tea or coffee and Christmas cake. Supper was drinking chocolate and assorted biscuits. Similar fare, with minor variations, was offered to the 2667 prisoners in custody at that point, 1159 of whom were special category (689 Republicans, 470 Loyalists). That year it cost over £70 a week to feed and guard each of them.

At the beginning of 1977, there were five H-blocks complete and the final three were under construction. By May, with the prison population up to 2800 and 109 male and ten female prisoners (the latter lodged in Armagh) refusing to wear prison clothes or work, the average cost of keeping each prisoner had soared to £120, mainly due to the labour-intensive design of the blocks and the need for large numbers of officers to maintain supervision and security around the steadily expanding Maze complex. Official figures also disclosed that the average salary for prison officers had risen to £10,000, much of it accounted for by long hours of overtime working.

With such a rapidly expanding workload and a high staff turnover despite the good pay – one in three officers resigned in 1976 – finding sufficient manpower to cope required constant effort. The age span, previously 21–45, was increased to an upper limit of 50, and there was constant and costly recruitment advertising by the Northern Ireland Office. In a typical week there would have been six 30-second commercials on Ulster Television, 25 spots on Downtown Radio and advertisements in about fourteen regional and local weekly papers.

'Why should I make the prison service my career?' asked the potential recruit.

'Because it's a great job. Let me tell you why,' replied the peak-capped prison officer. Using a comic-strip the advertisement showed the man telling his wife and child that there was job security and a pension; free housing or a rent allowance; training on full pay and a free uniform. In uniform now, he learned he could specialise as a hospital or clerical officer or a dog handler and that there was opportunity for advancement to higher grades.

'I enjoy the comradeship of fellow officers and I can earn £80 a week without overtime,' the new officer enthuses.

The financial package was certainly attractive: roughly twice what a firefighter or ambulance driver earned. While basic pay at this time was £39.20 for a 40-hour week, it was boosted by £3 a day 'danger' money, 12.6 per cent disturbance allowance for shift working, £6.60 for every weekend worked, a weekly rent allowance of £8 and 8.9 pence a mile travel allowance. 'Detached' officers, temporarily seconded to Northern Ireland from Britain, received a further £50 bounty monthly. It is said that one English officer who spent four years in Northern Ireland was able to return home and buy a hotel for £16,000. But the advertising did not portray the downside of the job. Apart from the growing danger and fear, prison officers recall the crushing boredom of the long hours and the constant intimidation and harassment from prisoners seeking to de-stabilise and unnerve them. There was also a more frequent resort to violence. One female prison officer who was attacked by a number of IRA women prisoners in Armagh jail was off for fifteen weeks on sick leave and then quit the prison service.

Sam Irwin, who joined the prison service in Britain before coming home to Northern Ireland after the troubles began, says, 'If you can relate to people and get on with people, then you'll get on in the Prison Service.' He continues:

'You were in constant contact with inmates, you were surrounded by inmates, you were bombarded by some of their thinking and all that sort of thing, and it can have an effect on people, and it did affect people. It turned people from law-abiding into criminals. You're living so closely with prisoners and it can creep up on you.

'The problem for the Prison Officers was, of course, they tried to bring you down to their level. One of the things I found in the prison was the language, foul, obscene language. And unfortunately some Prison Officers, to make themselves understood and to get things down, came down to that level too. Now the prisoner set out to bring you down to their level. Once they got you on their level then to them

Staff Parade, Crumlin Road prison, Belfast, *c.* 1950.

Main entrance gate, Belfast prison, *c.* 1965.

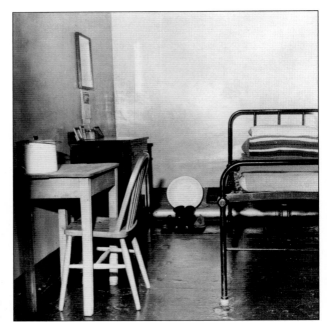

Standard cell, Belfast prison, throughout 1950s and 1960s.

Below: Long Kesh Internment Centre.

Aerial view of the Maze prison after the fire of 1974.

Maze prison, perimeter wall.

Maze prison, internal roadway.

H-block, architect's drawing.

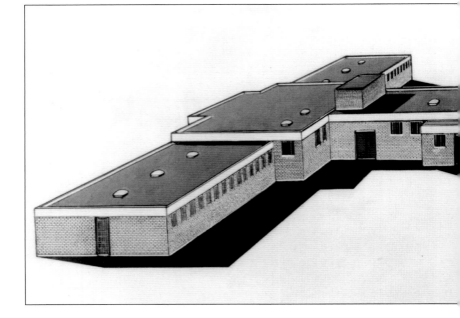

Aerial view of H-blocks.

Standard cell,
Maze H-block
c. 1977.

The 'dirty protest'.

Steam cleaning a cell during
the 'dirty protest'.

Protest march during the hunger strikes.

Loyalist mural, Maze prison.

Republican mural,
Maze prison.

Inside an H-block,
Maze prison, 1998.

you were no different. And the success of a Prison Officer who ran a good landing and kept discipline was the one who kept himself above all that. And all these evil people and notorious people – well you just dealt with them as individuals – but you didn't get in with them or that. You kept them at arm's length.'

The toll that the increasing stresses and strains were imposing on prison staff and their families was largely concealed from public view but, in a rare instance of outspokenness it was referred to at this time by the Reverend Bertram Livingstone, a Church of Ireland rector. He recalled the attractive television advertisement to recruit prison officers persuasively ending by showing a wallet of pound notes. 'What it does not say is that the prison service is going through a very bad patch. There is a very serious social problem being a prison officer.' Noting that many officers worked 29 out of 30 days, he continued: 'On the one day off they go and get drunk to get rid of the tensions and tiredness. Four out of five men on one shift crashed their cars on the day off within a short period of time.' The rector also referred to the problem of wives left all day with young families and the lack of provision for companionship and social life. 'This has resulted in two young women taking an overdose of pills. Three have had breakdowns in their marriages and three have left the country.'

At the time there were also some public glimpses of the situation emerging from the courts. Three prisons officers were fined between £100 and £160 each after behaving in what the resident magistrate said was an insulting, provocative and disorderly fashion in a bar at Moira, County Down in September 1976. The court heard how they were singing partisan songs and asking people their religion and then became involved in an assault with batons and bottles on a man and his two sons. A prison officer was fined £70 and disqualified from driving for five years after pleading guilty to possession of a loaded firearm and being drunk in charge of a vehicle in March in Bangor, County Down. In June 1977, a 27-year-old prison officer was given a two-year suspended sentence after accidentally discharging his legally-held firearm in a row with his wife. The flare-up came in the officers' club at Belfast prison when his wife slapped him across the face in front of colleagues after a row about the long hours he was working and her part-time job. He pulled his gun and was then disarmed by another officer but later, at their home, the gun was pulled again during a struggle and went off causing powder burns to her finger. Before his trial, the prison officer spent seven months on remand and was locked up for 22 hours a day for his own protection. The same month another court heard how two heavily intoxicated British prison officers serving in Northern Ireland, who had worked 344 hours in a 23-day period, had broken into their own social club at Magilligan and stolen over £1000 worth of drink and cigarettes. Both were fined. In another case a judge took a highly lenient view and dismissed charges against a prison officer who fired five shots from his legally-held gun during a violent row with his sixteen-year-old son about non-attendance at school in Bangor, County Down. The first shot was fired after the boy struck his father on the head with a poker and four more were discharged, although not directly at the boy, after he armed himself with a kitchen knife and confronted his father.

One experienced officer recalls the strains that were imposed:

> "When you went on duty you literally didn't know when you were going to get off again, because things blew up and you were maybe in prison for days before you got home. You didn't have the opportunity to switch off, and that was difficult. That is what led to the heavy drinking and irrational behaviour and the suicides. You had the Chief at the time saying now look you're going off at five o'clock but don't be going home. You go out there and get something to eat, I'm thinking now of the Maze, and of course there was a whole series of bars around the Maze. You could have got drunk, I'm sure, with one drink in each bar because you had all the Army Messes, Dog Section, Sergeant's Messes and you had our own officers' club. Then you had the wives ringing up. I used to always try and tell them, look, if you're going to the Club, ring the wife, let her know where you are, at least she'll know where you are. You see there was powerful pressure on the family and the wives at home. If they would do that then at least she knew that he was in the Club and if he didn't come home she would maybe ring somebody else and get him home. But it did put awful pressure on families, no doubt about that.'

The ongoing terrorist threats and direct attacks on the lives of prison officers and their families clearly intensified the personal pressures. In January, an army bomb disposal officer safely defused a booby-trap bomb attached to the underside of an officer's car while it was parked adjacent to Belfast prison. One night in March there was a wave of attacks on prison officers. An officer's wife, aged 24, suffered gunshot wounds to the neck after answering a knock at the door of their Belfast home. Scarcely 30 minutes later a small bomb exploded under a car owned by a prison officer while it was parked in the Shankill Road area.

Another officer's car suffered slight damage in a similar attack shortly afterwards. About the same time a number of companies supplying goods and services for the prison received a letter in the name of the Ulster Freedom Fighters warning them to sever all contracts because their companies were 'contributing directly to the system that has and is causing untold hardship to our comrades'.

The Provisional IRA suceeded in taking the life of another officer on 22 June. Wesley Milliken, 53, a Principal Officer at Crumlin Road and married with a grown-up son, was fatally wounded by a gunman who got out of a stolen Cortina car which pulled alongside him while he was walking home from work along Cliftonpark Avenue in Belfast. Six days later, the availability of a personal protection weapon undoubtedly helped save the life of another off-duty officer. That day, one of two men who came to see over his house, which was for sale at Oldpark Road, Belfast, pulled a gun. The officer saw them and fired a single shot through a window. The two potential killers, one of them wounded, fell over each other in their haste to escape and the uninjured one was captured a short distance away by an Army patrol. Almost exactly a month later, on 22 July, Graham Fenton, a Basic Grade Officer aged twenty at Magilligan, was shot dead by a gunman armed with a rifle who entered Molloy's Bar, near Ballymoney, and singled him out before firing nine times. A prison colleague was struck by two of the shots but survived the attack. Before the dead officer was buried at Ballyweaney Presbyterian Church, near Ballymoney, the Rev George Cromcy said there could be few careers more daunting and demanding than that of a prison officer. Their life had acquired a new dimension and they had become the target of terrorists. 'To the qualities needed for his normal work is added that of the courage of a front-line soldier or a member of the police or police reserve,' he said. 'His work is one of massive contradiction – to maintain human relations among men, some of whom show themselves less than human; to maintain some semblance of order and discipline of life, and to sustain their own ideals in an environment almost totally alien to the rooting or growth of honour and virtue.'

Desmond Irvine, aged 40, a Principal Officer at the Maze who was also chairman of the Prison Officers' Association, took part in a nationally broadcast television documentary programme the following September. The half-hour 'This Week' programme 'Life Behind the Wire' was broadcast on 22 September and examined the continuing problem of phasing out special category. Irvine said, 'One can think of wives who are now widows, children who are now fatherless and parents who have lost sons. That's the cost to the members of the Prison Service. We have paid for devotion to duty by the life blood of some of our members.'

In a subsequent letter to the programme makers he said, 'Congratulations have poured in from many sources including many messages from Great Britain. I was concerned about the reaction but there was praise from both staff and prisoners. I believe the programme will ease the burden borne by my members. To be told by the spokesman of the Provos they respected my frank answers to your questions and they would act in a reciprocal manner, gives me grounds for believing we are entering a new phase when co-operation between staff and prisoners will improve.' Before agreeing to take part in the programme at a time when only heavily guarded ministers were publicly speaking about the prison situation, Desmond Irvine remarked that those who might wish him harm already knew his identity and whereabouts, and that appearing in a television programme would add no extra risk to the risks he and his men ran every day. It was a bold and courageous initiative for which he paid a merciless price.

At 4.15 pm on 7 October, in Wellington Park Avenue, near Queen's University, Belfast, Irvine was shot dead as he drove out through the gates of the Public Service Alliance Headquarters (the Civil Service Union) where he had been attending a course. Two gunmen were involved. One opened fire from the other side of the street with an Armalite rifle; the other used a low velocity automatic weapon. His car windscreen was shattered as the victim was hit at least four times. Police found thirteen spent cartridge cases beside the car. The killers travelled in a van stolen earlier in west Belfast and accomplices held the driver and passenger hostage for several hours until the murder took place.

The Prison Officers' Association again imposed a ban on visits and parcels until after the funeral as a mark of outrage and respect. A Loyalist recently imprisoned for a double murder challenged the ban in the High Court, but Lord Justice Gibson dismissed the application for an injunction as being too vague and, noting the temporary duration of the ban, said that there was no evidence that any prisoner had been denied rights or privileges.

As 1977 closed there was still no sign of any break in the confrontation over the prison regime. The prisoners and the authorities remained in uncompromising deadlock on the issue and, despite the propaganda war being conducted by the two sides, there was little public concern or sympathy. Earlier in the year the *Belfast Telegraph* had noted in an editorial that 'what the protestors had failed to recognise is that people do not have the same sympathy for militants since the abolition of "political" crime. Paramilitaries are being charged with ordinary offences and cannot expect a special status in their communities.' But in the compounds and cells at the Maze and Magilligan and in Armagh, there was no lessening in the determination of the prisoners to continue waging their campaigns, not only for prisoner of war status but also for their wider beliefs. That Christmas, as a mark of solidarity with those 'on the blanket' in the H-blocks, 23 IRA and fifteen UVF prisoners among the 112 offered five days Christmas parole refused.

Republicans and Loyalists were now clearly deeply frustrated at the unyielding campaign of official attrition they faced. Outside in the community there was little sympathy or enthusiasm for their cause and, as evidenced by the large numbers of people being charged every month and queuing up to await trial, their ability to maintain the momentum of terrorism at its previously high levels was being significantly compromised. The number of deaths arising from the security situation had fallen steadily from a peak of 467 in 1972 to 112 in 1979. Over the same period the number of terrorist incidents had been reduced from 12,481 to 2224 while the number of persons charged with offences had soared from 531 to 1308. What was still going on was far from acceptable by any normal standards of law and order, but for Northern Ireland it represented widely welcomed progress.

Six weeks into 1978, the UVF renewed its demand for talks with the Northern Ireland Office about the special category issue accompanied by a chilling new threat to prison staff. Warning prison staff to 'pack their jobs in' or face 'serious physical retribution', the UVF Brigade Headquarters Staff described prison officers as 'lickspittles and lackeys' of the government. 'Is it worth the money to subject loyalist patriots to further physical abuse and hardships at the risk of losing your own life?' the statement asked. 'Before you decide whether or not to resign your job, think long of the physical pains you colleagues have inflicted on loyalist prisoners. Think long of the faceless men who expect you to don riot gear and beat loyalist prisoners and think long of your master, Roy Mason, sitting in Stormont surrounded by the might of the British Army for protection. What protection have you for the job you are given.'

Don Concannon, the minister responsible for prisons, assured the prison officers, during a statement in the House of Commons, that procedures and instructions had been drawn up to ensure their safety and protection. 'Neither money nor ingenuity will be spared in obtaining the best possible protection,' he pledged. At the same time the government was pressing on with its plans to put the prisoners in the system to constructive work. With some of the special category compounds in the Maze now unoccupied because of the release of short-term prisoners and the halt in new admissions, the huts were converted into workshops, and already woodworking and tailoring projects were underway. Furniture had been made and installed in the cells at a new Borstal for young offenders co-located with the prison service training college now formally established at Millisle. Prisoners were also at work tailoring and sewing items of the prison uniform that was so essential to the conventional prison regime the authorities were striving to establish. The authorities had also advertised for a £6000-a-year marketing manager to research and commercially exploit what products and services the captive prison labour force could provide.

In direct contradiction of these aims, the course of the ongoing protest inside the prison was significantly escalating. As Kieran Nugent recalls:

'We were in H1 and H2 until May 1977 and then got moved to H5. As soon as we got into H5 we were together – about 70-80 of us – and we reorganised. The screws didn't like that. Then we got the upper hand. Each wing had an OC – the men in that wing did what the OC told them to do. There was also a Battalion OC – a Block OC – who controlled the whole Block. Then all of a sudden men were getting removed to the punishment cells for nothing – taken there for the least wee thing. We got a shower once a week for five minutes. When we went out to the showers they were putting us against the wall and searching us, even though we only had to walk a few feet to and from the showers – what could you possibly have hidden in that space which they wouldn't have found before they started off with you? They were searching and kicking people about and brutally assaulting people. When you go up to the showers you go up to the slop-out as well, and when we were slopping out they were brutally attacking us and degrading us – like five or six screws round a naked man, making smart remarks, trying to degrade us, trying to boost their own morale.

'So we decided that this couldn't go on – we weren't prepared to take this treatment from anyone, especially screws. So we decided "OK, we're not going out." So we didn't go out. They then brought round plastic bowls with about half an inch of cold water in them for washing which were really stinking. We tried to use them but we just couldn't. They were coming round with a big plastic bin which they wheeled into your cell. They poured your pot into the bin and then pulled it out of the cell. Directly behind it was the food, and using the same gloves and protective clothing – and the gloves were really stinking – they were handling the food.

'This was late 1977 and into 1978. The screws were really starting to step up their harassment and we believe it came from British officials – to step up the harassment to break the protest. During the day they were coming in and kicking your pot over your mattress – the place was completely stinking. The only thing you had was a mattress and a blanket: we couldn't sleep in it – there were maggots running out of the blankets. So to save our beds and blankets – the only things we had – we decided to throw the slops out of the windows. But the screws went round the back and shoved it all back through the windows again – everything that was thrown out they threw back again, so it was all over the mattresses again. So we had no alternative but to put it on the walls – it was either that or on our beds and blankets. I would stress that we didn't like what we were doing: it wasn't self-inflicted – it was inflicted by others. We don't like living in those conditions – I don't think anybody would like living in those conditions – but it was forced on us: it was the only action we could take to save our own cells.'

This escalation, with prisoners smearing their own excrement on the walls of their cells with cubes of sponge ripped from their mattresses or strips of blanket, coupled with a refusal to wash or shave, was quickly dubbed the 'dirty protest'. Since lockers, beds, tables and chairs had been permanently removed from their cells in April, after a series of incidents when they were systematically broken up, prisoners now squatted on mattresses on the floor. The cells were otherwise bare and the only reading material was a bible. For the time being, however, far from sparking off any concern or sympathy for the prisoners, the dirty protest was instead widely condemned as grotesque and degrading. But at the beginning of August 1978 there was, for the government at least, a highly embarrassing intervention. On to centre stage strode Archbishop (later Cardinal) Tomas O'Fiaich, a blunt countryman from the border town of Crossmaglen, and a publicly committed Nationalist. After a pastoral visit to the Maze he issued a statement in which he said:

'Having spent the whole of Sunday in the prison I was shocked by the inhuman conditions prevailing in H-blocks 3, 4 and 5 where over 300 prisoners are incarcerated. One would hardly allow an animal to remain in such conditions, let alone a human being. The nearest to it that I have seen was the spectacle of hundreds of homeless people living in sewer-pipes in the slums of Calcutta. The stench and filth in some of the cells, with the remains of rotten food and human excreta scattered around the walls, was almost unbearable. In two of them I was unable to speak for fear of vomiting. The prisoners' cells are without beds, chairs or tables.

They sleep on mattresses on the floor and in some cases I noticed that these are quite wet. They have no covering except a towel or blanket, no books, newspapers or reading material except the Bible (even religious magazines have been banned since my last visit); no pens or writing material, no TV or radio, no hobbies or handicrafts, no exercise or recreation. They are locked in their cells for almost the whole of every day and some of them have been in this condition for more than a year and a half.

'In these circumstances,' [the statement continued,] 'I was surprised that the morale of the prisoners was high. From talking to them it is evident that they intend to continue their protest indefinitely and it seems they prefer to face death rather than submit to being classed as criminals. Anyone with the least knowledge of Irish history knows how deeply rooted this attitude is in our country's past. In isolation and perpetual boredom they maintain their sanity by studying Irish. It was an indication of the triumph of the human spirit over adverse material surroundings to notice Irish words, phrases and songs being shouted from cell to cell and then written on each cell wall with the remnants of toothpaste tubes.'

The Archbishop's furious outburst owed as much to what he regarded as an unreasonable snub by the uncompromising Roy Mason as to what he saw that particular Sunday. For some weeks before his visit he had been trying to persuade the Secretary of State to release a 70-year-old man suffering from terminal cancer so that he could die at home. The request had very recently been turned down and the Archbishop was visibly upset when he saw the elderly man, convicted with his son for possessing explosives, during his visit to one of the special category compounds. The episode signalled the width of the divide that had now opened up on the prisons issue, not just between the authorities and the prisoners, but between the more moderate nationalist community and the authorities. While the overwhelming majority roundly condemned IRA violence, there was a liberal ambivalence, which would intensify in the years ahead, about treating the perpetrators too harshly behind bars. Many members of the main nationalist party, the SDLP, took the view that deprivation of liberty was adequate retribution for crimes, however monstrous. The more broadly based stirrings of nationalist sympathy that rippled from the senior churchman's intervention revitalised the prisoners and those campaigning for them outside, gave new impetus to continuing the protests and clarified an important mindset that would crucially influence the way the protest developed and climaxed in the years ahead.

Liberal opinion was also stirred by the tough way Mason dealt with a pay claim from the prison officers the following October. The advent of the dirty protest, without known precedent in human history, created intolerable conditions for all involved. The Northern Ireland Office continued to stress the criminal calibre of the prisoners: of the 299 inmates on the protest in April, 74 were convicted of murder or attempted murder, 80 for firearms and 82 for explosives offences. It argued that as the appalling conditions were self-inflicted they would be ended at a stroke if the prisoners would conform and accept prison rules. But, as the Archbishop had pointed out, the Republican protestors were equally unyielding, their attitude being summed up by the slogan, 'Stone-Mason won't break us,' which appeared on walls and gable ends in several Republican areas.

For their part, the Loyalists were every bit as determined to regain political status and although they were pretty horrified by the IRA's tactics, they did not publicly disown them. Instead they chose to concentrate their campaign on the demand for segregation from Republicans which, if conceded, would have helped undermine the standard prison regime. Their demand was hammered home by frequent protest marches in Belfast with as many as 2000 people at a time taking part. From time to time the 200 Loyalists in the H-blocks also engaged in their own protest action, withdrawing cooperation from the prison staff and refusing to work, especially when given orderly duties which required them to clean cells used by Republicans.

The prison officers were thus 'piggy in the middle', as one later put it, having to deal directly with the distasteful consequences of the protest and the increasingly unkempt prisoners with their long uncut hair, unshaven beards and blankets draped round their bodies. In April, soon after the escalation, officers working in the H-blocks and dealing with the prisoners refused to bring or wear their uniforms home for hygienic reasons. Up to that point most officers had removed their caps and replaced their uniform jacket with an ordinary jacket or overcoat for the journey to and from work. As a result of the Loyalists' refusal to clean cells, the unpleasant task fell to the prison officers, and a routine soon developed where the 'dirty protesters' were periodically relocated in clean cells in another block to enable steam-cleaning to take place to maintain hygiene and prevent any infectious epidemic developing. As compensation for carrying out this task, the Prison Officers Association tabled a demand for an increase in their special allowance – 'danger money' – from £3 a day to £5. Not least because of its policy of restraining pay in the public sector, the financially hard-pressed government turned down the claim. Prison officers then slapped a ban on the reception of prisoners coming in from the courts, those returning from remand hearings or being transferred between prisons, and escorting prisoners to court, a course of action which brought them into direct confrontation with the courts and the government. Before long the police had to establish a temporary prison in army accommodation beside Magilligan – designated HMP Foyle – to hold prisoners denied admission to the prisons. The crisis came to a head when the High Court ordered the release of two prisoners who had been remanded in custody in their absence contrary to the existing law. Mason promptly used emergency legislative procedures to rush an order through parliament in London enabling prisoners to be remanded in their absence, incurring the wrath of some sections of the legal establishment with some insensitive remarks about alleged unprofessional sympathies with their clients. The dispute was defused and the prison officers lifted all industrial action at the beginning of November after the government agreed to refer their 'justified' claim for an increased special allowance to an independent national inquiry into the prison services throughout the United Kingdom, chaired by Mr Justice May. Their report was intended to set out a strategy for a more efficient and effective prison service and to bring an end to a period of deteriorating industrial relations in the prisons, especially in England and Wales.

Meanwhile, emphasising the extraordinarily difficult environment in which prison officers were working, the IRA's campaign against them continued. One off-duty officer narrowly escaped serious injury, although he sustained a leg wound, when a gunman fired several times at him through the front door of his south Belfast home on 24 September. On the evening of 26 November, Albert Miles, 50, was at home in Evelyn Gardens, off the Cavehill Road in north Belfast. He was listening to a country and western music programme on the radio in the kitchen getting ready to help his wife, Renee, make chutney with a new mincer she wanted to try out. Their 21-year-old son Alan, a Queen's University student, was on the telephone in the hall. When there was a knock on the door, Mrs Miles answered and was grabbed by the mouth by one of two unmasked gunmen who then shot her husband dead. The next morning Stanley Hilditch, the governor of the Maze, defiantly inscribed and signed the official prison journal in the red ink traditionally used to record serious incidents: 'Deputy Governor Albert (Bert) Miles was murdered last evening at approx 20.20 hours in the hallway of his home, and in front of his wife and son, by gunmen. His death is a great loss to me personally and the Prison Service generally and cannot be calculated in the compass of mere words. We will carry on in our task, as he did, with courage and determination in the face of provocation and danger from whatever quarter.' A couple of hours later, the IRA admitted the killing and said he had been shot dead for his role in disciplining prisoners in the H-blocks.

A week later, Kevin Artt was detained by the police and questioned for a week about the killing but he was released without charge. Three years later he was arrested again and, when confronted by detectives with the evidence of an IRA accomplice, broke down in tears and confessed to the murder and other serious offences in a lengthy statement. 'I have prayed many times for that man and for his wife. Why did it happen to me. I couldn't kill a dog but I killed that man. What is my wife going to think of me?' Showing detectives a scar on his wrist which he said was caused by broken glass from the door of the Miles home, he said, 'God gave me that scar. He gave it to me to remind me that I killed that man.' When Artt came to trial in 1983 he claimed that he had been subjected to inhuman or degrading treatment or torture and that the statement had been made under duress. Lord Justice Kelly rejected the claim and sentenced him to life imprisonment. Artt later escaped from the Maze prison and fled to the United States from where he continued to proclaim his innocence.

Three weeks after the Miles murder, on 11 December, John McTier, 33, a civilian clerk married with three children, was driving away from work at Belfast prison with two colleagues at about 6 pm. As they travelled round nearby Carlisle Circus, his car was overtaken by another and a gunman opened fire at them from inside. The back seat passenger and driver were both hit in the head and seriously wounded. The third occupant of the car, who was in the front passenger seat, was unhurt and later described how he first thought the sound of the shots was merely a car backfiring before he saw the other two slumped in their seats, bleeding from their wounds. Both were rushed to hospital where John McTier died three days later. (The other injured man survived, although he was off work for over two years as a result of his injuries.) The same day four parcel bombs, disguised as books and addressed to a dozen prison officers' families, were put into the Christmas post. In north Belfast, one officer's wife was injured when she opened the package, and across the city in Dundonald a postman received hand injuries when the device went off as he was putting it into a letter box. Two other wives were also hurt but after an urgent alert, broadcast over local radio stations, the others were detected and successfully defused by army bomb disposal experts. A few days later shots were fired into the home of a prison officer in north Belfast, narrowly missing a sleeping baby, and another officer escaped injury, although his car was destroyed, when a bomb attached to it exploded while he was driving from his home in Antrim to go on duty at the Maze. The Irish National Liberation Army acknowledged responsibility for this attack.

The inside front cover of the official journal of the Governor of the Maze for 1979 lists the continuing series of attacks on prison staff and their families as the seemingly intractable prison protest reached its third anniversary in September. The hand-written entries make grim reading, for that year nine serving and one retired officer were violently murdered as the IRA tried in vain, in what was a general election year in Britain, to shift the government from its criminalisation policy. It was a devastating low point for the service. The first casualty of the year was Patrick Mackin, aged 60, who died along with his 58-year-old wife, Violet, in their home at Oldpark Road, Belfast on the Saturday evening of 3 February. Their bodies were found the following morning when their son, an officer in the merchant Navy, arrived with his wife and two young children for a Sunday visit. The television was on, and the son found his father slumped in a chair and his mother lying dead on the floor, having been shot in the legs and abdomen during a desperate struggle for her husband's life. The IRA admitted the double murder a few days later and said that Mrs Mackin was an unintended victim. Her husband had retired two months earlier, having reached the rank of Principal Officer as head of the prison service training establishment at Millisle. A Liverpudlian, he had settled in Northern Ireland after the Second World War, during which he served in Africa and France, and had completed over 30 years service in Northern Ireland's prisons. The couple, he a Catholic and she a Protestant, were buried after a funeral service jointly conducted by a priest and a Presbyterian minister. (Gerard McClafferty, 22, was jailed for life in 1980 after admitting to police that he was the driver of the getaway car used by the killers.)

By this point the 1979 general election was under way in Britain. When the polls closed on 3 May the vote count overnight ejected James Callaghan's Labour government from office and propelled Britain's first ever woman prime minister into power. Margaret Thatcher promptly despatched Humphrey Atkins to Belfast to take over from Mason. He was not her first choice for the job. That had been Airey Neave, who was widely respected for his heroic exploits escaping from Nazi custody in wartime, but who perished at the outset of the election campaign on 30 March when the breakaway Republican group, the INLA, managed to plant a bomb underneath his car. It exploded while he was driving it out of the underground car park at the Houses of Parliament in London. By contrast with Mason, Atkins was a very relaxed figure who was largely content to take his policy cue from his officials rather than break any new ground himself.

Two more prison officers had died during the course of the general election. On 16 April Michael Cassidy, 31, an officer at Belfast prison for six years, was walking hand in hand with his three-year-old daughter Rosalynn in the grounds of St MacCartan's Catholic church at Ballinagurragh, near Augher, County Tyrone, after seeing his sister married. As he reached the car park a man with a rifle confronted him at close quarters. A single shot was fired, followed by six more from a second gunman. The officer was hit five times in the face, shoulder and trunk and died instantly. Another guest bravely tried to wrestle the rifle from one of the gunmen but failed. The dead man had survived a previous murder attempt at Christmas when shots were fired through the window of his home. Speaking at the funeral on 18 April, Dr Patrick Mulligan, the Bishop of Clogher, told some 500 mourners that the Cassidy family would always live with the suspicion that their own neighbours had played a part in the murder – 'had people they grew up with, and thought they could turn to in times of need, played a hand in this day?'

The morning after the funeral, four female prison officers collected their pay packets in Armagh jail and decided to treat themselves to lunch in the nearby Wagon Wheel pub. As they came out through the main gate complex at about 1 pm, they were chatting about how much they had earned that week and talked briefly to a group of five fellow officers before turning left towards the pub. They had scarcely covered twenty yards when 'a black Triumph car with the rear window removed pulled up beside them. A masked gunmen fired several shots at the officers from close range, killing Agnes Wallace, a 40-year-old mother of six who had only been a prison officer for three months, joining the service to 'take her out and have a bit of independence', her husband later said. The gunfire also injured her three colleagues before the terrorists lobbed a hand-grenade at the group and escaped from the scene. One of the injured officers was Mabel Hempson, 26, and if she had not already been felled by serious gunshot wounds in the chest, she would have died in the upward blast of shrapnel from the exploding grenade. She would never recover completely from her injuries and, to her lasting disappointment, was retired from the prison service two years later.

With a new government at Westminster, and a new Secretary of State at Stormont continuing Mason's uncompromising line on the prison protests and refusing to yield to threats and violence, the IRA chose the third anniversary of the start of the Maze blanket protest significantly to step up the violence against prison staff. On 10 September a prison officer escaped death when a bomb exploded under his car, parked in Landscape Terrace beside Belfast prison, while he was on duty. Four days later, four officers were returning the short distance to Belfast prison from the Buffs Club in Century Street, a regular lunch haunt, when their car was fired on from another vehicle. Eyewitnesses described how it was riddled with bullets and its windows shattered. The Maze Governor's journal bleakly records, 'Officer Foster dead; two officers injured; Officer Beattie uninjured. The dead officer, aged 30 and married with two sons of six and three years, had joined the service two years earlier after a spell as a soldier in the locally recruited Ulster Defence Regiment.'

It was only three days before the Governor had to record another death in his journal, the fifth of the year. 'Eddie Jones shot dead at lunch time at Agnes Street traffic lights,' he wrote without comment. Edward Jones, aged 60, who had been awarded the British Empire Medal, was an Assistant Governor at Belfast prison where he had served for some 33 years after wartime service in the Irish Guards. He was married with ten children and was probably one of the most widely known and popular members of a service that worked in a highly-controlled environment and had traditionally preserved its anonymity. His killers struck from a hijacked taxi while his car was halted at traffic lights beside the prison.

The two murders in the same location in quick succession deeply angered their colleagues who demanded far greater protection, including military patrols, for staff coming in and out of Belfast prison. They withdrew a threat to take industrial action, again disrupting the courts, on the promise of talks with the government about the security threat. However, a week later, before the talks had even taken place, the terrorists switched their attention to the Maze and fired on two officers coming off duty as their car traversed the Sprucefield roundabout a couple of miles from the prison. Neither was injured. On 13 October one officer was slightly injured when fourteen shots hit his car as he was travelling along the M1 motorway near Dungannon. Six days later two officers, again from Belfast prison, survived a murder bid, although one received gunshot wounds to his hand, when their car was ambushed and fired on in north Belfast.

The long-awaited report of the May Committee of Inquiry into the United Kingdom Prison Services was published on 31 October and was long on praise of the Northern Ireland prison officers. 'No one visiting penal establishments in Northern Ireland and meeting members' families can fail to be impressed by the remarkable calmness and determination of the men and women undertaking their duties. This is particularly so when it is borne in mind that these are duties which, although vital in any society, are bound to assume a special prominence in one where upholding the rule of law requires such peculiar tenacity.' Similar sentiments were expressed in the House of Commons by the Home Secretary, William Whitelaw, who referred sympathetically to the difficult conditions in which Northern Ireland officers had to work, and the Northern Ireland Secretary, Humphrey Atkins. 'Those who work in the prisons here have demonstrated a sense of duty and dedication to the job – sometimes in the most difficult circumstances – which should earn them the gratitude and respect of the entire Northern Ireland community.' (This was his first reference to the prison situation since taking up the Belfast posting.)

But the report singularly failed to meet the financial expectations of the Prison Officers Association despite recommendations which amounted to a pay rise of about a third. They had made a case for a 70 per cent increase, including the additional special allowance. The report said, "While we would not in any way wish to detract from the way in which Northern Ireland staff carry out their duty in very difficult circumstances we have to have regard to the fact that the allowance which they are now paid is more than three times the special duty allowance paid to the army and also over one and a half times the allowance of £500 per annum which the RUC receive. Taking all the considerations together, we have reluctantly felt bound to conclude that there is no sufficient case to justify increasing the daily emergency allowance from £3.30 to £5.00. Further, in view of the fact that the allowance is, at present rate, already considerably in excess of comparable allowances paid to the army and police, there is no case for either increasing it from its present level or changing the manner in which it is paid.'

One prison officer told the *Belfast Telegraph* that the tributes and words of thanks were fine, but 'if they think we're doing such a good job why don't they pay us a reasonable wage?' The prison officers' poor morale was dealt two more heavy blows within a few days. Just after 5 pm on 5 November, Thomas Gilhooley, 25, married with two children aged four years and ten months, was shot dead as he pulled into Landscape Terrace from a car park in the prison on his way home. The gunman had been waiting on the footpath and fired a shot through the car windscreen. When his victim slumped forward he walked closer and fired several more shots from point blank range. The dead man was originally from Scotland and a former soldier who left the Army and moved to Northern Ireland after meeting a local woman. The morning after the shooting the telex machines in Belfast newsrooms clattered out the customary statement of claim, this time accompanied by threats against four named officers. It was transmitted from the Sinn Fein and *Republican News* office in the Falls Road. 'We have been asked to issue the following supplied statement to our offices from Belfast Brigade, Irish Republican Army. 6-11-79. Belfast Brigade claims responsibility for the execution last night of the screw from Crumlin Road prison. This individual and others such as Sempy, Close, Huttley and Richie, to name but a few, have been involved in the beating and ill-treatment of POWs. Screws can rest assured that they will remain targets and will continue to die while they implement the barbaric penal policies of the Northern Ireland Office and the British government.' A day later at 8 am, David Teeney, aged twenty, a clerk in Crumlin Road prison, was shot dead while waiting at a bus stop in Clifton Street, virtually within sight of the prison. (Murder charges against two members of the INLA were dropped in 1980 after one pleaded guilty to possessing the guns used in the killing. He was imprisoned for ten years while the other was jailed for five years after admitting conspiring to communicate information about the victim.)

Speaking in defence of the two victims, the Reverend David Jardine, a full-time chaplain to the prison, accused the IRA of deliberate lies to justify the murders. Thomas Gilhooley worked in the reception dealing with relatives and had little contact with prisoners, while David Teeney was a wages clerk who never came into contact with them. 'They never ill-treated any prisoner,' he said. Prison officers, especially at Crumlin Road, which they now called Death Alley, were badly shaken by the two killings and the threats. The customary ban on visits and parcels after previous murders was now accompanied by a go-slow and work-to-rule, which caused delays in bringing prisoners before the courts, and there were tough talks between the Prison Officers' Association leaders and Northern Ireland Office officials and the security forces about improving protection for staff coming to and from the jail. A number of measures were quickly taken, including the introduction of undercover patrols, but the most visible was the construction of a fortified watchtower by the Army on 12 November. From there, military sentries could see up and down the Crumlin Road and along Oldpark Road, Agnes Street, Landscape Terrace and Cliftonpark Avenue, the immediate environs of the prison where the recent killings had taken place. Similar fortifications were quickly provided at the other prisons. At the Maze, cover-from-view screens, made from sheets of corrugated iron bolted to scaffolding, were built around the main gate and military patrols were deployed along the routes to and from the prison at the times when staff were coming and going to and from duty.

Despite the heightened security around Belfast and the other prisons, the Provisionals still managed to kill three more officers before the end of the year. They promptly changed tactics and attacked them at home, where they remained most vulnerable even though many were now being provided with alarm systems, bullet-proof doors and windows and security lighting. Gerald Melville, aged 45, serving in the Maze, was found shot dead at his Glengormley home on 24 November. Police broke in after midnight when colleagues at the prison raised the alarm after he failed to report for night duty at 10 pm. The dead man, a prison officer for seventeen years, lived alone. In a sneering statement the Belfast Brigade admitted responsibility and said, 'So much for the extra protection promised by the British for the mercenary services of the screws.' Their next victim died on 3 December. William Wright, aged 57, married with three children, was a Chief Officer at Crumlin Road and a veteran with 34 years' experience in the service and had been awarded the BEM. In the days before his death he was involved in planning the tighter security measures around the prison. He was ambushed and shot at his home in Lyndhurst Drive, Belfast while he was opening the garage door to put his car away after returning home from work. A year earlier he had narrowly survived a gun attack at his home and the previous September, in uniform, he had walked beside the coffin of his friend and colleague, Edward Jones.

Eight days before Christmas the Governor of the Maze entered yet another death in his journal, the ninth of the year and the seventeenth since the start of the H-block protest: 'Senior Officer Wilson shot dead outside Buff's Club at lunchtime.' Although two officers had been killed in a number of earlier shooting incidents in the vicinity of the club, and staff had been advised against using it after the recent spate of attacks in and around the prison, William Wilson, aged 58, defied the threat and continued his regular visits to the club, often walking the short distance as he did that day. As he reached the path at the front at about 1 pm a gunman fell in behind him and, just as he reached the steps of the three-storey building, fired several shots into his back. The dead officer had been a prison officer for 31 years and his son, one of his two children, had followed him into the service. The wave of killing, the most concentrated ever suffered by the prison service, continued into the new year. In the early evening of 18 January 1980 Graham Cox, 35, an officer at Magilligan, married with two children, was ambushed and shot dead on the main road between Limavady and Londonderry while on his way home from duty. His car went off the road, through railings and into a field where it lay until a fellow prison officer spotted it next morning on his way to work. (In March 1981, a nineteen-year-old man from Londonderry was jailed for life for the murder.)

Although they are not listed on the Prison Service's official memorials at Millisle or the Maze prison, about 50 prison officers have taken their own lives over the years, many with the handguns issued to them for their personal protection. Colleagues now recognise that they are as much victims of the conflict situation as those who lost their lives at the hands of terrorists. In that highly stressful year of 1979, two officers took their own lives. In January in Limavady an officer was found in his home with a gunshot wound to his chest, his legally-held firearm close by. He was rushed to hospital but died soon afterwards. Three months later in Belfast the body of a 24-year-old prison officer was found slumped in his car in a lay-by on Shore Road. He too had committed suicide with his legally held pistol.

Apart from so brutally targeting prison officers during 1979, the IRA also sought to make propaganda capital, at home and abroad, out of the release from prison of the first protestors to complete their sentences in the H-blocks. John Deery, a gangly 27-year-old from the Creggan area of Londonderry was first out at 8.25 am on 26 April. He would have been freed from his three-year sentence, for the possession of guns and ammunition, some eighteen months earlier in October 1977, if he had conformed to prison rules and not joined first the blanket, and then the dirty protests. It was another two weeks, until 11 May, before a long-haired and heavily bearded Kieran Nugent hobbled out of the prison gate clutching his possessions in a yellow plastic sack. He too had served his entire sentence, forfeiting his 50 per cent remission by leading the blanket and dirty protests. The night before his release, the Northern Ireland Office had tried to walk Nugent into their own pre-emptive propaganda strike by setting up an interview with one of the national television news programmes in a clean, furnished cell to counter what they correctly anticipated would be an unflattering account of his time in the Maze. Nugent, unsurprisingly, refused to cooperate and reserved his testimony for a well-trailed, Sinn Fein-hosted news conference later that day. For weeks prior to his release he had been coached in the prison, while outside Sinn Fein's wide-awake propagandists were planning to take him to Europe and, especially, the United States to whip up support for their political status campaign and to raise funds to promote it.

With the IRA so clearly making the running on the prisons issue, and taking the heat of the consistent condemnation of its tactics, the Loyalists were quite happy to sit back and let them do so. Andy Tyrie, the buccaneering Supreme Commander of the UDA, had said his men were prisoners of war and should be treated as such, but in an interview at the end of 1979 he menacingly reserved his position about prison officers: 'At this present time our policy is not to shoot prison officers but if we can make life a little uncomfortable for them without resorting to violence, we will do it. Some of the prison officers, not all, deserve what they get. It's no use telling lies about it. Some of them are animals.'

Whatever hopes the various paramilitaries had that the combination of intensified threat, violence and propaganda would at last provoke the overwhelming tide of public sympathy they wanted, or cause the British government to back down, were soon decisively dashed. Convinced by the fact that seven out of ten convicted persons coming into the prison system accepted the regime and conformed, and that a small number of prisoners were even coming off the blanket protest, the government believed that its unyielding stance was steadily grinding down the opposition to its policy. So, emboldened by this assessment, it decided to move to abolish retrospective special category for prisoners convicted of crimes before March 1976. Henceforth it intended that all new prisoners would go into the H-blocks, and that special category would soon disappear altogether, with the number of prisoners in the compounds steadily declining as they completed their sentences. In early 1980, there were 401 'special cats' (211 Republicans and 190 Loyalists), the lowest number for years. At this same point there were almost 400 protesting or 'non-conforming' prisoners.

But despite this toughening of its posture, the government was anxious and working secretly to find a face-saving formula not only to resolve the protests but also to pre-empt what it anticipated would be censorious remarks in a forthcoming adjudication from the European Convention of Human Rights. Although it was confident it would not be criticised on the fundamental point, the denial of prisoner-of-war status (or whatever else it might be called), Mason's unwillingness to be more conciliatory in tempering some of the conditions of the regime, to give the protesting prisoners a way out, was expected to be called into question. (The government had earlier modified the rules about regular cellular confinement and ended dietary punishment after legal advice that it could be in breach of the human rights convention.) Later they offered the prisoners pillows and bedsheets, which were quietly refused, and chairs, which were quickly smashed.

From the virtual outset of the protest there had, in fact, been discreet pressure on both the government and the paramilitaries from a variety of religious and political sources, and a series of mediation efforts. Thanks to obduracy on both sides, all had come to nothing. The most promising and influential dialogue had been initiated by Tomas O'Fiaich, since elevated to Cardinal, and Dr Edward Daly, the Catholic Bishop of Derry, soon after the Cardinal's angry 'slums of Calcutta' outburst in 1978. Since then the two senior churchmen had carefully monitored what was going on by making regular pastoral visits to all the prisons and talking to representatives of the prisoners. Early in 1980 they sensed a more flexible attitude from the government and, armed with the IRA's moratorium, had met Atkins three times in the early months of the year in a bid to broker a formula acceptable to both sides.

It was a particularly timely intervention. Atkins was increasingly uncomfortable about the local and international embarrassment the situation was causing for Britain. The signals from various sources all confirmed his analysis of wilting Republican and Loyalist determination to carry on, if a face-saving way out could be found. He was also anxious to blunt, if not forestall, criticism in the forthcoming human rights judgement. So on 26 March, adopting a new pragmatic, 'humanitarian' approach, he announced concessions in the form of additional visits and letters. The protesting prisoners would also be allowed to take exercise in physical training gear. A couple of days later, on 1 April, entitlement to special category for crimes committed before 1 Mar 1976 was formally ended.

The deal was put to the prisoners and their representatives but despite enduring what were undoubtedly appalling conditions, albeit largely self-imposed, the dirty protest prisoners immediately turned down the offer. In a bid to get their families to pressure them Michael Alison, the Minister responsible for prisons, wrote directly to their parents and next of kin to explain the new humanitarian measures. Atkins said they might have been misled by some of the reports which had appeared in the press about the new arrangements. The wounding of a 30-year-old prison officer in Newtownabbey on 21 May and the attempted murder of 48-year-old prison officer – who had survived a murder bid seven months earlier – outside his north Belfast home on 11 June, demonstrated Loyalists were far from content with the latest situation. That the initiative had indeed been finally rejected by Republicans, and the churchmen's negotiations had failed, was confirmed in an IRA statement next day. With Britain 'making no attempt' to resolve the protests, 'the unilateral decision' to halt attacks on prison officers 'to create the climate for a just settlement' was at an end. In a further sign of hardening positions, a conference in Belfast selected a thirteen-strong National H-Block Committee to steer a renewed campaign for the prisoners demands to be met. The main sticking points had been clothes and work. The prisoners would have accepted the equivalent of Category A top security status, which existed in British prisons for long-term inmates, and entitled prisoners to wear their own clothes. The work question could also have been resolved by accepting non-prison work, such as educational or training activity, as meeting the requirements of the prison regime.

The anxiously awaited outcome of the application to the European Commission of Human Rights seeking a declaration that Britain was in breach of Article of the European Convention of Human Rights which prohibits degrading or inhuman treatment finally came on 19 June. During the two years it had taken to wind its way through the legal process, Nugent, one of four prisoners taking the case, had put on prison uniform no less than 46 times to take visits from his lawyers to discuss it. But the ruling was, as the government correctly anticipated, a deep and fundamental setback for the prisoners. In a 105-page finding, the court decided that their conditions were self-inflicted and designed to create maximum sympathy and to enlist public support for their political aims which involved self-inflicted debasement and humiliation to an almost sub-human degree. But the British government's inflexible handling of the protest did come in for censure:

'It must have become clear to the prison authorities after a certain period that the applicants were not prepared to change their attitudes, to take exercise naked or to make use of prison facilities (such as the library or dining room) naked, or to wear prison uniform or underwear to see medical specialists. The result is that the applicants are confined to their cells on a permanent basis in conditions, though self-imposed, which must pose a significant threat to their physical and mental well-being. No doubt the authorities consider that to make concessions to the applicants will result in strengthening their resolve to continue their protest to a successful conclusion. However, the Commission must express its concern at the inflexible approach of the State authorities which has been concerned more to punish offenders against prison discipline than to explore ways of resolving such a serious deadlock. Furthermore, the Commission is of the view that, for humanitarian reasons, efforts should have been made by the authorities to ensure that the applicants could avail of certain facilities such as taking regular exercise in the open air with some form of clothing (other than prison clothing) and making greater use of the prison amenities under similar conditions. At the same time, arrangements should have been made to enable the applicants to consult outside medical specialists even though they were not prepared to wear prison uniform or underwear. [. . .]

'Notwithstanding the above, the failure of the authorities in these respects, taking into consideration the magnitude of the institutional problem posed by the protest and the supervisory and sanitary precautions they have adopted to cope with it, cannot lead to the conclusion that the Government is in breach of its obligations under Article 3.'

In addition, the Commission said that it did not consider close body searches – including examination of the rectum – to be inhuman treatment.

There was also talk about whether or not the 1949 Geneva Convention on the humanitarian laws of war would provide any basis for the Provisionals to claim prisoner-of-war status, but the British government was equally confident that its position was impregnable. In a controversial review of the convention three years earlier, the justice of the cause of recognised national liberation movements was acknowledged for the first time, even to the extent of allowing guerrillas operating in civilian clothes to become prisoners of war on capture provided they had openly carried their weapons before and after an attack. Britain, which had signed the convention but had not yet ratified it, believed the IRA could not fulfil the criteria laid down for the sort of national liberation struggle covered by the convention. To benefit from it, the Provisionals would need to have created 'an intensity of conflict' greater than the sporadic hit-and-run they conventionally engaged in, and, most importantly, required United Nations recognition for the legitimacy of their campaign. In practice, contemporary organisations like the Arab League and the Organisation for African Unity provided the bona fides for organisations within their sphere of influence. Thus it would be to the Irish Republic that the United Nations would have looked for approval of the Provisional IRA's cause and there were no conceivable circumstances, the British could envisage, in which any Irish Government would support the Provisionals in such a move.

Meanwhile, since February, the dirty protest had spread to the women's prison at Armagh, where thirty women were participating. Inside the nauseous Maze H-blocks, with their overpowering stench of urine, excrement and ammonia, the 350 protesting prisoners decided to resort to what they saw as the ultimate weapon in the Republican armoury – a hunger strike to the death.

Chapter Ten
Cynical brinkmanship

The hunger strike enjoys a unique and sacred status in the psychology and emotions of militant Irish nationalism. It is a holy enough thing to fight and die for Ireland but it is an altogether more worthy sacrifice to so selflessly, and painfully, take one's own life for the cause. As the Republican apologist Bernadette (Devlin) McAliskey, wrote in 1993 in a foreword to *Nor Meekly Serve my Time – The H-Block Struggle 1976–81*, 'I think of the power of such love as will lay down its life so resolutely, and I wonder what transforms ordinary young people into such universal defenders of human integrity.' The most revered and inspirational Republican martyrs are those who have been committed and disciplined enough to do so: 'Gallant patriots who died on hunger strike for national freedom,' according to the inscription on the hunger strikers' memorial erected by the National Graves Association at the Republican plot in Glasnevin cemetery, Dublin. In fact, imprisoned Republicans have consistently used the hunger strike since the early 1900s, against both the British and Irish states, to improve prison conditions or gain political status – and up to this point twelve had died – but the practice of using fasting as a political weapon actually has a much longer tradition.

Hunger striking to the death features in early Indian law and was still common in Nepal as recently as 100 years ago. If the hunger striker died the subject of his grievance could be prosecuted for murder. As far back as the eighth century, according to ancient Irish law texts, a ritual fast from sunrise to sunset was used by someone from a lower rank to enforce a legal claim against a high-ranking individual, such as a king, noble or poet. The fasting person maintained a vigil on the doorstep of the other party, who was also expected to observe the fast. Afterwards he was obliged to give a pledge or surety to guarantee that he would submit the matter under dispute to arbitration or he would become liable for twice the original claim.

The first documented use of a hunger strike in modern Irish history took place in 1912 when a cadre of suffragettes, then campaigning for female emancipation in Britain, trailed the British Prime Minister,

Herbert Asquith, to Dublin, where they staged a number of demonstrations to draw attention to their cause. After being imprisoned for attempting to burn down the Theatre Royal in the city, they were confined in Mountjoy, where they promptly launched a hunger strike. Augustine Birrell, the Chief Secretary of Ireland, commented, 'Personally I am dead against forcible feeding which always ends with the release of the prisoner long before her time. I want to keep these ladies under lock and key for five years and I am willing to feed them with Priests' Champagne and Michaelmas Geese all the time, if it can be done. These wretched hags are obstinate to the point of death.' Nevertheless they were forcibly fed for a time and eventually released because of ill health. Hanna Sheehy Skeffington, the leader of the Irish suffragette movement, said, 'Hunger strike was then a new weapon – we were the first to try it out in Ireland – had we but known we were the pioneers in a long line.'

The first use of the hunger strike by an Irish nationalist came in 1913 when the trade union organiser, James Connolly, who would later be executed as one of the key figures in the 1916 Easter Rising, engaged in a fast for better prison conditions during the 'Lock-Out', a protracted dispute between organised labour and the big Dublin employers. He was released from Mountjoy jail in Dublin within a few days. So too was Francis Sheehy Skeffington, who started a fast in 1915 after being sentenced for making a speech urging Irishmen not to enlist in the British forces fighting the First World War. But it was force feeding, rather than fasting, which caused the death of the first Republican to perish while on a hunger strike. Thomas Ashe, a school teacher by profession, took part in the 1916 Rising and was captured, sentenced to death, reprieved and then imprisoned for life. However, he was released in 1917 and quickly came to prominence in the new leadership of Sinn Fein and the Irish Volunteers, which had replaced those executed by the British for their part in the rebellion. With months, however, he was re-arrested during a crackdown intended to smother the growing Irish independence movement. Sentenced to two years' imprisonment for inciting the civil population, and lodged in Mountjoy, he immediately demanded political status. When it was refused, he led Sinn Fein prisoners into a hunger strike on 20 September. According to 'The Last Post', the roll of honour of the Irish Republican dead, 'he was determined to join in a sacred fast for liberty after being deprived of his bed, bedding and boots and being left thus to die in a dismal cell.' Five days later, Ashe collapsed while being force fed in the prison surgeon's chair. He was rushed to the nearby Mater Hospital, where he died five hours later. 'We have put up a great fight anyway,' he told priests at his deathbed. An inquest later censured those responsible for the way he was treated. The manner of his death, at the hands of the British, captured public sympathy and attention on a scale never seen before. His body, clad in the uniform of the Irish Volunteers, lay in state at Dublin City Hall and 30,000 people followed his coffin to Glasnevin, through throngs of others lining the streets of Dublin.

In April 1919, Robert Byrnes was sent to prison in Limerick for twelve months for unlawfully possessing firearms. He went on hunger strike to secure better conditions and was eventually moved to the local hospital where his comrades decided to mount an armed rescue but in the ensuing firefight with his guards, members of the Royal Irish Constabulary, the prisoner was fatally wounded. Hunger striking now became an increasingly common weapon but it was not until 1920, when three serious trials of strength between prisoners and the authorities developed, that its full grim value was learned by the Republican movement. In April that year 60 men demanding political status went on hunger strike at Mountjoy. In scenes more reminiscent of public executions, crowds gathered outside the prison saying the Rosary aloud and singing Fenian songs to encourage the prisoners. The authorities at first prevented relatives from visiting but relented in the vain hope that they would persuade the prisoners to give up. A week after the fast began, the pressure increased when a general strike was called to support them. Three days after that the prisoners were all unconditionally released.

The rapid success of the Mountjoy fast caused Sinn Fein prisoners at Wormwood Scrubs in London to go on strike for political status there. Once more huge prayer-chanting, singing crowds from London's Irish population gathered outside the jail urging the fasting strikers on. With the outcry over the forced feeding of Ashe all too fresh in their minds, the authorities again were powerless and freed them after eighteen days. However, a few months later in August they decided to take a tough stand when eleven IRA prisoners in Cork jail adopted the same tactics and started fasting. One of them was Terence MacSwiney, the Lord Mayor of Cork, who had been arrested under the 1920 Defence of the Realm Act and court-martialled on a charge of 'being in possession of documents the publication of which would be likely to cause disaffection to His Majesty'. Three days after the start of the hunger strike, MacSwiney was separated from the others and taken to Britain by warship before being sent to Brixton prison in London. Upon his inauguration as Lord Mayor in Cork City Hall, MacSwiney had said, 'The contest on our side is not one of rivalry or vengeance. but of endurance. It is not those who can inflict the most but those that can suffer the most who will conquer.

Those whose faith is strong will endure to the end in triumph.' His fast attracted worldwide attention and his widely quoted words became an aphorism for prison struggles and hunger strikers since. As MacSwiney's life steadily ebbed away, the British resisted widespread pleas for mercy. On 17 October, Michael Fitzgerald died in Cork followed eight days later by MacSwiney in Brixton on the seventy-fourth day of his fast. The same day a third hunger striker, Joseph Murphy also died. MacSwiney's death provoked an unprecedented display of public mourning in Ireland and Britain. At the height of the ongoing war of independence, it was thus of immense propaganda value to the Republican cause.

Having secured an Irish Free State by agreeing to partition, the fledgling Dublin government faced a civil war with those opposed to the settlement. It was they who faced the dilemma of either making concessions to prisoners – their former comrades in arms – or risking their deaths, when the hunger strike was next deployed in 1923. In March that year 91 female prisoners detained in Kilmainham jail in Dublin launched a hunger strike after their right to receive and send letters and communicate with their families was removed. Within seven days the authorities capitulated, the rights were restored and the hunger strike was called off. But in October the same year, when 424 male Republican prisoners, ten of them elected members of Dail Eireann, began fasting in Mountjoy, Kilmainham and other prisons throughout the country in protest at their detention without trial and generally poor conditions, there were no concessions. The protest was abandoned on 23 November by when three inmates had been allowed to die: Joseph Whitty, Denis Barry and Andrew Sullivan.

In 1939 Patrick McGrath, a veteran of the 1916 Rising, went on hunger strike for political status and the Prime Minister Eamonn de Valera, formerly the leader of the anti-partition movement, was forced to release him after 43 days by the tide of public support. But soon afterwards, in the run-up to Christmas festivities, when the breakaway IRA raided the Magazine Fort in Phoenix Park, Dublin, getting away (for a short time) with the government's stock of 1 million rounds of ammunition, special powers were introduced and the suspects were rounded up. This time, when a hunger strike was initiated in February 1940 to gain political status, de Valera took an uncompromising line. On 16 and 19 April, after two of them, Tony Darcy and Sean McNeela, died at Arbour Hill, some minor concessions were made. In 1946, with the world war at an end and the Irish prisons still packed with Republican prisoners, protest about the harsh conditions they had long endured flared again and a fast was started. For some time the prisoners at Portlaoise jail had been refusing to wear prison clothes and remained in their cells clad only in blankets. This time the leader of the hunger strike was Sean McCaughey, a convicted kidnapper who had been sentenced to death and reprieved in 1941. After nineteen days without food he began refusing liquids as well – a thirst strike – and died eleven days afterwards on 11 May 1946.

The hunger strike was not used as a weapon again until 1972, when, as we have seen, William Whitelaw conceded special category status to prisoners in Northern Ireland. The Republican leadership did not subsequently encourage hunger striking as a political weapon, although it supported the Old Bailey bombers who engaged in a prolonged hunger strike and endured force feeding to back up a demand that they be allowed to serve their lengthy prison sentences in Northern Ireland. The eight-strong team, led by the Price sisters, Marion and Dolours, carried out a series of attacks, killed one person and injured hundreds of others in central London, which coincided with a referendum on the future of partition in Northern Ireland in March 1973. After being convicted and sentenced to life imprisonment for their part in the plot, they fasted, and were force fed for 206 days, to secure political status and a transfer to serve their sentences in their native Northern Ireland. Hugh Feeney, another of the conspirators, fasted for 200 days until both strikes halted in June 1974.

In the same month Michael Gaughan, a member of Provisional Sinn Fein, who was jailed for seven years for his part in a bank robbery, died at Parkhurst Prison, Isle of Wight, having fasted from 30 March as part of a campaign to improve prison conditions. During his inquest, jurors were shown a plastic tube two feet long and three-quarters of an inch thick which had been forced down his throat to feed him. They were also shown a metal instrument used to force open his teeth and told how he was restrained, his arms pinioned behind his back, his legs forced out straight and his head held steady with a towel. The following month, the Home Secretary, Roy Jenkins, announced a major policy change arising from a review of the practice. In future any prisoners who took a rational decision to refuse food would be allowed to starve themselves to death if they wished, he said. In a statement to the House of Commons he said that if doctors were satisfied a prisoner's capacity for rational judgement was not impaired by mental or physical illness he would no longer be artificially fed. Instead he would be told that he would continue to receive medical supervision and advice and that food would be made available to him. 'When considered appropriate he would be moved to the prison hospital. But it should be made clear to him that there is no rule or prison practice which requires the medical officer to resort to artificial feeding whether by tube or intravenously. Finally he should be plainly and categorically warned that the consequent and inevitable deterioration in his health may be allowed to continue without medical intervention unless he specifically requests it.' In February 1976 Frank Stage was thus permitted to die in Wakefield jail on hunger strike, his fourth in two years, in support of his demand for political status and to serve his ten-year sentence (for conspiring to commit arson and IRA membership) in Northern Ireland.

It was against this highly complex and emotional background, therefore, that the British government and the protesting IRA prisoners in the Maze entered into what both sides saw as the denouement of their protracted confrontation. The start of the hunger strike was confirmed on 10 October 1980 when the following statement was smuggled from the prison. The message, like many others that would follow in the fraught weeks and months ahead, was written on sheets of toilet or cigarette paper, in tiny handwriting, with the ink tubes from pens, taken from visitors to the H-blocks, and then concealed by the prisoners. One priest recalls being surrounded by the men and having his pens removed when he went in to say Mass on a Sunday. Relatives visiting the men would then receive the 'comm', transported to the visit, wrapped in clingfilm, in a bodily orifice to foil the searches, and take it from the prison, again intimately concealed on the body. The authorities were constantly on the look out for the messages and a 21-year old female who was apprehended during a search in the visitors car park at this time was found to have a package of twenty 'comms', covered in human excrement, in her pocket. She was later fined £50 for attempted smuggling.

The highly significant statement announcing the hunger strike was written by Brendan 'Bik' McFarlane, serving life for five deaths caused in a gun and bomb attack on the Bayardo public house in the Loyalist heartland of Belfast's Shankill Road in August 1975. After he was sentenced in 1976 by Sir Robert Lowry, the Lord Chief Justice, for 'a most callous and indiscriminate crime', McFarlane enjoyed special category status but after trying to escape he was transferred to the H-blocks, where he became the public relations officer for the prisoners. He had revised his original draft three times before the prisoners' leader, Brendan Hughes was content for it to be smuggled out and published.

'We, the Republican Prisoners-of-war in the H-Blocks, Long Kesh, demand, as of right, political recognition and that we be accorded the status of political prisoners, We claim this right as captured combatants in the continuing struggle for national liberation and self-determination.

'We refute most strongly the tag of 'criminal' with which the British have attempted to label us and our struggle and we point to the divisive partitionist institutions of the six counties as the sole criminal aspect of the present struggle. All of us were arrested under repressive laws, interrogated and often tortured in RUC barracks and processed through non-jury courts where we were sentenced to lengthy terms of imprisonment. After this, men were put in the H-Blocks and were expected to bow the knee before the British administration and wear their criminal uniform. Attempts to criminalise us were designed to depoliticise the Irish national struggle.

'We don't have to recite again the widespread, almost total forms of punishment, degradation and deprivation we have been subjected to.

All have failed to break our resistance. For the past four years we have endured brutality in deplorable conditions – we have been stripped naked and robbed of our individuality, yet we refused to be broken. Further repression only serves to strengthen our resolve and that of our female comrades enduring the same hardships in Armagh Jail. During this period, many individuals, religious figures, political organisations and sections of the media have condemned the way in which we have been treated. Yet, despite appeals for a resolution of the H-Block protest, the British government has remained intransigent and displayed vindictive arrogance in dealing with the problem. They refuse to treat this issue in a realistic manner which is just another reflection of their attitude to the entire Irish question.

'Bearing in mind the serious implications of our final step, not only for us but for our people, we wish to make it clear that every channel has now been exhausted and, not wishing to break faith with those from whom we have inherited our principles, we now commit ourselves to a hunger-strike. We call on the Irish people to lend us their support for our just demands and we are confident that this support will be very much in evidence in the coming days. We call on all solidarity and support groups to intensify their efforts and we also look forward with full confidence to the support of our exiled countrymen in America and Australia and throughout the world. We declare that political status is ours of right and we declare that from Monday, 27th October, 1980, a hunger-strike by a number of men representing H-Blocks 3, 4 and 5 will commence.

'Our widely-recognised resistance has carried us through four years of immense suffering and it shall carry us through to the bitter climax of death if necessary.'

From that morning, the IRA leadership said later, seven men would refuse breakfast and begin a fast to the death. Each one who died would be replaced by another. The start day had been chosen with a view to the fast reaching its potentially fatal climax in the run-up to Christmas. More than 90 per cent of the Provisional prisoners, the leadership said, had volunteered to take part in the hunger strike. There had been exhaustive debate among the prisoners beforehand and a careful selection process. A prison chaplain, who witnessed the preparations for the hunger strike and the subsequent selection process, said it was 'as thorough as the Vatican's but the Provos were much better at identifying their strongest men.' McFarlane was rejected because of the negative propaganda that would be made from his involvement in a nakedly sectarian mass murder. Each individual volunteer was carefully assessed, and indeed questioned, about his commitment to the fast and willingness to go all the way to his death. At least one pulled out at this point, fearing he might let his comrades down by balking at the point of no return. The final shortlist thus consisted of individuals perceived to have the necessary commitment to forfeiting their life if necessary. The final seven choices were made by selecting one prisoner from each of the six counties of Northern Ireland and one from Belfast. It was felt this would enable their supporters outside to maximise support on the streets. In the tense weeks ahead there would be much talk of the prisoners' 'five just demands': the rights to wear their own clothes, to refrain from prison work, to associate freely with each other and organise recreational facilities, to receive a weekly letter, visit and parcel, and to have lost remission restored.

Outside the intellectually incestuous confines of the H-blocks, the IRA leadership was publicly supportive but privately unenthusiastic. More than once they had already discouraged prisoners from embarking on a hunger strike. After so long, they doubted that even the death of a hunger striker could shift the British government from its fundamental position. For its part, the British government was resigned, more in determination than in anger, to the coming confrontation. There would be no return to special category, the prisoners were living in self-inflicted misery and their ordeal could be ended at any time by accepting the prison rules. Addressing the House of Commons on 23 October, Atkins said the hunger strikers would not be force fed and could well die – in line with the 1974 Jenkins guidelines – but he reiterated the concessions recently offered to protesting prisoners not conforming to prison rules: three letters in and out each month; one hour's exercise a week in sports gear; access to books and newspapers in the association room where Mass was said on Sundays; closed visits as an alternative to the searches imposed before open visits; evening association once a week in prison uniform and compassionate home leave on the same basis as for conforming prisoners. That morning, in a last-minute bid to head off the fast, the British cabinet had actually approved another concession: prison uniform would be abolished in favour of civilian-style clothing.

This was precisely the sort of move earlier urged on the British by Cardinal O'Fiaich and Dr Edward Daly, the Bishop of Derry, who believed that it would have been enough to break the protest. That Friday they were engaged in a final effort to avert the hunger strike. The day before Daly flew from Belfast to London to link up with O'Fiaich, who had flown in from the Vatican, in Rome, where he had been attending a meeting of Bishops. Overnight they had talked to Cardinal Basil Hume, the head of the Catholic Church in England. The next day the two senior Irish clergymen were heartened by the lunchtime radio news which reported that morning's cabinet decision to allow all Northern Ireland prisoners to wear civilian clothing. But when they met Atkins that afternoon in the Northern Ireland Office, overlooking St. James's Park, they were bitterly disappointed. He explained the civilian clothes would be issued by the authorities who feared the Republicans and Loyalists would have set up the wholesale importation of black berets and khaki, military-style anoraks and that the authorities would have been faced with a terrorist prison population going around in virtual uniform.

The clergymen tried, but in vain, to convince him that if the prisoners were allowed to have their own choice of clothes, sent in by their families, then the imminent hunger strike and its potentially violent consequences throughout the community could be averted, Indeed Daly believed that that concession, on top of everything else in the package offered through their talks, would have been sufficient to head off not only the hunger strike but end the long-running blanket and dirty protests as well. However, the moment had already passed, the prisoners' mood had hardened, and the eleventh-hour concession was not enough and anyway had come far too late. The two clergymen returned home empty-handed and made another plea for the fast to be called off. But that Sunday evening the seven prisoners dined on steak and onion pie, baked beans, fruit, bread and margarine and tea. Later there was a two-hour morale building 'concert' with prisoners singing songs and reciting poetry. Some of them made rousing speeches, and there were two emotional addresses by two of the imminent hunger strikers. Everything was shouted through the windows and cell doors of the already notorious H-blocks. Next morning the seven refused breakfast – cornflakes, milk, tea, bread and margarine. 'Hunger strike began,' the Governor wrote and underlined in red ink in the margin of his journal.

The lead hunger striker was Brendan 'Darky' Hughes, who had given up his position as Officer Commanding the Provisional IRA inmates to take part. Hughes, who then lived at Arundel Street, Belfast, was a 52-year-old married man with a wife and child. In May 1961, as a juvenile, he had been fined 40 shillings and three shillings costs for larceny. When the troubles started, he came to the notice of the police and army and was detained in the Maze from where he escaped on 8 December 1973 and remained at large until his arrest on 10 May 1974 when he was the reputed Chief of Staff of the Provisional IRA. He was recaptured after a major surveillance operation when a quantity of firearms and explosives were found in a luxury flat in Myrtlefield Park, Belfast, which was occupied by Hughes and others. The haul also included plans of Belfast with certain areas shaded relating to Provisional IRA welfare plans in the event of widespread civil strife. The following December he appeared at Belfast City Commission where he was sentenced to two and a half years' imprisonment for handling stolen goods. At the same court on 5 February 1975 he was convicted on two counts of possessing explosive substances, firearms and ammunition with intent and received concurrent sentences of fifteen and twelve years' imprisonment. The prisoner refused to recognise the court and was not legally represented but he was convicted on the evidence of his fingerprints being found in and around the premises where the haul was made. Hughes again appeared before Belfast City Commission on 21 March 1975 and was convicted of escaping from lawful custody (on 8 December 1973). He received a further eighteen month consecutive prison sentence. Hughes served the first years of his imprisonment as a special category prisoner in the Maze compounds but on 20 January 1978, after he was sentenced to a further five years following an incident inside the prison when he and others seriously assaulted a Prison Officer, he lost his special category status and was transferred to the H-blocks where he promptly joined the protest. He was adjudicated on for refusing to work or wear prison clothing and his remission was reduced. At that point he faced his date of release being extended from 16 August 1985 to 15 May 1996.

The case histories of the other hunger strikers provided snapshots of the utterly violent and ruthless nature of the Maze population and the background they came from. Thomas McKearney, 28, a butcher from Moy, County Tyrone, was a lifer, with a recommendation from the judge that he should serve a minimum twenty years before release. On 27 October 1976, together with an accomplice, he posted a letter to a remote farmhouse near Pomeroy, County Tyrone. Overnight, armed with an Armalite rifle and a revolver, they took over the farmhouse and held the elderly occupants hostage as they lay in wait for the postman. When Stanley Adams, who was also a part-time soldier in the Ulster Defence Regiment, arrived, his van was raked with gunfire. McKearney then took a shotgun from the house and fired at the victim from point-blank range to ensure he was dead. Before leaving the scene, the killers took the bogus letter with them. McKearney came from a family who were steeped in IRA activism. One brother, Padraig, had recently been released from the prison after completing a seven-year sentence for causing an explosion and was already back in custody awaiting trial for another offence. Another brother, Sean, had earlier perished with an accomplice in a premature explosion while transporting a bomb. Not long before, Scotland Yard had publicly named his sister Margaret as their most wanted female terrorist suspect. Before beginning the hunger strike he had asked to be buried in Roscommon and remembered for dying 'an Irish soldier, not a British criminal'.

Thomas McFeely, 31, from Claudy, County Londonderry, was one of the four prisoners, with Nugent, who had mounted the unsuccessful case at the European Human Rights Commission. Married with three children between four and seven years old, he came from a family of eight boys and two girls, some of whom were also steeped in terrorism. A brother was serving a twelve-year sentence for manslaughter and causing an explosion and another was wanted by the RUC for questioning. McFeely, by trade a bricklayer, first came to the RUC's attention when he was charged with riotous behaviour after a civil rights march in 1969. He later went on the run and moved south where he was arrested by the Garda and found to be in possession of a firearm. One month into an eighteen month term for the offence, he escaped from Portlaoise jail in the Irish Republic in 1974, after IRA attackers breached the front gate with explosives and a mechanical digger. McFeely was serving fourteen years in the Maze for firearms offences and robbery. On 13 April 1976, two men, one of them armed, held up a country post office near Limavady. They took between £20 and £50 from the shop till and another £10 from the post office counter. A bread delivery man who arrived during the robbery was relieved of £500. During the incident a shot was fired narrowly missing the sub-postmaster. Two weeks later police who called at a cottage at Greysteel, a few miles away, were fired on. A shot creased the hair of a Sergeant. When the occupants refused to come out, police called reinforcements and surrounded the house. Three hours later a rifle was pushed out through the door and three men, one of them McFeely, gave themselves up. McFeely declined the services of a barrister and unsuccessfully defended himself when he came to trial in February 1977. On joining the H-block protest soon afterwards, McFeely twice conducted short-term hunger strikes protesting against the prison system, first a one-day protest and, later, a seven-day fast.

Raymond McCartney, 25,was a double killer. He had become actively involved in IRA activity early in the troubles after his brother was interned in 1971 and a cousin, Jim Wray, was among the thirteen unarmed marchers shot dead on Bloody Sunday, 30 January 1972. In February 1973 he was sentenced to six months' imprisonment for possession of a round of ammunition but walked free as a result of time served on remand. In October he was arrested again and this time interned without trial until March 1975. For a time he was involved in setting up and carrying out attacks in Britain but got away from a shoot-out with the police and returned to Derry, his home town, where, on 27 January 1977, he shot and murdered Detective Constable Patrick McNulty at Strand Road as the officer was leaving his car to be serviced. On 2 February he then killed Geoffrey Agate, the head of the Dupont plant and one of the largest employers in the area, who was shot five times at close quarters and killed outside his home as part of a campaign to sabotage the Northern Ireland economy. McCartney was sentenced to two life terms with the judge's recommendation that he serve a minimum of 25 years' imprisonment.

Leo Green, 27, a trainee accountant from Lurgan, Co Armagh, was one of six brothers and six sisters, four of the brothers being deeply involved with the IRA. John, who had escaped from the Maze in 1973 by dressing in the clothes of his brother Gerard, a priest, was shot dead two years later at a remote dwelling on the southern side of the Irish border. Another, Tom, was imprisoned three times in the Irish Republic for IRA member-ship. A younger brother, Lawrence, 23, currently serving twelve years was also a protesting prisoner in the Maze. The hunger striker was serving life with a recommendation of 25 years for the murder of RUC Inspector James Cobb, who was shot dead on 24 February 1977. Green joined the prison protest when he reached the Maze in April 1978 and declined all visits for two years because he would not wear the prison uniform.

John Nixon, 25, from Armagh, was an unemployed single man and the oldest in a family of five boys and five girls. One of the brothers, Leroy, was serving eighteen years, as a special category prisoner, for the attempted murder of a UDR officer. The family was steeped in Republicanism and at the outset of the Troubles he was associated with the Official IRA and engaged in petty crime, gaining several convictions for theft and burglary. In 1972 he was also convicted of disorderly behaviour. On 7 March 1973, in an incident which the Army described as an exchange with gunmen, Peter McGerrigan, 18, was killed and Nixon was seriously wounded. He was subsequently convicted of riotous behaviour and possession of firearms and imprisoned for five years. He was released in July 1976, having helped form the Irish Republican Socialist Party, a coalition of former members of the Official and Provisional IRA factions.

At 10 am on 31 August 1976 Nixon was one of three armed and masked men who entered a post office in Armagh and held up the staff. They made off with £60 in cash. Later that year, at 5.30 pm on 3 December, Nixon and another man, again armed and masked, entered a supermarket in Armagh and held up the staff. Nixon fired a shot into the ceiling as they made off with £1000. He appeared before the Belfast City Commission on 29 September 1977, where he was convicted on two counts of armed robbery and received sentences of twelve and fourteen years to run concurrently. He commenced protesting immediately and apart from losing remission he was also adjudicated for assaulting a prison officer by punching him in the face and chest.

The seventh of the hunger strikers was Sean McKenna, 26, from Newry, who was serving 21 concurrent sentences totalling 245 years for what the trial judge described as a whole catalogue of terrorist offences: belonging to a proscribed organisation, conspiracy to intimidate, false imprisonment, possession of firearms and explosives, causing explosions and wounding with intent. The most serious convictions were for the attempted murder of two RUC officers for which he had been sentenced to 25 years. McKenna's father, also named Sean, who died aged 42 in 1975, had been one of those subjected to in-depth interrogation after the introduction of internment in 1971. The two had been arrested on 9 August and Sean, then aged seventeen, remained interned until February 1975. He was again arrested in a dawn raid by undercover soldiers on 12 March 1976 close to the border at Edentubber, Co Louth, where he lived in a cottage just 600 yards into the Irish Republic across the fields. Like the other hunger strikers he had gone 'on the blanket' as soon as he was sent to the Maze after his trial in May the following year.

Forty-eight hours after the commencement of the hunger strike, Margaret Thatcher, then British Prime Minister, said in the House of Commons that the government would not make any concession to those on hunger strike. A few weeks later she was even more dogmatic: 'The government will never concede political status to the hunger strikers, or to any others convicted of criminal offences in the province.' The government was working to a confidential medical assessment that three of the hunger strikers would be at risk from around 6 December and the other four ten days later. The estimates were reached after considering the general health and weights of each of the prisoners. Initially they remained dispersed among the other protesting prisoners in the H-blocks but on 6 November they were moved, and isolated in the wing of H5, each in a separate cell. An official statement said, 'This wing has been reserved from the outset of the dirty protests to provide a clean area for prisoners who require a higher degree of clinical observation than is possible in the conditions pertaining in the dirty cells, but who do not require admission to the prison hospital. The move has not been occasioned by any significant deterioration in the prisoners' health. It will be a matter for clinical judgement as to when a prisoner should be moved to the prison hospital, should this be deemed necessary.'

In fact a number of what were described as sterile wings had been prepared and set aside in case the dirty protest and clearly unhygienic conditions resulted in an outbreak of serious or contagious infection. At this point the strikers were in good health. In *Nor Meekly Serve my Time*, Leo Green recalls the first ten days being the most uncomfortable of all. 'I experienced severe headaches and back pain. After that initial period the pain subsided and disappeared altogether.' But for three days around the twenty day mark he 'craved' food. 'To fight it, I occupied my mind with memories of past events in my life.' He also read the novels of Dickens and Hardy to occupy his mind. 'I read slowly and gave free rein to my imagination. Other than for those three days, food rarely again entered my head for the remainder of the hunger strike.' However, at every mealtime officers or prisoners acting as orderlies, usually from a Loyalist background, continued to bring meals to the hunger strikers cells in line with official policy that they should be offered food. The trays remained there until they were replaced at the next mealtime. 'That was to ensure that there was food available at all times if the hunger striker decided to eat,' a prison officer recalled. One of the Loyalists later described how his feelings changed from hatred of the hunger strikers – 'my first thought was to scald him or cut him with a razor' – to pity – 'he was wasting away, he weighed about five stone, and he was just lying on the floor on newspapers, with nothing in his cell except a piss-pot and a Bible and the full tray of food which I brought in and then took out.'

Whatever the extent of the ordeal the prisoners inflicted on themselves through their protests, the consequences for the entire prison service were enormous. Off duty, everyone concerned, and members of their families, suffered regular intimidation and were under a constant threat of attack from both Republicans and Loyalists. The hunger strike was a further unsettling factor for everyone feared violent retribution if the prisoners demands were not conceded and any of them died. For the governors and staff at the Maze, in the front line of the four-year confrontation, the hunger strikes compounded the problems of a penal protest unprecedented in its nature or duration anywhere in the world. The staff called the prisoners the 'hairy blanket brigade', and while some of them certainly clashed with the prisoners and made unsavoury and hostile remarks, especially when the fasts got under way, the majority acted professionally and with dignity. Privately the majority had a silent and grudging respect for the tenacity of the prisoners and the way they stubbornly endured such self-punishment for their cast-iron beliefs and found it difficult having to cope with such violently non-cooperative inmates. However much the prisoners resented the intimate body searches and other necessary indignities, the staff who had to carry the procedures out found them more thoroughly distasteful. It was also widely conceded that, whatever the unyielding official policy that they were no more than common criminals, these were no ordinary prisoners they were dealing with. 'The vast majority of the Loyalists would have ended up in prison for one crime or another but everyone understood that very few indeed of the Republicans would ever have seen the inside of a prison if it hadn't been for the troubles,' said one former Governor of the prison.

Patrolling the protest blocks required a strong stomach. In the drive to keep infection at bay, especially after the commencement of the dirty protest, medical officers visited the prisoners in their cells at least weekly but, however amicable they tried to be, they were generally treated with hostility. 'Their job may have been to provide medical services but they were still screws,' one former prisoner explains. Perhaps the most difficult task for the prison officers was the constant steam-cleaning of the fouled cells. In a drive to maintain hygiene, the dirty protesters were moved to fresh cells every ten days or so. Officers clad in spacesuit-style protective clothing used high-pressure water jets and powerful disinfectant to clean the walls, ceiling and floors of the cells, which were then repainted. At policy-making level and among the more thoughtful staff, there was frustration and a recognition of the futility of the situation. A senior prison official recalls, 'At that time on the mainland only one in five prisoners was serving a sentence of more than three years. We had four out of five serving three years or more. Many of them were very young. They had come into prison in their late teens and were facing terms of 25 or 30 years, which meant they would be virtually middle-aged when they got out. In the meantime life had to be made constructive and tolerable for them. If there were not very enlightened conditions, for such as the eighteen-year-old lifers we had in custody, there was a real risk they would have been destroyed completely. That is why it was so essential to get beyond the protests and into a more conventional type of prison regime.'

A Catholic prison chaplain at the time speaks of the 'amazing asceticism' he witnessed. 'They chose to deprive themselves of all the usual features and distractions of life. I am quite amazed at how they stuck it for so long and didn't go insane.' At the height of the protest, the high point of the week was Sunday, when they put on trousers and were permitted to attend Mass, which was said in one of the recreation/dining rooms in each of the three H-blocks where the protesting prisoners were confined. 'They were cut off from everything so I used to lace my sermons with bits of news and the football results to keep them informed.' He would also pack his pockets with cigarettes. Once when chided about this practice by one of the governors, he said there was nothing he could do if the prisoners crowded him and removed them. Sunday Mass was also used as a forum to exchange 'comms' and information between individual prisoners, wings and indeed blocks. The prisoners had also developed a code for tapping messages and communicating along the heating pipes that ran through their accommodation. Messages were also shouted from wing to wing, often in Irish to prevent the prison officers understanding. Indeed one of the principal ways the prisoners occupied themselves was teaching each other Irish, in 'Rang Gaeilgie' (Irish class). Words and phrases in the language, such as 'sceal' (news), 'pluid' (blanket) and 'stailc ocrais' (hunger strike), soon peppered their prison argot, 'Jailic' as it had become known to the language purists. At night 'Scealai' (storytellers) would recount their favourites out through the cell windows or doors for the others to hear. Sometimes extraordinary ingenuity was applied to finding ways to pass the long hours in isolation. A form of chess was developed using the cardboard centre of a toilet roll as an improvised board with pieces fashioned from chewed-up toilet paper.

Away from the prison, as the hunger strike gathered momentum, the National H-Block Committee and the Northern Ireland Office were engaged in a sustained propaganda onslaught against each other. From the outset Sinn Fein and the network of front organisations it had created or infiltrated worked to create an atmosphere of crisis and emotion around the issue. Every day there were at least columns, and some days pages, of 'Don't let the prisoners die' advertisements in the *Belfast Irish News*, listing the days the hunger strike had lasted and expressing support from local hunger strike action committees, ex-POW groups, and motley coalitions such as 'the concerned bakers and bakery workers of west Belfast'.

'Blessed are those who hunger for justice,' said many of the advertisements, while another, in the name of the Ardoyne Relief Committee, urged in stirring doggerel, 'Don't let our Irish brothers die; come out, come out, and join our cry; drop your pints and household chores to drive the Brits from our shores.' Every night there were torchlight processions, pickets, traffic hold-ups, sit-ins at public buildings, prayer vigils and demonstrations. Many of them were led by men and women clad in blankets. One male, blanket-clad protestor had, however, to be ushered away when women complained he was flashing at them.

A Sinn Fein leaflet published in Dublin urged people to write, telephone or send telegrams to people of importance urging them to lend support and to write or call newspapers, magazines and radio shows. It gave the telephone number of the British Embassy at Ballsbridge in Dublin so that supporters could call and 'let them know your feelings. Their lives are in your hands! Don't let them die! We want big protests not big funerals,' the leaflet exhorted. Ruairi O'Bradaigh, a veteran of the 1956–62 IRA campaign, who was Sinn Fein president, described the hunger strike as a 'showdown'. He said, 'They have thrown their frail human bodies in front of the juggernaut of imperialism as a last resort to challenge British policy towards the Irish people.'

The hunger strikes quickly touched a deep chord and roused the concern of the broad base of the Catholic community as no issue since the campaign for civil rights over a decade earlier, largely because of the leading role churchmen had assumed in trying to resolve the issue. There was also a surprising convulsion of support in the Irish Republic. When Gerry Fitt, then MP for West Belfast, voiced his concern that the subtle nuance differentiating their pastoral and humanitarian concern for the prisoners from outright support for the Provisional IRA (and therefore implicit approval of its atrocities) was not widely enough understood, he was targeted by protesters and night after night intimidatory torchlight vigils were held outside his home with people chanting 'Gerry Fitt is a Brit.' Fitt was also concerned at the potentially violent effect this perception of the Catholic church stand could have on hardline Loyalist opinion. Moderate Protestants were appalled by the prison protest. In November, Dr Armstrong, the Church of Ireland Primate of All Ireland, said the hunger strikers had a choice, 'and no amount of tortuous reasoning can prove otherwise.' He warned that decriminalising the activities of serious offenders on both sides and accepting them as political prisoners would negate Christian principles and constitute a move against the interests of society at large by giving a cloak of respectability and credibility to the perpetrators of violent crime.

Notwithstanding such reasoned sentiments, there continued to be a rising groundswell of interest and a tide of hitherto moderate support for the protest. Every week *An Phoblacht* and *Republican News* (which merged around this time) carried reports of solidarity protests from every county in Ireland, in many parts of Britain and many overseas countries. One week it was noted approvingly that Pravda had backed the prisoners and Soviet Television had referred to the 'courageous seven who are on hunger strike in the Long Kesh concentration camp'. Indeed the campaigning was not confined to Northern Ireland. Unarguably the most important of the overseas battlegrounds was the United States, where both sides invested heavily in getting their respective cases over. Former prisoners, including Kieran Nugent, were sent out to recount the horror of life in the H-blocks. Liberal campaigners, like Daniel Berrigan SJ, the anti-Vietnam war protestor who had been to Northern Ireland earlier in the year but was denied access to the H-blocks, was a prominent voice on their behalf, ironically from inside the Montgomery county jail, Pennsylvania. There he was staging a series of one-day support fasts while he awaited trial on charges arising from a protest at a US defence plant in the state when cones for Minuteman missiles were damaged. British ministers and MPs were also sent out to do the rounds in Washington and New York putting the British case and highlighting the 'criminal' backgrounds of those concerned. But it seemed the H-block protestors were everywhere. The Queen was heckled on a visit to Brussels. When Amnesty, the internationally respected prisoners rights organisation, denied reports that it had adopted the hunger strikers as prisoners of conscience and said that it was not considering doing so, it was an unnoticed setback.

The Northern Ireland Office was unusually proactive in getting across the government standpoints on the issue. It published detailed factual information about the hunger strikers and their activities to demonstrate their 'criminal' records and pedigree. In an unusually bold move, a camera crew from the ITV 'World in Action' documentary programme was allowed access to the hunger strikers wing in H5 and permitted to ask one question of Raymond McCartney: why did he and the other hunger strikers want the special status of political prisoners? He replied, 'The whole system in Northern Ireland, the special arrest system, the special court system, has proved to us beyond any shadow of doubt that we are not criminals. We are products of the political troubles in Northern Ireland. We are prepared to go through with this, and prepared to die, to prove that we are special prisoners.'

The ensuing shots of the mediaeval-looking, unshaven, long-haired, blanket-draped prisoners in their fouled cells and the gaunt, staring face of an unkempt McCartney were to become the defining pictures of the hunger strike and are among the most enduring images of the Irish conflict in the twentieth century. The television broadcast, on 24 November, was doubly significant, for it signalled clearly that the government had changed tack and was signposting a pathway out of the coming crisis. The prisons minister, Michael Alison, said, 'We will not make any concessions to blackmail and, if they are fighting for a great issue of principle, political status, as they see it, then they are banging their heads against a brick wall. But if they are, in a muddled way, saying "we want better conditions," well, that's a different story.'

These crucial words were largely overlooked the next day during the predictable outcry about McCartney being allowed to broadcast, but their full potential significance was explained to Pope John Paul II when he gave an extended 45-minute audience to Thatcher, who visited him at the Vatican during a visit to Rome for one of the two EEC summits that year. The meeting, overwhelmingly concerned with Northern Ireland and the hunger strike, reflected the pivotal role the church, both in Britain and Ireland, was playing in trying to resolve the confrontation, although Cardinal Hume, the head of the English church, had earlier struck an apparently discordant note with his Irish counterparts by describing the hunger strikes as 'an act of violence' in a pastoral letter which also called for politicians to find 'a just and peaceful solution'. From time to time the undercurrents of historic Anglo-Irish tensions surfaced. During one of their encounters at this time, Thatcher, the Iron Lady, the modern Britannia, asked the openly Irish Republican, Tomas O'Fiaich, why it was that Britain could be at peace with Germany and France despite their ancient enmities but still in conflict with Ireland. 'Well, Madam,' he replied, 'it's because you don't occupy the Ruhr.'

There was no hint of the government's new willingness to be flexible or reference to the slowly evolving settlement plan on 28 November when Atkins answered questions in the House of Commons: '[The hunger strikers] continue to refuse the food offered to them but are taking salt and water. They are medically examined daily and they have lost some weight, but their condition is not at present giving serious cause for concern. The prisoners will continue to be kept under close medical surveillance, and will be offered any medical treatment that may be necessary. This will be on the judgement of the doctors in charge, acting in accordance with the ethics of their profession. Medical treatment is not forced on a prisoner who refuses it. The Government has repeatedly made it plain that it will not be blackmailed by this hunger strike, or any other form of protest, into conceding that the motives for which the protesters committed serious crimes entitle them to treatment different from other criminals.'

Indeed, at this crucial point, the confrontation appeared if anything to be intensifying. For fear of prejudicing all the support that had been mustered, especially by killing civilians, the Provisionals had lowered the level of violence, although killings by Loyalists had actually intensified. In particular, five people actively associated with the H-block protests had been murdered, including Miriam Daly, a university lecturer who represented the IRSP/INLA interests on the National H-Blocks Committee, the main forum for coordinating the prison protest campaign. By the beginning of December, as the fast went on, there had been a marked reduction in IRA attacks, although the organisation was responsible for one in which two soldiers lost their lives. But on the evening of 2 December, a Territorial Army barracks at Hammersmith in west London was bombed and set on fire, while next morning in Brussels, Christopher Tugenhadt, the British Commissioner to the European Union (formerly the European Economic Community), was shot at while leaving his residence. IRA sources in Dublin quickly pointed to the attacks as indicative of their capability to strike again if their demands were not met or if any of the hunger strikers died. The attacks were consistent with what would become a classic IRA negotiating technique: underlining discussions with coordinated violence, especially on the British mainland. With what one television executive called 'Northern Ireland ennui' well established in the metrocentric London print and electronic news establishment, the Provos had correctly calculated that a well-planned, disruptive hoax device in central London was worth far more in propaganda terms than even a dozen deaths in Northern Ireland itself. The tactic had been first tried out to underpin the 1974–75 ceasefire negotiations and would be seen many more times in the years ahead.

The appearance of impasse was further reinforced when three women Republican prisoners in Armagh Prison joined the hunger strike. They were led by Mairead Farrell, 23, their Officer Commanding. Ten months after leaving school in June 1975, she took part in the bombing of the Conway hotel on the southern outskirts of Belfast. During the operation her companion was shot dead by an off-duty RUC officer and she was captured. Later she was sentenced to fourteen years' imprisonment. (In 1988 she was herself shot dead by British undercover soldiers in highly contested circumstances in Gibraltar while apparently making preparations for a bomb attack on a military ceremony.) Another hunger striker was 21-year-old Mairead Nugent, who was aged just seventeen when she took part in a a bomb attack at the weekend home of the then governor of Armagh jail. She helped transport the four lb bomb from Belfast to the property at Millisle on the County Down coast. However, neighbours spotted the break-in at the house and raised the alarm. About the same time as bomb disposal officers successfully defused the device, the two bomb couriers were arrested after their car broke down at Newtownards on its return journey to Belfast. Nugent was imprisoned for twelve years. The third hunger striker, Mary Doyle, 24, was serving a second term of imprisonment, this time of eight years, for explosives offences. She had already served a five-year term for causing an explosion and had been released in 1976. All had been on the 'no work' protest at Armagh since being sentenced and the previous February, after a violent clash with warders during a planned search of Armagh prison, they had launched a dirty protest in support of the political status demand.

Next day, 2 December, the seven Maze hunger strikers were moved from the clean wing in H5 to the prison hospital. A short statement from the Northern Ireland Office said, 'This move has been carried out to facilitate closer medical surveillance of the prisoners, not because of any significant deterioration in their health. While the prisoners are continuing to lose weight, their conditions do not yet give cause for serious concern.' But despite the reassuring tone of the statement and the carefully created impression of impasse, which both sides encouraged, the main effect of the transfer was to inject an even greater sense of urgency into the advanced work then ongoing to forge a settlement which both sides could accept.

Dr Edward Daly, the Bishop of Londonderry, in particular, had pricked up his ears at what Alison had said on the World in Action programme. He had long believed that a more flexible approach by the government would bear great fruit, a view he soon conveyed to John Hume, the leader of the SDLP, who had maintained close contact with the two church leaders throughout their recent talks with both sides. Hume now moved into a more open role, trying to persuade the government, in line with the European Human Rights Commission finding, to be more flexible and further relax the prison regime, as earlier outlined by Atkins, but without conceding the principle of political status. Hume also believed the prisoners could accept that without loss of face because they had brought the case. 'That was the first step, finding firm ground that everyone could stand on,' he later admitted. Hume travelled from Londonderry to Dublin and having got the Irish government on board – who, of course, did not want to concede political recognition themselves – flew to London to see

Atkins. They met on 4 December and later that day, in reply to a planted parliamentary question, Atkins published a lengthy document. Because of its central importance to the way events developed, then and in the watershed months ahead, it is worth reproducing in its entirety:

'Concern has been expressed on humanitarian grounds about conditions in the Maze Prison in Northern Ireland. I set out below the real facts about the living conditions which are open to all prisoners in Northern Ireland; and explain the special measures which have already been taken on humanitarian grounds in respect of the living conditions of the protesting prisoners.

'The ten prisoners in Northern Ireland are on hunger strike in support of a demand that all protesting prisoners be granted "political status," which would be intended to differentiate them from all other prisoners. The Government will not concede that demand.

'The specific demands by the male protestors are for five changes in their prison regime. They are the right:

(i)   to wear their own clothes;

(ii) to refrain from prison work;

(iii) to associate freely with one another;

(iv) to organise recreational facilities and to have one letter, visit and parcel a week;

(v)   to have lost remission fully restored.

Such changes would go far to give, and are intended to give, the protesting prisoners control over their lives in prison, and could not be agreed to by the Government, since to do so would be to legitimise and encourage terrorist activity. What the government is committed to is to ensure that, for all prisoners, the regime is as enlightened and humane as possible. This statement clarifies, in relation to the protestors' demands, how far this has already been achieved.

'Under Prison Rules, prescribed under statute by the Secretary of State, prisoners are entitled to certain rights and may, if they conform with the Rules, enjoy certain privileges. *Rights* may not be withheld although prisoners can – and some protestors do – choose not to take them up. *Privileges*, on the other hand, may be withheld if a prisoner is in breach of the Rules. If prisoners abide by the Rules, then the privileges are accorded as a matter of course. The rights and privileges compare with the protestors' demands as follows:

(a) Clothing: the protestors want the right to wear their own clothing at all times. Prison Rules require prisoners to wear prison-issue clothing (or special clothes appropriate to their work) during normal working hours on week-days (7.30 am to 5.00 pm), but, as a privilege, prisoners may, unless they are engaged on orderly duties, wear their own clothing for the rest of the evening during the week, and, throughout the weekend. They may also wear their own clothing when receiving visits. For security reasons, colour and design of prisoners' own clothing is subject to the discretion of the Governor. It will thus be seen that a prisoner conforming with the Rules may wear his own clothing for almost half the time he would expect to be outside his cell. For the remainder of the time, the Government's decision of 23 October means that conforming prisoners will be wearing civilian clothing issued by the prison authorities.

(b) Work: The protesting prisoners seek the right to refrain from prison work. Prison Rules require convicted prisoners to "engage in useful work", and four main types of such work are undertaken. *First*, some prisoners undertake domestic tasks in the kitchens, dining areas, ablutions and wings. *Second*, an extensive range of industrial employment is provided in prison workshops. *Third*, vocational training is available to teach a wide range of skills. Courses have been developed to the requirements of the skills testing service of the City and Guilds of London Institute. *Fourth*, education classes are provided *during working hours* (from 2 to 20 hours a week) to cover a wide range of prisoners' needs from remedial education to Open University courses. Classes in craft theory are given to complement the vocational training side whilst tuition is provided in a wide range of subjects enabling prisoners to study for RSA, City and Guilds Literacy and Numeracy certificates, GCE and A level certificates. In brief, while Prison Rules require a prisoner to "engage in useful work", work is interpreted to include orderly duties, industrial employment, vocational training, and education.

(c) Association: the protestors want the right to associate freely with one another. Prison Rules provide, as a privilege, that each week-day evening for *3* hours and throughout the day at weekends, prisoners have "association" during which, within each 25-cell wing they may watch TV, play indoor games, follow hobbies and exercise in the yard attached to each wing, and attend education classes. A wide range of evening classes is provided and there is some dove-tailing with daytime courses. Apart from text books the NI Education and library Boards provide well-stocked libraries. Books and newspapers may be taken to be read in cells. In short, there is *already*, as a privilege, association within each wing outside normal week-day working hours.

(d) Recreation: the protestors demand the right to organise recreational facilities. The prison regime already provides for the use of gymnasia and playing pitches in addition to the statutory exercise period of not less than one hour each day in the open air when practicable, during association periods, prisoners may use the Hobbies Room for supervised handicraft and artistic activities.

(e) Visits, letters and parcels: the protestors demand one visit, one parcel and one letter each week. Under Prison Rules, each prisoner enjoys *as of right* one letter and one visit per month. The Rules provide, as *a privilege*, seven additional letters per month at the expense of the prison, three additional visits, and a weekly parcel. Special parcels are also allowed at Christmas, Easter and Halloween. Thus the existing privileges are already more generous than the protestors' demand.

(f) Remission: the prisoners are demanding the restoration in full of the remission that they have lost while engaged in the protest. Prison Rules provide that a prisoner serving a term of more than one month receives remission, subject to good conduct, up to one-half of his sentence. This is a more generous rate of remission than is available elsewhere in the UK. Remission may be forfeited as a punishment for breach of Prison Rules; but it may be restored after subsequent good behaviour. The protestors have lost one day's remission for each day they have been in breach of Prison Rules. The opportunity to regain lost remission already exists.

'The above deals briefly with certain aspects of the regime; this regime is evidence of the Government's commitment to maintain and develop humane and enlightened conditions for all prisoners in its care in Northern Ireland.

'The protesters have forfeited a substantial part of the regime described above. Nevertheless, the Government, acknowledging the injunction of the European Commission of Human Rights to keep under constant review their reaction to the protestors, has in the course of this year taken the following steps:

(i) On 26 March the protesting prisoners who by their failure to conform with Prison Rules have forfeited the privileges afforded to conforming prisoners were nevertheless offered exercise in sports gear, 3 letters in and out each month in addition to their statutory monthly letter, and 2 visits a month instead of 1.

(ii) Since the late summer the protesting prisoners have been offered:

(a) an hour's physical exercise a week;

(b) one evening association a week in prison uniform;

(c) access to books and newspapers (which are available in the cell blocks but not taken) in the rooms where masses are held on Sundays;

(d) "closed" visits (ie in which the prisoner is physically separated from his visitor) as an alternative to a body search;

(e) compassionate home leave on the same basis as conforming prison

(iii) The protesting prisoners have never been denied their daily hour's exercise.

'Thus the Government has shown itself ready, despite the protest, to deal with the humanitarian aspects of the conditions that the protesting prisoners have imposed upon themselves.

'The Government takes no pleasure in the sight of young men and women inflicting suffering on themselves and their families. We agree with the European Commission of Human Rights that while there can be no question of their having political status, we should be ready nevertheless to deal with the humanitarian aspects of the conditions in the prisons arising from the protest. It is a matter of very great regret that changes made by the Government in response to the Commission have been rejected. We have always been and still are willing to discuss the humanitarian aspects of the prison administration in Northern Ireland with anyone who shares our concern about it.

'The Government remains determined that, subject always to the requirements of security and within the resources available, the progress achieved in recent years in the administration of Northern Ireland prisons should be continued to meet the legitimate needs of all concerned.'

With the force of the emotions now running over the hunger strike, there was extraordinarily tight security in Dublin on 8 December when Margaret Thatcher, making the first visit to Dublin by a British Prime Minister since Partition, flew in for a summit meeting with Charles Haughey, then her Irish equivalent. During the talks at Dublin Castle, once the seat of British power in Ireland, she was accompanied by Lord Carrington, Foreign Secretary, Geoffrey Howe, Chancellor of the Exchequer, and Humphrey Atkins. The main outcome of the meeting was a groundbreaking agreement to conduct a series of joint studies on a wide range of subjects examining the 'totality of relationships' between Britain and Ireland. Whatever was said in detail between the two sides about the accelerating efforts to end the hunger strike remained private. At a large rally in Dublin that night, after Thatcher and her high-powered team had departed, thousands of people cheered loudly when a Union flag was set on fire and effigies of Thatcher and Atkins were burned.

At the end of that week, having previously stayed out of the limelight, six members of the Ulster Defence Association in the Maze prison started their own hunger strike in support of their demand for segregation from Republican prisoners and were isolated in a wing of H1. Just what they wanted was unclear but the real reason for raising their profile was to stake a claim to ensure that they shared in any concessions the Provos might win. There were only 27 Loyalists 'on the blanket' (but most emphatically not the dirty protest, which horrified them). Now 143 other Loyalist prisoners refused to come out of their cells in solidarity with the hunger strikers. The protest was short-lived, however, and fizzled out after just five days, putting the full focus back on the IRA protest which, far from subsiding as everybody hoped, appeared to escalate again on 15 December when 23 further Republican prisoners joined those already on hunger strike. Among them were prisoners whose names would soon figure again: Francis Hughes, Thomas McIlwee, Kevin Lynch, Patsy O'Hara, Michael Devine, Raymond McCreesh, Martin Hurson and Kieran Doherty. The Northern Ireland Office reacted in a notably conciliatory tone: 'As in the case of the prisoners at present on hunger strike the government regrets the action taken. The government however remains committed to its policy of increasingly improving prison conditions while refusing to give any special status to particular prisoners.' The exit route was again being clearly signposted.

The lead hunger strikers had in fact reacted cautiously to the Atkins statement and so had their relatives but there was an innate distrust of the British government. 'Perfidious Albion' was an old Republican shibboleth. More recently, Republicans felt, they had been deceived during the secret talks after the 1974–75 ceasefire by purposefully ambiguous British diplomacy. The day after the Hume-Atkins meeting and the publication of the regime document, the relatives of the prisoners in a joint statement asked the British administration to enter into discussions 'with the representatives of the other protesting prisoners on whose behalf our sons and daughters are on hunger strike'. They said that if the door was really open 'the British administration will have the necessary will to resolve the crisis.' Hume knew the government was not going to enter into anything that looked like negotiations, with intermediaries openly shuttling between the two sides, nor would they begin to talk to the people regarded by the prisoners as their commanding officers. So he asked the prison authorities to make sure the men were in no doubt what the government was saying and to ensure Atkins' statement was fully explained to them. 'We took note of that,' says a senior Northern Ireland Office official. Next day, 6 December, a letter was sent to the relatives of every prisoner explaining the package on offer. Atkins then took another major conciliatory step on 10 December by sending a senior civil servant, a deputy under-secretary, to the prison. The seven hunger strikers, with pallid faces and long beards and hair, clad in pyjamas and dressing gowns, were brought to a recreation room from their single rooms in the prison hospital. Flanked by the Governor and the Chief Medical Officer, the official first read them the Hansard account of Atkins' statement about what was on offer and then answered questions for an hour. Next day, the prisoners smuggled a statement out rejecting the package while relatives said that now the ice had been broken, they hoped the official could go back for more dialogue. Despite the apparent deadlock there had been a major breakthrough. The prisoners had accepted they would not get political status but what they needed were gestures to present as a gain for there was nothing substantive on offer that had not been available well before the hunger strike began. While none of the prisoners was yet in a serious condition, there were signs that the condition of one was beginning to worsen. McKenna was showing the first symptoms of progressive blindness arising from vitamin deficiency and was having trouble focusing his vision. But despite the element of urgency this imposed, the arms-length dialogue broke down.

There were two points of contention. Ministers forbade the senior official to go back to the prison because the prisoners demanded he speak through Bobby Sands, the man who had succeeded Hughes as their commanding officer at the beginning of the hunger strike. Discussions in this fashion, recognising a spokesman for the prisoners, were not acceptable to the government. The Atkins package had promised further easements in the prison regime after the ending of the protest but the prisoners wanted this expanded in advance to present as a gain. However, despite the deadlock, the authorities facilitated Sands by allowing him free movement through the prison and hospital to talk to the Block leaders and the hunger strikers. A prominent Sinn Fein member was also allowed in to see Sands and the hunger strikers to recommend the acceptance of the package. Over the weekend of 13 and 14 December, prison chaplains and some relatives continued the pressure on both the government and the prisoners to move but the government position was firm. The 4 December package was the final offer. Take it or die.

Outside the prison preparations were underway to deal with the surge of disorder that would follow the death of one of the hunger strikers. Police leave was cancelled, the traditional round of pre-Christmas parties was postponed and the RUC Traffic Branch was issued with riot kit and redeployed from its customary breathalyser blitz on those who insisted on enjoying the excesses of the season and still driving their cars.

Fifty days into the fast, with their health steadily ebbing, the hunger strikers were holding out for more concessions. They still wanted to have their own clothes and to have recreational activities and educational courses deemed as fulfilling the obligation to work. Yet there was a serious lack of trust among them that they would get what was promised once the fasts were halted. Much midnight oil was burned in the Northern Ireland Office over the next 48 hours. John Hume had one twelve-hour session with officials exploring possible ways out of the deadlock. There were no new concessions being considered but it was hoped clarifications and refinements could clinch a deal. Cardinal O'Fiaich certainly thought so. On 15 December, after one of the periodic joint meetings between Atkins and the leaders of the four main churches, he was taken aside by officials to be asked if he thought they would run. Two days later he called on the hunger strikers to abandon their protest and appealed to Margaret Thatcher by telegram to intervene personally and help end the protest. Speaking in Dublin he said that he had seen a new document which seemed to improve the proportion of time that prisoners could wear their own clothes from half to three-quarters of the time.

By the next morning, the fifty-third day of the hunger strike, there was a real race against time at the Maze where doctors reported a notable worsening in the condition of the hunger strikers. Their eyesight and hearing was becoming impaired and although most could still walk, they were stooped, weak and very slow. McKenna, whose health had steadily deteriorated more rapidly than any of the others, was judged by doctors to have less than 24 hours to live and McKearney was also fading fast. The prison chaplain gave McKenna the last rites of the Catholic church. One prison officer remembers that the men looked like skeletons with skin stretched over their bones. Fr Brendan Meagher, a Redemptorist priest and one of the prison chaplains who had also emerged as a conduit between them and the politicians outside, told them he had been in touch overnight with the British and Irish governments and the leadership of the Republican movement. As a result, he reported, he was confident there was a deal they could accept and he was expecting to be able to come back later that evening to confirm it.

At that very time, the document, earlier shown to the Cardinal was in fact being finalised in the utmost secrecy in London as the centrepiece of a last minute initiative to break the impasse. The work had accelerated that morning after the intervention of Michael Oatley, the shadowy

British intelligence officer who had opened up a back-channel to the IRA five years earlier to facilitate the ceasefire negotiations. In the early hours of that morning, a go-between in Derry had renewed the contact after being approached by the prison chaplain. Speaking on the BBC Television series 'Brits' in May 2000, Oatley, by then retired from MI6, for the first time described what took place. 'I was rung up by a friend who said "This is the situation, I think we can do something with it." As usual the telephone call came at one or two in the morning. We spent two or three hours discussing the situation in veiled language over the telephone. I produced a set of proposals as to how the matter might be managed with a formula, and went the following morning with it to the Northern Ireland Office.'

There urgent discussions took place with Kenneth Stowe, the permanent secretary, and others in London and Belfast throughout the day. When they had finished drafting, there was an expanded version of the previous Atkins document, melting into the pot all the points raised by the hunger strikers themselves, John Hume and the secret mediator through Oatley. The text was then referred to Downing Street for personal approval by the Prime Minister. That done, Oatley was driven at speed to London Airport for the late evening shuttle to Belfast. But while Oatley was in transit with the document, there had been major developments at the Maze. At 2.30 that afternoon the Governor and the Prison doctor saw each of the seven hunger strikers and warned them in uncompromising terms of the medical consequences of their fast. They pointed out that the longer treatment was delayed the more their condition was likely to be irreversible. 'The brinkmanship is over. There is no reason to go on. There's nothing more on offer. Take it or leave it. The government has made its response,' they were told. The prisoners had heard similar warnings often before from one of their doctors whom they had renamed 'Mengele'.

Two hours later, at 4.30, a senior medical consultant was brought to the prison hospital to examine McKenna, who was lapsing in and out of consciousness. It was decided to move him eight miles to a closely guarded ward in the military wing at the Musgrave Park Hospital, where he could be more expertly cared for. At 6 pm, as he was carried out of the prison, according to eyewitnesses, he shouted, 'I'm away. Get off it.' Minutes later, as his ambulance escorted by a solitary RUC Land Rover, negotiated the layers of gates controlling access to the prison and headed out along the M1 motorway towards Belfast, the six remaining hunger strikers began what was to be a 56-minute discussion. Then they asked for Sands to be brought to them. The fast was being ended, he was told, to save McKenna's life on the basis that there was an improved offer on the way from London. Shortly after 7.30 pm Hughes asked to see the Deputy Governor. 'As far as we are concerned, the hunger strike is over,' he told him. The decision was recorded in the prison log at 7.46 pm on the fifty-third day of the fast. Sands had meanwhile left to visit H-blocks 3, 4 and 5 to relay the hunger strikers' decision. As he did so they were given tea and scrambled eggs in the prison hospital.

Meanwhile Oatley's plane had landed. 'I was required to have my meeting in Aldergrove airport fairly late in the evening, and that was a rather curious circumstance because there was nobody in Aldergrove airport at that time of night. The person who came to see me was a Roman Catholic priest who was in touch with the hunger strikers, was obviously known to be in touch with the hunger strikers and was clearly being tailed by a team of Special Branch officers. So we had this situation where our meeting took place in an entirely empty airport lounge with burly figures standing behind every pillar round about, which was quite grotesque and not exactly designed to keep the thing entirely discreet.'

Oatley's contact was in fact Fr Brendan Meagher, who was unknown to him. So the priest had been warned to look for a man wearing a red carnation. They met, had a brief discussion and the priest left the airport with a copy of a statement outlining what would happen once the hunger strikes ended and what was now a 30-page document outlining the details of the prison regime that would be on offer if the blanket and dirty protests finally ended. He travelled directly to the prison, where it was copied and distributed. In *Nor Meekly Serve my Time*, Leo Green, one of the strikers, recalled, 'He arrived back at the camp at midnight with a copy of the document. Typical of the Brits. The language in places was ambiguous. The deciding factor would be the spirit in which it had been drawn up. This would soon be tested. Relief that the hunger strike had ended without the loss of life soon turned to despair. The Brits, it became clear, had no genuine desire for a solution. Their sole concern had been to end the hunger strike and they had employed cynical brinkmanship to achieve it. Fifty-three days of hunger strike and we were no further on. Almost immediately a second hunger strike loomed on the horizon.'

Any hopes that the prisons were on the verge of a new era of serenity were further dashed by the Loyalists at 7 am on 30 December, when William Burns, aged 45, a married man with four grown-up children, was ambushed and shot four times in the chest as he left his home in Knocknagoney Park, east Belfast, to go on duty at Belfast prison. He died on the way to hospital. His killers escaped in a car. Fifteen minutes later, in another part of east Belfast, a second officer was hit in the arm and leg when a motorcycle drew alongside him in the morning rush-hour traffic and the pillion passenger opened fire. He survived the attack. Shortly afterwards a caller to Downtown Radio claimed responsibility for the attacks on behalf of an unheard group called the Loyalist Prisoners Action Force (LPAF). He said it was in retaliation for the ill-treatment of Loyalist prisoners. Later it emerged that the name was a flag of convenience for the UVF. For the hard-pressed men and women of the Northern Ireland Prison Service it was a grim end to a difficult year, but worse was to come.

Chapter Eleven
An unlikely model for a martyr

After four Christmases in the self-imposed isolation and discomfort of the H-blocks, the end of the hunger strike tempted some of the more optimistic IRA prisoners to think of a turkey dinner and watching television. While the more sceptical among them did not relax their guard quite that much, there was, at first, a wide consensus that the government's last-gasp, 30-page document, passed from the career spy to the priest, provided them with political status in all but name. Certainly that was the interpretation put on it by many of the prison officers. The commentators and editorials all complimented Thatcher and Atkins for standing firm on principle and showing parallel humanitarian flexibility. On an objective basis it seemed as if a classic compromise had been reached with both sides able to claim victory. The government had not climbed down on principle and granted political status. The prisoners had obtained significant easements of the prison regime, which went a long way towards their demands, and the promise of further concessions was on offer. Indeed they could fairly claim they had obtained the most liberal prison regime in the United Kingdom and, indeed, anywhere in Europe.

Bobby Sands, the leader of the prisoners, while recognising there was nothing concrete in the document, initially commended it to his fellow inmates as being so wide open he could drive a bus through it. But he was fearful that his negotiating position had been heavily weakened by the collapse of the fast, and veered in and out of the position that it would take another hunger strike to clinch things. Indeed he thought the hunger strikers had 'chickened out' at the vital moment when maximum pressure could have been exerted to gain concessions. The prisoners thus approached the Christmas and New Year period in a state of confusion and uncertainty about how the transition from protest to the new normality would be made. Their apprehension was reflected in a pre-Christmas statement: 'In ending our hunger strike, we make it clear that failure by the British government to act in a responsible manner towards ending the conditions which forced us to a hunger strike will lead to inevitable and continued strife within the H-blocks.'

Things got off to a discouraging start when a plan promoted by one of the prison chaplains for the prisoners to 'go sick' failed to materialise. According to the accounts of the prisoners, one of the senior governors had agreed to them declaring themselves sick, accepting dressing gowns, pyjamas and slippers, and availing themselves of toilet and washing facilities, thus ending the blanket and dirty protests. Over the following 30 days, as they 'recovered', the new regime would be progressively introduced. When this plan failed to materialise, and the prisoners spent their fifth Christmas on protest, it extinguished the tiny sparks of goodwill ignited by the promise of a new regime and nourished further the deep distrust that was rapidly gaining more ground. If the authorities hoped to gain a psychological advantage and blunt the resolve of the prisoners to continue and undermine the protest, they seriously miscalculated. But there is more compelling direct evidence of their good faith in trying to implement the Atkins plan. As soon as the hunger strike ended, prison officials were hastily sent on an £87,500 shopping spree to Marks and Spencer and C&A stores to buy civilian clothing in a wide range of styles and colours, which had since been stored in the prison awaiting distribution. For their part the government insisted that 'no undertakings were given to the hunger strikers, or the other protesting prisoners, before it or after. What the government had sought to do was to explain to all protesting prisoners what facilities and opportunities were available to them within the existing prison regime, which, as was also made clear to them, the government is committed to maintaining and, as circumstances allow, improving.'

'We were disappointed that Christmas all right but it only made us all the more determined to beat the bastards,' recalled one prisoner. 'We knew then that it would take another hunger strike and that, in all probability one of us would have to die to convince the Brits how serious we were.'

Although it was a primary article of faith on the part of the government and the prison authorities that there would be no acknowledgement of, never mind negotiation with, any prisoner leadership, that is precisely what happened in the early part of January. Sands and the Governor, Stanley Hilditch, engaged directly in interpreting what the new prison rules entailed. Out of this contact the prisoners understood there would be a gradual de-escalation of their protest accompanied by a phased introduction of the agreed new regime. In line with this understanding two wings of prisoners, ten in each, would abandon the protest in early January, wash and shave and cut their hair, and put on clothes supplied for them by their families outside. They would also move into clean wings, and make themselves available for work, provided it was of an educational or vocational nature or concerned with what was called wing maintenance, looking after their own accommodation. But again, according to the prisoners, the authorities reneged. On 27 January, Sands retaliated by ordering 96 prisoners to smash the newly provided furniture and fittings in their wings. In the immediate aftermath of this clash, according to the prisoners, there was a decisive confrontation between Sands and the Governor who said there would be no privileges for the prisoners until they conformed to the regime.

Sands now took the view that the British government had not only played poker with the prisoners lives but cheated. He immediately decided there would be a second hunger strike, he would lead it himself and, crucially, the back-up hunger strikers would only join in at intervals so that pressure could not be applied to a group if one was at the point of death. Sands made it clear to his comrades from the outset that he was not to be saved from death if the hunger strike was not achieving its full objectives. His plan was discussed and enthusiastically endorsed by the prisoners and, reluctantly again, by the Republican leadership outside. A smuggled statement on 5 February, announcing the second hunger strike said, 'Our last hunger strikers were morally blackmailed. Where is the peace in the prisons which, like a promise, was held before dying men's eyes?' Bik McFarlane then took over as leader while Sands prepared for his fast. Everyone involved knew that this time Sands, at least, would die if the five demands were not met and that others were equally prepared to do so if the British government still refused to concede. The scene was thus set for one of the most extraordinary, protracted and unprecedented confrontations ever between a government and terrorists.

By birth and background, Robert Gerard Sands was a most unlikely model for the revered, inspirational and visionary IRA figurehead into which the IRA's expert martyr-making choreographers would soon fashion him. Born in Newtownabbey, outside Belfast on 9 March 1954, he grew up in Rathcoole, a post-war housing estate on the north shore of Belfast Lough. It was a mixed community and although Sands was reared a Catholic and attended the local Catholic Stella Maris school, his friends came from both traditions. He also attended the Star of the Sea youth club, which was specifically cross-community. In the mid 1960s he starred in a football team which included players from both backgrounds, and won what he said was 'a lot of medals' for football and running. But in the aftermath of the early troubles, the mixed estate became a sectarian battleground and in 1972 the Sands family were intimidated and burned out of their house. They moved to the newly built Twinbrook estate, on the fringes of west Belfast, where many other Catholic families had also taken refuge, part of the largest enforced movement of a civil population since the Second World War. Sands had now started work as an apprentice coachbuilder, but once again he came up against the dark forces of Northern Ireland sectarianism and was driven from his job. Like many other young people of his age and generation, embittered by their experiences at that time, he soon became involved with the IRA, a move that would ultimately propel him from the obscurity of a prison cell to death and acclamation as a hero of the Republican movement. In one of the many articles, poems and pamphlets attributed to him, he recalls joining the Provos, aged eighteen and a half. 'My mother wept with pride and fear as I went out to confront the imperial might of an empire with an M1 Carbine and enough hate to topple the world.'

But the offences for which he first went to prison in 1973 after being convicted by a jury were distinctly vainglorious: two armed robberies at petrol filling stations and two attempted thefts. He was sentenced to five years' imprisonment and served his term as a special category prisoner until his release in April 1976. Barely six months later, a police patrol intercepted a car speeding away after a bomb explosion at a furniture warehouse in the southern Belfast suburbs. Gunfire was exchanged before the four occupants, including Sands, were captured. A gun was recovered from the floor of the vehicle. One of the four, Bobby Sands, was ultimately sentenced to serve fourteen years imprisonment for possessing firearms and ammunition. Another of the four, Joe McDonnell, would ultimately join the hunger strike and die in solidarity with Sands.

Sands chose 1 March 1981 to begin his fast, the fifth anniversary of the ending of eligibility for special category. That morning at 7.30 am he refused breakfast. A statement smuggled from the H-blocks set the scene:

> 'We, the Republican POWs in the H-Blocks of Long Kesh, and our comrades in Armagh prison, are entitled to and hereby demand political status, and we reject today, as we have consistently rejected every day since September 14th, 1976, when the Blanket protest began, the British government's attempted criminalisation of ourselves and our struggle.
>
> 'Five years ago this day, the British government declared that anyone arrested and convicted after March 1st, 1976, was to be treated as a criminal and no longer as a political prisoner. Five years later we are still able to declare that that criminalisation policy, which we have resisted and suffered, has failed.

'If a British government experienced such a long and persistent resistance to a domestic policy in England, then that policy would almost certainly be changed. But not so in Ireland where its traditional racist attitude blinds its judgement to reason and persuasion. Only the loud voice of the Irish people and world opinion can bring them to their senses and only a hunger strike, where lives are laid down as proof of the strength of our political convictions, can rally such opinion, and present the British with the problem that, far from criminalising the cause of Ireland, their intransigence is actually bringing popular attention to that cause.

'We have asserted that we are political prisoners and everything about our country, our arrests, interrogations, trials and prison conditions show that we are politically motivated and not motivated by selfish reasons or for selfish ends. As further demonstration of our selflessness and the justness of our cause, a number of our comrades, beginning today with Bobby Sands, will hunger strike to the death unless the British government abandons its criminalisation policy and meets our demand for political status.'

Twenty-four hours after the hunger strike began, the 439 Republican prisoners – including 28 women in Armagh – decided to call off the dirty protest, but not the blanket protest, to deny the British government any propaganda advantage from their decision and to help ensure that attention was clearly focused on the hunger strike and the five demands. So they began to use toilets and showers, shave and have haircuts. They also asked for bedding and furniture to be restored to their cells. The authorities agreed, but issued iron beds that could not so easily be smashed up. Over the succeeding weeks they would also be given access to library books and permitted to have radios in their cells.

The next day, Atkins signalled a predictably uncompromising line when he made a statement in the House of Commons in which he reiterated there would be no political status for prisoners regardless of the renewed hunger strike. The government line was that if Sands persisted in his wish to commit suicide that was his choice and medical treatment would not be forced upon him. Atkins revealed that overnight the women had been moved to clean cells and 240 male prisoners had been relocated and given clean bedding. The rest would also move as soon as more clean cells had been made ready. He added that since the ending of the first hunger strike, 80 prisoners had stopped protesting and were benefiting from the new regime outlined in his earlier statement. Privately it was said, by one of his officials, that Atkins felt like a man just released from hospital after treatment for a broken leg only to find himself straight back in bed with the other one broken.

When he commenced the hunger strike on Sunday 1 March, Sands, whose nickname was Geronimo, kept a diary written in biro ink on sheets of toilet paper. That day he wrote: 'I am standing on the threshold of another trembling world. May God have mercy on my soul.' Noting that before starting his fast he had eaten 'the statutory weekly bit of fruit' the previous night, he added, 'As fate had it, it was an orange, and the final irony, it was bitter. The food is being left at the door. My portions, as expected, are quite larger than usual, or those which my cell mate (Malachy Carey) is getting.' Later he wrote: 'I can ignore the presence of food staring me straight in the face all the time. It's not damaging me.' But he did admit to a craving for brown wholemeal bread, butter, Dutch cheese and honey. He also said he was praying – 'crawler, and a last minute one, some would say. But I believe in God and he and I are getting on well this weather.' Sands celebrated his twenty-seventh birthday on 9 March. 'The boys are having a bit of a sing-song for me, bless their hearts.' He does not mention the fact that he has spent almost a third of his short life in prison.

The diary concludes on 17 March, St Patrick's Day. Sands recounts a visit from the Governor. ' "I see you're reading a short book. It's a good thing it isn't a long one for you won't finish it." That's the sort of people they are. Curse them! They won't break me because the desire for freedom, and the freedom of the Irish people, is in my heart.' On 23 March, days later, having lost sixteen pounds in weight, Sands was moved to the prison hospital in the Maze. There he was befriended by an elderly prisoner orderly, serving time for financial offences. He slipped Sands some tobacco and cigarette papers but soon became alarmed at the rate the cigarette papers were being used while the tobacco was not being touched. Thinking that Sands might be eating the papers, he raised his concern and was relieved to be told they were in fact being used to write notes for smuggling.

Ever since a meeting in Dublin on 25 January, when 600 H-block activists were updated about the Maze situation, 250 groups had stood ready for renewed protest action in support of a second hunger strike, and the familiar round of marches, vigils, sit-ins and rallies now began again. So too did a bombardment of 'comms' from the prisoners to a wide range of political leaders, journalists, writers and other opinion formers. The messages were smuggled out to supporters and then put in the post. But on 5 March, in an incredible twist of fate, Frank Maguire, the independent nationalist MP for Fermanagh and South Tyrone, collapsed with a heart attack and was rushed to hospital, where he died. Maguire, a publican by trade was the proprietor of Frank's Bar in Lisnaskea, Co Fermanagh. He had been interned for a time in the 1950's and was an MP in name only. A man of active Republican views and sympathies, he rarely attended parliament and, although he had been a member since October 1974, had still not made his maiden speech in over six years.

The by-election was swiftly set for 9 April and immediately there was an extraordinary groundswell to put Bobby Sands up as a candidate. Although the Provos, at that time, maintained an abstentionist policy of not taking seats because they contested the legitimacy of both the British and Irish parliaments, they calculated that for Sands even to be a candidate in the election would dramatically publicise the hunger strike and put severe pressure on the British government. It was, most certainly, not out of the question that he could win it. The seat had a clear Catholic majority but, as with Maguire, Nationalists and Republicans needed to unite behind a single candidate to ensure victory. The Provos thus began a secret campaign of political skulduggery to ensure Sands got a clear run and won the seat.

The entire H-block issue posed a dilemma for Catholic opinion and divided it. There were those of a Republican disposition who saw the Provos fighting a just war and condoned and directly supported them. At the other extreme were those who shared the ideal of a united Ireland and the same sense of political and civil injustice but stopped short of advocating or approving violence to bring it about. In the middle was a large group of instinctive, but law abiding, Nationalists, who found their emotions in conflict with their consciences. The merits of the renewed hunger strike were far from clear to those outside the prison and even Dr Edward Daly, the Bishop of Derry, had publicly opposed it. Among more far-sighted Catholics there were the first stirrings of debate about what attitude they should take in the event of one or more hunger strikers dying. Would it be suicide? Should it be supported or condemned? There is no doubt that, despite a continued abhorrence of violence, some sympathy for the prisoners now began to germinate and a view that no one should die, or needed to, began to harden. For its part, the Republican leadership began to sense a real sea-change in attitudes to them beyond their own committed republican constituency. The main Nationalist party, the SDLP, nearly tore itself asunder deciding whether or not to put up a candidate. It finally accepted Noel Maguire, a brother of the dead MP, as the agreed candidate. But one prominent SDLP member, Austin Currie, who had wanted to stand, was worried, rightly as it turned out, that Maguire might back down or be forced out, so he completed nomination papers to slip in at the last minute if necessary to stop Sands having a clear run. Splitting the vote meant handing the seat to the Unionists, but at that stage, even though it was an unthinkable option, many moderate Nationalists would have preferred it to having a dying hunger striker as MP.

When the nominations deadline passed, however, Maguire and Sands were the two candidates, in opposition to the Unionist Harry West. But immediately after nominations had closed on 30 March, the Provos promptly cornered Maguire in the upstairs room of a public house. There, by threatening to smear him as a homosexual, they forced him to withdraw his nomination papers. The withdrawal, up to an hour after the close of nominations, was perfectly legal, but by then, of course, it was not possible for Austin Currie or anyone else to stand. In the subsequent straight electoral fight on 9 April, Sands beat West by 30,492 to 29,046, a majority of 1446. The election's far-reaching consequences for prison policy and the long term political landscape proved it to be one of the most defining moments of the years of conflict in Northern Ireland.

Protestants could not believe that so many Catholics could bring themselves to vote for a man whom they generally regarded as nothing more than a sordid terrorist gunman. Whatever the real explanation for Catholic support, and it was varied and complex, the international spotlight now switched to the fate of the man the west Belfast graffiti writers had instantly dubbed the Rt Hon Bobby Sands MP. It was richly ironic that the Provos, with their consuming hatred of everything British, should so revel in glorifying him as a British MP. In the United States of America Ronald Reagan, the President, said that he would not intervene in the situation in Northern Ireland but he was 'deeply concerned' at events there. The unyielding British government declared that the election would not change its position in regard to special category status and set about amending the Representation of the People Act to make it impossible in the future for prisoners to stand as candidates for election to parliament.

The election news was greeted with elation in the prison. The few with illegal crystal sets had them tuned in during the late afternoon anxiously awaiting the result. When it came it was tapped along the pipes in some blocks and loud cheers went up. Other nearby blocks, where there was no access to a radio, correctly deduced the news from the cheers. But in at least one block the news did not filter through until the next day, when prisoners returned from visits. Until then, thanks to a malicious prison officer the previous evening, the inmates were convinced the Unionist had won.

Community tensions soared sky high as the countdown to Bobby Sands widely expected death was relentlessly exploited by the Provos. On 20 April three members of the European Parliament, from the Irish Republic, were permitted to visit him and seek a way out of the impasse but Margaret Thatcher, the Prime Minister, resolutely refused to meet them. 'There is no such thing as political murder, political bombing or political violence. There is only criminal murder, criminal bombing and criminal violence. It is not political,' she proclaimed yet again. The Red Cross and other interested groups became involved. The private secretary to the Pope, Newry-born Father John Magee, flew from Rome and shuttled between the prison where Sands was slowly expiring in the hospital, Stormont Castle where he saw Atkins, and Cardinal O'Fiaich's house in Armagh. He presented Sands with a crucifix. 'All life is sacred and must be preserved as a gift from God. I therefore appealed, in the name of Christ and his vicar on earth, saying that violence of all kinds must be condemned in the clearest terms as being against the law of God,' the emissary said. It fell on deaf ears. Sands continued his fast.

The entire situation was utterly bewildering for Protestants, to whom it appeared the church, and Southern Irish politicians, were lined up solidly with the IRA. This frustration was given crude expression by the graffiti writers: 'Let the dirty bastards die.' In early May, as the entire community waited for Sands to die, the tension on the streets was almost tangible and there were rumours, deliberately planted and stoked-up, that the IRA was going to evacuate Catholics from flashpoint areas to save them from Loyalist mobs. In expectation of prolonged rioting and disruption in the aftermath, panic buying of bread and milk set in and there were hour-long queues at some supermarket check-outs. On 23 April Sands' sister Marcella made an application to the European Commission on Human Rights claiming that the British government had broken three articles of the European Convention on Human Rights in their treatment of Republican prisoners. Because of the urgency of the situation, two Commissioners flew to Belfast 48 hours later to visit Sands. However, they were denied access because Sands insisted on the presence of McFarlane, Gerry Adams, the Vice-President of Sinn Fein, and Danny Morrison, then editor of *An Phoblacht/Republican News*. The Commission later announced that it had no power to proceed with the case.

Finally, in the early hours of 3 May, Sands slipped into a terminal coma. On 5 May he died. The Northern Ireland Office immediately issued a terse statement: 'Mr Robert Sands, a prisoner in the Maze Prison, died today at 1.17 am. He took his own life by refusing food and medical intervention for 66 days.' In an accompanying statement, Atkins said, 'I regret this needless and pointless death. Too many have died by violence in Northern Ireland. In this case it was self-inflicted.' There had been intense debate within the Northern Ireland Office about the precise wording and its propaganda implications. In the end 'took his own life' and 'self-inflicted' were the terms decided upon, rather than using the word 'suicide'.

In a carefully planned operation Sands' body was immediately taken in an ambulance, escorted by a convoy of police Land Rovers, to the mortuary at Forster Green in south Belfast for post mortem. Later the Governor completed his journal: '5.5.81 Unlocked 965; Parole 3; Outside Hospital 6; Bobby Sands died this morning at 01.17 hours. Relatives present. Also priests. All parties informed and all arrangements went smoothly. His hunger strike started on 1.3.81. His protest action, declared repeatedly by himself and others, was directed to forcing HMG to grant special category status, in other words political prisoner status. Routines of today to be similar to a bank holiday.' For such a momentous event, the entry, surprisingly, was not in red ink.

During the day the prison was very quiet to the surprise of the authorities. 'Sombre and subdued,' was how one prison officer serving there at the time remembered it, but there was some tasteless early morning revelry in one of the nearby Army messes where a military chef had won a grim sweepstake for most closely predicting the exact moment when Sands would die. For their part, the prisoners had taken a decision that they would not show 'any reaction or emotion in the face of the enemy,' as one recalls. 'We were, of course, shattered and demoralised at the loss of our comrade but even though one of the screws was singing "Oh what a beautiful morning" we decided to let it pass.'

The Chief Constable, Sir John Hermon, who was asleep in his flat within the heavily guarded RUC Headquarters at Knock in east Belfast, was among the first to be informed of the death. The duty officer in the force control room who had passed on the message minutes afterwards was told: 'Well, you know what to do.' For months the RUC and Army had been planning to deal with the widespread disorder they knew would erupt once Sands died. While the Chief Constable was being informed, other officers flashed a coded message by teleprinter and radio to the formations of grey-painted armoured Land Rovers standing by to go into action. Each contained a sergeant and six constables, fully trained in new riot control techniques just developed by the RUC and being used for the first time. The police commanders initially hoped that the timing of Sands's death, after the last local news bulletins on radio at 1 am, would give them a breathing space until the radio stations came on air again at

6 am, but, before long Provo supporters in cars fitted with loudspeakers were out in their heartland areas broadcasting the news. In line with a headline in *Republican News* forecasting the consequences of Sands death – 'there will be fire and there will be fury' – the announcement prompted bin-lid bashing and whistle-blowing and then sparked riots and attacks on the security forces in many areas of Northern Ireland. But although there were deaths in the violence, the trouble, by Northern Ireland standards, was subdued. The Provos did not want to prejudice the unprecedented levels of sympathy and support they were attracting and, for their part, the Loyalists remained calm, judging that their best political interest lay in doing nothing. In what became one of the most widely recalled slogans of the Troubles, one Loyalist graffiti writer daubed a Belfast wall: 'We will not forget you, Jimmy Sands.'

The British government sent 600 extra British troops to Northern Ireland and on 7 May, the day of the funeral, the Irish News carried four pages of sympathy notices for 'Volunteer Bobby Sands MP'. An estimated 100,000 people attended the funeral in Belfast although it was a miserable wet day with incessant rain. A black beret and tricolour adorned the coffin, which was escorted by a lone piper and a masked guard of honour wearing camouflage combat jackets. At one point shots were fired in salute. Sands was buried in the Republican plot at Milltown cemetery beside other IRA martyrs of the Troubles. The Republican movement had built a scaffolding grandstand for the international multitude of camera operators and photographers to have an uninter-rupted view of the interment and the two-mile cortège led by his parents, his eight-year-old son and his sister, clad in black and bearing wreaths. The size of the crowd, probably the largest ever gathered for a single event in Northern Ireland, reflected the deep emotional impact the hunger strike was having on the entire Catholic community.

By now world attention was focused on the Maze and in particular the fate of Francis Hughes, who had commenced his hunger strike on 15 March, two weeks after Sands. Hughes, aged 27, a former painter and decorator from Bellaghy in south Derry, was serving life imprisonment and concurrent sentences, totalling 83 years, for the murder of a soldier and the attempted murder of another. The security forces, however, attributed at least one dozen murders, six attempted murders and upwards of four explosions to him during a four-year reign of terror in the south Derry area. In 1977 they paid him the distinction of featuring, with Dominic McGlinchey and Ian Milne, on the first ever 'wanted urgently' poster they had produced. He was finally arrested after a shoot-out with special forces soldiers in March 1978. One SAS officer was killed, another so badly wounded that he was confined to a wheelchair for the rest of his life. Although he sustained serious gunshot wounds in the incident, Hughes tried to outwit his trackers by lying up in a gorse bush in the fields in the Sperrin mountains, near Maghera, for fifteen hours afterwards before he was discovered and captured. He then spent ten months in a secure hospital undergoing treatment for his injuries which left him with one leg shorter than the other. SAS soldiers later expressed grudging admiration for his toughness and the ruthless skill which underpinned his terrorist exploits but at his trial, the judge admonished Hughes for being a dedicated and hardened IRA terrorist. On 10 April, six prison officers were tasked to escort Hughes when he was being moved from the H-blocks to the prison hospital. As he left his cell, he defiantly brandished his crutch like a machine gun at the warders and shouted 'Tiochfaid Ar La ['Our day will come']. Victory to the blanketmen.'

Hughes' death, at 5.43 pm on 12 May, after 59 days on hunger strike, prompted a further wave of rioting in nationalist areas throughout Northern Ireland, and in Dublin a group of 2000 people stormed the British Embassy. Nine days later, on 21 May, the third and fourth hunger strikers died within a 24-hour period. Raymond McCreesh, aged 24, an IRA prisoner from Camlough, Co Armagh, and 23-year-old Patsy O'Hara from Londonderry, who belonged to the INLA and led their prisoners, both died after fasting for 61 days. Two days earlier five soldiers, travelling in the second of two armoured Saracen personnel carriers, died when a massive 1000-pound landmine was exploded underneath their vehicle. The significance was unmistakable. The cruel attack, four miles from McCreesh's home, was an advance reprisal for his death. McCreesh was serving fourteen years for a series of offences including attempted murder and conspiracy originating in a shoot-out with soldiers near Belleeks in June 1976. O'Hara, whose older brother was also in the Maze serving five years for armed robbery, had been imprisoned for eight years for the possession of a hand grenade. The Governor at the Maze, having resumed the routine of recording major events in red ink in the official prison journal, noted O'Hara's death as follows: '21.5.81. At 23.26 hunger striker 18/80 P J O'Hara died in the prison hospital. Remains transported to Omagh for post mortem examination.' Next the Governor matter-of-factly recorded: '22.5.81: Unlocked 972; Parole 6; Outside Hospital 5; Normal routine operated today. Prison generally in a quiet state.' On the day of the funerals there were again pages of sympathy notices in the *Irish News*. A half-page advertisement on behalf of the Republican Movement, quoted O'Hara: 'We stand for the freedom of the Irish nation so that future generations will enjoy the prosperity they rightly deserve, free from foreign interference, oppression and exploitation. The real criminals are the British Imperialists who have thrived on the blood and sweat of generations of Irish men. They have maintained control of Ireland through force of arms and there is only one way to end it. I would rather die than rot in this concrete tomb for years to come.'

When Brendan McLaughlin, aged 29, serving twelve years for firearms offences, who had joined the hunger strike to replace Francis Hughes, was taken off the strike on 26 May 1981 after suffering a perforated ulcer and internal bleeding, there were brief hopes that the conveyor belt of death might be halted. These hopes were dashed when another IRA inmate, Martin Hurson, joined what it was now clear was a series of death fasts which the Provos were ruthlessly exploiting by fair means and foul. Security checks on those visiting the hunger strikers had been compassionately relaxed but when a picture, obviously taken in the prison hospital, of a gaunt, bearded O'Hara slumped in a wheelchair reached the front page of a Dublin newspaper, they had to be stepped up again. In a follow-up search a camera the size of a matchbox and a small tape recorder without batteries were found in McCreesh's single room in the prison hospital. Both items were concealed under the mattress and could only have been introduced by a close member of his family, the only permitted visitors.

There was further controversial propaganda about McCreesh when an account of a transcript of an alleged conversation between the dying man and his mother and brother, a priest, was published in the prestigious London *Sunday Times* newspaper. The disputed tape, of which the Northern Ireland Office denied any knowledge, portrayed McCreesh wavering not long before lapsing into his final coma and being urged not to give up his fast. Prison sources also say they do not know of a tape but recall that three times during the afternoon of 16 May, McCreesh, lapsing in and out of consciousness told medical orderlies he wished to end his fast. He signalled he would accept a glass of milk. The prison doctor was called and he asked McCreesh, 'Do you want me to save your life?' McCreesh replied, 'Yes.' The doctor was not prepared to act on the say-so of McCreesh alone because, as the Jenkins rules on hunger strikes require, he was not satisfied that McCreesh was sufficiently rational on his own account. Consequently he asked that the family be urgently summoned to his bedside. The dying man's brother, a priest, arrived and the situation was explained to him. He then went in to see his brother. The room door was left open and a prison officer at the door listened to the conversation and subsequently made a written report of what transpired to the Governor who informed the Northern Ireland Office. This was standard practice and had happened earlier when the three Irish parliamentarians and the Papal envoy had visited Sands. The prison sources will not disclose the details of the conversation but say that only one inference can be drawn from the priest's visit – that he did not discourage him from continuing with the fast nor did he himself request or authorise medical assistance to save his life. The McCreesh family strenuously denied that any such exchanges took place but the episode did underline the white-hot heat generated by the propaganda war between the government and the IRA as the death fasts accelerated.

On 28 May, Prime Minister Margaret Thatcher visited Northern Ireland and declared her belief that with the hunger strike the IRA was playing its 'last card'. It was an ill-judged and foolhardy statement which was quickly disproved. At the end of May the names of four prisoners on hunger strike, together with those of five other Republican prisoners, were put forward as candidates in the forthcoming general election in the Republic of Ireland. When the results were declared, after polling on 11 June, they showed significant support for the prisoners. Kieran Doherty and Paddy Agnew, had both been elected to Dail Eireann, the Irish parliament, representing border areas: Doherty for Cavan-Monaghan, Agnew for Louth. Another prisoner missed being elected by about 300 votes. Coming on top of the earlier electoral success by Sands and the deaths of the hunger strikers, there could not have been a clearer sign of the profound and troubling effect the issue was having on the entire Irish people. Emboldened by this latest electoral endorsement of its campaign, on 15 June, Sinn Fein declared an escalation of the protest with the announcement that a prisoner would join the hunger strike every week.

Attention was now briefly diverted to the Crumlin Road jail where eight IRA prisoners effected a daring and dramatic escape on 10 June. Seven of them were members of what had become known as the 'M60 gang', who were on trial for carrying out a series of deadly attacks using the M60 heavy-calibre machine gun, at the time the most powerful firearm in the hands of the IRA. The other was on remand, accused of murdering a UDR soldier and of three attempted murders. At 4 pm that afternoon, all eight had arranged simultaneous visits by their legal advisers so that they could trigger their carefully prepared escape plan. Indeed, 48 hours earlier they had carried out a last-minute rehearsal to ensure none of the elements had been overlooked. During the legal discussions, three of the prisoners suddenly produced miniature handguns which had been broken down and smuggled, part by part, into the prison over the previous four weeks. Solicitors were ordered to remain silent while ten prison officers supervising the visits were lined up at gunpoint. Two were ordered to hand over their uniforms, which two of the prisoners put on. The escape party then made its way to the first of three exit gates they had to traverse before linking up with getaway cars waiting outside the prison. They got through the first but the visits officers had by then raised the alarm and at the second they were confronted by a group of fifteen to twenty officers armed with batons. There were some scuffles, but the officers retreated after they were fired on and the first group of four prisoners managed to get out on to the Crumlin Road and link up with the getaway car waiting for them. The others came under fire from police and soldiers guarding the prison and the courthouse opposite, and ran off on foot through the car park of a nearby health centre, where passers-by including women and young children were caught up in a hail of gunfire. The second group of prisoners also succeeded in getting away when they commandeered a car.

The escape, by a gang of such exceptionally ruthless terrorists brandishing smuggled firearms, generated a political hue and cry in Parliament, where the government was forced to announce an independent inquiry. There was great concern about how the weapons had reached the prisoners and, almost immediately afterwards, security checks on professional visitors to the prisons were very significantly enhanced. William Pearce, the Chief Inspector of Prisons, was unable to conclusively establish how the weapons were smuggled but he eventually concluded that the escape was caused by a failure of the inadequate security procedures and by human error. He specifically criticised the lack of adequate and precise written guidance and instructions on security matters at all levels, within the prison from Governor to officers, and from the Northern Ireland Office to prison staff. He also criticised insufficiently rigorous application of existing security procedures by prison staff but took the view, that despite their collective failure, neither the Governor nor any individual should be singled out for blame. He did, however, commend the courage of the unarmed members of staff who, by their individual action during the escape, reflected great credit on the prison service as a whole. During the incident two officers were injured, one on the hand. The other required 30 stitches to a head wound after being coshed by one of the escaping prisoners.

Three days after the escape, there was another potentially serious security lapse at Queen's University, Belfast where Lord Gardiner, whose report in 1974 had recommended the ending of special category, was attending a legal function. A booby-trap device had been attached to the car he was being driven in, but it fell off without exploding.

Acknowledging responsibility for the attack, the IRA said he had been targeted because he was the 'political architect of the criminalisation policy and the H-blocks'.

By this point, with four hunger strikers dead and no end to the deadlock in sight, there was intense pressure on the British government from all sides to find a way out of the growing crisis over conditions at the Maze. There was now sustained worldwide interest in the situation and the Provisionals were well ahead in the international propaganda stakes. Fidel Castro, the long serving Cuban revolutionary leader, hailed the hunger strikers as Irish patriots in the process of writing one of the most heroic pages in human history. Lech Walesa, the leader of the Polish liberation movement Solidarity, described Sands as 'a great man who sacrificed his life for his struggle'.

Although Cardinal O'Fiaich and Bishop Daly were not as directly involved in efforts to resolve this hunger strike as they had been during the first one, both were seriously troubled by the seemingly unstoppable course of events and had continued to campaign and make their views known to the British government and others. With a fifth death looming, that of Joe McDonnell, they thus threw their weight behind the Irish Commission for Justice and Peace, a body established by the Catholic church in Ireland to campaign on human rights issues, when, at the beginning of June it launched a determined initiative to break the deadlock. Five individuals were involved: the Auxiliary Bishop of Dublin, Dermot O'Mahony, Father Oliver Crilly, and three lay people, Hugh Logue, Brian Gallagher and Jerome Connolly.

In line with the policy adopted by the two senior clerics in the past, and that rigidly maintained by the British government, the Commission came out against political status but called for easements of the prison regime to help meet the prisoners' five demands, a route to compromise that was already well signposted. With McDonnell's condition deteriorating, Michael Alison, the prisons minister, held lengthy meetings with the Commission on 23 and 26 June and 3 and 4 July. Altogether the discussions totalled sixteen hours. They also visited the hunger strikers and engaged in lengthy discussions with them, including one overnight session in the prison. Reflecting the substance of this renewed mediation effort, the British government issued a statement on prison policy in Northern Ireland on 30 June, saying yet again that it would not grant special category status and would retain control of the prisons. Recalling that changes in the area of work, clothing and association had been suggested in the hope of ending the hunger strike, Atkins then rambled on to say that 'the great difficulty about such a move is that it would encourage the hope that political status based on the so-called five demands could still be achieved.' However, a statement issued on behalf of the hunger strikers on 4 July appeared to indicate a notable shift in position. They did not object, they said, to any changes in the prison regime being enjoyed by all prisoners. With Republican prisoners therefore abandoning the demand to have 'special' status conferred exclusively on them, the way seemed to be clear for easing the regime towards the terms of the five demands.

That same day, after the last of their meetings with Alison, the Commission drafted a statement outlining the outcome of their discussions, as they understood them, and this was brought to Alison for approval on the evening of 6 July. According to the Commission, Alison accepted the draft statement, with one amendment, and agreed that one of his officials would go into the prison before mid morning the next day to clarify the 30 June Atkins statement and the Commission discussions to the prisoners – the negative as well as the positive. At 10.15, a call was made from Alison's office to a chaplain to inform the hunger strikers in the prison hospital that the Commission would not be visiting that night but that they should expect an official next morning. At 11.40 am the next morning the Commission were unexpectedly called back to Stormont Castle but declined to go when they heard an official had still not gone to the prison as promised. Shortly before they were due to hold a news conference at 1pm, they were informed an official would go in that afternoon. By 4 pm an official had still not been sent in and at 5.30 pm it became clear that the plan had gone wrong. The minister was now only prepared to send in a revised document, not an official. The Commission were now deeply concerned that their work, which the prisoners had accepted as 'the foundation of a resolution' would now be in vain. Given the history of contacts between the government and the prisoners in the context of the hunger strikes, there was a distinct lack of trust and an abundance of suspicion. The delay in sending in an official, the Commission feared, would compound that suspicion and only ensure that any document would be rejected.

They conveyed this view and their fears to Alison in telephone calls at 5.55 pm and again at 7.15 pm. At 8.50 pm they were told that, after all, an official would go in later that evening and stand by while a prison governor read out the new document. But by 10 pm the government had changed tack yet again. Alison personally telephoned the Commission to say that an official would not be going in until the morning, but that the delay would be to the benefit of the prisoners. The Commission were alarmed at the further delay as McDonnell's condition was continuing to deteriorate but Alison assured them he was not in immediate danger. However, at 5.11 the next morning, Joe McDonnell, 30, from Lenadoon, west Belfast, married with a daughter aged ten and a son aged nine, who had replaced Sands on 8 May, died after 61 days on hunger strike. He was serving a fourteen-year sentence for the illegal possession of firearms. In fact he was one of the four terrorists, including Bobby Sands, who were apprehended in a car speeding away from the bomb attack on the furniture warehouse in October 1976. Prior to that he had been interned on the *Maidstone* and at Long Kesh for two separate spells until 1974.

At 6.30 am the Commission were told that an official was finally on his way to the prison with a statement to be read to the remaining hunger strikers by a governor. Later in the morning, after Alison had said McDonnell was not expected to die so soon, the Commission accused the British government of clawing back what had been agreed by Alison. They said that the statement read to the prisoners could not be regarded as 'a serious attempt to seek a resolution in the light of the discussions we had and of the position clarified to us by the minister'. Atkins responded a few days later by sending the prisoners a note entitled 'What happens when the protest ends?' in which he set out again the regime available to prisoners conforming with prison rules but saying there was scope for further development but not under duress. The word 'not' was underlined and he ended: 'The only key to advance is for them to end the strike.'

With both sides now ever more deeply enmeshed in their uncompromising positions Martin Hurson died on 13 July after just 46 days on hunger strike. He was imprisoned in November 1977 for twenty years for the possession of two landmines and for causing an explosion at a quarry. He was one of those who joined in the latter stages of the first hunger strike and then volunteered to take part in the second. In a bid to alleviate the growing criticism that their unyielding position increasingly amounted to callousness, Atkins launched another effort to break the deadlock, this time involving the International Committee of the Red Cross. It was to prove equally unsuccessful. On 15 July, he announced that representatives of the organisation had been invited to carry out an investigation of prison conditions in Northern Ireland. They arrived next day, and over the next eight days met with the two sides to the dispute. The government allowed McFarlane and the hunger strikers to deal jointly with them but refused the strikers' demand, passed through the Red Cross, for direct negotiations to end the fast based on the prisoners' statement of 4 July. The hunger strikers then rejected any role for them as mediators with the British government, and warned the Red Cross that the British government would exploit them as they had recently done with the Commission.

The leader of the Red Cross delegation said the situation was deadlocked and in such circumstances they had no role to play.

The Dublin government, the Catholic hierarchy and the SDLP, who were now acutely concerned about the consequences of the continuing protest and the convulsion it was causing in the entire community beyond the prison, now urged the British government to engage in direct talks in a bid to break the impasse. Nowhere was the convulsion of conscience, emotion and horror of the hunger strikes more keenly felt than in the ranks of the Catholic church and at this point, Dr Cahal Daly, Bishop of Down and Connor and later to replace O'Fiaich as Cardinal, appealed directly to the hunger strikers: 'Your capacity for endurance, however misguided, is not so common in this materialistic age that Ireland can afford to be deprived of it.' At the same time Catholic priests and prison chaplains ministering to the dying prisoners stepped up their efforts to talk them off their fasts and pressure their families to authorise medical intervention to save their lives. Without explaining why, the prison leaders had specifically expressed their 'discontent' about the role of the chaplains in an earlier statement. In the end the work of the chaplains would prove to be the crucial factor in persuading families to intervene and halt the cycle of deaths.

Late on the evening of 20 July, with the condition of two more prisoners steadily reaching the point of no return, one of the prison chaplains orchestrated another initiative. According to the Northern Ireland Office, two senior officials were sent to the prison in the early hours of 21 July after the family of one of the expiring hunger strikers asked that he be allowed the personal clarification of the most recent proposals that Atkins had said would be available. A bald statement issued before breakfast time said, 'They saw the relatives of two of the hunger strikers and they also saw the five hunger strikers in the prison hospital. However, the hunger strikers, when asked, did not wish to take up the offer.' The sticking point turned out to be the presence of McFarlane. The hungers strikers wanted him there. The officials refused. The hunger strikers were equally inflexible with their own people on 29 July when they met representatives from Sinn Fein and the Irish Republican Socialist Party and turned down a suggestion that the strike be suspended for three months to allow time to monitor prison reforms.

Several more of the hunger strikers were now coming close to the critical point when faculties deteriorate and the final collapse of bodily functions sets in. The terrible pressures and anguish imposed on those closest to them became clear when the family of 27-year-old Paddy Quinn intervened on 31 July, the forty-seventh day of his fast, and asked for medical treatment to save his life. Quinn had been convicted of attempting to murder members of the security forces and sentenced to fourteen years imprisonment. The intervention proved to be a crucial turning point and, for a time, the human drama superseded the political confrontation. Although four more prisoners would die over the next three weeks, others would be saved from death by their loved ones, the futility of continuing the protest would become clear and the breakthrough made by the Quinn family would gather pace. But there was much more turmoil still to come.

Kevin Lynch, aged 25, died on 1 August after 71 days on hunger strike. A member of the INLA, who came from the Dungiven area of County Londonderry, he was serving ten years for taking part in an armed robbery and carrying out a punishment shooting. A day later, Kieran Doherty, aged 25, from Andersonstown in west Belfast, became the eighth faster to die after 73 days without nourishment. Doherty, a member of the IRA, was one of the two prisoners elected to the Irish parliament in June, and had been imprisoned for 22 years for the illegal possession of firearms and explosives. As was the custom, the Irish tricolour over Leinster House in Dublin was lowered to mark the death of a member. The next death, that of 23-year-old Thomas McElwee on 8 August, after 62 days on hunger strike, coincided with the tenth anniversary of the introduction of internment, and three people lost their lives in widespread disturbances over the weekend. McElwee, from Bellaghy, County Londonderry, had been imprisoned for life for manslaughter after a nine bomb onslaught in Ballymena on 9 October 1976. A young woman was burned to death when a blast incendiary device exploded in a boutique. Seven of the bombers were later captured after a device exploded in a car in which five of them, including McElwee, were travelling. He lost an eye in the blast. McElwee was a cousin of Hughes, the second hunger striker to die.

INLA member Michael Devine, aged 27, who died after 60 days on hunger strike on 20 August, was the tenth and last to die. He was serving twelve years for arms offences. The same day the family of Patrick McGeown, serving fifteen years for blowing up the Belfast Europa Hotel in January 1975, who had been on hunger strike for 42 days, agreed to medical intervention to save his life. He had actually been serving his term as a special category prisoner but lost it when, with McFarlane and another prisoner, he took part in an escape attempt dressed as a prison officer and was sentenced to a further six-month term.

But any government hopes that support for the prisoners was waning were firmly dispelled on 20 August when Owen Carron, who had been

Sands' election agent, topped the poll with an increased number of votes in the by-election in Fermanagh-South Tyrone caused by Sands death. Carron had been put up after the British government hastily introduced legislation to prevent prisoners standing but, in line with IRA policy, he did not go to London to claim his seat. During the course of the election two more prisoners had joined the hunger striker and another came off on 4 September, after 52 days, when his family asked for medical treatment to save his life. Matt Devlin had been sent to prison for seven years on three counts of attempted murder after the court heard how a police patrol were alerted and escaped from an ambush after Devlin had accidentally shot another terrorist while lying in wait near Coagh, County Tyrone in June 1976.

Despite their brevity, the entries in the Governor's journal concerning the hunger striker Laurence McKeown, who was serving five life sentences for causing two large car bomb explosions in Antrim and Randalstown and for the attempted murder of a police constable, vividly portray the horrible anguish of the family and the grim official protocols surrounding what had now become an unprecedented spectacle of confrontational terrorist theatre. On the sixty-ninth day of his fast, the Governor wrote: '5.9.81; Saturday; Hunger striker 454/77 McKeown continues to deteriorate. He was visited by his parents and parish priest. His parents have expressed a desire that he give up the hunger strike and accept treatment but the inmate is pretty coherent and refused treatment.'

The next day, McKeown's seventieth without food, the Governor recorded events: '6.9.81; Sunday; At approx 11.45 hours the medical officer informed the family of hunger striker 454/77 McKeown that he now considered him incapable of making a rational decision. At 11.50 hours Mrs McKeown, mother of the prisoner, asked the medical officer to take such steps as might be necessary to save her son's life. The written authority to intervene was signed by Mrs McKeown. The prisoner was conveyed to the RVH [Royal Victoria Hospital, Belfast] at 12.36 hours.'

At the end of September, in a cabinet reshuffle, Atkins was moved to the Foreign Office and replaced by James Prior, an avuncular business-man and skilled, experienced politician. He brought with him Earl 'Grey' Gowrie, as prisons minister. Within days of arriving in Belfast Prior went to the Maze to where he had a three-hour meeting with those on hunger strike. His arrival and the distinctly pragmatic note he set quickly transformed the atmosphere and two more prisoners soon came off the fast. On 24 September Bernard Fox, then on the thirty-second day of his hunger strike, began taking food again. Fox was serving twelve years for a series of explosives offences, including the triple bombing of a hotel in

Belfast which put 120 people out of work. His condition was deteriorating and Sinn Fein reported he was 'dying too quickly'. Two days later Liam McCloskey, then on day 55 of his hunger strike, gave up after his family said they would call for medical intervention to save his life as soon as he became unconscious. McCloskey was serving ten years for a series of terrorist offences and had been captured in October 1976 alongside Kevin Lynch, who had died earlier in the hunger strike, while conspiring to ambush and disarm a joint police and military patrol.

Family pressure now became the paramount factor and a meeting between the Republican movement, the families and a number of priests was set up in a west Belfast hotel at 4 pm on 27 September. In the background there had been intensive manoeuvring involving the new minister, Gowrie, Cardinal O'Fiaich, members of the families and the IRA and INLA. The mother of one of the dead hunger strikers told the mother of one of the dying, 'Take him off. They're being duped.' There were reports that another mother waved a household knife at a prominent Sinn Fein member and accused him of wanting more prisoners to die to build up the IRA. It was also reported that there had been a dramatic armed confrontation between IRA members during which guns were cocked and hardline Belfast Republicans were told there was to be 'no slagging' if any of the prisoners abandoned the death fasts. For their part, the hunger strikers were torn between a sense of loyalty and debt to their comrades who had already given their lives, and the concern of their own increasingly anguished loved ones. On Saturday 3 October 1981 the hunger strike finally ended when the six prisoners still refusing food decided to halt after each of their families indicated they would authorise medical intervention once the final deterioration had begun. Pat Sheehan (serving fifteen years for causing explosions and other offences) had been fasting for 55 days; Jackie McMullan (life for attempting to murder a police patrol) for 48; Hugh Carville (fourteen years for firearms offences and causing explosions) for 34 days; John Pickering (serving 26 years for the murder of a UDR soldier and other offences) 27 days; Gerard Hodgins (fourteen years for a catalogue of terrorist offences including possessing firearms, explosives, incendiary devices and armed robbery) after twenty days; and James Devine (twelve years for firearms offences) after thirteen days.

Fr Denis Faul, who had long championed the prisoners' cause but who was appalled at what he saw as a needless waste of life, had played a vital role in welding the families together to resist pressure from the Republican leadership, who regarded the views of the hunger strikers themselves as paramount. Indeed the fearless priest had been critical of the continuing hunger strike for months and had publicly complained about being 'snubbed and deceived' by the British on the one hand and 'rejected and mauled' by the prisoners' representatives on the other. They had even smuggled a statement out calling for him to mind his own business and to stop pressuring families to end the hunger strike. In August he had also claimed that three of the hunger strikers' lives could have been saved and pleaded for a change of tactic before 'their deaths became a bore and their names were not even noted'. (It was notable that the Republican movement death notices in the *Irish News* for McElwee and Doherty had come down to quarter-pages from the half-pages that had commemorated Sands and Hughes.) Ever after the priest's intervention was so resented by some Provo factions that he was known as 'Denis the menace'. The prisoners themselves confirmed the end of the strike a day later: 'A considerable majority of the hunger strikers' families have indicated that they will intervene and under these circumstances we feel that the hunger strike must, for tactical reasons, be suspended.' But it was made clear that despite the ending of the hunger strike, the blanket protest would continue.

With the duress of the death fasts at an end, the way was clear for Prior to begin to implement the promised easements to the prison regime, although, in the end, the prisoners got very little more than was on offer in Atkins' December 1980 document, passed by the spy to the chaplain long before any of the ten deaths. On 6 October Prior announced prisoners could wear their own civilian clothes at all times but with some restrictions – a blue suit that could be altered to look like a prison officer's uniform was not permitted, and nor were items of black or combat clothing that could be used to put prisoners in paramilitary uniform. Free association was not conceded, but two of four wings in each H-block were linked to permit wider contact although only 40 prisoners were to allowed in the exercise yard at any one time. The frequency of letters, visits and parcels was more generous than that asked for in the five demands and up to 50 per cent of lost remission could be earned back by good behaviour and conforming to the prison rules. The issue of prison work was not resolved at this stage but there were indications that this issue too would be pragmatically addressed, with a greater emphasis on education and training rather than industry, although prisoners would undertake orderly duties in the blocks, laundry, kitchens and in maintaining the prison complexes. The demand for segregation, which the Loyalists too were demanding, was not officially conceded but de facto segregation, which was already in existence at the Governor's discretion for 'the good order and running of the prison' would become the norm. By 25 October the blanket protest too was all but over, with only ten of some 400 Republican prisoners still refusing to conform. But the concession on clothing sparked bad feelings between some prisoners' families and the H-block committee, who had raised £140,000 in the United States alone on the back of the protest but said they had no money to help the families buy clothing to send into the prison.

Despite the major reduction in tension that flowed from the ending of the fasts, there was soon a minor clash with the prison authorities when the president of the Gaelic League, who was delivering Irish-language bibles to the prison, stormed out of a visit when supervising officers insisted he speak in English. (By this time many officers, especially those engaged on security duties, had learned some Irish and could follow the distinctive 'Jaelic' argot that the prisoners had developed. They never reacted but simply listened and smiled when the prisoners thought they were not being understood by lapsing into Irish.)

There was a potentially much more serious clash when Prior's 28-day transitional moratorium ran and the IRA prisoners were put into a work assessment scheme. About 36 prisoners did take part in the scheme and were assigned duties 'maintaining a high standard of cleanliness in their respective wings and ministering to the domestic needs of the rest of the men,' according to a smuggled statement. But when the authorities sought to assign other prisoners to what the statement called 'menial and penal work unfitting our universally recognised status as political prisoners', the Republicans refused to cooperate. In one day 63 had remission docked after appearing before the Governor and replying, 'No,' when asked if they would carry out any task ordered by him. McFarlane ended up with three days cellular confinement after a clash with a prison officer over the issue, which rumbled on in the background until late in 1982 when the authorities adopted a far more pragmatic attitude.

Lawyers representing the families of the dead hunger strikers attempted a final propaganda grandstand on the issues surrounding it when a joint inquest was convened at Hillsborough Courthouse on 1 December. In his opening remarks to the jurors, the Coroner for south Down, Albert Orr, explained that the system which up to a year earlier had charged juries to decide verdicts such as accidental death, suicide, or open verdicts, had been abolished. The new regulations placed responsibility on the jury merely to establish the identity of the dead person, the cause, date and place of death, the home address of the deceased, their marital status, the date and place of birth and particulars as to the registration of the death. Thus the Coroner, supported by Crown Counsel for the Northern Ireland Office, Robert Carswell QC, who was later knighted and became the Lord Chief Justice of Northern Ireland, prevented the jury from hearing any evidence beyond that required for their task.

During an eight-hour sitting, the jury was then told the story of the hunger strike by a succession of witnesses who were identified by number rather than name for security reasons. In each of the ten cases the governor or assistant governors of the Maze Prison gave evidence that the prisoners had at various dates announced that they were on hunger strike and had refused food. The jury heard that food was offered to them daily and was available at all times. The prison doctors said the prisoners had declined medical attention but had allowed blood and urine samples to be taken so that their condition could be monitored. Police officers who had taken charge of the bodies to convey them to the mortuary then testified, and the autopsy reports from the pathologists who examined the ten bodies were then read to the court.

The first inquest heard evidence on the death of Robert Gerard Sands. An assistant governor from the Maze Prison said Sands had been committed to prison on 28 August 1977, to serve fourteen years for possession of a firearm and ammunition with intent to endanger life. On 1 March he had said he was on hunger strike and the assistant governor reported that Sands was removed to the prison hospital wing on 23 March. A prison doctor who attended Sands said that from 22 April the prisoner had been given cold bottled aerated water, as he had had difficulty in keeping down fluids. Sands had become confused on 2 May and the following day lapsed into unconsciousness.

In cross examination the solicitor for Sands relatives asked, 'Can you think of anything that would have prevented his death?'

'Yes, eating and drinking,' the witness answered.

The evidence, in unemotional medical and factual detail, in the case of Raymond McCreesh was typical of what the jury heard. In making his deposition, Witness 1012, said, 'I am a Medical Doctor in attendance at HMP Maze. Raymond Peter McCreesh, DOB 25.2.57 was admitted to HMP Maze on 24.3.77. He weighed 10 stone on 30.6.76. On 22.3.81 he declared he was on hunger but not thirst strike. Weight 63.20kg, height 167 cms on 23.3.81. No abnormality detected in any major system. He was transferred to the prison hospital on 14.4.81. I monitored his condition daily. His last known weight was 45 kg on 16.5.81. His condition continued to deteriorate and he developed retention of urine with overflow on 18.5.81. On 20.5.81 he showed further depression on his brain stem and at 13.50 hours he had slow laboured breathing of 9 to 11 per minute. On 21.5.81 at 01.50 he was in extremis and I sat by his bed until 02.11 when I pronounced and certified life extinct.'

In cross examination for next of kin, the witness said, 'McCreesh refused medication. I saw the patient daily, examined him and reported on his condition. The patient allowed blood and urine samples to be taken voluntarily. McCreesh vomited a good deal and I had some difficulty in maintaining his salt balance. The first blood sample was taken on 16.4.81, and five further blood samples were taken at later dates. Urine sample was taken daily from the commencement of the hunger strike until the date of his death. His blood pressure was also taken daily from the commencement of the hunger strike. The last blood sample was taken on 15.5.81. The blood sample would have been taken from a vein in the arm by the insertion of a syringe. This would leave a puncture mark in the arm. The blood sample might be taken from either arm. There would be no need for the use of a hypodermic needle other than to take a blood sample.'

The pathologist who carried out the postmortem at Daisy Hill Hospital Newry at 5 am, some three hours after death, reported: 'The history indicates that this young man was on hunger strike from 22 March 1981 until his death at 2.11am on 21 May 1981, a period of about 60 days during which he apparently refused food but not water. At the beginning of the hunger strike his weight was approximately 10 stones and this had fallen to about 7 stones by the time of his death.

'Autopsy showed that he measured 5ft 8ins and was of wasted appearance. A thin layer of fat still remained over the body surface beneath the skin but the bones, for example the ribs and pelvis, clearly showed through and the cheeks were hollow. The examination revealed no evidence of pre-existing disease of any severity which could have caused or contributed to his death. He had had his appendix removed but this was merely an incidental finding. The bladder was distended and a slight degree of pneumonia had developed in the lungs, but these were terminal manifestations, to be expected in a person dying following coma in a weakened state.

'It can only be concluded, therefore, that death was due to the prolonged period of self-starvation which must have caused some upset of the biochemistry of the body in addition to the less of weight. The body surface was quite clean and there were no bed-sores or injuries, indicating that the deceased had been well cared for prior to his death.'

Having heard similar testimony about each of the deaths, the Coroner sent the jury out at 6 pm to make their findings. Twelve minutes later they returned to certify that in seven cases the deaths were due to 'starvation, self-imposed,' and in the cases of McCreesh, O'Hara and Doherty to 'starvation, self-imposed and terminal bronchial pneumonia'.

The huge sigh of relief with which the hard-pressed Northern Ireland Office and the prison service greeted the end of the hunger strikes was tempered that month by a serious disturbance in Belfast prison. Having remained quiet throughout the trauma of the year, the Loyalists seemed determined to provide a violent footnote. On Thursday 10 December, at the start of the evening association period a group of Loyalist remand prisoners in A Wing produced what appeared to be a gun (though none was subsequently found), took five prison officers hostage and barricaded themselves in the wing. While some prisoners climbed on to the roof of the wing to demonstrate, others systematically set about wrecking the cells, furniture and other facilities and equipment. One officer was released with a set of demands from the prisoners. When they were not granted further destruction continued on the roof and in the wing until 1.00 am on Saturday 12 December when the remaining hostages were released. At daylight, with the help of the police and Army, prison staff then moved in to take back control of the wing. The destruction they found was so comprehensive that the wing had to be completely evacuated until it was refurbished. The displaced remand prisoners were moved to the Maze from where convicted inmates were transferred to Magilligan into the third, previously empty, H-block, which had been completed during the year.

Despite the predominant focus on events in the Maze, there were other important developments in the service during the year. With the closure of the Borstal at Millisle, Woburn House was converted into the Prison Service Training College, providing high quality accommodation for this important function than the range of portable buildings it replaced. The conversion of former living quarters into residential accommodation also enabled more comprehensive training for new entrants, serving officers and Assistant Governors, who could now be recruited directly as well as by promotion from the officer grade, to take place. By the end of 1981, the prison service had grown to 2898, while the average daily prison population during the year was 2465 men and 56 women.

The 1981 hunger strikes had very important and far-reaching consequences for Northern Ireland and proved to be one of the key turning points of the years of violence. In retrospect, it can be seen that Sands' election changed one of the most fundamental tenets of IRA policy and laid the foundations for Sinn Fein, and indeed the Loyalist political frontmen, ultimately to emerge as new political forces driving the peace process of the late 1990s. The strategy the hunger strikes inspired was graphically articulated soon afterwards by Danny Morrison, the editor of *Republican News*, at Sinn Fein's annual conference in Dublin on 31 October: 'Who here really believes we can win the war through the ballot box? But will anyone here object if, with a ballot paper in this hand and an Armalite in this hand, we take power in Ireland?'

In the shorter term, however, the hunger strikes exacted a terrible price. The emotion and bitterness they engendered on both sides of the community plumbed new depths of division in a society already deeply sundered by sectarianism and apparently irreconcilable political aims. In addition to the ten Republican prisoners who had died inside the Maze Prison there had been an upsurge in communal violence outside, with the deaths of 64 people, half of them members of the security forces. Of these, seven were the victims of police and Army plastic baton rounds fired in a bid to quell street disturbances. Loyalists carried out four sectarian assassinations. Thousands were injured in waves of rioting and destruction that accompanied each death and caused many millions of pounds' worth of damage. The hard-pressed RUC was brought to the very brink of its capability to prevent a state of civil war rather than civil disorder. It was another element in the uniqueness of the Maze, where events in the prison so dramatically influenced those outside. In most societies prisons contain the dregs of society, those who are made outlaws because they cannot cope with the pressures of life or who flout the conventions of an ordered community by engaging in crime or endangering the safety of the law-abiding majority. But in Northern Ireland in 1981 a group of highly-motivated terrorist prisoners, convicted of a catalogue of the most brutal and ruthless offences against society and humanity, caused a major convulsion in their own community and massive political turmoil throughout the British Isles. It was a sobering and surreal experience for everyone involved. The prison service – the governors, medical and other staff – who had clearly come through a traumatic ordeal were commended in the service's annual report for showing 'qualities of humanity, resilience, dedication and resourcefulness of a very high order'. During the years of protest, the prisoners had constantly disparaged the prison officers who frequently returned the antagonism but, reflecting on the protests some time afterwards, one officer expressed a surprising respect for them. 'At first we thought they were dirty animals. The stench was incredible. Our stomachs turned when we went near the cells and we couldn't understand how anyone could live in such filth. But eventually there was some grudging respect for those on the protest. They were incredibly determined. I didn't agree with what they were doing but you had to admire them for sticking it out. At first I thought it would only last for a few days, or a week or two at the most, but they kept going for years and then queued up to give their lives. I don't think I would have been able to do it, no matter what the cause.'

Those closest to the unprecedented events in the Maze during the years of protest, but above all during the months of the hunger strikes, are still deeply scarred by the experience almost twenty years later. Some have erased it from their minds and profess not to remember much about it. Others simply refuse to discuss it. At least one could not cope with what he had endured. One of the doctors who had monitored and then watched these human beings so determinedly taking their own lives was so troubled by the conflict with the Hippocratic oath, according to colleagues, that he later committed suicide. The hunger strikes brought about a relative calm in the prisons after the years of protest and confrontation, but there were more traumas ahead.

Chapter Twelve
Amazeing

The Prison Service launched a new recruiting campaign at the beginning of 1982 and accepted 303 of the 2850 applicants for training. Another 102 successful candidates were put on a reserve list. Such massive demand for the job, despite its long hours, problematic working environment and omnipresent threat of intimidation or murder was, however, more of a comment on the endemically high rates of unemployment in Northern Ireland than a sign of any strong vocational commitment on the part of most of the applicants. The real attraction was the good money and the job security that then still characterised employment in the public sector. The reason for the massive intake of staff was part of the gearing-up process to take over the new high-security prison then under construction at Maghaberry, about seventeen miles west of Belfast and some five miles from the Maze. The game plan was for a streamlined system with a modernised Belfast prison holding remand prisoners. Long-term convicted inmates would go to Maghaberry and those serving shorter terms to Magilligan. Female prisoners would go to a separate institution within Maghaberry and young offenders would be accommodated in the newly opened Hydebank Wood centre on the southern outskirts of Belfast at Purdysburn. Armagh and Maze, Cellular and Compound, would all then close.

Maghaberry, like Long Kesh, was originally a wartime airfield. The newly constructed RAF Maghaberry went operational on 15 November 1941 and was used as an overflow and standby facility by units based at Long Kesh, which was very much its parent station. The aircraft based there, first fighters and then Wellington bombers, were mainly used for training and in exercises with the Army. However, on 15 October 1943, about 200 United States Air Force personnel arrived, in advance of the planned transfer of the station to that service which took place a month later with the customary colour-changing ceremony and march-past. The station was then developed as a ferrying base for the delivery of aircraft from the US to mainland Britain in the build-up to the 1944 D-day operation and some aircraft based there participated as an attacking force in a practice beach-landing in Northern Ireland by British troops. It was also used by casualty evacuation transports handling military patients from the US 79th Station Hospital at nearby Moira. During the American occupancy of Maghaberry, two personnel were decorated for an act of bravery in March 1944 when they risked their lives to rescue the crew from the burning wreckage of an aircraft which crashed on take-off. One survived but three others perished. The US forces handed the station back to the RAF on D-day, when it was put on a care and maintenance basis and made available for emergency landings only, although the Belfast-based aircraft manufacturer Short Brothers, who had been assembling Stirling bombers in hangars there for some time, was allowed to continue test-flights several times weekly. On 1 January 1945 the airfield was transferred to RAF Maintenance Command and used as an aircraft storage unit, accommodating several hundred Stirlings until they were eventually scrapped.

We have already seen that the need for a modern, purpose-built, secure prison in Northern Ireland had been identified as far back as December 1971 when a report prepared by Sir Charles Cunningham said that existing Victorian-era cellular prison accommodation for men at Crumlin Road, Belfast was already inadequate. Captain Terence O'Neill, the Prime Minister, said in a debate in the Northern Ireland Parliament on 11 January 1972, 'This is, of course, a long-term solution which, as the report makes clear, could not be put into effect for some years but the implications of the recommendation are receiving the Government's immediate and determined study.' Financial approval for the project was given a month later and a prison planning unit was set up to assess the staffing needs, the requirements of the police and courts and to decide the size and scale of the institution. By the time responsibility for the work passed to the Westminster government and the newly-established Northern Ireland Office, with direct rule in March 1972, the hunt was on for a suitable 50- to 60-acre site. By then, of course, the urgent need for an internment centre had been met by building at Long Kesh and, as the pressure for additional prison accommodation intensified, it was fulfilled by creating the Maze special category compounds.

Throughout 1973, with a working party set up to steer the project, the size of the planned prison grew from 60 to 100 and then 170 acres, and grandiose plans to have a single high-security male and female penal facility for Northern Ireland were conceived. The Northern Ireland Office team had studied sites at Temple Effin and Nutts Corner before finally settling on Maghaberry, when they discovered the owner refused to sell. Another possible site at the Palantine came on the market but it was rejected before the auction and no bid was made. Early in 1974 position papers for ministers ruled out any further development at the Maze and stated that Maghaberry was still the most suitable site. There were several site visits and they got permission from the owner in January to carry out soil tests but he changed his mind and refused the contractors access when they turned up with their drilling equipment on 11 April. In the meantime other possible sites at Kircassock, Cromkill and Ardmore were evaluated and turned down. A decision was also taken that wherever it was built, the new prison, with places for 447 male and 56 female inmates, would be modelled, with some security modifications, on the design of one then under construction at Low Newton, County Durham (later Frankland prison) in the north of England. The female accommodation was copied from the design for the Cornton Vale establishment in Scotland. A decision was also taken to maintain Belfast as a remand prison. The demands of security for high-risk prisoners could not be met there with a school, hospital and an undertaker all operating within the shadow of the perimeter wall.

With thousands of chickens now residing in twelve large broiler houses built along the disused concrete taxi and runways at Maghaberry, prejudicing its suitability and position at the top of the list, it was next decided to conduct a feasibility study of again expanding the Maze. However, because of the controversial notoriety the Maze had already attracted and his desire for a fresh start, Merlyn Rees ordered other government-owned sites to be investigated. Studies of sites at Castledillon, Bishopscourt, and Ballykinler were thus initiated, but after the Maze was burned down by the prisoners in November 1974, and an internee was shot dead in an escape attempt soon afterwards, an element of panic burst into the previously measured planning process. The day after the shooting Rees put Maghaberry back to the top of the list and, early on what turned out to be a very wet Sunday morning, sent his prisons minister, Lord Donaldson, to inspect the site along with an experienced prison governor. On 18 November 1974, at the end of a whirlwind week during which prison policy was completely re-appraised, he announced plans to Parliament for a quick-build, short-term prison, to be followed in time by a permanent, purpose-built, maximum-security institution. The cost of the project was estimated to be £30 million.

Meanwhile, the fact that not one brick of the ever more badly needed new prison had yet been laid attracted those excoriating remarks from Lord Gardiner in his January 1975 report. By then lawyers were working to compulsorily purchase the Maghaberry site, workmen had been escorted in to take soil samples, surveys had been carried out and preparations were going ahead to divert a water main, and a public inquiry was scheduled for March. But Rees was forced into an embarrassing climb-down in February when he was advised that the need to obtain planning and other consents, not to mention the actual land, made it impossible to meet his plan to have 700 advance accommodation cells, in five new H-blocks, ready for the phasing out of entitlement to special category in early 1976.

When the public inquiry opened at Hillsborough Courthouse on 18 March it emerged that, in the light of a security assessment, Rees had now decided to vest some 536 acres of land out to the edge of the minor rural roads surrounding the old airfield. Robert Carswell QC told the inquiry that fifteen old airfields in Britain had been converted into prisons and had proved to be eminently suitable for the purpose. Maghaberry, he said, was the most suitable of fifteen other possible locations. It was a rural area but still easily accessible for staff and visitors. Using a model he highlighted how the prison had been designed into the landscape to be unobtrusive and sought to reassure the 40 formal objectors that every contingency had been catered for, including the possibility of escapes. The poultry processing firm, Moy Park, which employed 630 people in its plant at nearby Moira, was the main objector. It said it was planning to double its £1 million investment in chicken-rearing capacity at Maghaberry, and that investment and jobs would be at risk if it was prevented from doing so. The inquiry lasted thirteen days and eventually, in September, the planning inspector approved the construction of the prison but ruled that the project should be accommodated within a 373 acre complex rather than the larger area the authorities intended to vest. He reduced the government's request for a security zone of 165 metres around the prison to one of 100 metres.

In November 1976 the new prison site was levelled and work began to put in water and sewerage pipes. The first priority was to build the seventeen-foot outside perimeter wall to secure the site, and this was completed by the end of 1977. At that time, the IRA had started to target contractors and construction workers, engaged in building and maintenance projects for the security forces. So when any police or Army base was being constructed, the practice was to secure the site first to enable the other work to go ahead in a more protected environment. Indeed, the threat was so serious that many contractors would not accept security forces work. In what became known as a 'cloak and concrete' operation, the government then secretly brought in specialist engineering and construction teams from the Army to work along with, and protect, some civilian firms who took on what had become highly dangerous work.

Taking account of such difficulties it was forecast that the state-of-the art prison would be completed by the end of 1981.

In the event, the building programme slipped, but although Maghaberry had not been taken over, or made ready for inmates as scheduled, its emerging presence on the near horizon as the symbol of a new era in the aftermath of the years of protest helped charge morale and create a sense of a change for the better in a battered service that, for years, had been forced by the pressure of events to lurch from crisis to crisis. A more immediate signal that the prisons system was at last being put on a more organised and up-to-date footing came in September 1982 when the government introduced the first major revision of the Prison Rules since 1954. The Rules, making provision for the management of prisons, the treatment of prisoners, the conduct of prison officers and the functions of boards of visitors, were updated, simplified and reduced in number from 219 to 108. They also brought the Northern Ireland Rules into line with those the Home Office set for prisons in England and Wales. The main changes included the abolition of the power to award dietary punishments, which had not been used for some years, and the award of remission on sentences of less than 51 days, which was introduced in England and Wales early in 1981. The clothing rule was amended to take account of the decision made in October 1981 to abolish the denim prison uniform and allow all prisoners in Northern Ireland to wear their own clothes, subject to some restrictions on the grounds of security. The number of letters which a prisoner was entitled to send and receive increased from one in four weeks to one a week, and the Secretary of State, in addition to the adjudicating authority (the Governor or the Board of Visitors) was given power to remit a disciplinary award. The rules relating to discipline were amended to specify a greater number of specific offences to reduce the number of occasions when prisoners have to be charged with the general offence of conduct contrary to security or good order. Similar new rules were also brought in affecting the young offenders centres at Hydebank Wood (for men) and Armagh (for women).

Another prison officer became a victim of terrorism during the year, but she was not singled out because of her job. At about 7.30 am on the morning of 7 October Freddie Williamson, a married man with three young children, was driving to the meat plant at Moy, where he was a foreman. Two miles outside the village, he came under fire from a hail of 21 bullets. He was not hit, but the car was, and as it spun out of control it collided head on with another vehicle being driven by Elizabeth Chambers, aged 28 and unmarried, who was on her way to work at Armagh prison where she was an officer. Both drivers died from injuries sustained in the crash: he from multiple injuries, she from brain damage. It was later established by the police that INLA terrorists had tried to kill the foreman because for ten years he had also served as a part-time member of the Ulster Defence Regiment. They had followed his car and opened fire when they could not overtake him. The gunman in the front passenger seat, who was later sentenced to fourteen years for conspiracy to murder the two, was aged seventeen at the time of the attack.

As was now inevitable in troubled Northern Ireland's prisons, any high hopes for a period of calm reflection and development with the ending of the protests were all too quickly dented by reality, and during 1982 two issues first emerged that would become as enduring as the demand for political status: segregation and strip searching. The campaign for segregation, largely driven by the Loyalists, had its origins in the gradual disintegration of the Republican no-work protest in the latter half of 1982. Tensions, some of them clearly manufactured and co-ordinated by the apparently rival factions, began to appear as more and more Republican prisoners moved into mixed accommodation. Citing fears for their safety, based on incidents involving crude prison-made incendiary devices, minor assaults and alleged tampering with food, prison staff noticed that both sides were establishing a self-segregated regime during periods of association, recreation and in the use of the gymnasium and other sporting facilities. Events came to a head in mid October, when more than 200 cells in the Maze H-blocks were damaged, this time by Loyalist prisoners. In some cases they were fouled with urine and excrement, forcing the prison officer to move inmates to maintain hygiene. The segregation campaign was replicated at Magilligan prison and, during December, a number of cells there were fouled by prisoners who claimed that their action was intended to force the authorities to segregate them from Republicans. At this time Northern Ireland Office ministers again it made plain on a number of occasions, as they had done in the context of the earlier protests, that the control of the prisons and their routines must remain in the hands of the prison authorities.

While the Loyalists were more concerned with segregation, the Provisional IRA prisoners were building up another issue of outrage. This time the women at Armagh prison were in the front line. All prisoners, whether convicted or on remand, and irrespective of the offence for which they have been convicted or charged, are subject to searches of their persons by one or more of four methods. Mechanical searches are carried out with a device, such as a metal detector, which is passed over the person's body. Rub-down searches involve the searcher passing his or her hands closely over the prisoner's body after outer clothing has been removed. Strip searches require the prisoner to remove all his or her clothing for examination followed by visual inspection of his or her body by the searcher while intimate searches supplement a strip search with an examination of bodily orifices. Prior to November 1982 women prisoners in Armagh were subject to strip searches on a routine basis only on first reception and final discharge. When routine searches were conducted on various other occasions they were either rub-down or mechanical. But on 22 October, in the course of a detailed search of cells in Armagh, two keys were found in the possession of two remand prisoners. Investigations revealed that the keys were from the doors of a court building to which the prisoners had been taken for a remand hearing and had then been removed and smuggled into the prison. As a result of this breach of security, it was decided to introduce regular strip, but not intimate, searching (in line with practice in prisons in Britain) when the female prisoners, who averaged about 30 at any one time, were attending court for remand hearings, making inter-prison visits or taking home leave. The decision triggered a controversy that was to rage inconclusively for several years and fostered a massive Republican propaganda campaign on behalf of the female prisoners who failed to cooperate with the search requirement. Although the searches never revealed much more than low level contraband over the next few years – some 60 tranquillisers, a phial of perfume, an uncensored letter and an illegally-held £5 note – the authorities persisted with them despite the sustained bad publicity, pointing out that therein lay their effectiveness.

Back at the Maze, meanwhile, Republican and Loyalist prisoners had effectively enforced de facto segregation by their own efforts and the unwillingness of the service to risk further debilitating confrontation by challenging them. Early in 1983, with seven of the eight H-blocks occupied, only seven of the 28 wings (four in each) contained mixed populations. Of the others, fifteen were exclusively occupied by Republicans and six by Loyalists. By then, too, a more sinister course of events was underway that would shake the prison system and the Northern Ireland Office to its foundations and prove to be every bit as significant a turning point in Northern Ireland's penal history as were the hunger strikes.

Although the numbers in prison had peaked at an average daily population of 2861 men and 86 women in 1978, and a steady reduction had set in, there were still on average 2426 men and 49 women in custody every day at the end of 1982. 833 of these, a large number among them ranking as the most ruthless, manipulative and dangerous prisoners in custody anywhere in the United Kingdom, were confined in the Maze. It had grown over the years into a complex, sprawled over 133 acres surrounded by a seventeen-foot high, grey concrete perimeter wall, with twelve 30-foot high watchtowers clad in corrugated iron at intervals of about 200 yards. They were manned by soldiers, usually units posted from Germany for ten-week tours as the prison guard force. The sentries were changed every few hours in daytime and more frequently at night to relieve the tedium of the constant vigil. One soldier remembers cold winter nights in the draughty towers where even standing close to the bottle-gas heater did not keep the cold at bay. Within that area there were now two prisons: the old compounds with their Nissen huts, at that time containing just under 200 inmates; and the infamous H-blocks with their 833 residents. There was an Army guard on an outer wire fence marking the edge of the prison-military complex, and patrols of soldiers constantly prowled the roads and countryside surrounding the prison, helping keep the prisoners in and accomplices or troublemakers well away from the area. Inside the perimeter wall, also guarded by the Army, there were still more layers of security. The prison was subdivided into segments by more walls and wire mesh fences and inside the segments, each compound or block was sealed off again by more walls and fences. There were also internal watchtowers, closed circuit television systems, electronic devices and sets of double airlock entrance gates in and out of each block or compound, segment and the main complex. Moving around the complex involved more checks at every barrier and barred grille. Prison officers carried metal tallies, one for each person they were escorting, and everyone carried bundles of keys. The sound of metal grilles being opened and shut and the jangling of bunches of keys was a constant sound in the prison. There were also regular overflights of the prison by a military surveillance aircraft taking infra-red photographs to show any recent underground disturbance which would reveal tunnelling.

Immediate responsibility for the good running of the prison was in the hands of two Governors, one each for Compound and Cellular, and altogether about 1000 staff, 929 of them uniformed prison officer grades. The vast majority were quite inexperienced. Half had less than four years' service, while only 40 of them had served for ten or more years. Despite their numbers, there was a heavy reliance on overtime to keep the prison going, with every officer doing an average sixteen hours a week, nearly half his basic 40-hour duty week. The high staff and supervision costs contributed greatly to the £27,571.41p annual cost of keeping each prisoner.

The ultimate responsibility for the safe custody and welfare of prisoners rested with the minister at the Northern Ireland Office, answerable to parliament for the prisons. He was the titular head of a 132-strong prisons department based in a 1960s glass-fronted, ten-storey office block at Dundonald House within the Stormont government complex in east Belfast. The senior civil servant, of Under-Secretary rank, presided over four divisions responsible for personnel, security and operations, regimes and a general division which handled education, supplies, prison industries and the building and maintenance of the prison estate. Its 132 staff, the vast majority in the lower administrative grades, also administered the annual prisons expenditure which then exceeded £70 million a year. It was a highly labour-intensive function and staff costs accounted for five-sixths of the total. With such a heavy reliance on human endeavour, therefore, there was endless opportunity for the dangerously subversive terrorist prisoner population to seek to undermine, manipulate and intimidate the staff for their own ends, a proposition all the more damaging because so many of the prison officers were so inexperienced.

One of the more experienced officers, who had served in Britain before the troubles and then returned to his native Northern Ireland, recalls the way prisoners sought to intimidate officers:

'It was amazing what they could find out about people and where you came from. You got a good prison officer doing his job, escorting an inmate to a visit or something and he just casually says to him: "I don't like the colour of curtains your wife has up now in that front room of yours, don't like that shade of green at all." He would know that there had been some surveillance and when you're hit with that and then you check it out and it's true, that's very unnerving. If there's children involved, a child gets a new bike or something and they say to you, "Those wee bikes are a good price now, it must have cost you a penny or two," it's very effective at getting prison officers very worried. Sometimes they would tell them old hard luck stories and all sorts of things to try and turn them, bring a letter to the wife, send a message to a girlfriend. Once they got them, locked them in, then they would ask them about things in the prison, what the procedures were, that sort of thing. Oh aye, that happened. There was a lot of it going on but thankfully, despite all the difficulties, morale in the Service was very high and you had this bonding together of prison officers. It was a "them and us" situation and while they got at some of them, we were all aware of what was going on and the actual number of prison officers, to my knowledge now, that actually gave them information and that ended up in courts themselves, wasn't very high.'

When the Governor arrived at the Maze on Sunday morning, 25 September 1983, there was no reason to suspect that it would be anything other than a normal day. The prison had been quiet and out of the headlines, albeit by its own turbulent standards, for some months as the more liberal and progressive regime promised after the hunger strikes was put in place. His journal that day records, 'Carried out morning rounds accompanied by Senior Officer on duty. Visited H3, H4, H5, H6, H7, H8 and prison hospital. Assistant Governor visited H1, H2, Cells and kitchen. Found all in order.'

At 2.30 that afternoon the normal Sunday routine was being followed in H7. Most of the 125 exclusively Republican prisoners were engaged in recreational activities, moving freely within each wing. 24 prisoners employed as orderlies were cleaning up and performing other tasks around the block. The full complement of 24 staff were on duty: two senior officers in charge, sixteen officers supervising the wings and six officers manning the fixed posts controlling movement around the block. There was also a hospital officer whose duties had taken him to the block. The next break in the routine would have come at 4 pm when tea was served. However, shortly after 2.30 five of the orderlies working around the circle at the centre of H7, each armed with a concealed handgun, set in motion a meticulously planned escape. Their first objective was to seize control of H7 and to ensure that each member of staff in the circle area who might press an alarm button was shadowed by one of them. One approached a senior officer, the second in charge, in the circle, and on the pretext of discussing a personal problem in private was taken into his office where another officer was busy at his desk. Meanwhile, another prisoner, who was standing in the locked and gated lobby at the entrance to H7, asked to be admitted in order to sweep the lobby. The officer unlocked the gate and let him in. At the same time a third armed prisoner took up a position outside the gated entrance to the communications room, where he could see another officer at work. The fourth and fifth armed prisoners entered the officers' tea room, where four members of the staff were having a tea-break. Once they were all in position the prisoners struck. The orderlies in the tea room produced guns and ordered the four members of staff to keep quiet. Another officer patrolling the circle area was called to the tea room and made to join his colleagues. The prisoner at the communications room pointed a gun through the locked grille and ordered the officer to unlock it and lie on the floor. Meanwhile the prisoner with the private problem drew his gun and kept the two senior officers covered. The sweeper in the entrance lobby ordered the officer there at gunpoint to lie down on the floor, and took his keys. At the same time, the visiting hospital officer, seated at the desk in the treatment room, looked up to find an armed prisoner standing in the doorway. He was ordered to crawl across the circle to the tea room, where he was held with the other members of staff.

While prison staff in the circle were being taken captive, there was coordinated action in the wings to overpower other staff. Two officers, who were operating the gate locks leading from the wings to the circle, were overpowered by two orderlies, one with a gun and the other wielding a screwdriver. An officer in C Wing was clubbed with a blow to the back of the head, while another in D Wing was stabbed with a handicraft knife. The remaining officers were also overcome. The last two members of staff still not under control were seized at gunpoint as they emerged from the toilets.

Some prison officers attempted to resist the takeover. The senior officer succeeded in knocking the gun away from the prisoner covering him but a blow to the jaw and a threat by another to shoot his colleague subdued him. The officer lying on the floor of the communications room, surreptitiously raised himself up in an attempt to reach his baton but his captor fired two shots at him and he collapsed on the floor with a bullet through the head. The sound of the shots did not carry through the closed doors of the block to the officer manning the gate lock at the entrance to the compound, so he was unaware of what was happening inside. One of the armed prisoners, using keys he had taken, then let himself and two accomplices out of the block, approached the gate lock and asked to be allowed in to sweep. Still suspecting nothing, the officer responded only to find himself faced with a gun and a demand to hand over his keys. The officer was then marched inside the block to join the rest of his colleagues. Twenty minutes had passed. The prisoners were in complete control of H7 and the alarm had not been raised.

40 minutes later, at about 3.30, the blue box lorry with a hydraulic tailgate, which delivered the meal trolleys from the prison kitchen arrived at the block and was admitted by a prisoner wearing a prison officer's uniform. The driver was quickly overpowered by other armed prisoners, 38 of whom then boarded the lorry, which he was ordered at gunpoint to drive to the main gate. Behind them the prison officers, stripped of their uniforms and wearing ponchos made from blankets with pillow cases over their heads, were prevented from raising the alarm by the remaining inmates.

On reaching the main gate, having passed through a number of internal checkpoints without being discovered, ten prisoners, now dressed in prison uniforms and armed with firearms and chisels, entered the Tally

Lodge. However, their efforts to overpower staff and take it over were hampered by the arrival of large numbers of officers coming on duty. In the ensuing fifteen-minute struggle some prison officers put up considerable resistance. One managed to push an alarm button, but when the prison emergency control room responded he was forced to say it had been an accident, so a full escape alert was not launched. At this point prison officer James Ferris, who had been stabbed three times in the chest, ran from the gate lodge in a bid to alert an officer outside to raise the alarm. Ferris, who had a history of heart trouble, then collapsed and died soon afterwards. A pathologist concluded that the three stab wounds contributed to a fatal heart attack. (The dead man, aged 43, the father of two teenage boys, had been a prison officer at the Maze for eight years and was described by his church minister as 'a quiet, courageous, devoted family man who would do his duty'. He was posthumously awarded the Queen's Commendation for brave conduct. Later, in April 1988, after a 35-day trial, sixteen prisoners were acquitted of murder after Lord Lowry, the Lord Chief Justice, said he could not be satisfied that the heart attack which caused death had been caused by the stabbing.)

These events were spotted by the soldier manning the watch tower overlooking the main gate, who reported to his operations room that he could see prison officers fighting in the gate area. The military operations officer telephoned the prison emergency control room to ask if they 'had any trouble'. The prison officer replied that an alarm had been set off accidentally and everything was all right. Shortly afterwards a prison officer who was being held captive in a back room of the gate lodge managed to bundle the gunman holding him out of the door and dial the emergency number to warn the emergency control room of the escape. This time, at 4.12 pm, nearly two hours after the escape had started, the alarm was finally raised, but it was too late.

The prisoners had by now succeeded in forcing the main gate open and were fleeing on foot. They had been prevented from getting away in the meals lorry, as planned, because two vigilant officers arriving for work spotted what was happening and drove their private cars across the opening to block it. As they did so, prisoners from the gate lodge and others who had been concealed in the back of the lorry continued to stream through the main gate on foot towards the outer fence some 25 yards away. Meanwhile, staff from the gate lodge, having regained control of the main gate mechanism, ordered the two officers to move their cars out of the way so that the gate could be closed again. No sooner had they done so than four prisoners outside the gate advanced on one of the officers to seize his car. He quickly threw away his keys but was knocked to the ground and given a severe kicking before one of the prisoners retrieved the keys and all four drove off in the car along the prison wall towards the external gate leading to the public road outside.

This episode was witnessed by yet another officer, who had just arrived at the prison car park, opposite the main gate, to go on duty. He immediately drove off again ahead of the prisoners' car, sounding his horn and flashing his lights to warn the staff at the external gate. When he reached it he swerved to one side, causing the speeding hijacked car to crash into him. The prisoners scrambled out of the car. Two escaped through the gate, one was chased and caught by a soldier and the fourth was detained before he could get away from the car.

A hot pursuit was also underway along the main road leading from the external gate towards Lisburn. A senior officer left the gate lodge and called to the group of staff outside the main gate to give chase. Three officers, later joined by a police officer and a soldier, soon found four of the escaped prisoners hiding in reeds at the side of the River Lagan, about half a mile from the prison. All were taken back into custody.

Meanwhile, back at the main gate, prison officers were pursuing prisoners who had not already reached the outer fence. One of them was shot in the leg by a prisoner, who was himself then shot in the leg by a soldier in the watch tower and recaptured. Another prisoner fell near the wire and was also recaptured. It was now about 4.18. The main gate was closed again and the prison secured. With the full escape alert in operation, soldiers in the adjoining military complex were on the move and police and Army patrols in the vicinity were converging on pre-arranged points to impose a cordon in a bid to contain the fugitive prisoners. Within minutes the first ring was in place, and within an hour checkpoints had been set up at strategic points within Northern Ireland and along the border.

According to the second part of his journal entry for the day, the Governor, who had gone home, was alerted immediately after the alarm was raised during the struggles in and around the main gate. 'At approx 16.26 hours in response to an urgent telephone message received at home that an escape had taken place from the prison I arrived in the emergency control room and was informed that a large number of prisoners had escaped by using the kitchen van and then by running through the main gate. Emergency procedures had been put into operation. The RUC, Army authorities and Compound Maze ECR were informed. Director of Prison Operations was contacted by the Duty Officer and he arrived at the prison 5.50 hrs. The Under-Secretary was also advised of the situation. All H-blocks had been instructed to lock up all prisoners and a head count of the prison was in progress. I was informed it was suspected that prisoners had taken over control of H7. Reports of a smoke alarm going off in that block were received at ECR. Staff were unable to make contact by landline or radio shortly after a message was received from Officer ** that Officer ** had been shot.' The Governor's priority now was to restore security and control of the prison and establish just how many prisoners were involved, those who had got away and who had been recaptured. It was soon established that 38 prisoners had been involved, making it easily the largest jail break in British prison history. During the breakout, and in the immediate follow-up operations by the police and Army, thirteen had been recaptured almost at once and another six were rounded up within days, but the other nineteen became long-term fugitives. Indeed several returned to active terrorism and two later perished in shoot-outs with undercover security forces. The prisoners left behind in H7 to hold the prison staff hostage after the lorry departed had ransacked offices, desks and filing cabinets in the interim, destroying pictures and records to frustrate those following up the incident.

But what happened after the hostages were freed and the prisoners were locked up again is one of the most shameful episodes in Northern Ireland prison history. Some of the thirteen prisoners who had been quickly recaptured were stripped, beaten and dragged along the ground near H7 by prison officers angered at the death of their colleague and the wounding and injury of others caught up in the violent events of the afternoon. A prison orderly who was on the kitchen lorry and detained along with the prison officers in H7 lost two teeth when he was batoned across the mouth by a prison officer. Reliable sources, including members of the Board of Visitors, priests, doctors and solicitors, gathered compelling witness accounts about the episode, including an incident when some prison officers wanted to go the gate armoury to get their own personal protection weapons and had to be restrained by more cool-headed colleagues. So that H7 could be thoroughly searched and examined by police scene-of-crime officers investigating the series of criminal offences committed during the course of the escape, it was decided to relocate the remaining 88 prisoners, who had not joined the escape, to the adjoining H8 block, which was vacant. What happened next was reconstructed in detail, some five years later, for Mr Justice Hutton, later the Lord Chief Justice of Northern Ireland, during the hearing of an action for damages for assault. The case was brought by Brian Pettigrew, who was in H7 serving a ten-year sentence imposed for robbery, firearms offences and IRA membership.

Pettigrew, who stated he was not part of the breakout, was in the handicraft room of the block when a hooded prisoner entered and ordered him and other prisoners, first to the canteen, then to their respective cells. Some hours later, after the escape, when prison officers finally arrived at the cell block, Pettigrew and his cell were searched. He was then removed from the cell, ordered to take off his shoes and socks and told to run up the corridor with other prisoners. At this point he injured his wrist when one of the prison officers attempted to run him against a grille. Two officers then pushed him into a toilet area, kicked him and told him to undress. He was then allowed to put on only his trousers after which he was handcuffed. His undergarments were thrown away and he was led away barefoot, with a chain attached to handcuffs and his shoes and socks tied to his wrist. During this time another warder kicked him in the rear end and he was struck on the head. In the prison yard he was nipped in the backside by one of two guard dogs, and the other dog attempted to attack him. In all between 80 and 90 prisoners, many barefoot and naked from the waist up, were forced to run a gauntlet between two lines of angry prison officers and dog handlers as they were transferred from H7 to H8, over a period of at least one hour after prison staff had called for armed police officers to be removed from the area. The dogs, all German Shepherds, were on long leads and were 'egged on' to attack the prisoners by their handlers.

Despite the fact that some twenty of the prisoners requested access to a doctor and others wanted to see solicitors, they were kept incommunicado for at least ten days in order, Hill told the court, to hinder any investigation and allow time for their injuries to heal. 'We say there was a deliberate cover-up among a large number of prison officers,' he said. 'This is not only a case for damages and aggravated damages but one for exemplary damages.' Nine other prisoners in H7 at the relevant time also gave evidence, including Sean McKenna, the man who went to the point of death in the first hunger strike and who, a doctor told the court, now suffered from mental illness.

The court also heard that after a public outcry about the prison officers' conduct, an investigation by the Deputy Governor into the allegations of ill-treatment and assault had come up against 'a wall of silence' on the part of the prison officers, who also failed to cooperate with a police investigation. Although an earlier case by another prisoner, who had recounted a similar course of events and described the mood of the prison officers that day as being 'unusually aggressive', had been dismissed by Judge Peter Gibson in 1985, this time the judge accepted the evidence and awarded £3000 exemplary and aggravated damages for oppressive conduct on the part of prison officers towards Pettigrew.

In his ruling the judge said, 'In the particular circumstances of this case as I am satisfied that there was a strong feeling of anger and hostility amongst the prison officers towards the remaining prisoners in H-block 7, as I am satisfied that the plaintiff was bitten as he alleged because prison officers who were dog handlers did not exercise proper restraint, as I am satisfied that the plaintiff's evidence that he was bitten was truthful, and as I am satisfied that a number of the prison officers who gave evidence about the actions of the dogs between H-block 7 and H-block 8 must have lied in the witness box, I consider as a tribunal of fact that there is also probably some truth in the plaintiff's allegations that he was kicked and punched and I hold on the balance of probabilities in this particular case that the plaintiff was assaulted by being kicked or punched at some stage or stages in the course of moving from his cell in H-block 7 to H-block 8.'

The judge gave a warning about the grave implications of the incident for the integrity of the prison service: 'The escape of the prisoners who had been convicted of the gravest terrorist crimes from H-block 7 and from the Maze Prison itself was a blow to the prison service of the greatest magnitude and of the greatest gravity. In the course of the escape one prison officer died, one prison officer in H-block 7 was shot in the head and seriously wounded, and other prison officers were injured. When the prisoners escaped from H-block 7 they left a number of prison officers tied up. It is clear that some of the prisoners who remained in H-block 7 and were subsequently moved to H-block 8 had helped in varying degrees those who succeeded in escaping. It is therefore understandable that the prison officers who were involved in moving the remaining prisoners in H-block 7 to H-block 8 would have had a deep feeling of anger towards those prisoners because of what had occurred. But those prisoners remained under the protection of the law and it was the duty of the prison officers, notwithstanding their anger, to ensure that they were not harmed. In this case I consider that the conduct of the dog handlers who deliberately did not restrain their dogs from nipping or biting the plaintiff and the conduct of the prison officers who kicked or punched the plaintiff was oppressive conduct by servants of the Government. Notwithstanding that the prison officers had real and understandable grounds for anger, it was their duty to restrain that anger, and in my opinion their conduct calls for an award of exemplary damages to mark the disapproval of the court, to teach that such conduct does not pay, and to act as a deterrent against this type of conduct against prisoners being repeated in the future.'

In all, 22 prisoners shared a £35,000 pay-out for injuries received at the hands of prison officers, and twelve of the recaptured prisoners later accepted a £45,000 settlement for ill-treatment. The award of £10,000 shared between two other prisoners awarded brought the bill for the Northern Ireland Office to over £90,000, with a sum of about half that also being paid in legal costs.

Meanwhile, back on that Sunday night in 1983, long before these shameful events became known, when it was publicly confirmed that 38 prisoners were involved, the ever more ingenious Belfast graffiti writers daubed the walls with '38 all out – the amazeing escape,' and 'Open up the Long Kesh gate, meals on wheels for thirty-eight.' The elation in the Republican areas was most certainly not matched among the angry prison officers. Next morning a Prison Officers' Association meeting decided the prison flag should fly at half-mast until after Officer Ferris's funeral, and that until then there would be a 23-hour lock-up for prisoners, who would receive no visits or parcels and have their meals served in their cells. The Governor noted the POA proposals and remarked that they could be regarded as ill-advised in the circumstances. The POA ignored him.

The scale of the escape, and the fact that a number of guns had been smuggled into a supposedly maximum-security prison for the second time in as many years, provoked an immediate crisis of confidence in James Prior, the Secretary of State for Northern Ireland, and his ministers. Prior ordered an immediate inquiry into the security arrangements that had failed to prevent the escape and, before the day was out, asked Sir James Hennessy, the Chief Inspector of Prisons, to conduct it. He arrived at Stormont the next morning to begin work and a day later set up an office at the Maze itself where he and a team of between nine and thirteen prison specialists, spent the next four and a half weeks interviewing the Governor and 114 Maze staff, including those on duty that Sunday, examining the physical layout of the prison from the ground and the air and taking evidence from a wide range of people and organisations concerned. They also interviewed some prisoners and received written evidence from another 28. (It should be noted that they did not investigate the events in the prison after the escape referred to above.) Through November and December, the team worked in the Home Office at Queen Anne's Gate in London, sifting through the mass of evidence they had accumulated, drawing their conclusions and writing their comprehensive report.

In a clear sign that the escape would prompt a major security crackdown, visits were cancelled and every prisoner remained locked in his cell from 9 am on the morning of 16 November until late that afternoon while hundreds of warders, drafted in from every other prison, carried out a methodical search of each of the 800 inmates, their cells and belongings. Nothing was found, but 48 hours earlier a pistol, wrapped in plastic and smeared in grease to preserve it in working order, had been found in a Loyalist compound. A few weeks earlier, on the post-escape crackdown, bomb-making components and items suitable for use in an escape were discovered in both the Maze and Magilligan.

Even before its conclusions had been drawn and published, the Hennessy inquiry sparked off a massive wave of recrimination between the Northern Ireland Office and the POA, whose members were placed in the firing line from the outset. Before the end of the first week, the Northern Ireland Office officials, who had masterminded the official propaganda response to the years of protest and the hunger strikers, planted a series of stories in the national newspapers, designed to save the political lives of Prior and his prisons minister, the affable Nicholas Scott, MP for Chelsea. They pinned the blame for preventing the escape firmly on the shoulders of the prison officers. The official line was that there had been no policy failures. If everybody had been doing their job properly, the escape could not have taken place. The POA publicly expressed deep resentment and said that internal classified documents and minutes of their own encounters with the prison management showed that, all along, they were the ones sounding the alarm bells. This material formed the substance of their written submission to Hennessy listing the occasions between July 1982 and July 1983 when the Association had raised its concerns with the Governor and the department at the Northern Ireland Office. The notes of one meeting on 27 August 1982 are typical: 'POA requested special meeting. Area Chairman present. Governor aware of paramilitary push for segregation. POA expressed consternation and fear among staff and indicated proposed internal disruption by inmates. Governor stated NIO were aware. Request for extra staff made. Refused by Governor. "Hazards of the job."'

At another meeting with the Governor in November 1982, they submitted recommendations for improved searching procedures and expressed concern about the high numbers in some of the blocks, specifically mentioning H7. Later they voiced worries that the regimes department at Dundonald House was 'at a loss to contain the segregation movement by protestant (loyalist) prisoners and to alleviate the situation in both Magilligan and the Maze Cellular, the policy implemented was to reduce the size of the protestant population in Maze by transferring many inmates to Magilligan and to create equal numbers of both factions in Maze. However, in so doing, the Maze became top heavy with republican prisoners and it is at this point that effective control was lost.' In all, the POA told Hennessy, at some thirteen meetings during the period they made 30 approaches 'with reference to security, manning levels and controlled movement. Staff were fully aware of the inherent dangers and in consequence made management aware of these dangers.'

Industrial relations, especially in the Maze, were decidedly fraught at this time. Not long before the escape there had been a POA walk-out on the August bank holiday Monday, in pursuance of a grievance over an allowance for travelling time, leaving the police to run the prison. Since the escape, to back up a demand for an extra officer to be deployed in wings of the H-blocks, the prison officers had imposed a number of restrictions on starting and meal break times and were refusing to move prisoners around the complex, except on a one-to-one escort basis. The normal ratio would have from one officer for two up to fourteen prisoners. This had proved to be highly disruptive to the day-to-day routine, slowing down visits (there were an average 150 a day) and work. The workshops making office furniture and cement blocks had to be closed down. Indeed, fearing a walk-out in the face of inevitably adverse comment when Hennessy's report was published, the government put the RUC and the Army's Spearhead battalion on standby to come in and run the prison if necessary.

Hennessy finally reported in January 1984 and, as Prior had promised, the report was published in its entirety save for the deletion of the names of prison officers and a few sensitive security details. As they say in Ireland, Hennessy and his team did not 'miss and hit the wall'. Their penetrating, trenchant but balanced analysis of the unprecedented debacle went well beyond the mere background to the escape. It also diagnosed the state of health of the prison service as a whole and made 73 recommendations in respect of three main weaknesses: flaws in the physical structure and design of the prison; inadequacies in the security and search procedures; and complacency and lax behaviour on the part of the staff coupled with fundamental management deficiencies. 'The difficulties in the prison had their effect on the work of the four divisions that go to make up the prison department in the Northern Ireland Office. Instead of being able to get on with their task of supervising and inspecting establishments and of ensuring the necessary improvements to security following the rapid concentration of so many terrorists in so few prisons, they were forced to spend much of their time dealing with disturbances and protests and the Parliamentary and international interest that they aroused.' The Hennessy report made sorry reading for the entire prison service.

Hennessy described how the Maze grew from the small temporary internment centre at Long Kesh in 1971 into the huge modern maximum security prison it had become in just over a decade, holding the largest concentration of terrorists in western Europe. He described it as:

'. . . A prison without parallel in the United Kingdom, unique in size, and in the continuity and tenacity of its protests and disturbances. In no other prison that we have seen have the problems faced by the authorities been so great. When terrorists are few in number they can be dispersed into small, secure pockets and absorbed into the general prison population. But when they are many the best solution is usually to be found in removing them from the area of conflict and incarcerating them in a fortress prison surrounded by armed guards. In Northern Ireland neither course is feasible.

'The prison is unique, too,' [the report continued,] 'in its population, which is totally dissimilar to the usual criminal recidivist population to be found in the nearest equivalent establishment in England and Wales. It consists almost entirely of prisoners convicted of offences connected with terrorist activities, united in their determination to be treated as political prisoners, resisting prison discipline, even if it means starving themselves to death, and retaining their paramilitary structure and allegiances even when inside. Bent on escape and ready to murder to achieve their ends. they are able to call on the help of their associates and supporters in the local community and – though increasingly less frequently – to arouse the sympathy of the international community; they are able to manipulate staff and enlist the support of paramilitary organisations in the process of intimidation.

'Against this background it is not hard to see that the Governor and his staff are faced with a singularly difficult and dangerous task, one that brings them into conflict with prisoners almost every day of the week. Nowhere else in the United Kingdom have there been such prolonged and wide scale protests of so horrendous a nature. Nowhere else has the media been so insistent, or international interest so widespread. And nowhere else have the prison authorities been more in the public eye, more engaged in satisfying public curiosity and consequently less able to concentrate on running the establishment.

'Nor has their task been made any the easier by the determination of the government not to give in to the terrorists' political demands: the determination to treat terrorists like all other prisoners – with all that that implies in terms of regime and privileges; and the determination to avoid, in the wider interests of peace, those measures which, although beneficial in security terms, might provoke further destruction, further protest or further conflict and loss of life.

'These pressures on the prison authorities, together with the troubles in the Province generally, provided the prisoners with the conditions they needed in which to lay their plans for escape – conditions where manipulation became possible, collusion could not be ruled out, intimidation could flourish, weapons could be smuggled in and messages passed out and orderlies could move freely about.'

Hennessy attributed blame for 'the state in which we found the Maze' to a variety of both physical and human factors contributing to weaknesses in security. He pointed to deficiencies in the design of the main gate complex and in the communications room in H7, weaknesses compounded by poor security procedure, including flaws in the system of searching prisoners, their accommodation, supplies and visitors; flaws in the system of controlling and escorting the movements of prisoners and orderlies in the H-Block; and flaws in the arrangements for responding to alarms. 'It was the responsibility of the Governor and his senior staff to ensure that such procedures were both adequate and effective. This they failed to do.'

Even where the security procedures were adequate staff often did not follow them, according to Hennessy. 'The human failures were many. Staff had become complacent about the dangers, and lazy practices had been allowed to develop. There were examples of security grilles being left unlocked, orderlies allowed over much freedom, vehicles unchecked, posts left unattended, alarms not properly answered – and so on, the list is long.' The report identified terrorist pressures as increasing this tendency for staff to turn a blind eye to such security-threatening activities. Hennessy said that effective security depends upon the constant alertness of staff and the consistent application of routine procedures. 'Responsibility for this rests upon all staff, however mundane their duties and whether or not they have direct contact with prisoners. Alertness is no less important in a prison like the Maze, which is equipped with a variety of security aids, than anywhere else. Staff who are punctilious in their work and use their intuition and initiative help security prosper; staff who are careless and unconcerned cause the breaches in security which lead to failure.'

He singled out for praise what he called conscientious men, professional in their outlook, ready to risk their lives in doing their duty, as setting a standard to be followed by prison staff everywhere. But he had harsh words for others. 'The Maze also harbours officers who show too little concern for their duty. We had ample evidence of this: of security gates being left open, prisoners not searched, posts left unmanned; we have quoted many examples. Then there were the complacent staff, ripe for manipulation by inmates, whose attitudes substantially impaired the performance of the security task, both directly and through their impact upon more conscientious staff.'

Another factor in poor staff performance was identified as the lowering of educational and physical standards and the emphasis placed on high earnings in the mid 1970s, in order to attract recruits at a time when the Prison Service needed to rapidly expand. 'With hindsight,' the report said, 'one may regret what happened, but we have little doubt that at the time, when the Prison Service was facing a real emergency, the measures taken were reasonable, and no one should be blamed for what was done. Nevertheless, it is clear that there are men in the Northern Ireland Prison Service now who lack the abilities required of a prison officer and the leadership qualities necessary for the more senior grade appointments – as well as men who are over-concerned with high earnings. And while such men may not be typical, they are nevertheless a factor of which the Prison Service must take account.' In further damning remarks, the inspector also pointed to the reaction of many ordinary prison officers to the government's decisions on prisoners' clothing and visits, 'decisions which many officers, despite clear statements of government policy, regarded as concessions to the terrorists; concessions which some appeared to think justified them in taking a laissez-faire attitude to prisoners. The restoration of a sense of professionalism in the staff must therefore be an immediate objective if security is to be improved. There are major problems here which strike at the heart of the Prison Service in Northern Ireland and the environment in which it operates.' (In this context, the prison service had been publicly embarrassed at this time when its recruitment methods – described by one official as taking anybody who could see a little and read a little – were found to have failed to detect an applicant who did not disclose a conviction for armed robbery on his application form, and allowed him to be offered an appointment to a post.)

When it came to apportioning blame, Hennessy concluded those who directed the affairs of the Prison Service in Northern Ireland, decided policy, issued guidance and instructions to implement it and inspected establishments to see that instructions are carried out must bear some responsibility. However, the report unequivocally indicted the Governor because the extent of the deficiencies in management and in the prison's physical defences amounted to a major failure in security for which he must ultimately be held accountable. 'He should have been aware of the deficiencies and he should have taken action to remedy them,' the report stated. But Hennessy acknowledged his 34-year membership of the Prison Service, including ten years as a Governor, and the mitigating fact that much of his time had been taken up with the constant crises that engulfed the prison. 'He has shown sensitivity and understanding in his handling of them. He is conscientious and hard-working, and we believe that he did his best. His achievements should not be underestimated. His personal qualities are of a high order, but much of his training and experience relate to a time when the service was smaller and the task less demanding.' The Governor, within a few months of his scheduled retirement, fell on his sword and resigned.

Later, in the House of Commons where the Hennessy report was debated on 9 February, Prior echoed the tribute:

'I would say to the House that he was close to retirement and I have made arrangements whereby he will not suffer as a result of his resignation so far as his retirement is concerned and I believe that that would be a proper recognition of, in many ways, holding the poisoned chalice at the time of the escape. I believe a man who has given honourable service in very difficult circumstances over a great period of time and is near to retirement should not be made to suffer unduly for what happened. But given the extent and nature of the security deficiencies within the Maze which the Report highlighted – and considering Sir James' conclusion that the Governor must carry ultimate responsibility for the state of the prison – I believe that it was right to accept his resignation.

'My responsibility now is to help the prison service in Northern Ireland to respond to the demands which will be placed on them. Running a prison of course requires more than just going by the book. It needs subtlety and imagination, motivation and high morale. And it is also essential that leadership is sensitive to the changing situation, and to attitudes among staff as well as prisoners. The report shows ways in which procedures can be improved and staff better managed. That guidance will be followed. But it must not be forgotten that as well as describing the pressures on the system the report emphasises the many qualities of the service and of the men and women who work in it – qualities of courage as well as of the highest professional standards. I attach great importance to the task the prison service has to perform for the community in Northern Ireland, a task which it is the continuing aim of the terrorist to undermine. That must never be allowed to happen.

'But I would not want the House to think that the work of the prison service can be taken in isolation from the community which it serves, The Maze is a product of the troubled history of Northern Ireland. It is a history of division and conflict as well as of resourcefulness and determination. It reflects a community which takes pride in its separate identities, but which shares, without always recognising it, a common heritage. This debate is about the Maze prison. But let us not forget that life in the Maze affects and is influenced by life outside the prison. If the proper lessons are learned from the Maze escape, as I am determined they will be learned and that they will be acted on, then we will go a long way to ensuring that such a catastrophe does not happen again.'

Prior and Scott escaped from the Maze with their political lives, but only just. The Prison Officers' Association accused the government of pursuing a policy of political appeasement and called for tough new measures to break the paramilitary grip on the prison. In particular it wanted a high-security block with a tough regime to house the recaptured escapees and other high-risk inmates. John Hall, the general secretary, said the prisons were not bartering houses. 'The Maze must be treated as a normal prison. We were betrayed by government policy. Now somebody has to be courageous and break the paramilitary grip. My members resent being made the "whipping boys" for failures at policy and political level,' he fumed. The Governors Association, with just 41 members, was so dismayed about the way the Governor, whose home had been bombed by terrorists in 1976, had been made the scapegoat that they took the extremely rare step of issuing a detailed public statement giving their side of the story. Like the POA, it said it had consistently warned Stormont that events in the Maze would inevitably create another crisis of some sort. The Governor, it said, had come under political pressure from Lord Gowrie, then the prisons minister, to find prison work for Brendan 'Bik' McFarlane, the leader of the IRA prisoners and a prominent mover in the hunger strikes and their aftermath, and other prisoners, as part of a deal to restore lost remission. The deal required them to conform to prison rules, including work, for three months. The Governors said that the Northern Ireland Office was well aware of the decision, criticised by Hennessy, to give McFarlane, and other equally high-risk IRA terrorist prisoners, orderly duties in the blocks, positions which they then exploited to plan and execute the breakout.

The mass escape, unequalled then or since, remains a landmark in British and Irish penal history, had far-reaching consequences. It ushered in what the prison service has come to call the years of containment, where the priority was to prevent the highly-motivated terrorist prisoners, who sought to carry on their campaigns from behind prison bars, from escaping, but at the same time to keep them constructively occupied while serving their sentences.

Hennessy had stated that the command of such a large and complex prison as the Maze required a man of exceptional ability with the energy to inject new life into the establishment, and the skill and experience necessary to manage what is probably the most difficult and important prison in the United Kingdom. It was a telling comment on the calibre of those concerned with running the prisons at the time that the only person who could be found to carry the 'poisoned chalice' of the Maze Governorship was the man who had run the prison through the traumatic years of the protests and the hunger strikes. Stanley Hilditch was therefore brought back to succeed the very man who had succeeded him early in 1982.

Chapter Thirteen
The Maghaberry Hilton

Late on the evening of 5 March 1984, two armed men and a woman overpowered the two elderly occupants of a house at Hawthornden Drive, off the Belmont Road in east Belfast, moved in and held them hostage. Overnight they waited and watched. At 5 am, the small car belonging to the now terrified couple was moved and positioned outside the house for a quick getaway. The waiting resumed. Three hours later the gunmen struck. Across the street, at 8.15 am, William McConnell, 35, was bidding farewell to his wife and three-year-old daughter at the front door, but as he turned and walked along the driveway to his car to leave for work two gunmen approached and opened fire. Their victim was hit in the head and face and died instantly. The killers then escaped in the car.

William McConnell was no random victim. He had joined the prison service in 1971 and was now an Assistant Governor at the Maze, responsible for security, and a few weeks earlier he had appeared on national television news, silhouetted to protect his identity, as the spokesman for the Governors' Association in the acrimonious aftermath of the publication of the Hennessy report. It was he who had publicly articulated their dismay at being disowned by their superiors and political masters at Stormont. In the run-up to his death he had been a troubled man. He had gone to the Ulster Unionist MP Ken Maginnis to confide his worries about the situation in the Maze and, indeed, the lack of progress in the completion of the new prison at Maghaberry, which was way behind its target opening date and still not ready to receive prisoners. The day after his television appearance, 3 February, he sat down and wrote a letter which was given to his cousin, the Reverend David McGaughey, to be read at his funeral if anything happened to him. His wish was respected. The poignant and cryptic letter was headed: 'Subject: my demise – to all in attendance'.

'I have decided to write this statement,' [McConnell wrote,] 'since I have come to the conclusion that the public interest is best served by knowing that whatever happens to me, I spoke the truth. I did not take the decision to go public on the matter of the Hennessy Report lightly. I realised the danger I was placing myself and others in, when, in consultation with my colleagues on the committee of the Prison Governors Association, I agreed to act as their spokesman.

'You will be gathered today asking questions which only a full investigation of the facts will reveal. Clearly, in attempting that process to continue, someone has decided that 1 should play no further part in the proceedings! I feel sorry for them, and can only pray that their part in the story will one day be revealed.

'My wife Beryl has been supportive of all I have done, I would commend her and Gail to your keeping and prayers.

'Finally, let no one be alarmed as to my eternal Security. In March 1966, I committed my life, talents, work and actions to Almighty God, in sure and certain knowledge that however slight my hold upon Him may have been during my years at school, university and the Prison Service, His promises are sure and His hold on me complete. Nothing can separate me from the Love of God in Christ Jesus our Lord.

'At our marriage ceremony we sang the hymn, "My hope is built on nothing less . . . " Please sing it today and may God be with you all. (Signed) Bill McConnell.'

The IRA had very quickly acknowledged their responsibility for the murder. It did not herald a renewed campaign against prison officers, they said, but 'should come as a salutary lesson to those in the administration presently advocating a return to a policy of beatings as a means of controlling political prisoners.' Prior dismissed the statement as 'garbage', and Fr Faul said it was 'absurd'. He had been killed because he was 'an easy target'.

By this time the police had the suspected killers in custody and had also arrested their accomplice, Owen Connolly, 63, a civil servant, who lived ten minutes' walk away from the McConnell home. A former Flight Lieutenant in the RAF, he had completed 30 wartime bombing missions over Germany as a navigator, but had later become embittered by lack of promotion in the Department of Agriculture where he worked. Five years before McConnell's murder, believing he was suffering from discrimination, he had offered to assist the IRA by spotting targets among the many police and prison officers who lived in the Stormont/Belmont area. After the shooting he had provided a safe house for the killers, purchased razors so they could shave off their moustaches and disposed of the gloves, wigs and guns they had used. He was jailed for life for murder and later testified against three men, one of whom was also convicted for the murder. The trial judge, who heard that Connolly had gathered information about the victim, including his car registration number, while walking his dog, said that Connolly had played a prominent and despicable role in the vicious murder plot.

McConnell's killing marked a turning point in the history of the Maze, with a move away from confrontation and a greater willingness on the part of the authorities to engage more directly with the prisoners through their command structures. One of the by-products of this was a greater interest in education, a development which would bear more fruit for many individual prisoners, and the community at large, than even its most optimistic advocate could possibly have foreseen. There had always been provision for education in the prison system but the bulk of it was low-level remedial teaching. 'It was just a case of someone from headquarters going out to the various prisons and taking soundings about what the prisoners wanted, doling out things like exercise books, pens, pencils and the odd textbook and stuff like that. There wasn't a structured education provision,' one official recalls. 'The prison education service in Northern Ireland really didn't take off until the monumental rise in the number of people who came in, both sentenced and detained. Then there was a big obvious need for some type of education provision and it started to get structured.'

But the pace of the rapid increase in the prison population and the need to dedicate resources to the more immediate problems of security and accommodation meant the educational programme suffered from periodic interruptions. At Belfast the classrooms had to be taken over and used as dormitories, and in Armagh, classes were suspended for a time because of overcrowding. When the Maze and Magilligan came into being, education provision had to be built up from nothing. Education had traditionally taken place in the evening after the normal working day, but with the introduction of internment in 1971 and special category in 1972 schedules had to be reorganised and staffed to provide daytime classes designed to meet the needs of an entirely new type of prisoner, some of whom were already well into third level courses. For instance, a trainee solicitor interned in 1971 was able to take his final law exams in Long Kesh. In March 1972 a central study hut was provided for twelve inmates who were students of the Open University, and by May each compound had been provided with a small study hut where students could prepare for GCE and other national examinations. A panel of volunteer teachers assisted with this work on two evenings per week, joined in 1973 by voluntary lecturers from Queen's University.

With the appointment of an education officer and two full-time teachers in 1974, the educational provision was in process of rapid expansion when the facilities were almost totally destroyed in the fire that year. During 1975 the rebuilt accommodation was more fully used as two further full-time teachers and additional part-time teachers were recruited. It was a similar story at Magilligan. In 1974 a group of part-time teachers was recruited and a full-time education officer appointed. By the end of 1976 three more full-time teaching staff had joined. Study huts and other facilities were provided, enabling educational programmes to be expanded. At that time there were 6579 textbooks available for students at the Maze and another 1750 at Magilligan as well as access to well-stocked libraries and the facility to borrow books from the public library service. It is interesting to note that the number of library books available at the Maze, 7694, was almost the same as the number of textbooks but that, at Magilligan, there were substantially more library than textbooks – 5800. In Armagh, the women prisoners had access to 1000 library books and 1188 textbooks. (However, a Maze prisoner did complain that among the textbooks there were only eight in the Irish language.)

By now there had been a complete reorganisation of education and vocational training with the appointment of a chief education and training officer, and a deputy, at the prison department headquarters in Dundonald House, as well as a training officer and a vocational training officer. The administrative staff was also augmented and additional teachers and civilian instructors appointed in each of the prisons. Apart from provision for academic studies at all levels from basic reading and writing to degree courses, there was also an increased emphasis on teaching prisoners trades or skills that could provide them with a living and help keep them from re-offending when they left prison. The range of training on offer was extensive and inmates could learn car maintenance, catering, carpentry, bricklaying, horticulture, painting and decorating and plastering. There was also furniture-making. Much of their labour was coincidentally directed into helping to operate and maintain the various prison establishments. The bleak Maze landscape was considerably improved in later years with flower beds, built by prisoners from kerbstones made in the prison and planted with flowers and shrubs grown in the horticulture area and the furniture for many cells and offices was manufactured in house.

We have already seen how the Maze had become a virtual university of terrorism, and, as their booklet 'Prison Struggle' clearly articulates, Republicans placed great importance on education from the outset. But their concept of prison education at that time was far from conventional and there were struggles with the authorities about books:

'Education for a POW begins when he enters Long Kesh. Inside the Cage, each Company Education Officer is responsible for seeing that every Volunteer gets an opportunity to study and learn the politics of the Republican Movement. This is done in a number of ways. A basic, education programme, drawn up by either Battalion Education Officer or Company Education Officers under his direction, is given to the men in lecture form. The lectures are given daily to squads of 15 men, each squad receiving one lecture a week.

'The purpose of giving lectures is not merely to impart facts, figures and dates, but to create an interest among the Volunteers so that they go into each aspect of politics and find out the answers for themselves. The role of the Education Officer is to co-ordinate and direct the interests of each man and to see that everyone benefits from the knowledge and experience shared by all.

'Each Company tries to maintain a library and everyone is encouraged to use it. The books are supplied by the men themselves and books of all shades of political thought are contributed as well as novels and biographies. It would be a dull library without a wide assortment of books so censorship is not practised; Mao Tse Tung to James Connolly, Fintan Lalor to Charles Dickens. It is an indication of prison policy when on occasions no attempt was made by the Authorities to stop cheap thriller novels, yet books of an educational nature are continually being turned away and not allowed in to us. The library gives Volunteers the opportunity to broaden their outlook and learn from the successes and failures of others throughout the world.

'Discussions are held regularly to debate the content of the lectures. The discussions held by each education squad are probably more educational in themselves than the lectures. Everyone has something to say and gets the opportunity to have points clarified and explained. Again the role of the Education Officer is to direct rather than instruct. The education programme organised and carried out by the POWs has had its successes. The purpose is not to produce indoctrinated cadres, but Volunteers who will return to the fight with a new determination based on the knowledge of their experience and the historical justification and universal right to wage war in the pursuit of their just cause.

'It is from this view that we point out that there are two sides to the education of POWs in Long Kesh in the same way as there are two sides to the struggle. There are the aims and objects which can be termed political and there are the means to achieve the aims which are military. The two cannot be separated; each is meaningless without the other. It is not entirely accurate to say that there is a programme of military education; the reason I say that is because what more can be taught to Volunteers than they already know and have learnt through fighting a guerrilla war in the North?

'The experience and practical knowledge of guerrilla warfare among the POWs in Long Kesh is probably the most extensive and most concentrated you will find in the Western World (Free World?) today. Within the confines of Long Kesh it would be possible to write volumes on the subject by simply asking questions and listening to the experience of each POW. These men have no need to be taught or lectured on any aspect of military training. The training which is carried out takes the form of physical training, drill instruction, with the commands given in Irish, as is the rule in most cases of activity where it can be applied. The drill is done not as a form of discipline but to maintain the structure and military nature of the organisation which functions in and outside Long Kesh.

'Lectures on weapons which do take place are merely for revision and tactics. This is not a Republican Sandhurst but with the War having lasted so long some men were captured before the more modern weapons were available so they get the chance to be brought up to date on the latest assault rifle or rocket. By combining the political lectures and military discussions it is hoped that men who return to the fight will look at the overall objective of a United Irish Socialist Republic and the dual importance of the armed means to bring it about.'

However, over the years, the Republican suspicion of the prison education service evaporated and they began to avail themselves of the opportunities it presented, although the education officer, who was once a key figure in their command structure, maintained close control over who could participate and what they were doing. Equally this officer was expected both to talent-spot and to stop lazy prisoners from wasting their time. Many individuals thus found themselves 'ordered' into education for their own good.

Gradually the emphasis on military training and revolutionary debate subsided and a more thoughtful, visionary and pragmatic brand of Republicanism ultimately emerged. This was based on some extraordinary soul-searching debate about the failings of their campaign, and a willingness to evaluate cherished Republican ideals and beliefs and adapt them to a more modern context. The Republican prisoners were all highly-motivated individuals and their innovative skills, which had driven the campaign outside the prison and extended the frontiers of terrorist tactics and improvisation, provided the basis for what amounted to a redefinition of Republicanism, which emerged from the Maze to stimulate the peace process of the late 1990s. When the 'whither Republicanism' debate gathered force within the organisation, several ex-prisoners proved to be influential voices and the views of the prisoners were given considerable weight because, in the Republican rationale, the prisoners had given their freedom for the cause just as some had given their lives. As they were still around to make their views known, their sacrifice entitled them to have their views heard and heeded. Thus the prisoners ultimately became a force for progress, and when the real political negotiations started their input was crucial.

Loyalist prisoners travelled on a parallel intellectual and political journey, as the former lifer Martin Snoddon recalled in *The Journal of Prisoners on Prison* in 1997:

'Regimental lifestyles that had existed were replaced with a commune-type existence where issues were openly discussed and a consensus of opinion sought and acted upon. Interaction between the factions, most notably between the UVF and the OIRA (Official IRA), increased and tribal feuds were submerged in political views which were amongst the most moderate and radical in the country. With Nationalists publicly espousing their credited phrase "ourselves alone", and Loyalists knowing the reality of its meaning, having been betrayed by their political leaders and finding themselves in the most unpleasant situation of being imprisoned by their fellow countrymen for fighting for their people, how much more remarkable it is then that their general morale remained buoyant in the face of adversity.

'Throughout the 1980s, they occupied themselves not by plotting and planning anyone's downfall, even though they endured unimaginable pettiness and psychological stress from members of the prison regime who tried to intimidate them into submission, but by continuing to cultivate their minds. Academic education, handicrafts, sport, and health and fitness featured heavily in their lives.

'Many partook in education. Meetings between a cage education representative and the prison education department administrator took place once a week, and over a cup of coffee, education requests forwarded by the cage rep were discussed and provisions and resources made available to enable a prisoner's chosen passage to be as obstacle free as possible. Most of the prisoners had no recognised academic qualifications at the time of their arrest. So over the years, full and part-time teachers were employed to go into the cages and teach eager students subjects found in any school curriculum. Irish language was surprisingly requested and taught to Fainne level in a UVF cage. Some chose not to sit examinations, but a significant number did bring many achievements at O and A levels.

'The Open University (OU), having first come into the camp in the mid 1970s for a few student prisoners, found a demand for their courses increasing in the 1980s as students climbed the academic ladder. They provided distance learning course material in prisoners' fields of personal interest such as mathematics, sociology, computing, technology, psychology, social sciences, philosophy, and history. Also tutors were sent in from the province's universities to discuss course units and prepare students for their three-hour examination. After many hours of solitary study, a number of students gained the required credits to entitle them to a degree from the OU (seven UVF prisoners graduated while in cage 21), others followed up their studies on release by going into full-time education at universities at home, in Britain, and in the Republic. Some, after having achieved their first degree, carried on to Honours degrees and even to postgraduate studies in the cages.

'The prisoners often joked about being a captive audience but what could not be laughed at was the dedication shown to attain a pass rate many of today's Further Education colleges would be proud of. The wire may have restricted the movement of their bodies, but their minds knew no bounds in their hunger for knowledge.'

Demand for Open University courses among Maze prisoners was proportionately ten times greater than in any other British prison. Indeed about five per cent of the prison population were either undergraduates or graduates, compared to less than half a per cent among the 47,000 prisoners elsewhere in the United Kingdom. Their success rate was also well above average with 66 students gaining seventeen distinctions in 1984 alone. At one time there were about 100 prisoners at various stages of Open University courses and some were pursuing research projects that would have been ambitious even for a student not handicapped by captivity. One prisoner was examining water levels and irrigation in the Sudan and arrangements were made for him to get satellite pictures from NASA to do the research. Another was investigating human movement and coordination, having been allowed the use of a computer. The Admiralty assisted yet another student who was investigating metal fatigue in large ships after two mystery sinkings on the high seas. By these standards, sourcing research material for the prisoner who was studying the way authors portrayed the troubles in modern novels was easy. Today, while prisoners are allowed laptops for educational purposes, they are only permitted to have supervised access to the Internet, again for security reasons:

'Thinking back to the Open University, we broke ground with the use of computers and the establishment of a telephone link with tutors on the outside,' [recalls one of the prison education staff.] 'That kind of thing was nearly unthinkable to the Prison Service at that time. There was always a tension between what the prison was there to do and what the education service was there to do. The Prison Service in Northern Ireland probably never really saw itself as a provider of education but it recognised its obligation. We, on the other hand, would have seen ourselves as obligated to provide the best possible service and that created an element of tension and education had to fight its corner and try to get the best possible facilities within the prison.

'Part of the tension arose from the security aspect. How can you provide a really proper education service when you're smothered by all the security requirements. Take the obvious ones like the chemistry degree or a degree in electronics, which could have a terrorist dimension. They would not have been permitted on security grounds but the broad range, arts, social, science, maths, humanities and, indeed, some science was allowed. It's absolutely wonderful for us, a tremendous success story when somebody comes in with no basic skills and then works his way through the relevant assessments and tests, up through GCSE and ends up doing a degree. I mean, it's a wonderful education and certainly in no way is that person the same at the end of that process as he was at the beginning. I remember one prisoner who did something particularly bad and came into prison and asked: '"What will I do with my time now, I'm doing to be here for a long time?" Apparently he had a mathematical bent and he did well in the maths class and went on to the higher maths. He then started to do an Open University. I think his first course was in technology but he was also going to vocational training at the same time, in welding or engineering workshops, and he got the highest mark of anybody in the UK in his year and he came out and he got his degree. [. . .]

'I think what you began to see towards the end of the '80s was the release of people who had been in the Maze and had received education and were going back into the community. And even though it might not have been a very big trickle of people, it was probably enough to make their presence felt and these people became key influencers back out in the community. The value of education, gained in the Maze, was beginning to be recognised. I was approached by a prisoner in Maghaberry, one of those people who has achieved well beyond what he thought was his capability. He came in as an uneducated prisoner, did science, did a few other areas of study, and then the Open University. He quite openly admitted to me, nearly with tears in his eyes, he was a fairly emotional guy, that it was a life changing experience for him, because if had he not come in to prison he would have never had the opportunity to avail of education. This door would never have been open to him and his life would therefore have continued to be a dark life.'

About half the prison population took the opportunity for education and the staff providing it for them expanded to 80, including full- and part-time teachers. In some cases the prisoners' educational achievements were all the more praiseworthy because the facilities set aside for them to study were far from distraction-proof. In one of the UDA compounds the study space was divided from the recreation area by a flimsy wall. 'All you could hear, when you were sitting in there reading a book, was the budgies, canaries, cockateels and parrots screeching and chirping from the other side of the wall,' recalls the educationalist.

Among the most enthusiastic beneficiaries of a prison education were the lifers. One of the most unusual features of the Northern Ireland prison population was the large number of prisoners serving life sentences for murder, indeed a high proportion of them for multiple murder. By the end of 1983, according to RUC figures, there had been 2356 murders attributable to the security situation. Another 184 non-terrorist murders had also taken place. For a variety of reasons many of them still remain unsolved, but at the end of 1984 there were 424 prisoners serving life or detained at the Secretary of State's pleasure for their part in this catalogue of violent death. This represented one in five of the sentenced prison population, compared with the situation in England and Wales where only one in sixteen prisoners was a lifer. Before the troubles, there were only a dozen lifers among the average daily Northern Ireland prison population of about 300 – one in 25.

Even then the question of capital punishment or life imprisonment was a matter of intense public debate. On the evening of 28 May 1969, while the Troubles were still at what could probably be described as the overture stage, the Stormont parliament was in session, handling the Committee stage of the Theft Bill. Based on the Theft Act 1968, its aim was to bring the law on theft, robbery, blackmail, burglary, fraud and the handling of stolen goods in Northern Ireland into line with Great Britain.

For once there was a wide-ranging, reasonable and, indeed, thoughtful debate about the issues raised by the legislation. Paddy Devlin, the Northern Ireland Labour MP for Falls, said, 'I think that in Western Europe, in England and elsewhere the movement is towards the idea that we should be less heavy-handed with the criminal than we are at the moment. In the context of Northern Ireland we should take into account that we have a community where we could possibly afford to be much more generous, liberal and more adventurous in our new legislation in this field.' In particular Devlin wanted life sentences reduced to a maximum fifteen-year term.

Similarly liberal sentiments came from Roderick O'Connor, the Nationalist member for West Tyrone, who called for a more lenient sentencing policy in Northern Ireland. 'I take the view that a sentence of imprisonment should not in any circumstances be longer than what gives a man at least the hope of living to come to the end of it and having enough life, energy and hope left in him to enter the world and rejoin the family to which he belongs. I believe that terms not exceeding fifteen years would be appropriate. In this country we have not the same number of professional, hard criminals as elsewhere. I find it difficult to believe that a period of fifteen years' imprisonment is not enough for any of the criminals of which we have had experience in the past. I see no reason to think that the criminals of the immediate future would be of a different type from those to which we have been accustomed.'

Robert Porter QC MP, the Minister of Home Affairs, added, 'Perhaps I should point out that in Northern Ireland no general intimation has been given as to the normal practical duration of a life sentence because ... it is very rare that it would mean the duration of the person's life, as is quite often the case in places like the United States of America. The reason why there is no general intimation in this country is that the number of persons affected is not large enough to enable such generalisations to be drawn.' O'Connor's views about the calibre of future criminals were soon to be proved spectacularly erroneous. Like the other speakers that night, he could not have imagined the savagery and callousness that was about to be unleashed and how the narrow database of experience in handing the unique problem of lifers in a prison system would be so spectacularly shattered.

With the abolition of capital punishment in Northern Ireland in 1972, life imprisonment became the mandatory sentence for murder committed by a person aged eighteen or over. It can also be imposed as the maximum for other serious offences including attempted murder, manslaughter, causing an explosion and the most serious firearms and sexual offences. A person convicted of murder who is under eighteen at the time of the crime is not sentenced to life imprisonment but, as an equivalent, is ordered to be detained during the pleasure of the Secretary of State wherever, and under such conditions as he might direct, which could be in a training school, a young offenders centre, or an ordinary prison later or from the outset.

While a life sentence gives authority to detain a person for the whole of his or her life, it is only in the most exceptional circumstances that a prisoner would remain in custody until he or she died, although, especially in the context of violent terrorism in Northern Ireland, there are many who believe this should be the case. In practice what happens is that the Secretary of State exercises power to release the prisoner on licence, subject to such conditions as he thinks fit and after consulting the Lord Chief Justice and the trial judge, if available, as he is required to do by law. In passing a life sentence for murder the judge may recommend a minimum period which should elapse before the prisoner is released and, while such recommendations are not binding, they naturally weigh heavily with the minister in deciding if a lifer should be freed.

While judges had four times stipulated life should mean natural life in a number of particularly vicious murder cases and laid down minimum terms of between twenty and 35 years in others, many lifers were simply jailed without any recommendation. Similarly, there is no fixed period of detention under a life sentence or a sentence of detention during the Secretary of State's pleasure, nor is there any form of 'tariff' against which the length of imprisonment is measured. All cases were reviewed periodically within the special life sentence unit, part of the regimes branch in the prisons department at the Northern Ireland Office, in the light of all the relevant factors, including the circumstances of the crime, the prisoner's age and background and the reports over the years of his behaviour and attitude in prison. In practice, a life term had come to mean a period of between twelve and fifteen years in prison. Before authorising the fixing of a date for the release of a prisoner serving a life sentence, the Secretary of State must be satisfied that the period served is sufficient to reflect the seriousness of the crime and that there is no significant risk that the prisoner will repeat his offence or commit another crime of violence. The overriding consideration is the need to protect the public from the risk of further offences of violence.

Prisoners serving indeterminate sentences get about twelve months' notice of their release on licence, but it is subject to continued good behaviour and to satisfactory arrangements being made for resettlement in the community. During this period, prisoners take part in a phased programme to prepare them for release. After a long spell in prison they need to adjust to the changes in society and come to terms with simple things like changes in prices and fashions, improvements to lifestyles through technology, and even how old familiar landmarks in their neighbourhoods might have disappeared through redevelopment. When released, the prisoner is always subject to whatever conditions may have been included by the Secretary of State in his or her licence. Although it can subsequently be varied or even cancelled, the licence remains in force for life and the licensee may be recalled to prison at any time if the Secretary of State is satisfied that this course is necessary in the public interest. From 1968 until the end of 1982, twenty life sentence prisoners and two prisoners detained during the pleasure of the Secretary of State were released on licence. Five of the 22 were released on medical grounds. During the same period two licensees were recalled to prison.

This workload clearly did not strain or overburden the system for keeping the cases of lifers under periodic review and releasing them in due course. But by the early 1980s the pressure of keeping the cases of the surge of lifers imprisoned in the 1970s under review was consuming more and more time and resources, and the burden was set to increase as these lifers progressively reached the point where their release would have to be considered. Towards the end of 1982 an increasing number of prisoners had reached or were approaching the ten year stage of their indeterminate sentences, so it was decided that the machinery for reviewing their cases on a regular basis, which had been in operation since the early '70s, should be revised. With such a heavy and, for any modern prison administration, unprecedented workload looming for many years ahead it was essential to ensure consistency and fairness.

With the terrorist groups to whom the lifers owed their allegiance still active, there had been fears expressed that the release of proven killers would increase the risk to the community. There had also been criticism of inconsistencies in some releases that had already taken place. In one case, where two people were involved in the same crime, the older, sentenced to life, had been released after serving thirteen years while his co-accused, the younger, who was being detained at the pleasure of the Secretary of State, remained in custody. The prisoners themselves, and their families, had also complained about the lack of information they were given about the review process. In a bid to create a framework, a Life Sentence Review Board was established and held its first meeting on 8 March 1983. It was chaired by the Permanent Under-Secretary of the Northern Ireland Office, and its other members were senior officials from the life sentence unit at the Northern Ireland Office, a consultant in forensic pyschiatry, a principal medical officer of the Department of Health and Social Services and the Chief Probation Officer. The board met on four occasions in 1983 and held a further four meetings in 1984. In January 1985 published an explanatory memorandum, setting out in simple language the background and procedures followed in dealing with life-sentence prisoners. It was the first step in a more humane process to give the lifers more information about the system that determined when they would be freed and to give them some idea of how close they were to getting a date and, if not, why and what they had to do to impress the board.

The introduction of the new review procedures was accompanied by the creation of a structured programme to prepare the lifers for release and help them to make the transition from prison back to the community. As the review board got into its stride, and more and more lifers were given a provisional release date – some nine to twelve months ahead – these prisoners moved into the phased pre-release scheme, designed to enable them to make the difficult transition to freedom from a prison term that would have lasted on average a dozen years, but often much longer. The first phase entailed short job-seeking visits out from Belfast prison with a probation officer. Early every morning for the next three months, they would slip discreetly through the heavily-fortified front gates of the prison to go to the jobs found for them by welfare agencies or the Probation Service. Some engaged in community work while a number went to university or a training scheme before returning to the prison at night. They were allowed to spend weekends at home with their families. However, for the final three months before release, they were allowed to remain at home and attend work, only reporting to the prison once a week.

Between 1983 and 1998, when diferent release arrangements came into force, 456 lifers, and other prisoners who were under eighteen when they were convicted and sentenced to be detained at the pleasure of the Secretary of State, were released from custody on licence. They all knew that should they commit another offence or participate in any unacceptable conduct or activity they would be recalled to prison. For the successive Secretaries of State who had to sign the release papers it was a major political gamble. If any one of the licensees had ever killed again, even in a non-terrorist situation, it would have meant the end of the Secretary of State's political career. In the event, although the violence continued until the terrorist ceasefires were called in 1994, only one has been recalled and convicted for committing a further offence – common assault. (Since 1998, another 98 lifers or 'pleasure' prisoners have been freed and only three have had to be recalled for further offences including, handling stolen goods, assault, causing criminal damage and possession of drugs.) The way that the prison system has handled its lifers problem is now the subject of international study and commendation as an example of best practice in handling what is probably the most demanding and difficult of all penal dilemmas.

The years from the mid 1980s to the mid '90s, when the Republican and Loyalist ceasefires were declared, were comparatively quiet and tranquil in the prisons compared with what had gone before, but, of course, were not without incident. In August 1984, 34-year old Benny Redfern, a Loyalist serving life for the sectarian murder of two Catholics, who was married with a child, and another life sentence prisoner concealed themselves in a 'wheelie bin' in their compound at the Maze. When the refuse lorry arrived to empty it they were dumped into the rear, but became enmeshed in the compressing mechanism. Redfern sustained serious injuries and died 24 hours later in hospital. His co-escapee only sustained a shoulder injury. The Coroner later described the episode as 'a hopeless attempt to escape', for ever since previous use of the refuse lorry to get out of the prison, all the rubbish was dumped internally, searched and only then taken out to the public dump for disposal.

The years until the ceasefires have been described as the years of containment, during which the emphasis, after Hennessy, was on creating an effective security cordon around the prisoners while allowing them a pretty liberal existence within it. Among the improved facilities introduced were the provision of microwave ovens, toasters and gym equipment in each wing of the H-blocks, and the prisoners were also allowed to have a personal stereo, as well as a radio, in their cells. For some time previously there had been access to television and video recorders in the wings. Later innovations would include summer, as well as Christmas, home leave schemes and more liberal granting of parole.

But there were still repeated efforts to escape on an ongoing basis although the emphasis on tighter security meant that these attempts were invariably thwarted. In May 1989, an escape alert led to a two-day search of the Maze and the same year, on 7 October, an elaborate IRA plot for a mass breakout from Belfast prison was foiled by the police. All of a sudden that Saturday afternoon, fifteen vehicles were hijacked and set on fire in several Republican areas of Belfast, sparking off four hours of riots and street disturbances. During the clearly organised clashes, police became suspicious of a JCB excavator parked adjacent to the prison and discovered that it contained a 750-pound bomb in the front bucket. About the same time they swooped on six cars parked suspiciously at various points around the prison. By now they had established the rioting was a cover for a major escape, the bomb was to be used to blast the prison perimeter wall and the cars were to take away the escaping prisoners. 76 of them were at that very moment enjoying afternoon exercise in the open on the other side of the wall where they were preparing to detonate a small bomb to clear a path to the planned breach in the wall. An immediate clampdown took place inside and in follow-up searches the four-pound Semtex high explosive device and some ammunition were quickly uncovered. Later a loaded pistol and more ammunition were uncovered. The searchers also found that the heels of several inmates' trainers had been hollowed out and, they believed, used to smuggle the explosive and the weapon into the prison.

Notwithstanding these attempts, the reduction in serious incidents reflected not so much a change in the objectives of the prisoners but rather a shift in their strategy. The nature of their perennial challenge to the authorities was changing from the direct confrontations of the 1970s and early 1980s to a more subtle campaign characterised by attempts to secure concessions by pressurising staff and exploiting the legitimate grievance procedures, supplemented by outside support groups.

In December 1984, for instance, the Secretary of State's office was hit by a torrent of petitions on conditions in the prisons. Soon afterwards, a document captured from an IRA prisoner in H4 illustrated the way the organisation conceived its propaganda policy and motivated its members to implement it. The paper described how all IRA prisoners should pool their efforts in drawing up the material for a campaign to embrace complaints about every possible aspect of the prison system from 'petty things like ignorance to visitors to refusal to replace damaged darts or whatever,' to 'beatings by riot squads, long periods on the boards [in the punishment cells], searching of visitors, forced integration, compassionate parole and life reviews.' Not only were past events to be catalogued; those still occurring were to be much more thoroughly documented for propaganda. The organisation felt this was necessary to counter the 'Brit/SDLP/ Father Faul' line that conditions in prisons were improving. The paper outlined the broad theme to link the threads of the campaign as being to put the blame on the system: the Governors, Chiefs and NIO Prison Department Officials and of course the Judiciary. It said they should demonstrate the links between Judiciary and the Governors here, show how they both co-operate in torturing POW's. 'Mo Chara [my friend], the emphasis is not to be put on the Screws, people already see them as bigots. What we have to try and show is that the Brit system is very carefully manipulating the prison conditions to torture POWs and then pressure the IRA.'

The content of the letters was to be carefully and methodically thought out. Those organising the 'torture' were to be emphasised – 'the Governors, Chiefs and NIO Officials'. Prisoners are instructed to 'name names when giving incidents of Governors violence and bigotry, give case histories of refusals of Compassionate Parole and how the POW was insulted by their bigoted attitude, etc.' Very sound stylistic advice is given – 'Don't crowd a letter. Pick one topic per letter and give it all the details you can put together.'

The campaign was predicated on fully exploiting recent relaxations to the rules which now, for instance, allowed prisoners to write to newspapers: 'The censorship rules have been amended and we are now able to write to the papers. I want you to make sure that any spare letters in your wing are used up every week, with short letters to local papers, avoid any ideology type letters. Just comment on local issues in which Sinn Fein are involved, and more or less praising their community work. It's only three months to the elections, so we can't afford to ignore the opportunity existing in these letters.' The paper concludes with an exhortation that all are required to play an active part – 'This is not another PR exercise it's an important army (IRA) activity, each of us has a duty to expose exactly what the Brits are at and what part in their plan they have for prisoners. The feachtas [campaign] starts now.'

One multi-faceted protest campaign was mounted against the prison authorities for banning fluent Irish language speakers from wearing the Fainne, a silver or gold brooch, or even a new cloth version because they feared it would open the door to the wearing of paramilitary insignia. Later, in October 1987, two former prisoners were awarded £50 damages each in compensation for Irish-language bibles being seized from their cells in 1985. They went to court claiming £5000. Indeed the agitation about the authorities apparent hostility to all things Irish led to the appointment of an Irish-speaking censor in April 1987 to handle the growth of Irish-language material being demanded by the prisoners. This was yet another sign of the way the internal regime was liberalised while the security landscape was reinforced.

There was still constant intimidation of staff inside the prison and targeting by terrorists outside. In 1986 there were 300 actual or threatened attacks outside the prisons, including one massive vehicle bomb explosion at a housing estate in Limavady, occupied by many prison officers' families, which devastated 60 homes and left six families homeless. Virtually every day, at the gate lodges where they reported for duty, the security department would post notices warning staff to avoid certain bars, restaurants, petrol stations and localities where there were indications of terrorist-spotting going on. From time to time, more specific threats emerged. One group of Maze officers had to call off an annual reunion function after the RUC Special Branch got wind of a plot to attack the hotel with a blast incendiary bomb during the evening. More and more officers were given permits to carry a firearm for personal protection, some were issued with body armour and, over the years, several thousand had physical security measures installed at their homes: bullet-proof windows and doors, panic buttons linked to the local police station, under-car booby-trap detectors, and fire extinguishers and fire blankets to deal with petrol bombs. Despite all this, sometimes individual officers, and their families, would be whisked from their homes and given temporary accommodation at Millisle when their names turned up in intelligence reports suggesting there was an immediate risk to their lives.

The Prison Officers Association complained that the stress their members suffered was compounded by the increasingly long hours they were required to work, 90-hour weeks in some cases. The average was 17.32 hours' overtime per officer which earned some £10,000 on top of the annual basic pay of almost £6000. Hennessy had remarked, with some admiration, on the way that prison officers discussed their lifestyle, with its incredible dangers, stresses and strains, in such a matter-of-fact way. But not every officer could resist the intimidation and stand the acute strain.

One such was John Blair Barr, 46, a former soldier who saw action with the Royal Ulster Rifles in Borneo and who had later joined the prison service in 1977. In May 1984, two IRA prisoners in one of the H-blocks tried to get him to provide information about an escape plan they were hatching. He was first told they would keep him and his family off their hit-list if he cooperated, and then offered £250, which he accepted. He gave the prisoners his home telephone number and a photograph of himself and they said he would be contacted outside by a woman called Alice. In July she contacted him and, over the course of two meetings, he checked over a six-page sketch plan and answered a two-page questionnaire about the proposed escape, for which he was given another £250. However, 'Alice' was known to the security forces as an active terrorist and was under surveillance. Barr, who was working long hours and drinking heavily, was identified by the police, arrested and confronted with his treachery, to which he confessed. When he came to trial, the court heard that after being suspended from duty he had tried to commit suicide three times. Judge Peter Gibson sentenced him to two years imprisonment for corruption after hearing that he had disclosed details of the plan to the authorities and helped block potential deficiencies in the security of the prison. He served his sentence away from Northern Ireland.

The pressure on the prison staff manifested itself in other ways. The Chief Medical Officer committed suicide by putting a twelve-bore shotgun to his head in June 1986. He had been deeply affected by the hunger strikes, which left him fearful of terrorist attack and, as a doctor, deeply troubled about having to watch the succession of young men taking their own lives. A deputy governor at Magilligan prison, aged 32, became estranged from his pregnant wife after becoming obsessed about his personal safety and engaging in violent rages and bouts of excessive drinking. His behaviour was so bad that his wife asked superiors to confiscate his firearm. One evening in September 1987, while heavily intoxicated, he shot himself through the heart in the grounds of his cricket club in Belfast. Another officer took his own life with his personal protection weapon after drinking too much at a family barbecue and assaulting his mother, who required two stitches to an eye wound. In other excessive behaviour, a 31-year old prison officer from Magilligan, driving a top-of-the-range, high-performance car, was given a twelve months' suspended prison sentence and fined £1000 after admitting causing death by reckless driving. Two passengers in his car were killed when he crashed at high speed. Another prison officer got into trouble for taking his firearm across the border and smuggling a radio into one of the prisons. During the interview he confessed to losing his gun to a prostitute in 1982, and police later discovered she had sold the Webley revolver for £30 and that it was later used by Protestant gunmen in a series of sectarian murder attempts. There was a major security investigation after two strippers were smuggled into the prison complex for a night of rowdy high jinks at the officers' social club in May 1987. The fact that they had also performed in Republican and Loyalist areas raised fears that officers might have been compromised. Psychiatric counselling and training to withstand the pressures of their job became available to prison officers in 1990.

The murder of Patrick Kerr on 17 February 1985, the first such attack for almost a year, was yet another stark reminder of the constant terrorist hostility to prison staff. That Sunday morning, his thirty-seventh birthday, as he was leaving St Patrick's Catholic Cathedral, Armagh after 10.30 Mass with his two youngest children, a daughter aged five and an eight-year-old son, two masked gunmen approached and shot him four times in the head at point blank range. A doctor from the congregation rushed to his aid and the priest, who had just said Mass, gave him the last rites, but he was declared dead, from extensive brain injuries, on arrival at hospital in Portadown. His wife and eldest child, his eleven-year-old daughter, were told of the killing at a family funeral they were attending across the Irish border. The dead man had joined the prison service in 1969 and had served in several establishments before becoming a Principal Officer at the Maze H-blocks. In 1981 he had been awarded the BEM for his brave service. As a Catholic he was highly vulnerable, and in 1976 the family had moved to a different part of Armagh after their home was raked with gunfire. A short time after the shooting, the IRA claimed responsibility in the following terms: 'In March 1980 we called a halt to attacks on prison officials but we reserved the right to take action against those specific individuals involved in beatings. Kerr was one such person.' In a second, more detailed statement 'exposing' Kerr's involvement in 'brutality within the H-Blocks', said that 'the days of torture and repression must end. If not, someone must pay the price.' His outraged colleagues leapt to his defence and dismissed the claims as an unjustified slur on a brave officer.

More prison officers would lose their lives in future years before terrorist ceasefires were declared. At 8.55 pm on 23 March 1987, Leslie Jarvis, aged 61, a civilian instructor at Magilligan, who had been with the prison service since 1983, was shot dead in his car outside Magee University College, Londonderry, where he was studying psychology at night classes. About 50 minutes later, two RUC officers, Detective Inspector Austin Wilson and Detective Sergeant John Bennison, who had been called to the scene to launch a murder investigation, were also killed when a bomb in the car exploded without warning. The Secretary of State, Tom King, described the killings, where the body of the first victim was callously used to lure the others to their deaths, as 'one of the vilest deeds in the catalogue of terrorism'. John Griffiths, aged 37, a hospital officer in the prison service, who lived near Loughgall, County Armagh and had served for twelve years in the Maze and then Maghaberry, perished when a booby-trap device under his car exploded as he was leaving home to travel to work on 4 May 1989. The dead man, married with two children aged sixteen and seven, was so badly mutilated he could only be formally identified from dental records. In both cases the IRA acknowledged responsibility for the deaths, as they did for that of Brian Armour, a prison officer of fourteen years' service, based at the Maze, and also vice-chairman of the Prison Officers Association, who died in a similar under-car booby-trap blast in east Belfast on 4 October 1988. But it was another prison officer, Christopher John Hanna, who had betrayed him and who would ultimately go to jail for his murder.

Prison officer Hanna was an incorrigible womaniser. 'You know me,' he told one of his superiors. 'I'm a chaser. I can't keep my trousers up.' It was a fundamental weakness that made him easy prey, for an amoral actress, who was an IRA spotter, led him to betray at least one colleague to his death and cost him his £38,000-a-year job in the Northern Ireland Prison service as well as his freedom. He ended up behind bars, an inmate of the prison system in which he once held a position of trust, guarded by former colleagues he once commanded. Ironically, the actress who lured him to his plight remained at large because Hanna inexplicably refused to save himself by cooperating with the RUC to turn her into a double agent. (She did, in the end, pay her debt to society when she was imprisoned for another serious offence.)

Hanna, aged 45 at the time of these events, was born and grew up in the staunchly Protestant Donegall Road area of Belfast. He left the local Linfield Secondary School and spent the next ten years working as a shopfitter before joining the prison service in 1971. He suffered his share of the risks facing prison staff in Northern Ireland, both on and off duty, and was once on sick leave for five weeks after having his throat cut while helping to foil a terrorist escape from Belfast prison. In a separate incident, he and his wife and three young children had to abandon their home on the outskirts of Belfast, under Army escort, after he escaped almost certain assassination by IRA gunmen when he managed to slam the front door and keep them out. From the witness box Hanna's wife later described him as an 'embittered Loyalist' who 'absolutely hated Catholics', and others say the incidents deepened his existing bigotry. After successive postings to the Maze, Belfast prison and the Young Offenders centre at Hydebank, in 1982 he was posted back to the Maze having reached the rank of Principal Prison Officer, the most senior uniformed grade. From a security point of view, although he was suspected of associating with known UVF activists, nothing emerged to his detriment. Indeed, he was regarded as 'competent and reliable', in the words of one superior, and quickly climbed the promotion ladder.

By day at the Maze, he was in charge of H-block 1. When he was on regular night-shift his duties were prison-wide, necessitating access to the central key room, the nerve centre of the prison security network. It was a senior position requiring a high degree of trust and responsibility. Hanna acted the tough man with the inmates especially when governor-grade officers were around, but it did not impress the more perceptive of them who saw his behaviour as an attempt to impress them: especially dangerous conduct in a volatile prison like the Maze.

Ever since joining the prison service in 1971 Hanna had quickly earned a reputation as an off-duty 'raker', the Ulster word for a playboy. Indeed he was such an incorrigible womaniser they openly joked about his 'trouser trouble'. Unwisely for a man in his position, he frequented bars and clubs in dangerous areas, drinking heavily and chasing women. His compulsive behaviour knew no boundaries. Wives of colleagues were endlessly propositioned at functions, even when their husbands were sitting nearby. His prolonged absences from home understandably caused trouble with his wife. Hanna manufactured every excuse to cover up his activities, even using as an alibi his membership of a Masonic Lodge, which he joined but rarely attended.

Eventually he split from his wife and moved in with a highly respectable middle-aged spinster, but he continued to cheat, and she was devastated when he effected a reconciliation with his wife after some ten months and returned home. At this time one of his daughters, Susan, aged twenty, left home and, after drifting round various flats and the Salvation Army hostel, took up with a man who had IRA associations and became pregnant. Hanna thoroughly disapproved of the relationship, refusing to enter the house the couple shared when he went to visit his daughter and baby grandson in the Poleglass area of west Belfast, an area where IRA support was much in evidence with graffiti and murals on gables and flags and posters on lamp posts.

Hanna wanted his daughter and her baby to come home but failed to persuade her. Any wise man would have realised the security implications of the situation and sought advice or assistance, but Hanna continued to frequent the area, sitting in his car outside the house, chatting to his daughter and grandson. By doing so he undoubtedly sowed the first seeds of his own downfall. It was inevitable that the IRA, which closely monitors the community in the areas from which it operates, learned who his daughter was and not only the significance, but also the weaknesses, of her father. In the latter part of 1987 the IRA struck. One day a prisoner called 'Juice' McMullan asked about Susie and Martin as Hanna pushed him through the doorway into a gymnasium. 'We need a wee job done,' McMullan said. 'If necessary we can arrange for the child to come home in a wee brown box. Innocent people die in wartime situations.'

Over the next few weeks, according to Hanna, McMullan, whose sentence was coming to an end, put pressure on him to make prison key impressions in a bar of soap and told him that in due course, after he was released, someone describing himself as Hanna's 'cousin' would be in touch to arrange a meeting. Hanna told nobody about the approach or the intimidation, a clear breach of the rules laid down by the prison authorities. After his arrest he said he had acted out of fear, but later he told the court he was 'bouncing with confidence' that he could deal with the problem. Whatever his real state of mind, it was a most serious mistake.

When they finally exploited Hanna, the Provos played an expert hand. Over the next few months the 'cousin', a man, telephoned him at his office in the prison several times. In September 1988 he arranged a Saturday night rendezvous at the Beechlawn Hotel in Belfast's southern suburbs but when Hanna turned up as instructed he was instead approached by an attractive blonde woman who said her name was Anne. The honeytrap was complete. Hanna thought she was a schoolteacher, found her 'attractive and very gentle' and said he tried to impress her by showing off his knowledge of ancient Greek mythology. Over drinks she talked about James Joyce and Ulysses. Hanna was convinced the woman had given him the 'glad eye', so he gave her a lift home and after 'a few hugs and kisses' in the car divulged his telephone number and extension at the Maze. He later told a disciplinary hearing he was hoping for a sexual relationship with her. 'I was trying it on to see how far I could get with her,' he said.

Over the next four months, recklessly ignoring his own safety and the prison security rules, he met her three times at Blaris Cemetery, a mile from the Maze, slipping away at lunchtime with a civilian jacket pulled over his uniform shirt and trousers. During these meetings they had what he described as 'a good court. She put her head on my shoulder. She thought it better to create the impression of a courting couple.' Although he subsequently denied it in a thicket of lies and contradictions in court, Hanna told the police after his arrest in June 1988 that, tantalised by the promise of a weekend with her in the north coast seaside resort of Portrush, he passed on the names and addresses of several colleagues, and that they discussed his planned role in a potential mass breakout from the Maze. He was to use his senior position to facilitate smuggling guns into the prison. These would be used to stage a takeover of blocks H6, H7 and H8, adjoining the prison perimeter wall. Then a vanload of explosives, which he would meet and escort into the prison, would be set off to breach the wall. At that point, a helicopter would land to take away the most important IRA prisoners. 'Anne' was named in court as Rosena Brown, aged 45, a mother of seven children, separated from her partner, who earned her living as an undistinguished jobbing actress. She had appeared in a couple of stage plays in Belfast and had parts in one or two films and commercials including, with supreme irony, a television advertisement for crime prevention commissioned by the Northern Ireland Office.

Unknown to her, and Hanna, her real-life performance as an IRA targeting agent was also being photographed. The RUC Special Branch had long suspected her of active involvement with terrorists and she had been the subject of undercover police surveillance for about a year before Hanna crossed her path. The couple were photographed leaving the Beechlawn Hotel after the first encounter and at the subsequent meetings in the cemetery. Throughout this time the police, who had quickly identified Hanna, asked the prison authorities to keep him at his post and careful checks were made on all his activities and duties. Even his bank accounts were checked but no misconduct or discrepancies were detected.

It was only after the death of one of his colleagues and an attempt on the life of a prison governor in October 1988 that the scale of Hanna's extraordinary treachery came to full light. Brian Armour, 48, married with two children, a former soldier, had been a prison officer for fourteen years and was the Vice-Chairman of the Prisoner Officers Association. He had been warned he was in danger after an IRA communication was intercepted on its way out of the prison the previous July. He was murdered on 4 October, when an explosive device went off under his car as he was driving near his home in east Belfast. When he braked to avoid two dogs fighting on the road in front of him, the sharp jerk dislodged the mercury in a tilt switch, completing the electrical circuit that detonated the two pounds of Semtex high explosive attached to the underside of his car. The car was blown along the road for 50 metres before crashing into a stream in an allotment garden. The next day a governor and his wife had a lucky escape when they discovered a similar bomb under their car. It had failed to explode while it was parked outside a supermarket in Lisburn, not far from the Maze.

Some weeks earlier Hanna had boasted to a junior officer that he was going to give the names of four officers, including Armour and the Governor, to the Provos. After the first of two incidents the officer kept quiet because he thought Hanna had only been joking, but because it 'preyed on my mind' after the second he reported the conversation. The growing suspicions about Hanna were soon confirmed when he asked this prison officer to 'ride shotgun' at the cemetery to ensure he was not being set up when meeting the woman again. This request was also reported and the police mounted surveillance of the encounter.

Hanna was not finally confronted with his treachery until May 1989 when he was interviewed by senior Special Branch officers. They wanted him to continue meeting the woman with a view to them entrapping her and turning her into a double agent. Inexplicably, Hanna refused this lifeline which would have protected his freedom though not his job. Shortly afterwards he was dismissed from the prison service and charged with twelve criminal offences including aiding and abetting in the murder of Brian Armour. During his 27-day trial in 1990, the detectives who questioned Hanna told Mr Justice Campbell that during their interviews he was often laughing and jovial and showed no remorse.

Hanna, who went into the witness box to defend himself, cut a pathetic figure with a bizarre claim that he was a member of a secret group of civil servants and former members of the security forces working for an independent Northern Ireland. He said they had let him down, refused to name them and stated that he would go to prison because their work must go on. The court heard psychiatric evidence that he had a 'grandiose' opinion of himself and believed he had been playing a 'shrewd game' with the IRA. A clinical psychologist gave evidence that his performance in specific intelligence tests was only slightly better than that of a mentally handicapped person. A consultant neurologist confirmed that he was suffering from multiple sclerosis, a wasting disease which causes progressive mental and physical impairment. But the judge accepted the psychiatric evidence that he was not suffering from mental disease, convicted him and sentenced him to life imprisonment for aiding and abetting the Armour murder. The decision was upheld on appeal after three judges rejected a plea that insufficient weight had been given to medical evidence that he was ill. They said that the trial judge had had the benefit of seeing him in the witness box for seven days where he did not seem to be mixed up or confused. Hanna's health steadily deteriorated in prison and he died in hospital on 27 December 1992 from the effects of multiple sclerosis.

Although Hanna was far from the stereotypical prison officer, the case was a parable of its time for the prison service. Despite Hennessy, improved training and a greater awareness of the difficulties the service faced, enough weaknesses in organisation, philosophy and security were now highlighted to shake the organisation to its bones. The debility was understandable. For over twenty years, up to that point, the prison service had been engaged in constant firefighting. There had been neither the time nor the opportunity, in the face of unyielding circumstances, to stop, take stock and, after a considered process of internal debate and discussion, define policy for the future. During 1987 and 1988, therefore, the Prison Department launched a thorough review of its strategy. The initial outcome was a statement setting out, for the first time, what the service should be doing:

'The aim of the Northern Ireland Prison Service is to hold in secure and humane confinement persons who have been given into custody by the courts and to reduce the risk of re-offending by encouraging them to take full advantage of the opportunities offered during their confinement.

'Within that aim specific objectives are:

(a) To keep in custody, with the degree of security and control by staff appropriate to each individual, persons committed to custody by the courts; and to produce or release them as required.

(b) To provide for all prisoners the necessities of life, including accommodation, food, exercise, health care and freedom to practice religion; and to provide the opportunity to engage in constructive activities, such as work, education, training, hobbies and sport, to fill at least the working day.

(c) To enable all prisoners to retain links with their families and to assist sentenced prisoners in their preparation for release into the community.

(d) To treat prisoners as individuals regardless of their religious beliefs or political opinions; and, as far as possible, to offer them the opportunity to serve their sentences free from paramilitary influence.

(e) To manage the resources allocated to the Prison Service economically and efficiently and, in particular, to enhance the morale and abilities of staff by providing the appropriate conditions of service, management structures and training.'

Within this framework, the next step was to set some 'Principles of Conduct' for the staff. After two years' work, 3000 pocket-sized booklets were published and distributed in June 1990 setting out the professional standards and conduct expected of members of the Northern Ireland Prison Service. The guide, the product of a working party which included serving prison officers and governors and was chaired by a senior governor, is divided into four main sections headed 'Duty to the Service', 'Duty to the Community', 'Duty to Prisoners', and 'Duty to Self/ Colleagues'. It outlines very specific standards expected of the Prison Service, including the impartial treatment of prisoners regardless of political or religious belief, staff behaviour on and off duty, and loyalty to the service.

By now there was an unprecedented service-wide consultation process under way to produce a more comprehensive vision and strategy for the way the service should develop. Using a computer-based planning model, five one-day workshops were held, involving 80 staff, with a sixth for outside organisations concerned with prison issues. A full record of the discussion and the ideas and opinions expressed was maintained and carefully analysed in the preparation of the final document. When it emerged in June 1991, it had been entitled 'Serving the Community' to reflect that way in which the earlier 'Aims and Objectives' had been expanded into a more comprehensive mission. The priorities of the service were listed as being: to protect the community through holding securely those committed to its charge; to ensure that life in prison offers prisoners opportunities to develop their physical and mental well-being and to prepare them for release thus contributing to peace and stability in Northern Ireland; to ensure that the effectiveness, commitment, self-esteem and morale of prison staff match the challenge of their varied and demanding roles; and to manage the resources allocated to the Service effectively and efficiently.

The advent of Maghaberry, it was hoped, would be the principal theatre to give expression to the bold vision for the prison service that had now been articulated. Despite the original high hopes that the prison would accept its first inmates in 1981, work on completing Maghaberry had slipped ever more steadily behind schedule and the cost had increased in stages from the projected £20 million to £50 million by the time it opened seven years later. In 1981 the prison authorities occupied the central services unit, which provided the basic utilities for the institution, staff quarters and the recreation club. In 1982 the 560-place men's prison was handed over to the prisons department for fitting out to receive prisoners, followed a year later by the separate 56-place women's prison. A governor and 60 staff were posted there to guard the complex and supervise the specialist work. The new target was for the progressive arrival of prisoners from beginning of 1986.

However, more security work was then prescribed because of Home Office modifications to the design of Frankland prison in County Durham, on which Maghaberry was being modelled. The 1983 escape and the Hennessy recipe for even tighter security caused further setbacks but the need for the work was underlined by an exercise involving Special Forces troops, who exposed many weaknesses by managing to get in and out without detection. As a result of all this, a number of additional measures were put in place: a high, wire perimeter fence around the entire complex; internal partitioning to prevent the inmate population from being able to gather together in the central quadrangle; relocating doors and bullet-proofing windows; and installing closed circuit television and other surveillance equipment.

In fact the Maze escape started a frenzy of claims by MPs and others that escape mechanisms had been built into the new prison by IRA sympathisers among its 600-strong construction force: traps in sewers, defective brickwork, and deliberate weakening of doors and windows. The hue and cry, fed, it has to be said, by certain senior people in the prison service including Assistant Governor McConnell, was such that the Northern Ireland Office invited a delegation from the Security and Home Affairs Committee of the Northern Ireland Assembly to inspect the site for themselves. One of the members, Gordon Mawhinney, reported on the visit to the full Assembly on 6 May 1984. Referring to the claim that secret shafts had been built into the sewers, he said, 'May I mention that the deputy chairman preceded me twenty feet deep into the bowels of the earth in the centre of the prison and we did endeavour to crawl down the drains. I will say only that the preventive measures are more than adequate, and it will save any prisoner, who might attempt the exercise, the trouble, if I tell him now that his chances of success through that particular route are simply nil. I am by no means an expert on prison security, but I think it will present a formidable task for anyone to by-pass the physical and electronic barriers in the prison at Maghaberry.'

The first inmates were admitted to the prison on 18 March 1986 when the female establishment opened and the 200-year-old Armagh prison finally closed. The women moved into a series of two-storey houses, split into seven self-contained units for seven inmates. Each unit has a kitchen and other facilities and a mother-and-baby cell. There is also a communal chapel, hospital, gym and library. The first male prisoners arrived at Maghaberry two years later, in March 1988. The prison was now on its fifth Governor even though there had been no inmates for much of that time. Numbers quickly built up to 100 at Maghaberry, where they found a purpose-built, state-of-the-art, modern prison where the old practice of the morning slop-out was ended with the provision of a toilet and hand basin in every cell. There were also low-voltage power points and before long some prisoners were allowed television sets. There were four houses, Lagan, Bann, Foyle and Erne, each built around a landscaped quadrangle, with 108 cells in each divided into six units of eighteen. The dining and association rooms were carpeted and painted in bright colours and there was a wide range of facilities for sport and recreation, including football pitches and multi-gyms. From the outset there was a conventional prison regime, where the prisoners worked every day. Some tasks were the mundane cleaning and cooking essential to the running of the prisons but other prisoners carried out a variety of more useful work ranging from the laundering of linen from incontinent patients at local hospitals to the cutting of braille texts for blind people. It was not for nothing that it quickly became known as the 'Maghaberry Hilton'. In December 1991 Judge Stephen Tumim, the Chief Inspector of Prisons, said that the establishment was not only the flagship of the Northern Ireland prison service but that it was also a 'shining example' of what prisons elsewhere in the United Kingdom should become.

With financial disciplines now bearing down on the cost of security in Northern Ireland, the security forces and the prison service were now, for the first time, having to face a good deal of financial stringency. From that point of view too, Maghaberry was a worthwhile proposition. Its operating cost was only half the £40 million a year it took to run the Maze. By far the most expensive component of the prison system was the Maze special category compounds, where, in 1985, there were 500 staff looking after 170 prisoners, all but twenty lifers, at an annual cost of about £60,000 per prisoner. With Maghaberry looming on the horizon, the authorities began secret moves to negotiate an eventual end to special category, which had peaked with 1500 prisoners in 1975, and enable them to finally close the costly compounds. By June 1988, with the cost per prisoner having soared to £80,000 compared to £50,000 in the H-blocks, they had secured understandings with the prisoners. The 92 remaining at that time moved into H1 and H2 blocks, where they enjoyed an unrestricted lifestyle not dissimilar to that they had voluntarily left. This enabled the closure of the compounds to take place, bringing to an end one cycle of the history of the Maze. By September 1991, their numbers had dwindled to seven, five Loyalists and two Republicans, all serving indeterminate life terms. These two had the run of one 25-cell wing in H1, while two UDA prisoners occupied a second and three UVF inmates a third. With it costing an estimated £42 million to maintain them in an H-block capable of accommodating 100 prisoners, they were pragmatically given release dates and moved from the block to the pre-release scheme on 18 September.

The ending of special category and the opening of Maghaberry encouraged many prisoners, including lifers, to sever their paramilitary links and move to the new prison. Indeed, lifers were directly promised more favourable terms for doing so. Within two years of Maghaberry's opening, 180 had done so and the authorities took to committing all newly-sentenced prisoners there in a bid to run down the 700 population of Maze Cellular even more. The new prison was run along strictly conventional lines, with all prisoners conforming to the rules, albeit in an extraordinarily liberal regime, by the standards of prisons in Britain at the time.

Back at the Maze there was now an undisputed de facto acceptance of segregation where virtually every demand the prisoners made was conceded. The priority for the prison staff was simply to ensure that they did not escape. A glimpse of the life they led was exposed after a BBC Television crew was allowed into the prison in 1990 to make an observational documentary. That November, viewers saw the Republican prisoners' spokesman complaining to the prison authorities about the fact that the sausage rolls were getting smaller, as well as the Loyalists' Twelfth of July celebration in one of the wings with a band wearing improvised uniforms, beating drums made from waste-paper baskets and plastic water containers and playing real flutes, which had been allowed into the prison. The corridors and recreation areas in all the blocks were seen to be extensively painted with murals and other illustrations depicting either the Republican or Loyalist culture of violence. How deeply embedded it remained was well emphasised in April 1992, when the Governor of the Maze was seriously assaulted when visiting a UVF wing in H8. Before he arrived prison officers had been threatened with violence themselves if they warned him or intervened. But when two masked prisoners attacked, felling him with blows to the head and kicking him on the ground, one senior officer went to his aid and suffered similar treatment. If he had not done so, it later emerged, the Governor would have been scalded with boiling water.

The full extent of the liberal regime, so graphically portrayed in the groundbreaking documentary, was all the more astonishing because meanwhile, at Magilligan and Belfast, the prison service was still desperately seeking to hold the line which had first been drawn in 1976 against demands for segregation. From time to time, spontaneous violent incidents would erupt to draw attention to the demand. Some were undoubtedly collusive play-acting by both sides to reinforce their calls for segregation but more were clearly symptomatic of the deep hatred and hostility that existed between the two main Northern Ireland communities outside, which the prisoners imported when they were arrested, convicted and sent to prison.

Magilligan was very much the forgotten prison in comparison to the Maze, and the average 300 inmates, medium-security risk and short-term prisoners, who resided there caused proportionately far less trouble. But, following the destruction of a wing at Belfast by Loyalists at the end of 1981, the consequent pressure on accommodation led to some highly disruptive prisoners being transferred and, not surprisingly in the fully integrated regime maintained there, a series of incidents followed.

In November 1984, there were two hunger strikes, one of 31 days' duration. On 16 June 1986, two Loyalist prisoners embarked on a hunger strike, followed by another pair every fortnight. They basically wanted segregation but, more immediately, an improvement in conditions, which they said were far harsher than those in the Maze. There was also a demand for a fully-equipped family centre for visits, similar to facilities provided at Belfast and the Maze. By the time of the Twelfth of July commemorations, when tension inside and outside the prisons traditionally soars, eight were fasting and another 100 had launched a three-day sympathy food strike. Outside the prison pressure was applied by a series of attacks on officers' homes but, again, the authorities refused to bend and the protest collapsed. Soon after a Loyalist prisoner was shot in the side and wounded on 30 January 1987, the prisons minister, Nicholas Scott, said, 'I am quite clear that the paramilitary organisations are prepared to quite cynically use their own members and even to injure prisoners on their own side to bring about segregation. The two sides are in collusion.' For three months around that time, prisoners refused to accept visits in a new room and there was a bout of damage to fixtures and fittings, including televisions and snooker tables provided for the prisoners. The most serious incident, which lasted for four days began during a Free Presbyterian church service on the morning of Sunday 5 April 1987, when the minister, a Catholic prisoner and a prison officer were taken hostage by 28 Loyalist prisoners and held in the barricaded wing of one of the H-blocks. The authorities called in a special police unit in case it became necessary to rescue the hostages but the incident ended peacefully, and without concessions, when the food in the tuck shop ran out.

The focus of the segregation campaign then switched to Belfast where, despite the official policy, the prisoners separated themselves by custom and practice with the acquiescence of the staff. Republicans and Loyalists exercised alternatively in morning and evening and took association only every other night. There were few incidents until 1990 when 80 officers were hurt in a series of clashes. However, for no apparent reason, in August 1991 Loyalists launched a gun attack in Armagh on a bus taking Republican prisoners' families on a visit to Belfast prison. Nobody was killed but two women were wounded and Republican anger surged. A month later, on 21 September, Loyalists started a fire in the prison dining hall and, a day later, Republicans wrecked furniture and fittings. Thirteen officers suffered from smoke inhalation during the fire as they raced to unlock prisoners from cells nearby and above. These exchanges, which caused £100,000 worth of damage, sparked off a series of clashes. Two Loyalists were beaten in their cell by prisoners who overpowered an officer and took his keys. Another two Loyalists were scalded when boiling water from tea urns was thrown over them. In another incident an officer was scalded and sustained very serious eye injuries.

The trouble came to a violent head at teatime on Sunday 24 November. During the afternoon a group of Republican prisoners had been using the C wing canteen where many had watched a televised football match on television. The eye-level TV set was inserted into a cavity in the wall, protected by reinforced glass which could be protected by a sliding sheet shutter if there was trouble. Below it and a little to the left there was a slim central-heating radiator attached to the wall with a shallow gap behind it. The Republican prisoners were allowed to remain a little after 5 pm to see the end of the match, which had gone to extra time. This delayed the Loyalists' scheduled arrival in the room. By 5.15 pm, however, the Republicans had left and 28 Loyalists had moved into the canteen. One of them, Robert 'Rab' Skey, aged 27, awaiting trial on kidnap charges, approached the corner with the TV remote control in his hand. As he did so, precisely at 5.16 pm, an eight-ounce Semtex bomb exploded, triggered by a timing device. It had been placed behind the top right-hand corner of the radiator. The explosion tore the metal radiator off the wall and punctured the top right-hand corner which broke into a shower of shrapnel. Skey took the force of the blast and was killed immediately, his death serving to protect others. Another prisoner, 23-year-old Colin Caldwell, accused of conspiracy to murder and firearms offences, later died of his injuries, and three other prisoners were seriously wounded. The IRA acknowledged responsibility. In a clear reference to the earlier Armagh shooting, they said it was a reprisal for earlier attacks on Republican prisoners and their relatives.

Lord Colville, a judge with experience of Northern Ireland through conducting the annual review of emergency legislation, was then appointed to report on 'The Operational Policy in Belfast Prison for the Management of Paramilitary Prisoners from Opposing Factions'. He completed his work in March 1992 and endorsed the government's policy. Secretary of State Peter Brooke accepted the report and told parliament:

'Lord Colville brings out very clearly the increased risks posed to security by segregation. He says (and I quote): "All the lessons from history suggest that segregation facilitates escapes, and escapes will give freedom to Paramilitary fanatics, of both factions, who will kill and maim outside prison." On security grounds I am satisfied that Lord Colville's recommendation is right. Moreover I am also satisfied that segregation would make it more difficult to offer constructive regimes for inmates, as it already has at the Maze. It would constrain the flexible and effective use of the available accommodation. And the opportunity which segregation would provide the paramilitaries to reinforce their cohesiveness within the prison would have an adverse effect on the morale and self-esteem of staff.

'Segregation remains a key objective of the paramilitaries. In resisting campaigns by both factions, prison governors and their staff have implemented the policy of successive administrations. There now have been three major reports by respected and independent figures which say segregation is wrong. Lord Gardiner, in his report published in January 1975 on measures to deal with terrorism, recommended that special category status – segregation writ large – should be ended and that the influence of the terrorist leaders must be reduced. Her Majesty's Chief Inspector of Prisons, Sir James Hennessy, in his 1984 report into the Maze escape of the previous year was in no doubt about the increased threat to security posed by segregation. Lord Colville having taken evidence from a wide range of people has come to the same conclusion. My predecessors accepted the recommendations of Gardiner and Hennessy and I in turn have concluded that I should accept the recommendations of Lord Colville. I do not believe that it would be acceptable to this House for the clear stand which has been taken over the years against segregation to be set aside as a result of paramilitary violence and in the face of unequivocal advice from three such distinguished sources and the powerful arguments that they have deployed.'

With the government's line now clear – pragmatism in the face of overwhelming prisoner power in the Maze and integration elsewhere – events in all the prisons settled down for a time, although there were sporadic incidents. In July 1993, in separate events in H3 and H8, two prison officers were stripped, had their heads shaved and were covered in paint by Loyalists complaining about conditions in Belfast prison. The next serious flare-up came when Loyalist anger erupted in the Maze in August 1993 after a Loyalist prisoner was refused compassionate parole. The decision triggered a wave of violent responses. 24 staff officers and seven prisoners were injured during a riot in the Maze when the UVF wings had to be retaken by force and the UVF then publicly threatened to take more 'appropriate action'. A few days later, on 1 September, 44-year-old Liverpool-born Jim Peacock, a prison officer in B wing at Belfast prison, who was nicknamed 'Big Bird', was making a bedtime drink for his wife, Sandra, at their home in the Oldpark area of north Belfast. Their thirteen-year-old daughter, the youngest of five children, was upstairs in her room reading. Suddenly there was what Mrs Peacock later described as 'an almighty thud and glass breaking' followed by the sound of a single shot. She ran to the kitchen where she found her husband slumped on the floor by the fridge. There was a bullet hole in his t-shirt. As he lay dying, his daughter cradled him in her arms and stroked his hair. 'I was crying and crying and he tried to say something to me but couldn't,' she said later. The same night, in quick succession, cars belonging to prison officers were petrol bombed and set on fire in the Rathcoole and Rathfern estates in Newtownabbey, shots were fired through the window of an officer's home in Antrim, narrowly missing his wife and three children, and the car and garage were set alight and destroyed at another officer's home in north Belfast.

The Peacock family, like so many others among the 3332 prison officers and the 316 civilian support staff, were no strangers to the intimidation and violence that had become such a corrosive element in their lives. At Jim Peacock's inquest, Sandra told the coroner they had lived with a barrage of threats from Republicans and Loyalists for years. They had moved home once after an IRA threat and again after one from loyalists. At other times their house had been petrol bombed and its windows broken. For two months before the murder there had been daily anonymous telephone calls. In that same year, 1993, 212 threats were reported and 112 officers given assistance. Recorded incidents included one case of attempted murder, ten petrol bomb attacks and four gun attacks on homes, and two gun attacks on individuals. Officer J A Peacock's name became the thirtieth to be entered on the roll of honour and chiselled into the stone of Northern Ireland Prison Service memorials at the Maze and Millisle. There, every year, in the week before Remembrance Sunday, as the Prison Service Pipe Band plays sombre music, an inter-denominational service of commemoration takes place and wreaths are laid to mark their sacrifice.

Almost exactly a year after the Peacock murder, in August and September 1994, the IRA and Loyalist paramilitary groups both declared open-ended ceasefires. The declarations were the most carefully nurtured and hard-won components of a joint drive by the British and Irish governments over several years to end violence in Ulster and create a durable political settlement. It could be said to have started after the Remembrance Sunday bombing in Enniskillen in November 1987 when eleven died and 63 were injured. The scale of the revulsion was so overwhelming and widespread that John Hume, the leader of the SDLP, judged the time was right to initiate talks with Gerry Adams, a former

Maze inmate, who had since become one of the most influential voices in the Republican movement.

Hume and Adams soon enunciated a new agenda, based on political advance towards Republican objectives, but only by peaceful means. Given the centuries of distrust of Britain within the Republican constituency, which had been consolidated during the years of conflict, there was much to be done on both sides to change traditional mindsets and nourish what was now being called the peace process. But it gathered real, albeit for the time being secret, momentum after Peter Brooke took over as Northern Ireland Secretary in July 1989. He judged there was a new 'window of political opportunity', but he was not after a short-term fix. He wanted to build on the 1985 Anglo-Irish Agreement, which had given the Dublin government, for the first time, a highly influential role over events in Northern Ireland. His real aim was to forge new political arrangements redefining, more fundamentally than at any time since Partition in the early 1920s, the complex triangular relationship between London, Dublin and Belfast. Above all, he reasoned, the violence must be halted if progress was to be made. In a surprise move marking his first hundred days in office, Brooke sent a remarkable public signal to the IRA that if they renounced violence then the Government would be 'imaginative' in dealing with them. The message was secretly reinforced through intermediaries, the first signs of flexibility since the collapse of a ceasefire in 1975.

Mr Brooke then set out to methodically pummel the politicans and gunmen from a state of weary deadlock into a clear effort to find solutions. The strategy was pursued along parallel paths. In public there were 'talks about talks' with the Irish government and the four principal political parties in Northern Ireland. There were regular exchanges with the IRA, first through Catholic clergy as intermediaries, later also through the SDLP leader, John Hume. In both processes, however, there was only inch-by-inch progress from the shackled positions of Irish history.

On 26 March 1991 Brooke finally lined up the parties and two governments and hopes were high that, come early July, the parties would be signing an historic new agreement. The prospects of being frozen out of a political breakthrough were not lost on the IRA, which began what was to be a protracted policy change from what William Whitelaw called the 'absurd ultimatums' first presented in 1972 to the highly pragmatic Republican policies that had since evolved. But when the first round of Stormont talks quickly became bogged down, Brooke halted them, reasoning that an orderly end to the first inter-party contact for sixteen years would enable the process to be rekindled again. By the end of 1991 a new round of 'talks about talks' was under way. More significantly, a deep understanding was being forged between the two Prime Ministers, John Major and Albert Reynolds, who jointly adopted a problem-solving posture, both with the politicians and the IRA, with whom both were now deep in secret, albeit indirect, dialogue. But there was great frustration at the IRA's unyielding posture.

After the general election a new Northern Ireland Secretary, Sir Patrick Mayhew, took the chair when the talks resumed at Stormont in April 1992. In July, now including the Irish government, they moved briefly to London, the first time that all the constitutional parties to the Irish conflict had sat around the same table for more than 70 years. After a summer break, more new ground was broken when the Ulster Unionists took part in discussions at Dublin Castle, the first time they had ever ventured south.

These talks ended inconclusively in the autumn of 1992, but, Sir Patrick said, 'Things are never going to be the same again. Historic watersheds have been reached and left behind us as we have moved on.' Both strands of negotiation now moved into private and largely secret phases until John Hume and the Sinn Fein leader, Gerry Adams dramatically announced they had agreed a formula for peace in late 1993. The two Prime Ministers, John Major and Albert Reynolds, instantly swooped on the potential deal and, in the aftermath of one of the worst ever bouts of tit-for-tat sectarian savagery in Ulster during the autumn, the Downing Street declaration was signed that December.

After that both governments worked assiduously to draw the strings of the public and private peace processes together. The IRA fought hard for concessions to persuade its members to support an open-ended ceasefire. The constitutional politicians fought equally hard not to concede anything in advance. With the ceasefires finally put in place in August (by the IRA) and September (by Loyalists) both governments unveiled a framework document outlining a new agenda for political progress, this time including the IRA. It was the outcome of six years of patient preparatory political dialogue, but it was to take another four years of inter-governmental and inter-party talks for the sort of comprehensive political settlement envisaged by Brooke to emerge. It finally did so as the Belfast Agreement, which was concluded on Good Friday, 10 April 1998. Ultimately it would have long-term implications for all the people of the British Isles but, in the short term, it had a major impact on the prison service and its highly-politicised clientele.

Chapter Fourteen

A powerhouse of peace

When Princess Anne visited the showpiece Maghaberry prison in May 1992, the first ever royal visit to a Northern Ireland prison, she chatted to four life sentence prisoners who told her how they had turned their backs on terrorism and were committed to working for peace. Indeed peaceful imperatives gathered increasing force among the terrorist-aligned prison population – an estimated 1400 of the 1700 behind bars – throughout the early 1990s, and their view that it was time for an end to violence heavily influenced events outside. One IRA prisoner, writing to a Belfast newspaper from the Maze, in the context of the collapse of the Iron Curtain, asked, 'Why is it that the rest of Europe is settling its differences with flowers and the Provos are still using Semtex?' Every political development outside the prison was picked to pieces inside and exhaustively analysed by both Republicans and Loyalists. They urged the officials to make sure more extensive contacts were made with their free counterparts. 'Sure if you can talk to us in here you can talk to them out there,' they argued. Emissaries brought views back and forward at crucial stages, as the prison authorities privately adopted a highly cooperative stance in enabling what were to prove to be negotiations of vital political importance.

As it had so authoritatively been a university of terrorism in the past, the Maze was now proving to be a forceful powerhouse of peace. There was, of course, a high degree of self-interest in promoting a new agenda, for, alongside the debate about ceasefires, the parallel proposition that prisoners had to be part of any peace process was gaining ground. The words 'early release', and even 'amnesty', were frequently mentioned in this context. Once the Provisional IRA declared its open-ended ceasefire from midnight on 31 August 1994, followed by the Combined Loyalist Military Command, with effect from midnight on 13 October, the prison dimension became ever more prominent. Its centrality to the now political process was publicly underlined three days earlier when the Loyalist leadership, nearly all ex-prisoners, trooped out to the Maze to see the prisoners to gain their approval for the imminent announcement.

At an exploratory meeting with officials on 23 December, the political frontmen for the Loyalist organisations submitted position papers putting the demand for the phased release of prisoners at the top of their agenda. Sinn Fein, the political mouthpiece of the IRA, as the turbulent history of the prisons amply demonstrates, had long given the highest priority to the plight of its own prisoners.

But the question of how to deal with the prisoners was a highly sensitive, controversial and complex one. The Northern Ireland Association for the Care and Resettlement of Offenders published a timely report on the topic in March 1995, entitled 'Release and Reintegration of Politically Motivated Prisoners in Northern Ireland'. The authors, Brian Gormally and Kieran McEvoy, researched comparative experiences in other conflict situations in South Africa, Israel and Palestine, Italy and Spain as well as both parts of the island of Ireland, in compiling their report and setting out an agenda which heavily influenced the subsequent treatment of prisoners:

> 'Our first and overriding conclusion is that the issue of early release of politically motivated prisoners is crucial to any peace process which follows a violent political conflict. Whatever the particular positions taken up by negotiating parties at any given time, we would argue that until the question of the prisoners is agreed then nothing that will create a final solution is agreed.'

> 'We do not attempt to minimise the legal, philosophical and political difficulties involved in a consideration of early release. The extent to which the interests of society in a political resolution of its past conflict can be squared with a continuing adherence to the rule of law, is dealt with in some detail in the report. We have noted the very real problems which other jurisdictions have had with this issue, but we believe that they can be overcome through the application of existing legal norms and precedents. Moreover, we argue that the opportunity can be taken to use prisoner release as a positive way of encouraging peace and reconciliation.

> 'We do not think it is for us to come to any prescriptive conclusions on what methods should be used. What we can say is this: our clear view, and that of the experts we have consulted, is that any legal, technical or administrative factors which are held up as obstacles in the way of the early release of politically motivated prisoners are fundamentally obfuscatory. If the political will exists, the means to accomplish it exist within the legal and administrative paradigms of our criminal justice system.

'Our study also shows that the social and economic reintegration of ex-politically motivated prisoners should be an integral part of the process of release and of rebuilding our community in general. Again, some of the issues involved are anything but easy to resolve. However, we should not let these stand in the way of trying to prevent future division and destabilisation by developing appropriate and sensitive programmes which encourage ex-prisoners to play their full part in civil society.'

During the first fragile years of the ceasefires the future treatment of terrorist prisoners in Northern Ireland jails became an increasingly central issue as the fragile Northern Ireland peace process slowly consolidated. The IRA was especially concerned to ensure that the remaining 26 of its members serving sentences in British prisons would swiftly be transferred to Northern Ireland where – like the 29 who had already been moved – they would be under the jurisdiction of the Northern Ireland Office rather than the Home Office and thus be able to benefit from any future release package. Their numbers included men and women who had carried Northern Ireland's troubles to the streets of London and other British cities, staging a series of gun and bomb attacks which had cost at least 120 lives. One of them, Patrick Magee, serving eight life sentences, was a modern Guy Fawkes, who had come close to murdering Margaret Thatcher and almost her entire government when he planted a bomb in the Grand Hotel, Brighton, which exploded without warning during the Conservative party conference in October 1984. While the leaders of both Republican and Loyalist terrorist groups had often stated that an unconditional amnesty must form part of any overall settlement, privately they indicated they were prepared to settle for a more gradual approach to the problem. The Reverend Roy Magee, one of the handful of discreet peace-brokers who had helped midwife the ceasefires, called for a Commission to be set up to direct the phased release of paramilitary prisoners.

For its part, the Government made it known that it would not countenance any path which undermined the standards of justice or the law and order process, as an amnesty would. It had to underpin the credibility of the judiciary and legal process and be mindful of the effect on police and Army morale if it was simply to throw open the gates of the prisons. There was also the general public reaction to take into account. The voices of the victims of violence and the relatives of the deceased were increasingly coming to the fore and the community at large was seriously apprehensive about the prospect of hardened terrorists being released en masse. The scale of the grief and hurt that had engulfed the entire community for three decades, a period three times as long as the ten year total of the two world wars in the twentieth century, was immense. It took four walls of a gallery in a post-ceasefire exhibition at the Old Museum Gallery in Belfast to accommodate the typewritten lists naming the 3500 who by that time had lost their lives violently in connection with the political differences in Northern Ireland.

While the Irish government more readily accepted the integrity of the ceasefires from the outset, the British government adopted an altogether more cautious stance. John Major, then Prime Minister, said he would work to consolidate the peace process on the 'working assumption' that violence was indeed at an end. From this perspective, a gradual policy of responses had the added advantage of locking the terrorist groups further into a ceasefire mode because the prisoners and their families would act as a further restraint on any hardline elements who might wish to resort again to violence. Against this background officials therefore signalled there would be 'administrative flexibility' in dealing with prisoners as the post-ceasefire situation developed but that a general amnesty was ruled out and, for the time being at least, releases would not take place.

The great advantage of adopting a pragmatic approach to the prisoners, from the point of view of government, was that any concessions would apply to both sides. There was also considerable scope for making concessions through changes to the rules and regulations governing the prison regime. With so many of the powers discretionary to the prison authorities, adjustments, as they had been in the past, could easily be made. So in June 1995, in what was presented as a development of the policy of helping prisoners to maintain their family links, but was clearly a response to bolster the ceasefires, a number of moves were started by the prison authorities. Access to card-phones, already conceded to the other prisons, was extended to inmates at the Maze. (This was pretty symbolic, for many of the inmates in the H-blocks already had access to unauthorised mobile phones and chargers. Some had been confiscated during searches but were soon replaced.) That summer, mothers and partners were allowed to join the summer and Christmas family parties, previously confined to just the children of prisoners. There were also three easements of the compassionate parole scheme: release for the funeral of a close relative was doubled to 48 hours; leave would also be granted to visit a close relative who was seriously ill; and prisoners serving six, rather than ten, years would in future be permitted absence to visit a close relative who had been unable to visit the prison for eighteen months or more. The scheme was also renamed as Compassionate Temporary

Release. That autumn the government also restored the rate of remission for longer-term terrorist prisoners to half. It had been cut to a third in 1988 by the then Prime Minister, Margaret Thatcher, after what can only be explained as a fit of pique in response to right-wing elements in her party, soon after eight soldiers were killed and 28 injured in an IRA attack on a bus at Ballygawley, County Tyrone. As a result of the restoration, 83 prisoners were set free on 17 November, when it came into force and over the next twelve months, another 75 also benefited. Before the end of 1996, the government made further adjustments to prison conditions. Christmas home leave was extended from seven to ten days for prisoners serving more than twelve years. Pre-release leave was increased and, in addition to the provisions of existing pre-release scheme for lifers, they were given fortnightly home leave as soon as their provisional release date was set. In addition, many prisoners were to be allowed to attend hospital without an escort. These conditions were further eased in September 1997, when another day's funeral leave was granted and the home leave allowance for long-term prisoners was increased by another three days. The benchmarks for releasing lifers were also lowered when the maximum period a case could be deferred for review was reduced from five to three years. The succession of concessions prompted one cynical prison officer to remark that the prisoners would henceforth be spending more of their sentences at home than in prison.

As had now become customary, prisoners continued to resort to the courts to extend the frontiers of their conditions even further. In January 1997, a convicted murderer, kept in solitary confinement for his own safety, successfully persuaded a judge that he should have his own television in his cell in Maghaberry because he could not use the communal television rooms. In another application, which confounded the prison authorities when they found out about it, a male prisoner at Maghaberry, serving ten years for robbery, applied to be present at the birth of his child, due to be born in April 1997. The complicating factor was that the mother, whom he had married and impregnated, was, at the time also serving a sentence (in Maghaberry women's prison) of seven years for armed robbery. There was an investigation into the circumstances in which the couple had been able to consummate their marriage in a regime which, despite its extraordinary liberalisation, still did not officially provide for conjugal encounters. It transpired that during one of their 'closely supervised' fortnightly visits they had been left alone for three minutes. The 6lb 4oz baby boy was born safely on schedule, but his father was not present since the judge had ruled that the prison regulations did not provide for temporary leave for births.

Despite the terrorist ceasefires and the tidal lap of concession after concession, the situation inside the prisons remained as volatile as ever and a final chapter of disorder and murder would soon be added to the already astonishing history of the Maze. After the IRA murder of the two Loyalists in Belfast prison, followed by regular attempts to attack Republican prisoners and cause damage to cells, the decision was taken to abandon it, and in July 1994 the remand prisoners were all transferred to the Maze. 'Belfast 2000', an ambitious £42 million plan to renovate the 150-year-old institution and provide integral sanitation in every cell, was torn up and the gates closed for the last time in March 1996. As Sir David Ramsbotham, the Chief Inspector of Prisons, was later to observe, 'While this achieved the prisoners' objective of segregated living conditions for unconvicted prisoners, it also met the Government's objective of confining such conditions to the Maze.'

In the early summer of 1994, when the ceasefire negotiations were in an eleventh hour precarious state, the prison service anticipated that television coverage of the football World Cup, with many matches beginning at 9 pm, would lead to difficulties in enforcing the night-time lock-up. In line with their now well-established, highly pragmatic approach to regime issues, they therefore backed away from confrontation and conceded what they regarded only as a temporary 24-hour unlock. True to form, the Maze prisoners exploited the move and made it clear they regarded it as a permanent feature of the regime. Recognising the reality of the tremendous physical and political cost that would have to be paid to claw it back, the management, and the minister responsible for prisons, decided to allow it to continue, subject to an undertaking negotiated with the prisoners' leaders that staff should be able to visit all parts of the wing daily to carry out security checks. The development was then concealed behind the barely adequate fig leaf that it was affording prisoners night time access to sanitation in accordance with the recommendation of Judge Stephen Tumim, the former Chief Inspector of Prisons. But as his successor, Ramsbotham, was later to wryly observe, 'By 1997 many prison statutory rules were no longer operative, or were respected only when it suited the prisoners to do so.'

There were further major disturbances at the Maze in March 1995, when Loyalist prisoners rioted following a search by prison officers. The riot caused extensive damage to one H-block, and about 200 officers suffered smoke inhalation or other injury, resulting in a large number of them going sick for lengthy periods. A few days later the homes of six prison officers were attacked and damaged but no one was injured. But the authorities' worst fears about the loss of security and control inherent in the round-the-clock, open door regime that flourished in the H-blocks were realised in March 1997 when another elaborate escape plot, centred on H7, the scene of the 1983 escape, was uncovered – but only by accident. On 23 March, a very wet evening, a dog handler was patrolling the area between the chain-link wire fence surrounding H7 and the layers of fences and walls that marked the outside perimeter of the prison complex, when he came across a large hole in the ground where the earth had collapsed halfway between the two boundaries. On investigation it was found to be the digging face of an elaborately constructed tunnel, leading back some 32 metres to cell eighteen in the block's A Wing but still some 30 metres short of the outside walls of the prison. The newly-dug section that collapsed in the wet, swampy Maze undersoil had not yet been shored up with the component parts of beds, wood supplied for handicrafts and dismantled furniture that supported the completed sections of the square-metre sized tunnel, nor yet fitted with light fittings stripped from the block. In a follow-up search, prison officers found two cells packed to the ceilings with 25 tonnes of rubble and spoil. The most worrying aspect of the affair, from the security point of view, was that 95 inmates in the block had been able to improvise tools, chip their way through several inches of concrete and hardfill, drop a seven-foot shaft and dig and dispose of the spoil for weeks on end without a single prison officer spotting anything suspicious.

There was a 'Who runs the Maze?' outcry in the newspapers, and the government appointed John Steele, the former controller of prisons who had since moved to become director of policing and security at the Northern Ireland Office, to head an urgent enquiry. However, even before he had reported, the IRA released pictures taken of the digging operations in the tunnel, which caused a renewed hue and cry about the competence of the prison service. When he reported on 28 April, Steele attempted to put the best possible face on the situation. Although the prisoners had effectively gained control of the wings over the years through intimidation and constant pressure on prison staff, he said, the high degree of perimeter security, involving the military guard force, had prevented any successful escape for fourteen years.

Steele's report stressed the importance of introducing procedures and systems that were realistic and sustainable in the unique circumstances oft the Maze but, above all, a purposeful staff presence in wings. This, he suggested, should involve twice-daily fifteen minute lockups, with associated headcounts and random checks in which the fabric of cells would be examined. There should also be a system of full block searches organised on a frequent and unpredictable basis. Movement of prisoners between blocks would be strictly controlled and prisoners undertaking such moves searched, he added. Steele also called for better systems to control and audit supplies issued to wings, for cell furniture to be constructed out of soft materials unable to be adapted for illicit purposes and a fresh risk assessment of all handicraft tools as well as enhanced CCTV coverage of wings to better maintain security and the safety of staff and prisoners.

The Steele report prompted a massive security crackdown in the prison which inevitably caused more trouble. On 29 April, Loyalist prisoners went on a three-day protest rampage and caused considerable damage to their three blocks. Some, wearing masks, took to the rooftops of blocks H1 and H2 with banners saying 'Loyalist victims of IRA sins'. Their spokesmen outside the prison said they were refusing to cooperate with the new security measures which should only be applied to the IRA prisoners. For their part, a number of Republicans threatened to go to court to challenge the legality of their visits being halted after the escape plot was uncovered. The protest coincided with the general election in Britain, which ejected the Conservative John Major from office and brought Labour leader Tony Blair, to power. He appointed Dr Mo Mowlam as Secretary of State and Adam Ingram as security minister. With both Republicans and Loyalists again threatening Maze staff (the homes of three prison officers were firebombed) and warning that the ceasefires were in jeopardy, the new ministers ordered a compromise. After negotiations with the leaderships of the factions in the prison, it was agreed that the twice-daily headcounts would take place in the dining halls with the cooperation of prisoners and that random cell checks would also be carried out during this period. This formula brought the protests to an end for the time being but tension continued to simmer dangerously in the prison.

Much of it surrounded a highly charismatic Loyalist figurehead from Portadown, called Billy Wright, aged 37, who was known as 'King Rat'. Although the police could never sustain serious charges against him, they had good grounds for suspecting that he, and a small band of equally fanatical associates, were responsible for at least a dozen chilling sectarian murders and massacres in the mid Ulster area over the previous several years. Wright was very much a marked man and, apart from constant police attention, he had survived six IRA attempts to murder him. His apparent immunity came to an end in 1997 when a Protestant woman neighbour in Portadown, infuriated that her son had been viciously beaten by the UVF, identified two of the assailants to the police. Wright sent a message that she'd be 'a body bag job' if she didn't withdraw her statements and, next day, drove up in his flashy, red sports car to reinforce the threat in person. The woman courageously refused to back down, and additionally agreed to testify against him. As a result, in March 1997, Wright was jailed for eight years for threatening to kill her. The judge said that Wright was a sinister man whose evidence of his innocence was incapable of belief. The woman witness was resettled in England with a new identity for her safety. At the time of his imprisonment, Wright was facing a UVF death sentence for his opposition to the ceasefire and was therefore placed in the segregation unit at Maghaberry for his own protection. Aware of the potential support within the Loyalist prisoner population for his breakaway Loyalist Volunteer Force, the authorities were now faced with a number of dilemmas.

With Wright and his henchmen pushing for recognition and segregation, a practice the authorities did not want to take root in Maghaberry, there was a real apprehension that they would resort to protest and violence to achieve it. An intelligence assessment of Wright pointed to the very real possibility that he would go on hunger strike, to the death if necessary, and they dreaded all that that entailed, particularly as it looked as if he would time it to climax in early July when community tensions would be aggravated enough by the marching season and what had become an annual confrontation at Drumcree in Wright's Portadown heartland. At the same time, the LVF had made a specific threat against a named prison officer in pursuance of their demand.

But the clear alternative to locate them in the Maze was fraught with its own additional difficulties. The LVF were not welcome, and none of the Republican or Loyalist factions would give ground to accommodate them. The problem was compounded by pressure on accommodation. There was a rolling programme of refurbishment and the options were further limited because the block, from which the IRA tunnel was dug the previous month was closed for repair. In any case a new visits area would be necessary to keep Wright and his supporters safe from their many enemies. After weighing all these factors, it was finally decided to put the LVF in H6, allocating them C and D Wings, opposite those in A and B occupied by the breakaway Republican group the INLA. Six steel grilles and gates separated the two groups. So, over the weekend of 26/27 April, Wright and three of his henchmen were transferred to the Maze.

The hardline Republicans were far from happy. Twenty-four hours later, in protest, two of its members back in Maghaberry produced guns, one an improvised home-made 'zip' gun, the other a mini-Walther pistol, and held an officer hostage the entrance 'airlock' to one of the accommodation blocks for four hours before freeing him unharmed and surrendering. They made conflicting and confusing demands during the siege but, outside the prison, in an unambiguous warning that was to prove all too ominous, their organisation said that the move was 'a grave error and the authorities must be prepared to accept whatever chain of events, inside and outside Long Kesh, that they have set in motion.' If the authorities in the prison service and the Maze thought that their share of problems for the year were over they were wrong. In fact, they were only just beginning.

Children's parties were first introduced in the early days of Maghaberry prison as part of the stated policy of helping prisoners maintain family ties. The benefit was extended to prisoners in the Maze in 1994 and, thereafter, there were a series of summer and Christmas parties attended by prisoners' children up to the age of sixteen. They were organised on a block by block basis and held in the gymnasium where Quakers and welfare volunteers looked after the guests. In the summer of 1996, UDA prisoners refused to attend their party unless wives and partners were also allowed. The authorities promptly relented.

In the run-up to Christmas 1997, there were three IRA block parties. H8 prisoners had their party on 10 December, and at 6 pm, after it was all over and the wives and children had gone home, the IRA Officer Commanding and his second-in-charge approached the senior prison officer and told him that Liam Averill had escaped. It is probable they only did so after receiving telephone confirmation that he was safely over the border. Averill, a murderer serving a double life sentence for mercilessly shooting dead a former UDR soldier and his friend, had only been in prison for two years. During the party he helped serve tea and hamburgers before slipping away to change into a wig and dress and put on make-up. Overnight he had shaved his legs in preparation for his escape by mingling with the departing women and children. The Duty Governor immediately ordered a standing headcount and established that a prisoner was indeed missing. There was then a face-to-face identification check of prisoners from photographs held on what were known as 'T-cards'. It was then confirmed that it was Averill who was missing.

Martin Narey, the director of regimes for the England and Wales Prison Service, was called in to report on the escape, which had shattered the most positive element in the Maze's infamous reputation, its record of fourteen escape-free years. Narey painstakingly reconstructed the events of that day. At 9.30 am, an unusually high number of IRA prisoners had been moved from H8 to the gymnasium to prepare for the party. Prison officers described the prisoners coming out of the wings in 'a mass exodus'. Not all were named on the lists and they had problems counting prisoners and checking them against their T-cards. The gate officer recalled how it was difficult for him to count prisoners in the van taking them out. 'They were obscured by containers and parcels; they were moving around and trying to make it as difficult as possible for me.'

The visitors arrived at the prison between 9.15 am and 11.25 am. There were 47 women and 103 children ferried inside the prison, by bus or van, to the party after being given rub-down searches by male and female officers. Averill was only attending the party as a 'helper' and had attended another party two days earlier with his own family when, it was later discovered, he had taken the opportunity to carry out a reconnaissance and perfect his own escape plan. Narey established that while the visitors had arrived in numbers which made counting manageable, the nature of their departure en masse made counting difficult. He suspected that there may have been a deliberate effort on the part of, at least, some of them to crowd together, making it possible for Averill to slip through as part of a group on the first bus, which left the gymnasium at seven minutes past three. He said: 'The procedure for counting visitors out was fatally flawed: there was a gap of 53 minutes between the departure of the first and last vehicle and by the time the final vehicle was being loaded and counted, the first vehicle was clear of the prison.

Even had the final count revealed one more adult visitor leaving than had arrived, Averill would have already escaped. Moreover, the practice of allowing prisoners to stay behind to clear up after the visitors had left was misguided. Prisoners had argued that it was inhumane for their children to see them being loaded on vans and ferried off to their cells. This reveals the threat posed by the conditioning of staff. Prisoners should be safely located and accounted for before visitors are allowed to leave.' But staff described even greater confusion as prisoners returned to the block. When the third vehicle arrived outside the block it waited to let the second empty vehicle out and prisoners got out and walked through the gate on either side of the empty van. The gate officer recalled, 'I was not physically able to get a count. With hindsight they were trying to create as much havoc as possible.'

Narey concluded that no particular blame should be attached to any individual involved in the supervision of prisoners on that day, nor was he critical of the principle of the family parties. But, he said, there was a general sloppiness in procedures which Averill was able to exploit. 'We believe that the laxity in procedures may, in part, have resulted from a perception amongst staff that there was a tacit agreement with all the factions in the jail that the privilege of the parties (like parole) would not be abused. This perception was not valid.' Averill had more than two hours to get away before his escape was reported, more than enough time to reach the Irish border before any alert was put out. He was never recaptured. (In March 2000 the *Sunday World* newspaper tracked him down to the Donegal town of Ballybofey, where he was living in a bedsit and working as a roofer.) But before Narey had completed and published his report on Averill, his remit was urgently widened to include an investigation into the murder of a prisoner in custody, which ranks equally with escapes as the most serious occurrence for any penal system. The victim was Billy Wright.

After Wright's move to the Maze in April, prison staff running the shared block tried to ensure that prisoners from the opposing factions never came into contact with one another. They could not see each other from the exercise areas on the outside of the long cell 'bars' on each side of the 'H', and when they had to move through the common circle and forecourt areas there was a general effort to avoid encounter. In a reflection of the extraordinary demands placed upon those in charge of such an unconventional regime, the Governor also spoke with leaders of both factions on a number of occasions and consequently formed the view that neither would launch a first strike against the other. Initially both factions coexisted without difficulty but by July prisoners from both sides were complaining about being in the same block. Staff also expressed their concern after a clash when rival prisoners did come into contact. Two vans, one holding a single INLA prisoner and the other four LVF prisoners, arrived outside the block simultaneously and all prisoners disembarked. The LVF prisoners abused the INLA prisoner but returned to their wings. Later that day the INLA Officer Commanding lodged a complaint with the Principal Officer for failing to ensure the safety of an INLA prisoner. He also warned that had the ratio of prisoners been reversed, there would have been a violent response.

The LVF prisoners set fire to their wing and caused extensive damage on 13 August 1997. They were disgruntled about visiting facilities and said their wing conditions were inferior to those provided for other groups. They were moved to H6 for a time, while their cells were repaired, but their return prompted vigorous protests from INLA prisoners. However, while the antagonism between the groups increased, and staff remained aware of the potential for violence between them, there were no overt signs that their enmity would reach as grave a climax as it did.

Over Christmas 1997, the Maze was unusually quiet. The number of inmates had steadily dwindled from some 1300 at the time of the 1981 hunger strikes to 547 and 160 of those were absent on ten days' Christmas home leave. Many staff were also off for the holiday, so on the Saturday morning of 27 December, in the after-Christmas calm, it seemed to be a routine enough decision for the duty governor to re-deploy the H6 watch tower officer, overlooking the INLA exercise yard, at 9.15 am to help make up a shortfall of eight staff in visits. It was a decision that would have fateful consequences and, long after, would be invested with great significance by Wright's elderly father, David, who believes that it was the cornerstone of a high-level political conspiracy to murder his son.

There was, in fact, an agreement between the Governor and the Prison Officers Association that officers occupying towers overlooking the H-blocks could be removed to alleviate staff shortages but, because it was the only block in which there were opposing factions, the H6 tower was exempt. So, that morning, when the officer there received the instruction to make his way to visits, he was concerned and contacted his POA representative, who duly confronted the duty governor about the move. According to the Narey report, the duty governor insists that while he ordered the officers in the watchtowers to be stood down he did not intend to include H6, and that his instruction had somehow been misinterpreted. Faced with the fact, he then ordered that the officer should make his way back to the tower.

At that precise moment, shortly before 10 am, Billy Wright and another prisoner, having been called to attend a visit, had boarded a transit van in the common block forecourt and were sitting in the back with an escorting officer. As the van was waiting to enter the first of the two gates in the vehicle lock to leave for the visits complex, three INLA prisoners jumped down from the roof of A wing. One of them opened the sliding door on the side of the van and, as Wright and his companion kicked out at them, discharged a firearm, hitting Wright several times in the chest. As Wright slumped in his seat, gravely injured, they climbed back on the roof and returned to their own wing exercise yard. The tower officer had now reached his post again and had climbed into his position just in time to witness their getaway.

It was 9.59 am when the Emergency Control Room received information from H6 that there had been a shooting incident in the block forecourt. The duty governor was told and immediately took charge while another governor grade officer was despatched to the scene. By 10.07 he reported back that it was Wright who had been shot and seriously wounded. An ambulance was called, but despite the work of the paramedics he was pronounced dead at 10.53 am. Meanwhile H6 had been surrounded and sealed by members of the Maze Immediate Response Force (IRF), a team specially trained and equipped to respond to incidents, and the INLA prisoners had asked for the Catholic Chaplain. One of the killers then informed a governor grade officer that an INLA operation had been carried out, the incident was now over, and staff were not under threat. Two firearms and a pair of bolt cutters were handed over and three prisoners emerged voluntarily from the wing and were removed from the block. By 2.55 that afternoon all INLA prisoners had been searched and transferred to H3 and a police murder investigation was under way.

In October 1998, Christopher 'Crip' McWilliams, 35, John 'Sonny' Kenneway, 35 and John Glennon, 32, smiled as they were sentenced to life imprisonment for Wright's murder and twenty years for possessing the firearms and ammunition used to kill him. McWilliams was already serving life for the murder of a Catholic barman in 1992. Soon after being convicted for killing Wright, McWilliams and Kenneway were also jailed for seven years for taking the Maghaberry officer hostage after Wright was moved to the Maze.

Wright's murder sparked off a series of tit-for-tat sectarian killings outside the prison, which sucked both the UVF and IRA into violence and rocked the credibility of their ceasefires. With political negotiations predicated on an end to violence and the participation of the political frontmen, the blood-letting threatened the continuation of the talks and, indeed, the peace process itself. Once again, recognising the unparalleled position of the Maze as the hub of the peace process, the Secretary of State, Mo Mowlam, took the initiative and went in to talk directly to the prisoners on 9 January 1998. In a conditioning move, a group of journalists and photographers was allowed in the day before. They were entertained to tea and chocolate biscuits in a Loyalist block and held a news conference with the entire IRA prison leadership in one of their blocks. Mowlam's 'courage' in entering the lions' den to ensure the lions continued to support and preach peace was all the more widely understood, supported and successful. The violence subsided, the cease-fires were reinforced and the peace process remained firmly on track. In some ways it was a grotesque spectacle to see a government minister bartering with terrorist killers, but her mission was decisive in saving the peace and with it further lives.

But the Maze was again plunged into a third crisis in as many months when another Loyalist prisoner was murdered in H6, this time by members of Wright's LVF. David Keys, 23, was remanded in custody accused of two murders. He was alleged to have been involved in a gun attack on the Railway Bar at Poyntzpass, County Armagh on 3 March 1998 when two men, one Protestant, one Catholic, were shot dead by the

LVF. Keys was one of those arrested and charged within a week and could have awaited trial in Maghaberry. But on 11 March he requested and signed a form opting to transfer to the Maze. The LVF inmates accepted his request to spend the time in their wings, where there were now a dozen prisoners, and he was transferred the same day. At 8.30 am on 15 March his body was found hanging in a cell in C Wing, suspended from a concrete window post with a sheet. His wrists had been slashed, he had extensive external and internal body injuries and his hands and feet had been mangled. At first it was thought he had committed suicide, but a post mortem later in the day established he had been choked to death before he was strung up to make it look as if he had taken his own life. It was clear he had been brutally tortured, probably because the LVF suspected he had cooperated too freely with the police investigating the pub shooting. A police investigation followed and, in March 2000, two men were released when David Patterson, the main prosecution witness, who had been in the next cell to Keys, first changed and then refused to carry on with his evidence, causing the ten-day murder trial to collapse. A third man, accused of offering Patterson £5000 to withdraw his police statements, was also freed. When the judge said the trial could not go on a man shouted from the public gallery, 'Justice has been done today in this court.'

The Averill escape and the two murders in the Maze in the space of three months had once more focused the intensive news spotlight on the prison and its extraordinary penal environment. By now the government no longer maintained the pretence that everything in the Maze was normal and rosy. Replying to widespread calls for the restoration of a normal regime there, on 16 March 1998, security minister Adam Ingram warned the House of Commons of the stark realities: 'The consequence of change in the administration of the Maze would clearly have a significant impact among the prisoners, possibly leading to major disorder in the prison, as we have seen time and time again in the Maze. Also, because of the large-scale support that those prisoners have outside the prison, in the communities from which they come, there could well be major public disorder in the estates of Northern Ireland. If that is the kind of change that local politicians want, and if those are the consequences that they want for their community, they should say so now.' It was the first time that any government had so explicitly conceded their powerlessness in the face of organised paramilitary prisoner power. Ingram's exasperated analysis was tantamount to classifying the Maze as a human zoo, where the dangerous inmates had to be confined in first-class conditions or else they would rise up and cause their kin outside to do the same. It was also an implicit admittance that the officers of the prison service were no more than artisan custodians, locking and unlocking gates, patrolling walls and fences, peering from watchtowers and monitoring security cameras lest their dangerous charges should escape. Less dramatically, one highly-disillusioned prison officer described the Maze as 'being like Butlin's and we're the bloody redcoats.'

One of the most regular features of the post-ceasefire period had been the ever more critical voice of Finlay Spratt, the chairman of the Prison Officers' Association, speaking out in defence of his besieged members and articulating their fears and frustrations about being 'the football in the middle being kicked about by both management and paramilitary prisoners' and the constant 'climate of fear' in which they were required to work. Indeed, alongside their predictably hostile relationship with their charges, there was a long history of an equally acrimonious and confrontational intercourse between the officers and the prison service management, most notably after one celebrated incident in 1986 after a Maze prison officer was found asleep at his post. Most of it had been about conventional issues, like pay and allowances, but some of the disputes had been protracted and accompanied by walk-outs, work-to-rules, overtime bans and the threat of industrial action, which had disrupted the running of the prisons and regularly forced the government to put police and troops on standby to move in and secure the prisons.

With three officers for every two prisoners, and two to one in the Maze, the Northern Ireland Office was appalled at the confrontational way the POA routinely conducted itself. In the later 1980s, in a bid to capitalise on the fall in the prison population and the heavy cost of and reliance on overtime working, it unveiled a 'Fresh Start' programme designed to cut costs and improve conditions. Talks dragged on for over a year, erupting into an overtime ban and other action, and even then the POA dragged its feet about holding a ballot of its members. It was drawn into national controversy in 1996 when it emerged that a cadre of officers at the Maze and Belfast had attempted to rig the election of their national chairman by withholding about 150 ballot papers and submitting them in the name of one candidate who won the election by only 78 votes. The poll had to be rerun, at a cost to the entire association of more than £100,000. In January 1997 the 2600 staff unanimously passed a vote of no confidence in the management after twelve of them were suspended for refusing to report for duty to take part in an emergency search. The authorities dismissed the charges and accused the staff of ganging-up to influence the disciplinary process. The immediate reason for the clash was not significant.

What was at issue was the way the staff felt betrayed and overwhelmed by the regime they were required to operate at the Maze. Spratt had been scathing on the subject, accusing the authorities of losing control to the point where they could not even verify the numbers of prisoners locked up every night.

Relations were not helped by a report from the Chief Inspector of Prisons accusing staff of abusing the sick leave system at Maghaberry, where absenteeism was running at a steady rate of one in ten officers. It was the same story at the Maze with around 100 of the jail's 1220 officers absent sick on an average day in April 1998. Spratt pointed to the figures as evidence of the poor morale of his members and the stress they had to endure. In his report on the Averill escape and Wright murder, Narey did not completely exonerate the staff but he did express sympathetic understanding of their plight:

'The reality of the Maze is that the prisoners – whatever their status – have to be treated very differently to non-paramilitary prisoners. Their organisation, discipline, community support, ability to intimidate and, most of all, the fact that they at all times act collectively necessitate an alternative approach.

> 'Our view is that, although we have concerns about security at the Maze, as well as anxieties about the general air of apathy which pervades much of the establishment, the current Governor's approach to managing the prison, which involves a series of monthly consultative meetings with the Officers Commanding each of the five prisoner factions, is founded on an honest recognition of the unique nature of the Maze. There is no point in pretending that it is a normal prison. This pretence has, in large part, been the basis of the very negative publicity about the prison which has followed the escape and the shooting. The differences in the running of the Maze should be publicly acknowledged. This will allow staff to stop feeling ashamed at their perceived failure to run the Maze like a "proper prison" – something which causes many staff considerable distress – and will perhaps allow them to reflect that although it is different, until 10 December 1997 it has, for fourteen years, contained a difficult and extremely dangerous population safely and without a single escape.'

Sir David Ramsbotham, the Chief Inspector of Prisons, who carried out a major inspection of the Maze from 23 March to 3 April 1998, largely endorsed Narey's analysis in his report:

'Prisons are meant to be safe – safe for staff and safe for prisoners. The Maze is not safe for prisoners, as the recent murder of two prisoners within the prison demonstrates, nor is it safe for staff, as evidenced by their continuous intimidation, both inside and outside the prison, as part of a deliberate campaign against them by the paramilitaries. [. . .] Unless things are right for staff, things will not be right for prisoners. In the case of the Maze, the staff are the real victims, many of the normal Prison Rules being inoperable and Prison Service Headquarters not being as understanding or supportive as one would wish. The Army only allows soldiers to serve operational tours of a certain length, in recognition of the pressures of active service. I am aware of the pressure on policemen, but it is not the same as that put on prison staff, who are in face to face contact with prisoners throughout their time on duty. Some of the staff in the Maze have been there for twenty years, and it tells; they are worn down and worn out, and it is not surprising. I realise that the Northern Ireland Prison Service is a small service, but I would have expected that someone would have had the wit to realise what such continual exposure to stress entailed, and have made arrangements for them to be relieved for periods, possibly by exchanges with other Prison Services in the United Kingdom.

'Once the final decision is taken to close the Maze for good staff will require proper psychological and financial support. That said, the Maze has to remain in being until it is emptied, and I am reporting on a living and not a dead prison. I recommend most urgently that the key to the future is to acknowledge and accept conditions as they are today, and not indulge in any witch hunt or blame attribution for how that came about, however much one may abhor the situation, not least because it would be wholly counterproductive, and take time which would be better spent in improving the situation. A line should be drawn, and progress made from there.

'Every day, on their way into work, staff pass a memorial to their colleagues who have lost their lives during the Troubles. This is the most vivid reminder of what has been expected of staff over the years, and it is to their credit that there have been so few escapes or major incidents for much of that time. Good staff/prisoner relationships are the foundation of any prison, being the bedrock on which all activities with prisoners are built. This has never been possible in the Maze, whose prisoners have regarded themselves as being at war with the staff, accentuating the fact that it is not, and never has been, a normal prison within the meaning of that term. We were left with two abiding impressions. Firstly that the Maze is in need of strong leadership, from the Governor, with equally strong understanding and support from the Northern Ireland Office and the Northern Ireland Prison Service, secondly admiration and sympathy for the vast majority of the staff, who have been "piggies in the middle" between unsupportive management and implacably opposed prisoners for so long.'

Ever since the late 1980s, when John Steele, as Controller of Prisons, had first begun to create an esprit de corps and give the Prison Service the sort of long-term vision it had lacked for so long, there had been a continued effort to achieve the aims and objectives he had helped articulate but a great deal still needed to be done. The work had coincided with the Conservative government's ideological drive to inject more commercial instincts and create both a management and financial performance culture within the public service.

Thus in the annual report for 1993/94, Alan Shannon, who had succeeded Steele, talked for the first time about 'our business'. A year later, when the annual cost of keeping a prisoner in Northern Ireland had reached £79,000, three times what it was elsewhere in the United Kingdom, the government designated the Northern Ireland Prison Service as an executive agency from 1 April 1995. The security minister, Sir John Wheeler, announced a number of key performance targets for the agency to achieve in its first year. It had to ensure 100 per cent security for prisoners in high- and top-risk categories and at least 99.5 per cent security for medium- and low-risk prisoners. Significant breaches of order and control must not exceed 159, the average for the previous three years. The proportion of prisoner places having access to sanitation at all times of the day and night should go up from 70 to 80 per cent, while the time available for vocational training and occupational services should increase from four hours per day to five hours and for education from four and a half hours per day to six. Wheeler also decreed that the average annual cost per prisoner should not exceed £73,122. 'The Prison Service is primarily concerned with the custody and care of its prisoners, but it also has a duty to ensure that funds allocated to it are managed efficiently and effectively. I believe that the move to agency status offers the best opportunity to achieve these objectives,' he said.

Thereafter the closely typed, carefully worded content of its annual report gave way to pages of coloured charts, tables and diagrams setting out whether and how the targets had been met. There was also a rolling corporate and business plan, a prison service charter and a visitor's charter. Later, in moves to improve efficiency, cut costs and improve the services to prisoners and their families a number of innovative developments would take place. The prison service set up a comprehensive internet site. Live secure video-links were set up between the remand accommodation at Maghaberry and the courts in Belfast to avoid the need and inconvenience of conveying prisoners to routine pre-trial hearings. A service enabling visitors to use the Internet to pre-book visits to relatives serving sentences at Magilligan was introduced.

The new financial emphasis was heavily reflected in a hard-hitting report on the workings of the service, compiled by the dozen members of the House of Commons who comprised the Northern Ireland Affairs Committee. During the preceding months, under the chairmanship of Peter Brooke, the former Secretary of State, they had used their powers to call for information and summon ministers, officials and others to give evidence. They confirmed, what had now become the main thrust of policy, that the service must move from a management culture of thinking about short-term problems – 'make-do-and-mend' management – and concentrate on its long-term future. 'The service has been operating under considerable pressure for a long time. This has left a deep mark on the staff which it will not be easy to remove.' The problem of staff morale, they added, was therefore the most immediate problem which management needed to address, but they expressed considerable cause for concern about the ability of the managers in the service to cope with the demands on the system which likely reforms and changes will require. The report went on:

'The combined problems of low morale and high sickness levels reveal a basic lack of professional pride on the part of officers in the Service. A properly instituted training system which is geared to improvement of officers' skills can do much to change attitudes. The present training programme is clearly failing; no training that is systematically avoided by staff can be effective. To this end, the present arrangements for training, which are based on training plans produced by each establishment annually, should be supplemented by a Service-wide training scheme with common steps which all staff see as a ladder to promotion to the highest levels in the Service. It is vital that such a system is perceived by staff as a route to advancement within the Service rather than as a means only of achieving a paper performance target. At present, it is not so regarded.'

The MPs said that the political developments which culminated in the Belfast Agreement had brought the Northern Ireland Prison Service to a turning point in its history. The comprehensive deal concluded on Good

Friday, 10 April 1998, after some two years of inter-government and inter-party negotiations, was the most radical and far-reaching since Ireland was partitioned in 1922. It provided for a completely new north-south constitutional relationship between the two parts of the island and interlocked cooperation on a wide range of common issues such as tourism, transport, energy and so on. One section of the agreement, which was overwhelmingly approved in simultaneous north-south referenda a month later, dealt specifically with the issue of prisoners:

> 'Both Governments will put in place mechanisms to provide for an accelerated programme for the release of prisoners, including transferred prisoners, convicted of scheduled offences in Northern Ireland or, in the case of those sentenced outside Northern Ireland, similar offences (referred to hereafter as qualifying prisoners). Any such arrangements will protect the rights of individual prisoners under national and international law.
>
> 'Prisoners affiliated to organisations which have not established or are not maintaining a complete and unequivocal ceasefire will not benefit from the arrangements. The situation in this regard will be kept under review.
>
> 'Both Governments will complete a review process within a fixed time frame and set prospective release dates for all qualifying prisoners. The review process would provide for the advance of the release dates of qualifying prisoners while allowing account to be taken of the seriousness of the offences for which the person was convicted and the need to protect the community. In addition, the intention would be that, should the circumstances allow it, any qualifying prisoners who remained in custody two years after the commencement of the scheme would be released at that point.
>
> 'The Governments will seek to enact the appropriate legislation to give effect to these arrangements by the end of June 1998.
>
> 'The Governments continue to recognise the importance of measures to facilitate the reintegration of prisoners into the community by providing support both prior to and after release, including assistance directed towards availing of employment opportunities, training and/or re-skilling, and further education.'

As required by the Agreement, the British government moved swiftly to bring in the Northern Ireland (Sentences) Act to give legal effect to its side of undertaking and establish the Sentence Review Commission. (A parallel release programme was also implemented by the Irish Republic.)

With the Act in force from 28 July and a set of statutory rules effective on 31 July, Sir John Blelloch, who had been the top civil servant at the Northern Ireland Office from 1988 to 1990, and Brian Currin, a South African lawyer with international experience of mediation and political transformation, were appointed as joint chairmen. Eight other commissioners were also appointed, one of them a consultant psychiatrist who had taken a special interest in how victims of violence had suffered.

As had been laid down, they quickly issued guidance notes and an application form to all prisoners. Within a month there had been 446 applications for early release and the total eventually reached 558. The Commissioners formed into panels of three to begin individual consideration of each qualifying case, taking account of a submission from the Prison Service on behalf of the Secretary of State. In a small number of cases where there was a conflict, oral hearings to determine whether particular prisoners qualified and could go free was provided for. It was an essential feature of the scheme that the prisoners were only freed on licence. Any breach of the law, especially in the context of terrorist activity, and they would be recalled.

The first early release prisoners were freed on 11 September and for the next two years there was a steady flow from all the prisons and especially the Maze. By July 2000, two years after the signing of the Agreement, 342 prisoners had been freed – 173 Republicans, 157 Loyalists and twelve others. On the cutoff date, 28 July 2000, the remaining 78 qualifiers walked free from the Maze. Another seven were released from Maghaberry and one from Magilligan. There were 46 IRA prisoners, fifteen UDA/UFF, eleven UVF, seven INLA affiliates and seven others.

Relatives and supporters gathered early in the car park outside the Maze visiting centre, to await the first releases, phased over a two and a half hour period from 9.30 am so that the rival factions would not meet. First out were the UVF prisoners, who dispersed quickly and quietly without 'glorifying the occasion', as their political representative, William Smyth, put it. As the first Loyalist prisoner into the compounds in 1972, exactly 28 years earlier to the day, he said, 'We are the Alpha and Omega, the beginning and, we hope, the end.' The LVF prisoners were next out and they too slipped away quietly, several of them masking their faces with their clothing, dark glasses, baseball caps or the large brown paper bags containing their personal effects. The 100-strong UDA/UFF supporters were, however, far from discreet or sensitive. They welcomed their prisoners in a frenzy of flag-waving and cheers, repeatedly chanting 'U-U-UFF, U-U-UFF.' Their chants and catcalls drowned out their spokesman, double murderer John White, who insisted without the slightest trace of irony or embarrassment that there was nothing 'triumphalist' about their behaviour. The IRA prisoners, 'free from this prison camp, proud republicans, unbowed and unbroken,' in the words of their commanding officer, Jim McVeigh, were showered with confetti and champagne as they emerged from the prison in single file through the clanking turnstile gate. None of the prisoners or their spokesmen apologised to their victims or the surviving relatives of those who had died by their hands during the years of conflict, but there was a general recognition that the releases would not be universally welcomed.

The Northern Ireland Secretary, Peter Mandelson, said that the releases were 'a bitter and very difficult pill to swallow. I don't feel easy or comfortable in what is happening here today but I justify it because it's a necessary part of the peace process.' One Unionist politician deplored what he described as 'a week of shame'. The veteran nationalist politician Lord (Gerry) Fitt, who led the civil rights campaign 30 years earlier and who had consistently opposed terrorist violence from every quarter, spoke of the anguish being experienced by the relatives of the victims. 'There is no early release from the graveyards or the suffering of those left behind. Is it too high a price to pay for peace in Northern Ireland? There are many people who think so,' he said. That evening, as the prisoners were feted at a series of boisterous release parties in their Republican and Loyalist heartlands, the *Belfast Telegraph* expressed what was clearly the predominant view in the community:

'The release today of 86 prisoners from the Maze marks the end of another disturbing chapter in Northern Ireland's troubled history. Nobody, apart from the prisoners and their supporters, can be happy to see terrorists walking free after serving such a brief portion of their sentences. Once again, the abnormal becomes the norm.

'Those who are being freed should be reflecting on their good fortune. Many are hardened terrorists who by rights should have been behind bars for years to come. Instead they are being freed thanks to the Good Friday Agreement and, as Peter Mandelson says, it is a bitter pill for people to swallow. The gain had better be worth the pain. The inmates who are being freed should not cast themselves in the role of prisoners of war. The reality is that they are men whose hands are stained with blood, convicted of heinous crimes. Far from being freedom fighters or patriots, they were for the most part thugs who were up to their necks in a squalid and sordid terrorist campaign. The only consolation for the public is that their release brings to an end the life of ease which the prisoners led. Although they were deprived of their freedom, the conditions in which they were held were far from punitive. The taxpayer will be saved the £70,000 a year it cost to keep each inmate in the style to which he was accustomed.'

Further afield there was little approval of the releases and doubts that they would bolster the peace process and the ceasefires. The *Scotsman* described them as 'a cold-blooded trade-off', and there was a thundering leader, headed 'The Hardest Day – Stomachs are turned across Britain as the Maze empties' in *The Times* in London:

'The last mass release of terrorist prisoners was always going to be the hardest day of the peace process. Pain has been compounded by the absence of regret, let alone remorse, on any side of this conflict. While warm words, or aspirations at least, have been offered for the future, there is not the slightest hint from the former occupants of the Maze that their brutality was improper. The IRA members who left their cells for the last time yesterday lauded themselves as "unbowed and unbroken republicans". John White, a loyalist murderer, produced the pious hope that in years to come men like him would not be "forced into war in defence of our community". It was as if those who in their terms "responded to the call to arms" were the real victims of the Troubles, rather than the families of those they had coolly condemned to the soil.

'This bitter pill has been swallowed in the belief that without it there would not have been a political accord at all and another generation of murders would have made orphans and premature widows. This is not the most principled of arguments but it has undoubtedly had its practical benefits. Northern Ireland could hardly be described as "normal" or "peaceful" today in the sense that this would be understood in mainland Britain. But it is less abnormal and violent than it was a decade ago.'

There were now only fourteen prisoners left in the Maze with 120 officers guarding them. By the end of September 2000 they had been either freed or transferred to other prisons. Since the releases began, one licence has been revoked after a Republican prisoner was apprehended conveying a large cache of explosives into Belfast in March 2000, the only known instance of a prisoner becoming re-involved in terrorist activity. In August, the Loyalist Johnny Adair was recalled to prison after engaging in provocative publicity stunts and helping to trigger a violent feud between rival Loyalist factions. Nine other early release prisoners had also been arrested and charged, but with non-terrorist criminal offences.

Among those who regained their freedom on 28 July was Torrens Knight, 30, a Loyalist killer serving twelve life sentences for his part in two UFF sectarian massacres in 1993. Four Catholic workmen were shot dead in a van at Castlerock, County Londonderry and eight people died in an indiscriminate gun attack on customers in the Rising Sun public house at Greysteel, near Londonderry. Knight had been in jail for seven years. Pastor Ian Major, a Baptist minister, said that he had 'found God' while in prison and would be 'an asset to the community' on his release. Such views were not popular or widely understood, but it is one of the most remarkable features of Northern Ireland's turbulent prison history that of these ex-prisoners – a group which includes more than 450 former lifers – only a miniscule minority offend again once they are released. Neither the prison service nor the police can say for sure how many ex-prisoners there are. Some people were in the Maze and other prisons, three or four times during the course of the years of conflict. However, an authoritative estimate puts the figure at about 25,000 – one in 64 of the 1.6 million population.

Despite the emotions and understandable prejudice it excites, it is now generally agreed that the resettlement of these ex-prisoners back into the community is, however painful, an essential element in the process of post-conflict peace-building and reconciliation. Indeed it is one of the key funding areas in the European Special Support Programme for Peace and Reconciliation, created after the ceasefires to help foster new levels of cross-community reconciliation and tolerance in Northern Ireland. Since then ex-politically motivated prisoners, as they prefer to be called, have played an important role in community development work in their own neighbourhoods and, in many cases, have been highly active in community relations work, seeking to build bridges of reconciliation with their former opponents. One such group, 'Seeds of Hope', has brought Republican and Loyalist prisoners into contact and dialogue after their release. They have staged an arts and craft exhibition, promoted cross-community and cross-border contact between children and organised a music project composing and performing peace songs. The driving force behind the project is a former Belfast nurse, Anne Gallagher, née McGlinchey, four of whose brothers became involved in the Troubles and went to prison. One of them, and his wife, were later shot dead.

Another project in which ex-prisoners from both sides of the conflict play a major role is the Springfield Inter-Community Development Project whose mission is 'to initiate, encourage and enable inter community development and community action and promote greater understanding and the reduction of community divisions along the Springfield/Falls/Shankill interface.' Its work straddles what are now universally known as Belfast's 'peace walls', which remain an ugly scar on the landscape, underlining the city's rigid sectarian geography and its continuing divisions. Apart from stimulating effort to ease the effects of 30 years of violence and civil disorder which have left a legacy of long-term social hardship, endemic poverty, illness, especially stress-related, spiralling crime levels and significant under-achievement in the schools, the project plays a more practical peace-keeping role. From time to time young people clash across the peace-line, throwing stones and endangering passers-by and property. The trouble is not always motivated by sectarianism or political factors but even minor stone-throwing incidents can significantly affect relationships within and between communities. In a bid to defuse this tension and build trust across the walls, a network of monitors (some ex-prisoners) equipped with mobile telephones has been set up. They promptly move to the scene of any incident and make telephone contact with a counterpart on the other side to provide first hand information to defuse tension. 'It is very much reconciliation in action,' says one of those involved. In a development, virtually confined to Loyalists, some ex-prisoners, including convicted killers like Knight, who 'found God' in prison, have become pastors and preachers after release.

The funding, from Europe, the government and other private and philanthropic sources, has nourished what has quickly developed into a veritable ex-prisoner industry. In the last six years, demand for community-oriented and employment-related training led to a change of emphasis in the range of courses available to prisoners in the Maze. For example, Road Transport Competence training (a preliminary to learning to drive heavy goods vehicles) was introduced. There were also new classes in assertiveness training and how to start up a business. Prisoners were also given access to computers for information technology training from very basic to advanced levels. Outside the prisons, the respected Northern Ireland Voluntary Trust, one of the funding bodies, has supported ex-prisoner projects since 1996. Avila Kilmurray, the director, says, 'The importance of providing support for the reintegration of ex-prisoners was recognised within the terms of both the EU Special Support Programme for Peace & Reconciliation and the Good Friday Agreement. NIVT established a broadly-based Politically Motivated Ex-Prisoner Advisory Committee in 1996, and has been funding community-based self-help initiatives since that date. Currently some 40 projects serve ex-prisoners whose allegiances range from the IRA to the UDA, and from the UVF to the INLA. A number of groups also work with non-aligned ex-prisoners.'

Among the programmes of work the groups undertake are schemes to address the need for employment and training, counsel ex-prisoners and their families, and provide help in dealing with welfare and housing issues. The Trust organised a seminar in Louvain (Belgium) to gain a greater understanding of EU structures and aspirations and a conference, in November 1998, which brought together 180 ex-politically motivated prisoners to discuss their common issues and concerns. In an evaluation of eighteen ex-prisoner projects, completed in June 1998, researcher Liz McShane found that in all of them a similar pattern of need emerged when prisoners coming out of jail, especially after long sentences, experienced the shock of release and the trauma of readjusting to another lifestyle. A parallel set of needs is experienced by families, partners and children trying to help the ex-prisoner to cope with the stages of resettlement and adjustment to a different set of relationships. Ex-prisoners generally had no money and were unprepared to cope with the complex task of filling in forms to claim the appropriate welfare benefits. McShane found that for long-term prisoners there is the feeling of having been in a time warp: prices have risen dramatically and the value of money has changed. One project worker described collecting a prisoner on release and finding that among the personal possessions returned to him were Belfast bus tokens that had long ago been discontinued.

Housing and accommodation was also a problem, and jobs almost impossible to access given ex-prisoners' records and the fact that many live in areas of high and long-term unemployment. Concerns about personal security were paramount, often limiting their access to places of education. employment, recreation and even hospital care. Prisoners were often suspicious, frequently lacking in confidence, restless, always on edge. McShane also found ex-prisoners, used to masking and controlling emotions as a coping mechanism in prison, continuing this pattern within the family. 'Children have grown up and the ex-prisoner has had no experience of their childhood or teenage years; rules for behaviour have been established and attempts to change these can be resented. Difficulties in communicating with children about prison, and answering their questions, were common. Children can display behaviour difficulties, or experience stigma and bullying at school,' she reported. But, on the positive side, ex-prisoners are generally very committed to the development and regeneration of their areas. 'They are keen to help other ex-prisoners, and to discourage young people from engaging in paramilitary activity. They have worked out their own political positions and have views on the problems of their own communities and how to tackle these. They possess recognised skills in areas such as conflict resolution, negotiation and organisation.'

The ex-prisoners' support projects attempting to tackle these problems had all evolved out of small-scale local prisoner aid groups, originally formed to provide help with transport to prisons, food parcels and events for children. They developed in response to a large level of unmet need and an unwillingness to deal with bodies like the Probation Service, which they perceived to be lifelines for 'ordinary decent criminals' and did not want to share. EPIC (Ex-prisoner Interpretative Centre), which runs a self-help centre for Loyalist prisoners and their families in north-west Belfast, is one such group awarded funding from NIVT: £80,000 in 1996–97. Its objectives are to identify the needs of prisoners and their families during the post release period, provide resources and facilities which will help them in the process of reintegration into the family and community and to link ex-prisoners and families with other existing agencies and support them in making use of their services.

The European Funding programme, run by the Community Relations Council was another source of funding for EPIC. One of the most difficult problems most ex-prisoners encounter on release is finding employment. So travel expenses were therefore approved for two delegates from EPIC to attend a conference in Spain where they were able to hear how similar groups, concerned with the situation in Corsica and the Basque country, addressed the question of reconciliation arising from their own conflicts, and to investigate how ex-prisoner employment and other issues were handled.

Another grant was approved to enable an EPIC delegate to make a fact-finding visit to three Victim/Offender Reconciliation Programmes at Oakland, Fresno County and San Joaquim County in California. These schemes, which had their origins in church settings but developed into non-religious contexts, bring an offender face to face with a victim through a trained mediator. In the process, the victims are enabled to deal with their trauma and the offenders have to face up to the consequences of their offence and make recompense, usually by doing work. The EPIC delegate took part in a training course for mediators and, on his return to Northern Ireland, compiled a report about the schemes and their potential use as a mechanism for reconciliation in Northern Ireland.

The fact that ex-prisoners appeared to be carving out a role for themselves as arbiters of justice in their own communities created tensions and controversy in both Loyalists and Republican areas. The prospect of the released terrorists running alternative police services and receiving official sanction to continue kneecapping and assaulting people for 'anti-social behaviour' terrified the law-abiding majority. But the very sight of freed ex-prisoners walking the streets and lanes in a comparatively small community and society, where people know their neighbours, caused a great deal of hurt and renewed the grief of those who had suffered at their hands. The relatives of those killed, their victims, scarred physically and mentally, people who had suffered loss and inconvenience, were all affected. A businessman who had to rebuild his warehouse after a devastating bombing was horrified to see the man who had done it on his premises. A widow in a country area now sees the man who killed her husband several times a week. The exodus from the prisons as part of the peace process was difficult enough for the victims to endure, but the subsequent disproportionate largesse has more deeply offended them. By the end of 2000, £4.3 million from the European Union Peace Package had been allocated to ex-prisoners' groups compared with only £2.8 million for helping their victims.

Finlay Spratt, the chairman of the Prison Officers Association, is particularly angry about the way his people, in particular, have been treated. 'I'll give you an example. I was with Sandra Peacock down in the court the time the settlement for her husband's death was being pursued. When they were totting up the money, they calculated that she no longer had to feed him or clothe him as he was dead. That's how callous the calculations were. A lot of widows out there are living in poverty. They were left with young families. They had to educate them, put them through school on their own, all on the paltry pensions that they were getting from the Prison Service.'

Former prison officer Mabel Hempson is severely disabled and still suffering from the chest wounds she received outside Armagh prison in April 1979 on the day Agnes Wallace was murdered. She is one of the forgotten victims Finlay Spratt refers to. 'She's in a wheelchair, and the prison service thought she was dead ten years ago,' he says. 'She's now forty-six and she was twenty-six when it happened. She was just sitting in the wheelchair all day long, nothing for her at all. When she eventually contacted us I went out and it was unbelievable what she was enduring. We put a ramp at the back of her house, and tarmacked it. Then we got her an electric wheelchair and a van, adapted for the disabled, to get her about.' Mabel can now go swimming and get outside to the greenhouse where she grows tomatoes at table height so she can tend to them.

Mabel is diabetic and suffers constant pain, but the worst aspect of her traumatic ordeal was the court case to settle her compensation. Disgusted and upset by the haggling between the judge and the lawyers about the extent and effect of the injuries to her wounded breasts and body, she fled the court, refused to return and instructed her lawyer to accept the money on offer. The experience still troubles her to this day and she breaks down trying to describe it. 'Of course the prisoners need to re-build their lives but I say what about the people who have suffered?' asks Finlay Spratt. As for the prison officers, a former Governor of the Maze believes they were like the soldiers in the First World War. 'They were used as cannon fodder by governments and put in the frontline of a battle for the false aim of criminalisation that was always going to fail. In the end, they learned at a terrible price that you could only run a prison like the Maze with prisoners like that with their consent.'

The early release programme and the rundown of the Maze left the prison service significantly over strength. By July 2000 a £125 million voluntary severance programme had reduced their numbers by some 200, and another 900 had departed by March 2001. Their years of dedication and courage were recognised in August 2000 when the Secretary of State, Peter Mandelson, announced the award of a Northern Ireland Prison Service Medal to all staff who had served five years or more. At the same time, in another sign of changing times, six cellular transporters, used to carry prisoners from the jails to the courts, were auctioned in Belfast for between £1300 and £1500. The new owners said they intended to tear out the ten cubicles, covered with partisan and sectarian graffiti, and use the vehicles as mobile shops or horseboxes. The eventual closure of the Maze had first been publicly foreshadowed by Robin Halward, as far back as November 1998, soon after he replaced Alan Shannon as Director-General of the Northern Ireland Prison Service. Halward, aged 47, who came to Dundonald House from being head of the Secretariat to the Metropolitan Police Committee in the Home Office, was a prison governor by profession. He had served as Governor of Armley prison, Leeds from 1990 to 1992 and Strangeways, Manchester from 1992 to 1995.

'There are few in Northern Ireland and further afield who will be sorry at the prospect of the Maze closing,' Halward said in 1998, 'but it should also be remembered that the Maze has played a crucially important role in protecting the community from convicted terrorists in an environment which makes it totally unlike any other prison establishment in the UK. Until last year there had been no escapes from the prison for fourteen years. A truly remarkable achievement given its population. We owe a debt of gratitude to all who have served in the Prison Service, particularly those who have served at the Maze. The Service itself must now look to the future. The nature of the prison population is changing and we are looking forward to a more "normal Prison Service, so long as circumstances allow that to develop. The prison estate will be smaller, but

Maghaberry, with its two new accommodation blocks, will represent the largest and most modern of our prisons. The organisation may well be smaller,' he said, but it would be able to 'concentrate on its prime objectives of holding prisoners securely and to develop their physical and mental well-being and to prepare them for release.'

The prison service intends to keep the Maze in mothballs – 'warm storage' – for at least two years until it is clear that the peace process is so firmly established that a resurgence of violence can be firmly ruled out. What will happen to it in the long term remains to be decided. Republicans want it preserved as a museum and shrine to the hunger strikers and all they endured there. Others think it should be preserved as a grim reminder of the price of a society failing to resolve its differences peacefully. There is a school of thought that it should be turned into a tourist attraction. Another suggestion was for it to be converted into a race track and named in memory of the world champion motorcyclist Joey Dunlop. Loyalists have called for the fleet of minibuses which operated the transport service around the 130-acre site to be donated to community groups. Most, however, appear to favour its demolition and the redevelopment of the site for a more worthwhile purpose. Sir Reg Empey, the minister responsible for economic development in the Northern Ireland administration, believes it should be turned into an industrial centre. But even if it is eventually bulldozed into rubble and cleared, the Maze has left an indelible legacy on the history of Northern Ireland and its people and will always rank with the likes of Alcatraz, Robben Island and Spandau as one of the most notorious places of incarceration in the history of the twentieth century.

Index

Index prepared by Mike Leach